How Nashville Became Music City, U.S.A.

50 Years of Music Row

Cover design by Hal Leonard Creative
Interior book design by Snow Creative Services
Back cover photo: Music Row co-founder Owen Bradley in bronze. Photo by Adam McKeown.

Published by Hal Leonard Corporation
7777 Bluemound Road
P.O. Box 13819
Milwaukee, WI 53213

Trade Book Division Editorial Offices
19 West 21st Street
Suite 201
New York, New York 10010

Library of Congress Cataloging-in-Publication Data
Kosser, Michael.
    How Nashville became Music City, U.S.A. : 50 years of Music Row / Michael Kosser.— 1st ed.
        p. cm.
    Includes index.
    ISBN 0-634-09806-3
    1. Country music—History and criticism. 2. Music trade—Tennessee—Nashville. I. Title.
ML3524.K67 2006
781.64209768′55—dc22

                                                                        2006004095

Printed in the United States of America
First Edition
Hal Leonard books are available at your local bookstore, or you may order through Music Dispatch at 1-800-637-2852 or www.musicdispatch.com

HOW NASHVILLE BECAME MUSIC CITY, U.S.A.

50 YEARS OF MUSIC ROW

by
Michael Kosser

HAL•LEONARD®

Acknowledgments

I would like to thank the following for their cooperation, candor, and contributions: Harold Bradley, Buddy Killen, Marty Brown, Jack Jackson, Jerry Bradley, Bob Saporiti, Jim Foglesong, Brien Fisher, Shelia Shipley, Ed Penney, Pat Rolfe, Bob McDill, Don Cook, Ray Baker, Jimmy Bowen, Troy Tomlinson, Tom Collins, Walter Campbell, Shelby Singleton, Ralph Murphy, Jerry Kennedy, Jack Clement, Charlie Monk, Joe Galante, Herky Williams, Tim DuBois, Don Cusic, Bobby Braddock, Frances Preston, Cliff Williamson, Ray Stevens, Ed Seay, Glenn Meadows, Bill Denny, Woody Bomar, Dick Frank, Kyle Lehning, Dane Bryant, Ronnie Pugh, John Egerton, Bob Beckham, Charlie Fach, Kerry O'Neil, Lou Bradley, Pat Higdon, David Ross, Arthur Buenahora, Norro Wilson, Glen Sutton, Norbert Putnam, Gordon Stoker, Mark Wright, Billy Sherrill, Pat McMakin, Bob Johnston, Jana Talbot, Martha Sharp, Brett Beavers, Brenda Lee, Bob Titley, Charlie McCoy, Allen Reynolds, Bob Doyle, Paul Worley, Jo Walker-Meador, Mike Curb, Guy Clark, Jerry Crutchfield, Kay Smith, Ron Chancey, Hank Cochran, Robert Oermann, Alan Mayor, Terry Wakefield, Greg Matthews, Mike Whelan, Judy Roberts, Walter Campbell, Larry Butler, Dale Dodson, Tom Long, Reggie Becker, Vince Candilora, Scott Johnson, Peggy Lamb, Gina Putnam, Adam McKeown, and Adam Engelhardt.

Thanks also to the Hal Leonard team: Keith Mardak, Brad Smith, and John Cerullo for their faith; Belinda Yong and Jenna Young for all their assistance in production and publicity; and Mike Edison for his extraordinary talent and understanding while editing this book. And an especial thank-you to my wife, Gina, for being there—I mean really being there, every single moment.

This book is dedicated to Donna Hilley. For twenty years I have dreamed of writing this book. A single phone call from her made it possible. I am forever grateful.

CONTENTS

INTRODUCTION

Just a few blocks uptown from Nashville's business center is a ten- or twelve-block area that fifty years ago was just a faded residential neighborhood. Today this area is known the world over as Music Row.

Music Row began in 1955 when two brothers built a studio in one of the many little homes that lined 16th and 17th Avenues South. Most of those homes are still there, but today they house recording studios, music publishing companies, record companies, management companies—all the supporting businesses that make a commercial music industry go.

The area is also peppered with office buildings reflecting the huge amounts of money that have passed through on the way to banks in L.A., New York, London, Tokyo, and Berlin. The businesses here and downtown include finance, insurance, health care, and Christian book publishers.

But the world neither knows nor cares about those aspects of Nashville. Even much of the business community and high society here has been not-so-secretly ashamed of the country image that Music Row has given the town, one unfortunately pigeonholed as a "hillbilly heaven." Nevertheless, Nashville has also generated a lot of pop records, and most of those records have been made by the same musicians—minus the fiddles and steel guitars—as those who have played on the country hits. Artists as diverse as Paul McCartney and Bob Dylan have made signature recordings here.

It's an odd place to pursue a living, a town filled with music business veterans who all know each other, but few of whom enjoy unbroken and prosperous careers. The industry waxes and wanes; people get fired and lose their deals; they get hired and find new ones. Songwriters drift from publisher to publisher, and then out of the business altogether. Sometimes it's the peaches, sometimes it's the pits.

Too often the suits are making the decisions and the creatives suffer. Great songs go unheard and mediocrity reigns because that's the most direct route to radio. But every so often, something wonderful breaks through. There's always a chance that something special will change the landscape. Somewhere between Division Street and Wedgewood Avenue lurks another "Heartbreak Hotel," or "Oh, Pretty Woman," or "Crazy," or "Friends in Low Places."

Why, of all the cities around America that took their turn to shine in the world of popular music, did Nashville survive, while Chicago, Detroit, and Memphis, for example, become anachronisms?

Many people think Nashville is about the spotlight and celebrity. For fifty years, fans and casual listeners have been conditioned to believe that *artists* are the only talent and everyone else *serves*. There are even great producers with successful careers who believe that myth. Show business may indeed be about stars—stars are the brand names of pop music—but Music Row is about *songs*.

Every workday on Music Row the songpluggers check to see who is scheduled to record. They measure which of their best songs would be most appropriate for these artists, and they hustle. They burn CDs and they make appointments. Sometimes they carry the CDs over to the labels or producers and leave them in in-boxes, but mostly the songpluggers want to play the songs live so they can do a little gentle prodding and get an immediate *yes, no,* or *maybe*. Of course, a *yes* is never as final as a *no*.

And the folks on Music Row listen. One producer I know swears he listened to two thousand songs in order to find ten he eventually recorded for his last record.

The people who speak in this book run the gamut of the industry, from the creative souls who can sit down in an office on a Monday morning and emerge with sixteen inspired lines set to music to the folks who see that the final plastic product makes its way to radio and retail outlets. Some of them are gifted with the vision of what makes the music good *and* popular. Some just do what they're told and get the job done.

The men and women of Music Row are not like other people. They are gamblers. Many of them have no sense at all, or they would have chosen a more sensible way to make a living! Almost all of them came to town without knowing anyone, fully aware that in a year or two they might be slouching home all tuck-tailed and the people they grew up with laughing at them for having had the nerve to believe that they could make it.

I have been in Nashville for thirty-five years, writing songs and writing books, watching the industry ebb and flow, hearing the music change. But the most continually fascinating part of the industry is the ever-changing cast of characters. They have their entrances and their exits. Sometimes they percolate with inspiration, sometimes they betray themselves for the silly and childish creatures we all are. I was determined to let them tell this story in their own words.

They shared the secrets of how Music Row really works—why some singers become stars while others don't, and who's responsible. These are the folks you never heard of, the folks who turned Nashville into Music City, U.S.A.

CAST OF CHARACTERS

Ray Baker—Nashville publisher and producer of roots country singers, like Moe Bandy.

Bob Beckham—One of Nashville's pioneering music publishing figures, critical to the career of Kris Kristofferson.

Jimmy Bowen—Record producer and executive who dragged Music Row kicking and screaming into the modern world of big money. Some loved him. Some hated him. Nobody ignored him.

Bobby Braddock—One of Nashville's most unique hit songwriters, and a producer of hit records by Blake Shelton. He's the only songwriter I know who had hits in the '60s, '70s, '80s, '90s, and '00s.

Harold Bradley—Pioneering studio musician and co-founder of Music Row.

Jerry Bradley—Son of Music Row co-founder Owen Bradley, successful executive with RCA Records and Acuff-Rose Publishing Company. Also Music Row's most creative and devastating practical joker.

Lou Bradley—Longtime studio engineer at Columbia Records, best known for his work with star producer Billy Sherrill. (No relation to Harold, Owen, and Jerry Bradley.)

Marty Brown—Savvy country boy from Kentucky who turned an okay record deal into a long, successful music career.

Dane Bryant—Son of songwriting greats Boudleaux and Felice Bryant, later Music Row's foremost real estate authority.

Larry Butler—Record executive, United Artists, producer of some great Johnny Cash records and the man behind many of Kenny Rogers's biggest hits.

Ron Chancey—Producer of numerous hits by the Oak Ridge Boys, Crash Craddock, and many others.

Guy Clark—Artist and songwriter revered for his talent and his determination to write from his heart, not for the charts.

Jack Clement—Engineer and producer at Sun Records in Memphis, songwriter of early Johnny Cash hits, producer of early Charley Pride hits, founder of JMI Records, which launched Don Williams. One of Music Row's great characters.

Hank Cochran—Wrote numerous country and pop standards. The songs he wrote and published were the bedrock of Patsy Cline's recording career.

Tom Collins—One of Nashville's most successful independent publishers. Produced major hits on Barbara Mandrell and Ronnie Milsap.

Don Cook—Long-term successful songwriter and producer of many Brooks & Dunn hits.

Jerry Crutchfield—Music publisher, record executive, and producer of many Tanya Tucker hits.

Mike Curb—Founder of the most successful independent record label in the history of country music (Tim McGraw, LeAnn Rimes, Hank Williams, Jr.) and later a prime mover for preservation of historic Music Row. Also former lieutenant governor of California.

Don Cusic—Belmont University professor and an expert on the history of Music Row.

Bill Denny—Son of Music Row pioneer Jim Denny, head of Cedarwood Publishing and later head of Nashville Gas Company.

Bob Doyle—Manager and co-architect of Garth Brooks's career.

Tim DuBois—Accountant-turned-songwriter, president of Arista Records in Nashville (Alan Jackson, Brooks and Dunn, Pam Tillis, and others), and co-founder of Universal South Records.

John Egerton—Southern historian with strong interest on the role of country music in the Southern culture. An intellectual with an edge.

Charlie Fach—Longtime record executive for RCA and Mercury, signed Roger Miller to his star-making deal at Smash Records.

Brien Fisher—Independent record executive and producer of the Kendalls.

Jim Foglesong—One of Music Row's most respected and beloved record executives (Dot, MCA, Capitol). Survived everything Music Row could throw at him, except Jimmy Bowen.

Dick Frank—Powerful Music Row attorney for many years.

Joe Galante—Longtime head of RCA Records in Nashville—a dominating force with an unparalleled knack for creating stars.

Donna Hilley—Longtime head of Tree and SONY Music Publishing, one of Nashville's best major publishing executives.

Jack Jackson—Studio musician and studio executive.

Bob Johnston—Staff producer at Columbia, best known for producing classic Bob Dylan albums. A genuine Nashville rebel, then and now.

Jerry Kennedy—One of Nashville's top studio musicians, record producers, and record executives. He was playing guitar on hit records before he was twenty-two.

Buddy Killen—The moving force behind the early success of Tree Publishing and producer of Joe Tex's many R&B and pop hits.

Brenda Lee—Early hit pop artist for Decca Records in Nashville as a teenager, later a country star.

Kyle Lehning—Studio engineer and producer of many artists, pop and country, from England Dan and John Ford Coley to Randy Travis.

Charlie McCoy—One of Music Row's very best and most versatile studio musicians. Came to town singing like Chuck Berry, and stayed to become country's greatest harmonica session player.

Bob McDill—Writer of many classic country hits ("Amanda," "Baby's Got Her Blue Jeans On"), known for his powerful songwriting talent and work ethic.

Pat McMakin—Studio engineer on many country hits.

Jo Walker-Meador—Longtime head of the Country Music Association, which did so much to save Nashville's music industry.

Glenn Meadows—Studio owner and engineer. At one point he was mastering most of the recordings in Nashville.

Ralph Murphy—Hit songwriter and ASCAP staffer.

Robert Oermann—Nashville's best known and most respected expert on country music's history.

Kerry O'Neil—Powerful music business accountant and business manager.

Ronnie Pugh—Veteran country music scholar and author.

Norbert Putnam—Studio musician and co-owner of Quadraphonic Studios, known for its success recording pop acts like Joan Baez, Dan Fogelberg, and Jimmy Buffet.

Allen Reynolds—One of Nashville's greatest record producers (Don Williams, Crystal Gayle, Kathy Mattea, Hal Ketchum, Garth Brooks).

Bob Saporiti—Record promoter and executive at Warner Bros. Records, revered for his honesty, clarity, and candor.

Ed Seay—One of Nashville's most respected studio engineers, especially renowned for his mixing talents.

Martha Sharp—Hit songwriter turned A&R executive for Warner Bros., a key figure in the career of Randy Travis.

Billy Sherrill—Nashville's dominant record producer of the '70s (Tammy Wynette, George Jones, Charlie Rich, Tanya Tucker, Johnny Paycheck, many others).

Shelia Shipley—First female major label head (Decca Records, late '90s).

Shelby Singleton—A&R head of Mercury Records in the early '60s, when Mercury was recording a lot of pop music in Nashville. Later successful independent label owner.

Kay Smith—Longtime staffer, Columbia Records.

Ray Stevens—One of Nashville's most unique, independent, and successful crossover artists. Early A&R staffer, studio musician, later Music Row studio owner and real estate mogul.

Gordon Stoker—A founding member of the Jordanaires, the most dominant backup group in the history of country and pop music.

Glenn Sutton—Hit songwriter and producer of Lynn Anderson's all-time classic "(I Never Promised You a) Rose Garden."

Bob Titley—Manager of Brooks and Dunn. One of Music Row's deep thinkers.

Troy Tomlinson—Longtime record executive at Acuff-Rose and Sony/ATV Nashville publishing companies.

Herky Williams—Capitol Records A&R staffer, later staffer at ASCAP.

Norro Wilson—Unsuccessful recording artist, successful record executive, and very successful songwriter and producer.

Paul Worley—Musician and studio owner turned publishing and record executive. The man behind the success of Big and Rich.

Mark Wright—Songwriter and producer who grew from Music Row bad boy to one of the Row's more reliable record executives. Latest major success: Gretchen Wilson.

THE ROOTS
OF MUSIC ROW

Like many American cities in the nineteenth and early twentieth centuries, Nashville had its share of music publishers, mostly specializing in printed arrangements of songs for folks to play at home on their pianos. But what would make Nashville shine among other budding music centers was WSM, a radio station that took to the air on October 5, 1925, and would become home to the Grand Ole Opry.

WSM was not Nashville's first radio station, but it was special in that it had *quality* dollars behind it, unusual for early entries into the uncertain broadcasting industry. The station was owned by the National Life and Accident Insurance Company, which was co-founded by the Craig family. Edwin W. Craig, the son of the company's president, suggested to his father that a radio station might help sell insurance, and his father convinced the company board to invest in his son's project. "One of the things that made WSM unusual," says country music scholar and journalist Robert Oermann, "was the Craig family and WSM's commitment to making it first-class all the way." The early WSM studios and offices were unusually swanky. "There were beautiful velvet drapes, first-class microphones, just a gorgeous studio," Oermann continues. "From the very get-go, it had one of the most powerful signals in the South." In the beginning, WSM was rated at 1,000 watts, which put it in the top 15 percent of radio stations around the country, and gave it exposure in locales hundreds of miles away. The studio was located in the brand-new National Life headquarters in downtown Nashville, at 7th Street and Union. The music publishing and recording industries in Nashville would evolve virtually on its doorstep.

The Grand Ole Opry show began about a month after the station started broadcasting. Early on it was called the *WSM Barn Dance*, a direct imitation of the *WLS Barn Dance* in Chicago. Over the next three decades there would be many well-known Saturday-night country-music shows on radio and TV, in cities like Shreveport, Wheeling, Knoxville, and Springfield, Missouri. Most of these shows paid their stars very little. The artists considered their appearances to be commercials that would allow them to book into schoolhouses and gyms around the local areas. They didn't make a whole lot of money on those live shows, either.

The *Opry* was different from the other radio shows. For one thing, its reach across America was huge. "In 1932," says Oermann, "they built a tower that is still there at Concord Road [in Brentwood, a city a few miles south of Nashville], and at the time it was the tallest radio tower in the world. At that point they upped the signal to 50,000 watts, clear-channel status, again, wanting the station to be first-class all the way. They flooded that area around the tower. I don't know anything about electronics, but somehow this goosed the signal even more.

"In the '40s, still wanting to be the best and the biggest, they went on this massive talent drive to attract all of the hot hunks of the day. Red Foley, Hank Williams, Eddy Arnold, Roy Acuff, you know, all these guys that were the hottest thing goin', were basically brought to the Grand Ole Opry to make it the most star-studded of all the barn dances. That in turn attracted the record companies to Nashville, because it became easier to bring the equipment here and record, rather than to keep taking the artists to Chicago or Dallas, which was a very big recording area for country music, particularly for Columbia.

"A lot of Acuff's early stuff was cut in Chicago; Eddy Arnold went to New York several times before he began Nashville's modern recording era in December 1944, when the Victor people came to town to record Eddy, who at that point was a hot star. And one of the songs he recorded on that occasion was 'Cattle Call.'

"There was one earlier attempt at recording in Nashville. In fall 1928, Victor came to town to record the *Opry* acts: The Gully Jumpers, Clodhoppers Orchestra, DeFord Bailey, the Vaughn Quartet, several people were recorded at that time. None of them were breakout smash hits—it is one of the great mysteries of the old-time era why Charlotte and Bristol and Memphis and Atlanta had multiple sessions for old-time music acts but not Nashville. They just had that one session.

"The recording locus of country music shifted three times before it settled in Nashville. In the old-time era, by far the biggest recording center was Atlanta. That's where many of the labels recorded, from 1921 to just prior to World War II. It shifts northward to Chicago because the *National Barn Dance* was the most popular and the first network radio barn dance, with Patsy Montana, Lulu Belle and Scotty, and early Gene Autry. And then there is a shift to the West Coast during the singing cowboy era in the early '40s. Gene Autry is there now, Roy Rogers, the Sons of the Pioneers, and a billion other people. Finally, in the post–World War II era, it settles in Nashville, where it has remained.

"It was the arrival of Acuff-Rose [publishing company] in December '42, and the Victor recording team in December '44, that were the first steps toward Nashville becoming a music business center," says Oermann.

Lou Bradley, who would engineer some of Nashville's greatest country sessions of the '60s and '70s, recalls another event that led to the advent of the Nashville recording industry.

Often when Lou was in the studio mixing records, producer Owen Bradley (no relation) would drop by and visit. "I'd just pick his mind. He'd talk right straight from the shoulder about anything you asked him. He wouldn't mince words or sugarcoat it or whatever, he'd tell you just like Peter wrote it on the rock.

"I asked him, 'Owen, you've seen the whole music business evolve'— he'd been playin' music here from the '30s on through, so he'd seen a lot happen. And I said, 'Can you point to one thing that really lifted the recording off the ground and got it going?' and he didn't hesitate a millisecond. He said, 'Ernest Tubb chose to record here in 1947.' He went on to explain that Tubb was a big star when he came to the Opry, and could have recorded wherever he wanted. And he said, 'I'll record here.' When he did that, it gave Nashville credentials."

Just off Music Row stands the brick building that houses the offices of the American Federation of Musicians, Local 257. President of this local is Owen's brother, Harold Bradley, who has been a session musician for six decades. He is also, with Owen, the co-founder of Music Row.

"My career started when I was about twelve years old," Harold recalls. "My dad was building a house on a lot next door to where we lived in East Nashville at 120 Lucille Street. He brought a carpenter down from the country who played guitar, and I got him to teach me 'Steel Guitar Rag,' the first song I learned. But that was about all he knew.

"Then Billy Byrd came along. He was dating a girl who lived down the street, and he took an interest in me, started teaching me guitar. Really we were just jammin'. He'd bring two guitars and an amp and I'd play rhythm for him and he'd play electric, then he'd play rhythm and I'd play electric. We were copying Charlie Christian, the first electrified jazz guitar player."

Harold must have learned a whole lot from Billy Byrd, who was best known for his years of playing lead guitar with Ernest Tubb's road band the Texas Troubadours. Though Byrd carved a career in country music, he was heavily influenced by the great jazz musicians Stephane Grappelli and Django Reinhardt. Harold shared Byrd's love of jazz, but the summer of 1943 found him touring with Tubb. Harold was a seventeen-year-old at the time. Nowadays country purists look back at Ernest Tubb as being "pure country," but we can only imagine what the mountain string players of the Grand Ole Opry must have thought of Tubb's electric guitar, his drums, and his honky-tonk songs.

After high school graduation Harold served in the Navy, returned to Nashville, and started pursuing a degree at Peabody College, a teacher's college that many years later became a part of Vanderbilt University. "In 1946," he says, "there were no recording studios in Nashville, although there were a few sessions that had been recorded here, some in the studios at WSM."

Most commercial country sessions were being recorded in Chicago or New York. Harold played his first recording sessions with Pee Wee King in 1946, in RCA's Chicago studios on East Wacker Drive.

That year Nashville finally had a decent studio to call its own, in the Tulane Hotel, at the corner of Eighth Avenue and Church Street. It was called Castle Studio, after WSM's nickname "Air Castle of the South." The studio was assembled by three WSM engineers: Aaron Shelton, Carl Jenkins, and George Reynolds. In early 1947, the studio was home to a huge pop hit by Francis Craig and His Orchestra, "Near You." Ernest Tubb cut his first Nashville sessions there at the end of that year.

Buddy Killen, future president of Tree International, one of Music Row's great publishing companies, recalled Castle as it was when he first came to Nashville in 1951: "You talk about a modest affair, just a little ol' tiny board like they had at a radio station. You didn't have echo, it was just dry as a chip. You didn't have all that fancy equipment and stuff, and yet they had hits. But what you had to do, because we were cutting on those big ol' discs, big transcription discs—you'd get started and if somebody screwed up you'd have to stop and they'd have to move the needle over and put it back down and start all over again. It wasn't like today when you can just go in and make all the mess you want to and say, 'Ah, don't worry about it, we'll fix it,' and you just punch it in a bar at a time or a note at a time.

"Castle was built out of equipment that was bought to record an Eddy Arnold radio show," says Lou Bradley. "Those guys [Shelton, Jenkins, and Reynolds] were really good, they had a touch and an ear. They recorded to disc—before tape. They bought a really good Scully lathe. They had a Presto lathe, too. The Scully was the Cadillac and the Presto was the Ford. They did recordings on the stage of the Ryman during the week, 'cause it sounded so good." The Ryman Auditorium, located in downtown Nashville, was the legendary home of the Grand Ole Opry for three decades, and its acoustics were—and are—revered. "Bing Crosby cut there. The Four Aces, Red Foley, they would go over telephone lines back to Castle.

"They'd just gotten a tape recorder—Owen was telling me this story— they played it back and it sounded bad. He says, 'I think they had the tape on backwards.' Something went wrong and they said, 'We'll fix it, we'll equalize it, whatever.' Owen said, 'I know what they did. With tape bein' so new, they'd rolled the disc along with the tape just to be safe, and they transferred the disc back to the tape.'"

One day in 1947, Owen called Harold to play a session at Castle, and when Harold arrived at the studio he found, in addition to his brother, drummer Farris Coursey and George Cooper. The singer on the session was Snooky Lanson, who would later earn wide acclaim on the national network TV show *Your Hit Parade*. "It was a jingle," Harold remembers, "for a jeweler, Harold L. Shyer, and it was written by Hank Fort, a very nice lady here in town who wrote songs and belonged to the Belle Meade Country Club [Nashville's most exclusive country club]. That was the first recorded music in the first real commercial recording studio in Nashville."

Harold and Owen continued to play sessions at Castle, but it wasn't until 1950 that Harold played on his first major hit, "Chattanoogie Shoeshine Boy," a Red Foley smash especially memorable for the rhythmic shoeshine rag slaps by drummer Coursey. In spite of that record, and other sessions, there still wasn't all that much recorded music being made in the place that would become known worldwide as "Music City, U.S.A." Reportedly, radio announcer David Cobb had first coined that term back in 1946, and within a decade it would seem nothing less than prophetic.

"In 1951, I was mostly just sitting around the house, there wasn't that much to do," says Harold. One day Owen said, 'Why don't we build a recording studio?'"

Just like that.

"I said, 'Well, Castle's owned by our buddies, how would that work?'

"He said, 'Not everybody wants to record there. We'll just rent our studio to whoever doesn't want to go down to Castle to record. We'll do a film and recording studio.' And I said, 'Well, okay, I'm not doing anything, you know.'"

The following year they rented a lodge hall at Second and Lindsley, in downtown Nashville, just a stone's throw from the Cumberland River. Working with great diligence, they sealed up all the windows to keep the traffic noise out, hung a lot of burlap, and otherwise refurbished the building. "We experimented with videos, with a camera—I do remember we had a Magnacorder, but I really can't remember any recordings that we did there. We probably never did a session there, probably Owen and I played and our engineer Mort Thomasson just fooled around with the equipment." Like the Wright brothers learning to fly with gliders before actually applying engine power to their creations, the Bradleys were learning the recording business the only way they knew how, by playing music into a recorder and listening to find out how it sounded. The video experimentation was built around a strong belief at the time that television was the coming thing, that it would soon replace radio, and that when it did, producing visual works would be the way to make a living.

"At the end of that first year, the landlord came around and tripled the rent," says Harold. "Tried to up us from twenty-five to seventy-five dollars a month. We were insulted, so we left." They moved uptown to a building near 21st Avenue South, in an area called Hillsboro Village. The building was a low brick edifice in an alley, a building that would later be known as the home of the ACME School Supply.

The Bradleys must have been really desperate—the building had very low ceilings. "We actually built the concrete block walls ourselves. We made some industrial films there for Genesco and Springfield Woolen Mills. The problem was that when you put the flats in there for a set, it changed the sound. And of course with those low ceilings you couldn't get the lights up high enough."

They stayed with their Hillsboro Village studio for a couple of years before an ultimatum from a WSM executive would turn Nashville into the most enduring and dynamic music center in the history of the recording industry.

2

THE OPRY PUTS ITS FOOT DOWN

I n August 1955, John H. (Jack) DeWitt, president of WSM, issued a directive to employees demanding that they make a choice: Choose between WSM and your outside interests—you can't do both. At the time, several key employees of WSM and the Opry were using their station connections to branch out into their own businesses, such as music publishing and recording studios. DeWitt wanted those practices stopped.

One of the key Opry figures at this time was Jim Denny, who ran the Opry talent agency. His son, Bill Denny, later told country scholar and professor Don Cusic that in order for country music to grow, it had to get away from being just the Opry. Over the next year, the men who ran Castle Studio decided to stay with WSM and to shut down Castle. "That gave Owen Bradley the opportunity to take over the business that had been Castle's," says Cusic. "When Owen first set his studio up, he really was trying to make what we today would call videos, because emphasis was switching over to television. Remember, there was a freeze on TV licenses because of the Korean War, so WSM didn't get one until, I think it was '53 or '54. The engineers at Castle wanted to work in TV, it was a new challenge to them, and they pretty much gave up their studio right away." Their decision to close the studio left Nashville without a top quality recording facility.

Around this time, Paul Cohen, vice president and head of country music recording for Decca Records, told Owen that he was thinking of moving his country recording business down to Dallas, where a man named Jim Beck had a highly respected studio. By this time Owen was session leader on many of Cohen's Decca sessions. But Owen was a lot more than that. In these classic days of radio, much of the music was live and Owen was one of three orchestra leaders at WSM, which was not a country radio station during most of its broadcasting hours. His days in Nashville were filled with a profitable music schedule—Owen also had a dance band, and he might be directing his radio band in the morning, working a session in the afternoon, and playing a date at a country club or dance club at night. Cohen wanted Owen to be his session leader for the Decca studio dates down in Dallas, which would have caused him to miss a considerable amount of live playing in Nashville. "We had a wonderful dance band," Harold remembers. "Snooky Lanson was the vocalist. Dottie Dillard, Anita Kerr sang with the band; two of the all-time great arrangers, Bill McElhiney and Cam Mullins, were in the band; Bob Moore and myself."

All these people became key performers in the early Nashville recording scene. Anita Kerr was the leader of one of Nashville's great backup vocal groups, Dottie Dillard was a successful background vocalist, and Moore and Harold Bradley were A-team studio musicians. "There was so much talent already in Nashville," says Harold, "and a lot of that was because of the Grand Ole Opry. You already had the singers, the songwriters, the musicians, and the engineers. . . .

"Owen said to Paul, 'Harold and I have already had two studios. What if we build you a studio that you like, then you won't have to move. What if I put in fifteen thousand dollars and you put in fifteen thousand dollars, and Harold continues working for nothing, you know, giving his time?' Paul said okay. So Owen borrowed fifteen thousand dollars on his life insurance and Paul never came up with the money." This probably didn't bother Owen all that much. The only justification the Bradleys had for building the studio was Cohen's guarantee of Decca's business.

"Later, when we decided to sell the studio, then he did pay Paul some money," says Harold. "I don't know what percentage he got. Owen did really love Paul. He didn't want to go into the Country Music Hall of Fame when they chose him. He said, 'Paul ought to be going in before me,' and I said, 'Paul's time'll come, you need to go down there tonight.' He wasn't even gonna go to the CMA show."

Paul Cohen had come to Nashville in 1947 as a one-man office representing Decca "because he figured it was cheaper for one man to come here than it was to take Red Foley's band to Cincinnati or to New York to record them and have to pay their per diem and travel. So he would come down here from New York and he'd stay a month," says Harold. "And we'd record everybody during that month. Once the songwriters found out that Paul was in town, they'd all come looking for him. When he was here we'd work night and day and he'd thrive on that."

Owen and Harold had decided to buy a piece of property for the next studio. Owen wanted a location close to downtown, but in a neighborhood that was not expensive. "The real estate agent was Park Owens," Harold remembers. "They drove down 16th [Avenue] here, and then they drove on out behind Belmont College, and Owen said, 'Let's go back to that other section back there.'" The house they finally chose was located at 804 16th Avenue South. It cost them $7,500.

"The house had a couple of nice columns out front, which we got rid of. Later on, somebody in the neighborhood was calling, wanting those columns. I don't know what happened to them. The house had a long concrete front porch. When you walked in, there was an office on the right. To the left, at the end of the office, was a door. You went in that door and made an immediate right, then down the steps, into the basement.

"Owen had knocked out most of the middle floor, so that basement studio was a small studio, but it had a high ceiling. When we were recording, when you added to the basic rhythm section—Boots Randolph and the Anita Kerr Singers or the Jordanaires—you didn't have the isolation, and the music would start bleeding into the singer's mic."

"The board was just a little console like you'd use at a radio station and I'm sure he added a little thing or two to it," added Buddy Killen in an interview done in his 17th Avenue office. "He had that room out there where we all sat around and played. Wasn't much separation, but it's an amazing thing how good the sound was comin' out of there. And he put in a little echo chamber. I bet that echo chamber wasn't any bigger than that fireplace right there." He stretched out his arm toward a tiny office fireplace.

"He started cutting those records and huge hits started coming out of there. 'Gone,' by Ferlin Husky was one. I produced 'White Lightning' with George Jones in that room, tore my fingers off [playing bass].

"That's how modest everything was, but slowly technology started happening and success kept happening for everybody, where they could afford to do a little bit more."

Almost immediately after the Bradleys had transformed the house into a studio, they added a Quonset Hut to the back of the building. A Quonset

Hut is a large, prefabricated metal building with a curved roof that was used extensively by the military in World War II. For $7,500 they bought the kit and had it assembled. This one was about seventy-eight-feet long by thirty-five-feet wide by thirty-five-feet high. Owen was still enamored of video production, and that was to be the main purpose of the Quonset Hut, but the cramped quarters of the little house studio up front got their clients thinking in other directions. Originally the complex was known as Bradley's Film and Recording Studio. Eventually, sound recording would crowd out the film business.

"[Columbia record producer] Don Law wanted to experiment with recording in the Quonset Hut, so we did a session in there but he didn't think the voice was out loud enough, so Owen and I had to pay for the session to be done over again," Harold recalls. "I believe it was Mel Tillis. That was a burden at the time, boy, took us months to pay for that."

The demand for audio recording in the Quonset Hut caused changes in the Bradleys' plans. Owen still had video on his mind, and early on they did do some film business. "We did some *Country Style, U.S.A.* shows for the Army Air Corps," Harold says, "and we did some for the Navy."

The engineer, Mort Thomasson, and Owen were not studio architects, but once they understood that there would be a demand for audio recording in the Quonset Hut they set to work transforming the metal building into a useful recording site. Harold recalls the hit-or-miss nature of the transformation.

"They did all of that by their ear. They knew that the bass would rumble around the room, so they trapped the bass sound with big curtains in the corners and they would just work here and there with baffles to separate some of the sounds. Owen got very sophisticated when we got back into the Quonset Hut," Harold continues wryly. "He had a rheostat on the light where you turn it down dim. You come in at ten o'clock in the morning and it's like one o'clock in the morning, you know, to get the singer in the mood. He came up with the 'shed houses' I call 'em, which were isolation booths. When it was mono it was all mixed together, but when he went to stereo and he could separate the sounds, he could hear either the bass going into the drum mic or the drums going into the bass mic, so he put a baffle between 'em. It was about this high [maybe waist high] so they could see over it, then he could get some separation between the bass sound and the drum sound."

More improvements came as the result of another Don Law session. "It started raining hard," Harold remembers, "and the sound of the rain on the metal roof was so loud that we had to stop recording. When it quit raining we started recording again. After the session, I went to tell Owen about the rain, so he had a carpenter build a framework near the ceiling and we draped some green burlap over the framework."

Owen's son Jerry adds this detail: "The key thing was, where it was curved [the metal ceiling] they made this square louvered thing that was held up by chains, and they got an old curtain, which they threw up there, so when the sound hit the floor or the walls and it went up, it never came back down, it didn't reflect. One of the interesting stories about that is, when CBS bought it, Goddard Lieberson [head of Columbia] and a couple of pin-stripe-suit guys—CBS was very limo-organized at that time—they all came down, they wanted to buy the studio. Owen and Harold decided to sell it to them. The executives wanted to know, 'How do you get that sound? What's up there? It doesn't seem like it oughta work. How are you guys making it work? We wanna know what's up there.' They told them, 'This is just an old curtain.'

"Anyhow, they did the closing, they wrote the checks, and Daddy had left the property, but he left something back in the studio and he went back in. He saw these two executives, one was on a ladder and the other one was lookin' up over the louvers there and he told the other one, 'Hey, there ain't nothin' but curtains up here.' Daddy said, 'I told you!' "

Harold doesn't know where Owen got the idea for baffles, or bass traps, or any of the other things he did to turn a corrugated metal building with no acoustic merit into a studio that would be the home of hit records for more than two decades. "He had the idea that instead of running the mic cables out on the floor, where if you step on the connection after a while it's gonna go bad, he ran them up the wall, through a pipe and out to the end of the pipe. He was very clever.

"After we did that first session with Mel Tillis, even Owen started recording back there [in the Quonset Hut]," says Harold. "That's where we did Patsy Cline—the hits—her career only went eighteen months or so, so I'm gonna say that in '62 we moved her sessions from the small studio into the Quonset Hut. We started doing all of her sessions there. We did go back into the small studio and did Jack Greene on 'The Last Letter' when he was the drummer in Ernest Tubb's band, and the recording got him out of the Texas Troubadours. It kind of launched his career before he had 'There Goes My Everything.' "

After a time, only "very small groups would record in the small studio," he says. "Basically we moved all our recording to the Quonset Hut."

Slowly but surely, on very lean budgets, the Bradleys removed the flaws from the Quonset Hut. "When we started recording back there, the studio had a tile floor and it had a 'ping' in it, a bad echo bounce off of the tile floor, and we didn't know exactly what to do with that. Then Al Gannaway rented out the studio for some programming he was filming. He wanted to build a set in there, so he put up wood along each side, I'd say two-thirds of the way down so the camera would be able to catch it there. And at the very end he put up a barn door. And what that wood did, it evened out the sound and made it a fantastic studio. It was live enough that your instruments or your voice sounded great, but it also absorbed the sound better than any way you could have planned it."

The wood remained there throughout the Quonset Hut's career as studio B for Columbia Records. When they closed it down people bought pieces of the wood for souvenirs. "I was not one of those people," Harold adds sadly. "I didn't go over there, it would have been like going to a funeral. However, Owen was smarter than me and he had more money than me, he went over and bought the piano." After the Bradleys sold the 16th Avenue studios to Columbia in 1962, they opened a new studio in Mount Juliet, in the country just a few miles east of Nashville. Harold believes that the piano from the Quonset Hut wound up out there. "There are two pianos there," he says, "and one of them is the one on which Floyd Cramer played the famous opening licks to 'Crazy,' " Patsy Cline's biggest hit and one of the biggest earning copyrights in the history of Music Row.

In 1959, Bobby Braddock was a teenager, the son of an orange grower, who hailed from Auburndale, Florida, and had a burning ambition to make it in the music business as a performer, musician, or songwriter. In the winter of that year, Braddock made his first appearance on Music Row. "I was playing piano with Chuck and Betty, a duo on Decca Records. I went with Chuck into Nashville and we went into a recording session that was in progress at the Quonset Hut. Harold Bradley invited us in. We didn't sit in the control room, we sat in the studio with the musicians. All my heroes were there: Floyd Cramer, Buddy Harman, Hank Garland, Bob

Moore, and Ray Edenton." These were charter members of what came to be called the "A-Team," the most requested studio musicians for many of the Music Row sessions.

"Red Foley was doing an album à la 'Sing Along with Mitch.' 'Pack Up Your Troubles in Your Old Kit Bag' was the one they were singing, and they had booked the Jordanaires and the Anita Kerr Singers to give it a real sing-along feel. Owen Bradley was the producer and he was definitely ruling the session with an iron fist. In fact, he was giving the rhythm section a bit of a hard time, so much that he gave a little bit of an apology at the end of the session to the musicians, saying something to the effect of, 'This is strictly business and nothing personal and I hope nobody had their feelings hurt.'

"Looking back now, that's pretty amazing that we were allowed to come in and sit in this session in the studio. If we'd coughed or sneezed or something, it would have blown everything.

"My impression of Music Row early on was that it certainly did not look like a commercial part of town at all, it looked strictly residential," says Braddock. "There was only one building that looked like an office building, and that was the RCA Building, which even then was referred to as 'the house that Chet built.' Of course it was all magic with me."

In 1956, the year after the Bradleys opened their studios on what would become Music Row, one of the single most momentous events in music history occurred just a couple of blocks away, on McGavock Street. RCA Records had bought Elvis Presley's contract from Sun Records and immediately brought him to Nashville to record. There was a studio on McGavock, called Trafco, operated by the Methodist Film and Television Board, and it was used in those days by RCA, even though it was not considered to be of especially high quality. Elvis recorded "Heartbreak Hotel" there, one of the most important records in the history of rock 'n' roll.

In later years Harold would play on numerous Elvis sessions, but somehow he missed that one. The musicians on "Heartbreak Hotel" were Floyd Cramer on piano, Scotty Moore on guitar, D. J. Fontana on drums, and Bill Black on bass. If you listen to the record, you can't help but notice the stark simplicity of the instrumental tracks, as well as the raw echo sound that gave it a haunting quality unique for its time—or any other time. Harold recalled that the echo chamber there "was in the shape of a concrete cylinder that went all the way through the building, and if the secretary flushed the toilet at an inopportune time," then the recording would sound even more unique.

"Heartbreak Hotel" was released in early 1956 and by the end of March it had sold more than a million copies. It was the record that made Elvis a huge star and gave rock 'n' roll the next big step up toward capturing the soul of American teenagers. The building was torn down in January 2006. It was never treated as a shrine or a tourist site. In fact, few people who work on Music Row even know about Trafco. It's just a place where, one day, a group of musicians and an inspired artist caught lightning in a bottle.

There was at least one other sound studio in town, called Brown Brothers Transcription Services, which Harold remembered as being located downtown at Fourth and Union. "I remember doing one session there," says Harold. "'Tennessee Stud' with Eddy Arnold." At that time Steve Sholes, head of RCA's country division, was doing most of his recording there, but RCA would soon have its own Music Row recording facilities. Harold did not regard Brown Brothers as primarily a recording studio. Mostly they did radio transcriptions there—fifteen- or thirty-minute radio shows. "I remember they used to get people off the street to be the audience for shows that we did there. We did Eddy Arnold, Slim Whitman, and the Oklahoma Wranglers."

An artist who was part of Music Row almost from the beginning was Brenda Mae Tarpley, a singer we know as Brenda Lee, one of the founding figures of the rock 'n' roll era. Brenda was born in Atlanta, was a regular on the *Ozark Jubilee* TV show, and signed with Decca Records in 1956 at the age of eleven. In 1959, she began her string of hits.

Between 1958 and 1968, Owen Bradley produced all of her Nashville sessions, and during much of that time she was as big as it was possible for a female pop artist to be. When her pop career waned, she weathered some health issues then moved over to country and scored steady success. Lee was blessed with much more than a great voice, she was blessed with an easy disposition and a natural understanding of what in life has value.

"Owen could be very stern, but he was so kind to me," she says. "Maybe that had a lot to do with that I was a child, but he respected my opinions, he respected my choices in music, he respected my knowledge of who I was musically and what I could do...he was different in that he actually cared about his artists, he had a good personal relationship with them, as well as professional. My father had died when I was seven, so other than Dub [Albritten, her manager], Owen was one of the most prominent male figures in my life."

Kay Smith, who has been working in the Nashville record industry since 1972, grew up with Brenda Lee. "We used to babysit her brother and sister together," Smith recalls. "And when she'd go out on the road, she'd get me autographs and bring pictures back. In school she and Rita Coolidge were the cheerleaders and I was the basketball player. We've stayed friends since."

Lee's first major hit, "Sweet Nothin's," was recorded in the Quonset Hut, and of course, Lee remembers the musicians. "We had Buddy Harman on drums, Bobby Moore on bass, Ray Edenton on rhythm, Grady Martin on guitar, Hank Garland on guitar, Floyd Cramer on piano, Boots Randolph on sax, Harold Bradley on tic-tac [bass guitar], and the Anita Kerrs on vocals," she says.

In those easy early days before the music was deeply segregated into genres, Bradley did not point his young singer in definite directions, country, pop, or otherwise, she recalls.

"No distinction was made with me, which was great," Brenda enthuses. "What Owen tried to do was find the best material that he could for me, and then I sang it the way that I sang, and then, you know, the record company did what they wanted to, but we never went in with the forethought, 'Oh, let's make this country or let's make this this, or let's make this that,' which really was great because it didn't hinder our decisions on songs, we were pretty free to choose whatever we wanted to.

"There was lots of camaraderie, lots of passion and love for the business, and what we were doing and what we were creating; there was naïveté too. If somebody said to me, 'Okay, you can be a success in any decade, which decade would you want?' I would choose exactly the one that I was in, because the music was so influential. Finally, we youth had a music that we could identify with, we had people our own age that were making hits, it was no longer listen to what your parents listen to, it was our own brand of music.

"And we had the greats, you know, in every field, we had the greats in country music like Patsy Cline, and those wonderful people that were recording in the Quonset Hut, and even some rockers came to town in those early years and recorded. It was just a time when artists were friends with each other and saw each other a lot.

"I was much younger than a lot of them. I wasn't drinking with them or carousing with them, but I used to hang out at the Opry. So I was really good friends with Minnie Pearl and Patsy Cline and Faron Young and the Everly Brothers and Jimmy Dickens and Carl Smith and Goldie Hill, and, well, you name 'em and I was friends with them, because I was kinda like a mascot, you know, I'd hang out hopin' they would let me sing a song.

"Patsy and I became friends first off because I did a tour with Patsy, she was headlining and huge, and we became friends even though, I think, she was twelve years older than I was. I thought so much of her, I wanted to name my first child, if I had a girl, which in fact I did, I wanted to name her Patsy. But Loretta Lynn, who was also a friend of Patsy's, beat me to the punch and she had twins and named 'em Patsy and Peggy, so when I had my first little girl I named her Julie after Patsy's daughter Julie.

"And, you know, we never talked show business, we just always talked girl talk. She was like my first big sister, starting from when I first met her in '56. She was—and I say it very affectionately—just the last of the broads. She just had the biggest heart—she was a mother to everybody."

Music Row through the eyes of a child. Brenda Lee had a view of those early days unlike anybody else who ever worked on 16th Avenue.

"Owen was just so precious," Brenda continues. "When we did 'Rockin' Around the Christmas Tree,' which I think we cut in July, oh, he had the Quonset Hut all decorated with a Christmas tree and he turned the lights down low and got the air-conditionin' on full blast, and we all got in the mood and it was so great. He did stuff for me like that all the time. He let me have the Quonset Hut one night to have a school party, and he cleared all the instruments out so we could dance.

"Most of the sessions that we did, the main thing I remember was just how giving everybody was, how giving all the musicians were of their creative talents and their thoughts, no jealousy, no bottom line, no agenda, just everybody helpin' everybody is what I remember."

By the time Brenda Lee had become a star, a number of other music operations had begun to develop in downtown Nashville, businesses that would eventually form the nucleus of Music Row.

3

IT ALL BEGINS
WITH A SONG

I n Nashville there is a saying: "It all begins with a song." Music publishing is the heart and soul of the music business. A hundred or more years ago the song publisher was like a book publisher: he found a writer, took the work of that writer, printed it up, and sold it to the public. The book publisher's product was the book. The song publisher's product was a piece of sheet music for piano.

But as more and more people bought records and stopped buying sheet music, the role of the song publisher changed. Gradually the record manufacturer took over the role of presenting music to the public by signing artists, recording them, manufacturing the records, and distributing them to retail outlets. The music publisher no longer had direct contact to the public. He was now the middleman. His job was to find songs and persuade record companies and artists to record those songs.

In 1942, Nashville had a very successful national radio show in the *Grand Ole Opry*, but it had no important record companies. And it had no significant song publishers. That year in Nashville, the *Opry*'s biggest star shook hands with a reformed alcoholic, who was an extraordinary songwriter. That handshake was the beginning of the Nashville music industry.

Roy Claxton Acuff was a hillbilly singer from Maynardville, in the mountains of East Tennessee. By 1942, he was about as big as you could get in country music, with a spot on the Grand Ole Opry's national network portion, lucrative touring dates, and a presence on the silver screen. That year, his income rose to the neighborhood of $200,000, an enormous amount of money then, especially in the still-impoverished South.

Fred Rose was a Tin Pan Alley–style songwriter from Chicago who had moved to Nashville and had his own radio show. In spite of Rose's alcoholic past, he had a great reputation in Nashville as an honest man who knew songwriting and publishing. His songwriting resume included not only pop standards like "Deed I Do" and "Red Hot Mama," but recent success in the cowboy-song field with co-writers like Gene Autry and Ray Whitley.

"I was selling a lot of songbooks and had some good shows going on the air, and I had accumulated a little extra money which I had in the bank," Acuff told a *Billboard* writer many years later. "I wanted to make some kind of an investment, and I knew that there wasn't anyone in Nashville publishing country music—at least not in a big way. So I approached Fred Rose on the idea."

After a short period of reluctance, Rose agreed to form a partnership with Acuff. Their first year, Acuff-Rose scored with a pair of Bob Wills cuts, and in 1945, the company had two of the top seven charted country songs. Over the next decade there would be some big things in store for Acuff-Rose, including numerous Fred Rose–written hits and some standards penned by Pee Wee King and Redd Stewart.

But the defining moment for this company was the arrival in Nashville of a skinny, nearsighted kid from Montgomery, Alabama. His name was Hiriam King Williams, but he called himself "Hank."

On September 14, 1946, Hank Williams and his wife, Audrey, took a train to Nashville and found their way to the tiny downtown Acuff-Rose office. What made him zero in on Acuff-Rose? Possibly because it was co-owned by Hank's musical hero, Roy Acuff, or possibly because Acuff-Rose was already the most prominent publishing company in Nashville.

Did he interrupt a ping-pong game between Fred and his son, Wesley, when he walked in? Maybe. For some reason that ping-pong game has become very important in country music mythology.

Fred liked some of Hank's songs, and got Molly O'Day to record a couple of them. Fred liked the way Hank sang and got him a record deal on a very small New York label called Sterling. Hank's Sterling recordings did not launch his career, so Fred started pitching Hank to major labels. As would happen to many future country stars, Hank was turned down.

But Fred Rose was resourceful. He had a friend named Frank B. Walker, and Walker was running a brand-new record label called MGM. With the war over, the traditional major labels—RCA, Columbia, and Decca—were facing challenges from all directions. MGM the movie company realized that record labels were making money on songs that had been exposed in its films, and the company wanted a piece of that action, so it decided to start a record company. Frank B. Walker liked Hank, and he also liked the deal Fred offered: Fred would supervise Hank's recording sessions at no charge, and he would record Acuff-Rose songs, but instead of charging the statutory publishing rate of two cents per record, Fred would only charge a cent and a quarter.

Hank's first release on MGM, "Move It on Over," became a big country hit in late 1947. Over the next couple of years, his recording career did fairly well and he became a regular on an up-and-coming barn-dance-type show from Shreveport, Louisiana, called *The Louisiana Hayride.*

Meanwhile, his personal life went from crisis to crisis. In the more than fifty years since his death, writers have speculated on what was eating Hank: his relationship with Audrey, his relationship with his mother, his relationship with alcohol, his aching back. His behavior could certainly be extreme. I once asked Jack Stapp, one-time general manager of the *Grand Ole Opry*, if he was really the man who fired Hank Williams from the *Opry*. His answer? "Oh, I fired Hank lots of times." Whether or not that statement was literally true, it is clear that Hank could be a real pain in the butt.

Hank was an inspired singer/songwriter, but the greatest inspiration of his career was an old song that had been written for the New York stage more than twenty-five years before. The song was "Lovesick Blues," and it would be to Hank's career what "Heartbreak Hotel" later was to Elvis Presley's.

The most basic truth in commercial music is that nobody *knows* a hit before it's a hit. Some producers, publishers, or artists know better than others, but everybody in the business will miss one once in a while. In the case of "Lovesick Blues," it was the near-rookie Hank who guessed right. The great songwriter/publisher/record producer Fred Rose, who would guess right an awful lot over the next three years, was dead wrong this time, and so were the veteran musicians on the session.

Nashville was still studio-poor in the late '40s—in 1948 Castle Studio was still brand-new, and maybe Fred Rose didn't have confidence in the operation. Or maybe it was booked during the time Fred wanted to record Hank toward the end of 1948. Whatever the reason, Fred recorded Hank in Cincinnati. With about a half hour left to go in the session, Hank introduced the musicians to "Lovesick Blues."

By some accounts he had learned the song from a Rex Griffin record. He had played it a lot on *The Louisiana Hayride,* and the huge fan reaction had given him tremendous confidence in the song. Rose did not share that confidence. Soon the mentor and his protégé were at it hot and heavy.

"That's the worst damn song I ever heard!" said Fred, according to Jerry Byrd, steel player on the session.

"You might not like that song, but when it gets so hot that I walk off the stage and throw my hat back on the stage and the *hat* encores, that's pretty hot!" replied Hank, according to Clyde Brown, another musician on the session.

Colin Escott, one of country music's best historical authors, writes that Jerry Byrd felt the song was "all out of meter," and indeed some of it was. "That's the sorriest thing I ever did hear," he is supposed to have told Hank.

Hank was not backing down. He was determined to record the song, and Rose probably figured he could spend the rest of the session time arguing with Hank or give in and get something recorded. Although he must have been especially annoyed because "Lovesick Blues" was not an Acuff-Rose song, wisely, he let Hank have his way.

"Lovesick Blues" was released February 11, 1949, and within two and a half weeks it had sold almost 50,000 copies. Less than two months later, it hit the top spot on the country charts and stayed there for sixteen weeks. At a time when ten thousand copies was pretty good for a country record, "Lovesick Blues" sold like a pop hit and, in fact, it was getting played on a lot of stations that normally did not touch country. With its out-of-meter phrasing, its yodels, and its hard country instrumentation, it was pretty strong stuff for the American public, but not only did many non-country fans embrace it, it paved the way for Hank Williams to become a wildly successful crossover artist.

After "Lovesick Blues," Hank Williams emerged as the greatest singer/ songwriter in the history of country music. At least one well-respected studio engineer today said that he thought the later Hank Williams sessions recorded at Castle were pretty bad from a sonic point of view, even for that era. But there is no mistaking the success of many of those records, which again and again transcended the genre. Fred Rose had a great relationship with Mitch Miller, who had become head of A&R for Columbia, and his association with Frank B. Walker opened up the ears and minds of the music people at MGM. Time and again, the country hits of Hank Williams resurfaced as huge pop hits, songs like "Cold, Cold Heart" (Tony Bennett), "Your Cheatin' Heart" (Joni James), "Jambalaya" (Jo Stafford), "I Can't Help It" (Guy Mitchell), and "Hey, Good Lookin'" (Frankie Laine and Jo Stafford) were among the many pop covers of Hank Williams songs.

Since that time, hundreds of Nashville songs that were originally written to be country songs have crossed over into pop, R&B, jazz, and other genres, songs like "Slowpoke," "Release Me," "Crazy," "Green Green Grass of Home," "Lucille," "The Gambler," "She Believes in Me," "Wind Beneath My Wings," "I Will Always Love You," and so many more.

Despite all of the studios, record labels, booking agencies, publicity companies, radio stations, and other music organizations that make up the Nashville music business, Music Row is first and foremost a place where songs are written and published. Most people on Music Row regard songwriting as a noble calling. The songs of Music Row are like messages in a bottle, written, demoed, and sent out to the world by the thousands in the fervent hope that some of them will surface not only as money-making copyrights for their creators, but also as memorable works that will enrich the lives of listeners who get to hear them. Most Music Row songwriters regard their songs as their children, and treasure the best of them.

Hank Williams and Fred Rose were the founders of this glorious tradition. From that time forward, Nashville's music business, and later Music Row, would be built around relationships between songwriters and their publishers.

One of the longtime debates that has raged among traditionalists in the country world is the question of how much of the great Hank Williams song catalog was written by Hank, and how much was written by Fred Rose. It's a very emotional debate. There are Hank Williams fans who simply do not want to consider the idea that Hank did not write all of "Hey, Good Lookin'," "Jambalaya," or "I'm So Lonesome I Could Cry." But Richard H. Frank, a Nashville attorney who did considerable work for Acuff-Rose and knew many of those within the company, has some strong opinions that are worth considering. Sitting in the dining room of the University Club at Vanderbilt University, between bites of catfish, Frank, who was born and raised in Middle Tennessee, and eventually became one of the key movers and shakers of the Country Music Association, said the following:

"Hank Williams was a grammar-school dropout, who was an alcoholic before he was old enough to join the Boy Scouts, which he never did. He was from South Alabama. He was from a family background that was intellectually deficient to his own, which put him pretty much in a negative territory.

"Think of the lyrics of some of the songs. 'The silence of a falling star lights up a purple sky.' Have you ever heard a redneck hillbilly from South Alabama use language like that?"

Rose, on the other hand, had a stellar and varied songwriting background that included numerous pop hits in the '20s and some classic country and western songs for Gene Autry and Ray Whitley. "He was a very, very accomplished songwriter, and like most really good songwriters, his product had certain fingerprints on it," says Frank. "I think that there was no question but that there was a streak of musical genius in Hank Williams. A very raw streak. He would have ideas, hooks if you like, and bring them to Fred and they would massage them, which is a polite way of saying Fred would write it up.

"I have a tape at home with the Drifting Cowboys [Hank's band], who of course knew more about Hank and his habits than anyone, they traveled with him all the time. Well, after his death they got drunk one night in the studio and put down this tape, called 'The Ballad of Fred And Hank.' It has a number of lines in it that are very illuminative. One is a narration thing, back and forth [between two of them]. It said:

> Now I just wrote the next song that you'll record
> And it's called 'Your Cheatin' Heart'
> Now don't you go and [bleep] it up and change it all around
> You just sing the goddamn thing
> The way I wrote it down

"If you're familiar with Fred's work, you can see his fingerprints all over those songs. He wasn't the only one, that was one thing publishers did in those days. They did not wait for a completed song to come in and say, 'Wait a minute, get me a lyric page and get a better tape of this and then I'll look at it.' Writers would wander into their offices with a half-formed idea, play some chords, a verse or so, and they would brainstorm it. I'm sure a certain amount of that happened between Fred and Hank."

They died within two years of each other, at the beginning of 1953 and the end of 1954, respectively. Their deaths left a hole in country music that paved the way for its near demise, that's how much they meant to the genre.

Fred's son Wesley moved to Nashville and joined the company in 1945. Wesley was not a musician, he was an accountant, and there must have been those who thought that Acuff-Rose would not continue to grow after Fred's death. In fact, Wesley would take the company to new heights.

"Wesley had been estranged from his father for many years," says Frank. "He told me that Fred was a drunkard and mistreated his [Wesley's] mother badly, and he was very bitter about it. Wesley was a bookkeeper for Standard Oil. Fred kept trying to approach Wesley, and Wesley kept rebuffing him. Finally he agreed to come down for a couple of weeks. Well, the books at Acuff-Rose were in such bad shape that he couldn't leave them alone. So he went in to set up the books and records and so forth—it was a typical bookkeeper's reaction. In doing so he got to understand his father better, and they became very close. By that time Fred had married again, converted to Christian Science, and was not drinking at all.

"Wesley appreciated the broader boundaries of music. He was instrumental in forming what became a close friendship with Mitch Miller, who really expanded so-called country music into the pop field. Wesley foresaw, way ahead of his time, the international impact of country music. Acuff-Rose was the first Nashville company to have offices around the world, which were staffed by Acuff-Rose people. Now, a number of companies would have subpublishing arrangements with foreign companies, or might even have their name on the door, but in all the major territories, Wesley had an individual who was an Acuff-Rose representative with no other duties. As a result they created a lot of European markets, although nothing like what exists today."

Indeed, there was a whole lot more happening at Acuff-Rose besides Hank Williams. In 1946, Pee Wee King and Redd Stewart wrote "Tennessee Waltz," and within five years, the song became one of country's greatest copyrights.

Another great Acuff-Rose hit was "Chattanoogie Shoeshine Boy," a huge crossover hit for Red Foley in 1950, a number-one hit on both pop and country charts. There is a lot of myth surrounding this song, but two things we pretty much know are that Fred Rose wrote the song, and Harry Stone and Jack Stapp wound up with the writer's credits.

In the mid-'70s, Jack Stapp and I were riding a very slow elevator from the ground floor to the third floor of Tree International, of which Jack was the chairman of the board. I asked him how he had come to write the song, and he replied, "I didn't write it, Harry Stone gave me half the song."

"How did he come to write it?" I asked.

"He didn't write it either. Fred Rose gave it to him."

Ironically, in making a gift of that song, Fred Rose might have furnished the seed money for the publishing company that would some day supplant Acuff-Rose as the premier music publishing company in Nashville.

NOW WE HAVE AN INDUSTRY!

Jack Stapp was a longtime radio veteran and one of the general managers at the Opry. But he had a vision that went far beyond his job. There are those who suggest that when Stapp began to receive royalty checks on "Chattanoogie Shoeshine Boy," the light went on. One could make big money in the business of publishing songs.

Stapp had many friends in the music and broadcasting businesses, one of whom was a CBS TV executive in New York named Lou Cowan. Even from where he was sitting, Cowan could see a music industry taking shape in Nashville, and he suggested to Stapp that they start a music publishing company there. Nashville mythology credits Cowan's wife, Polly, with coming up with the name "Tree Publishing" for the new company, which opened for business in 1951.

Stapp had a long, illustrious record in the broadcasting business, but he knew little about music and even less about publishing. His great assets were his uncanny ability to recognize desire and work ethic in an individual, and his ability to make that individual believe in himself. Jack Stapp was a great motivator. It would take him a few years to find the right man to run his publishing company, but when he found him he nurtured him with patience and understanding. The man he anointed was a very young bass player from northern Alabama named William D. "Buddy" Killen. Together they created the most dominant homegrown music company in the history of Music Row.

Killen had been making a bare living playing bass on the road and on the *Grand Ole Opry*, and also scuffled on the *Wheeling Jamboree* as part of a comedy trio with veteran performer Cousin Jody.

Shortly after his return to Nashville from Wheeling, a couple of WSM announcers with songwriting aspirations had contacted Killen. "Before

I left here to go to Wheeling I had done some demos for them, just took my guitar and did 'em for free on a little Wollensak recorder. They called me and said, 'Hey, you helped us for free when we asked you before you left town, and we can get you ten dollars a night to sing some of our songs. Owen Bradley's puttin' in a recording studio and he needs somebody to sing. Mort Thomasson is testing the equipment, we'll get the studio for free, and Tree will pay you ten dollars a night to sing."

The recordings were made in the Bradleys' new studio in Hillsboro Village. Studio time was free because they were still working the kinks out of the studio.

The sessions were taking place overnight, and Stapp came by a couple of times, just to visit. Killen did his work seriously, earnestly, and Stapp took notice. Soon thereafter, he called Buddy and asked him to check out a singer/songwriter who was playing the lounge of the Andrew Jackson Hotel, a downtown landmark that has since been demolished. Killen liked her songs enough to take her to the Bradleys' studio and demo a couple of them. To Stapp, that was initiative and the following day he asked Killen to work for Tree.

"I don't know anything about publishing," Killen told Stapp.

"I don't either. We can learn together," was Stapp's reply. Killen's salary would be thirty-five dollars a week. He had a few songs to work with, but no office and no writers.

One of Tree's early rivals was Jim Denny's Cedarwood Publishing Company. "Jack DeWitt and Jim Denny were strong-willed personalities who didn't get along," says Denny's son, Bill. "My dad went to WSM and asked them if they wanted to get into souvenir sales and they told him no, they didn't want any part of that, so he started selling souvenirs himself, selling songbooks, pictures and things, and the concessions. They were upset that he was doing it and obviously making money out of it."

When Jack DeWitt sent out his memo demanding that employees cease their outside businesses, Denny decided to ignore it. DeWitt did not do anything about Denny at first, but, says Don Cusic, "Finally, I think it's September '56, DeWitt nailed Denny, called him in the office, and fired him because Denny wouldn't choose."

Denny immediately formed his own booking agency, and now the artists had to choose between Denny and the Opry. "Denny's the guy puttin' food on their table," adds Cusic. "And there was something else: the country record business had progressed to the point where Opry exposure maybe wasn't as critical as it had been. Besides, Opry pay was poor, and the *Opry* was on Saturday night, the most lucrative booking night of the week." So many of the artists chose Denny over the Opry.

By this time, Cedarwood was already established in a building on 7th Avenue in downtown Nashville, and the Bradleys were long gone from Hillsboro Village. Their studios on 16th Avenue South were up and running, and much of the recording business in town was going their way. Denny could see the future of the Nashville music industry revolved around the Bradley studios, so he decided to find new offices close to the Quonset Hut because that was where the action was. Besides, one of Denny's key artists, Webb Pierce, was recording for Decca, and that was the label where Owen worked. Denny spotted a furniture store located across the street from the studios, a one-story building with large plate-glass display windows in the front. He bought the building and moved the publishing company into it, along with the newly established Jim Denny Artist Services.

Denny had chosen his location well. Just a couple of buildings down from Cedarwood, Owen had built the new Decca headquarters, and across the alley facing on 17th, RCA had built the new RCA studio, later known as the fabled Studio B. It was the first modern, built-from-the-ground studio in Nashville, and it would be home to hundreds of classic hits by artists like Elvis Presley, Jim Reeves, Don Gibson, the Everly Brothers, Charley Pride, and Dolly Parton, just to name a few.

Bradley and the RCA studios, Decca offices, Cedarwood—these were the bare bones of a tight little community that would become Music Row. The year was 1957. From here on in for many years, in good times and bad, Music Row would grow. And Nashville would become the undisputed center of country music.

There were other music offices in town, of course. Acuff-Rose was doing business on Franklin Road. Franklin Road was an extension of 8th Avenue and not all that far from Music Row, but far enough that as the Row grew into a very sociable little community, the writers at Acuff-Rose would begin to feel left out of the mainstream. Not until after Gaylord Entertainment bought Acuff-Rose in 1985 would that company finally move to Music Row.

There was another little cluster of music companies in town, located in the Cumberland Lodge Building downtown. The Cumberland Lodge

Building held the offices of an active young company called Sure-Fire, owned by the Wilburn brothers, who eventually would become involved in the career of Loretta Lynn. Buddy Killen recalled some of the other music business offices in the building.

"You had John Kelly, he was a booking agent. There was Gary Walker, he was working for one of the New York companies. Then Billy Sherrill came up [from North Alabama] and built what later became Sam Phillips's studio upstairs. And we were there. That became a real hot building. I had all these stars hanging around my office up there. The Everly Brothers before they happened, Buddy Holly—it became the place to be, on 7th Avenue across from the War Memorial Auditorium. Jim Denny was down below, on the corner of 7th and Church, I think. That was about it, and the other [publishing] companies like Hill & Range, Peer, they'd just send their representatives in. Al Gallico would come in and what they'd do, they'd check into a hotel and they'd call around. The songwriters would come to see them, bring their songs, and if they liked the songs, then they'd take the songs and get them recorded or get them played on the radio.

"And that's when I started signing people. Roger Miller in 1957. Dottie West. Bill Anderson in 1958. In the late '50s was when I really started cookin'. It was such a modest time. You didn't make much on a record. If you got a record cut, the maximum you could get on a song was two cents [half of that for the writer] and the record label would try to get you to take a cent and a half, or a cent, half a cent, quarter of a cent, and they'd say, 'If you don't take our offer, we won't put the record out.' So it was a real struggle, and performance royalties were very, very small, too. So back in those days we just weren't making a lot of money. Today you can make enough off one song to retire."

Buddy Killen grew up poor in Florence, Alabama. There must be something in the waters of the Tennessee River that glide through the lands of northern Alabama where lay the towns of Muscle Shoals, Sheffield, Tuscumbia, and Florence. A little later, in the '60s and '70s, a group of Southern white musicians from the region would record some of the greatest rock music of their time, backing up black artists like Percy Sledge, Wilson Pickett, and Aretha Franklin, as well as white pop stars like Bob Seger, Paul Simon, the Rolling Stones, and Rod Stewart.

But long before the Muscle Shoals Rhythm Section played its way to musical immortality, a number of talented young musicians from that area moved up to Nashville in search of fame and fortune—or at least a living. One of those was Killen, and he couldn't wait to hit the road that led north to Tennessee.

"I got out of school at the end of August. I finished in summer school because I had screwed away my time playing music and everything. I just didn't love school. Down in Alabama, at that time, when you got out of high school you either went to work at the Reynolds Aluminum Company or you went up to Detroit on the assembly lines in the automobile plants."

He was, in fact, scheduled to enlist in the Air Force the following Monday, but the Sunday before, while sitting in his father's café having breakfast, he got a call from Nashville offering him a job playing bass. So on September 9, 1951, Buddy's father drove him and his bass up to Nashville to take his chances.

Once Jack Stapp had hired Killen to run Tree, the youngster found that the publishing business suited him fine. One reason was the open attitude of acceptance and inclusion that was part of the early Nashville music scene. "It was so friendly back in those days," Killen says, his voice gentled by soft nostalgia. "Once you were in, you were in. I mean the stars didn't have this standoffish attitude. They'd hang out with you—we'd go to the Clarkston Hotel and sit around over there, drink coffee, and have a greasy hamburger. There was a camaraderie among all of us that existed that I don't think happens today."

In 1956, Buddy Killen and Tree hit an exceptional lick, a song that would launch rock 'n' roll's greatest star and change the face of popular music forever. "It's down at the end of Lonely Street...."

5

WHEN COUNTRY MUSIC ALMOST DIED

In 1955, Killen and his wife, along with his friend, writer Floyd Robinson, and Robinson's brother journeyed to Daytona Beach, Florida, to play a place called the Mello Club. While they were there he had an opportunity to visit with Mae Boren Axton, a schoolteacher who also wrote songs and did some publicity work. Recently she'd been doing publicity for a very young Elvis Presley, who happened to be performing in the Daytona Beach area at the time. One night, Mae took Killen and his little group to the auditorium where Elvis was appearing along with Hank Snow and Andy Griffith. After the show Mae returned to the club where Buddy and his group were working. Between sets Killen asked Mae the question he always asked songwriters in those early days: "How about writing a song for my publishing company?"

Axton said that she had a song called "Heartbreak Hotel," a song she and a man named Tommy Durden had written. She said she thought it would be good for Elvis, and that was good enough for Killen. Although Elvis had yet to become a national star, he was already a powerhouse in the South. When Killen returned to Nashville, he found a small tape reel in his mailbox. He listened to the song, liked it, and pitched it to a few artists in Nashville without success, then he sent a copy of the song to Memphis, to Bob Neal, who was Elvis's manager. Neal heard the song and promised Killen that he would make sure Elvis heard the song. Almost immediately thereafter, Neal sold Elvis's contract to a hustling promoter named "Colonel" Tom Parker, and Sam Phillips sold Elvis's recording contract to RCA.

This brought a change in plans for Buddy. Instead of contacting Sam Phillips, he contacted the head of RCA's country division, Steve Sholes, and asked him about the song. Sholes had heard it and said he liked it.

Axton had also been active. She had played the song for Elvis, and, says Killen, Elvis had told her, "Hot dog, Mae, play it again!"

The voice on the demo was that of a singer named Glen Reeves. According to Killen and others, Reeves had heard enough of Elvis that when he demoed the song he made a genuine attempt to sing the song in what he thought was Elvis's style. Elvis in turn listened carefully to Reeves' version and copied *it* when *he* recorded it in the Trafco studio.

RCA released "Heartbreak Hotel" early in 1956, and by the end of March it had sold more than a million copies. For Tree, "Heartbreak Hotel" was an incredible piece of good fortune. A tiny publishing company had, for no expense, obtained what would become one of the most valuable copyrights of the early rock 'n' roll era.

Mae Axton and Tommy Durden gave one-third of the writer's rights to Elvis, even though Elvis had nothing to do with the writing of the song.

In the tough, gritty world of music publishing, one would have thought that the buzzards would be circling over Tree, attempting to snatch chunks of publishing from the tiny Nashville publishing company. Yet Buddy Killen insists that no such thing was ever attempted. The closest thing to it was that Hill & Range, which handled Elvis's publishing, offered to buy the copyright from Tree. Killen says that he and Stapp discussed the offer, that Jack asked for Buddy's opinion, and Buddy stated that a publishing company could not prosper if it sold off its most valuable copyright. Even though the company was crying for a cash infusion, Killen and Stapp chose to wait for their royalties. It was as good a decision as any ever made in the Nashville music publishing business.

For rock 'n' roll, "Heartbreak Hotel" was the *necessary* record, the one that transformed the new music from a fad into a phenomenon.

Through 1954 and 1955, as rock 'n' roll gained momentum, the vast majority of its stars were black. The appeal of the music was to a degree sexual, but in the culturally segregated America of the time, it was inconceivable that most middle-class white kids could relate to black artists.

By this time, Bill Haley had established himself as a white rock 'n' roll star, but he was over thirty and did not exude the sex appeal of an Elvis. Then came "Heartbreak Hotel" and Sam Phillips's dream of finding a white boy who sounded black had turned into a sonic revolution. Elvis's looks, his voice, his moves simply overwhelmed the industry and paved the way for a host of young white singers who would reshape the image of rock 'n' roll.

One man who was on the spot when Elvis became *the man* was Charlie Fach, who was born and raised in RCA's hometown, Camden, New Jersey, and was working for RCA at the time "Heartbreak Hotel" first surfaced.

"I went to work for RCA the day after I graduated from college—designing office forms," he says. "My objective was to get into the record department. So I did some forms for the record department, and about a year later they asked me to come to New York City to design a production control system for them—this was the mid-'50s, the early days of LPs—to coordinate all the work from the recording to jacket design and manufacturing. Back then, most of the jackets were printed with a four-color process and it took a very long time to have the proofs made correctly, and then to do the one-color-at-a-time printing. So from the day that RCA had an idea for doing an album, we would schedule the release six months later.

"I designed this very complex system for them to schedule all the recording, liner notes, jacket.... The system was so complex that I was the only one who understood it, and they moved me to New York City. It was an administrative job, but because all this production was so critical, I sat in on all the A&R meetings, all the scheduling meetings, the production and promotion meetings. I was there when they signed Elvis Presley. There was a guy who was a regional man for the label out of Charlotte, North Carolina, and he called Steve Sholes and the people in New York and he told them, 'Hey, this Elvis Presley thing is selling like crazy on Sun.' And he had heard the rumor that Sam Phillips wanted to sell his contract.

"Steve Sholes sent two men down to either hear Elvis or make contact with Phillips, and then they got into discussions about buying the Sun masters. The guy who originated it all was Brad McCuen."

Brad McCuen went on to a fine career in the music industry in New York and Nashville. Among other things, he was the head of Mega Records when Mega artist Sammi Smith had her incredibly successful hit, "Help Me Make It Through the Night." "He's one of the unsung people of the record business," adds Fach, himself one of the unsung people of the record business. He has been in the business for fifty-three years and his eyes sparkle as he tells his stories. It's obvious that they mean the world to him.

"When 'Heartbreak Hotel' came out," Fach continues, "RCA thought they had a big *country* act with Elvis Presley, they had no idea he was going to be anywhere near what he was. So when it came time for 'Heartbreak Hotel' to go out, they pressed 35,000 singles at their three plants around the country. Every distributor had to have their order in on the same day, and the records would be shipped so that every distributor got them on the same day, too. Part of my job was, I'd come into the office every day about twenty minutes before everybody else in the sales and promotion department got there, and I would have three teletypes in from the plants, showing yesterday's sales and what they had in inventory. If there was anything unusual, I'd take it into my boss and the sales manager to adjust production up or down.

"So we'd pressed 35,000 copies of 'Heartbreak Hotel.'—I went in the morning and I added up the first day's orders on Elvis, and they came to 62,000. My boss came in about ten minutes later and I said, 'Dave, Dave, we got 62,000 orders on 'Heartbreak Hotel.' He said, 'Call those simple sonsofbitches back at the plant and get a confirmation on those numbers!'

"It took me about a half an hour to get through to all three plants. I went back into my boss and said, 'Dave, that 62,000 figure is incorrect, it's now a little bit over 90,000!'"

In response to Elvis's unbelievable single sales, RCA made a quick decision to put out an album of all the Sun sides. "We were gonna do our regular schedule, which meant it would take six months," Fach recalls. "We were having a joint meeting with the distributors, so my boss says, 'We've got this Presley album gettin' ready, it's gonna be out six months from now,' and one of the distributors cries out, 'We need it right away!' So he explained to them the four-color process, *da-da-da-da*, it takes so much time...' The distributor says, 'How long does it take to make the record itself?' The plant manager says, 'Well, we can make 'em overnight.'

"The distributor says, 'I'll tell you what to do. Press those Elvis Presley LPs, put 'em in a plain white sleeve, ship 'em to me, and I'll sell 'em like that!' That's why that first Presley album only had a black-and-white photo of him, with pink lettering down one side and green lettering the other, they could do that almost overnight." Fach says the album sold out almost before they could be put on the shelves.

"We had a studio at 23rd Street in New York City—the record department headquarters was on the ground floor, and one of the young engineers grabbed me one day, says, 'Charlie, stick around tonight, Elvis Presley's comin' in to record.' So I stayed around that night, and Presley came in and recorded two sides. That's all he ever recorded in New York City. 'Hound Dog' and 'Don't Be Cruel,' which went out back to back—in my mind, the greatest single record ever released.

"I remember that session, I stood there in awe of the fact that *Elvis Presley* was in complete charge of the session. He told the musicians what to do, the engineers what to do, like he'd been in the business all his life." Presley was twenty-one at the time.

For country music, the coming of Elvis was a disaster. As the standard soundtrack for many Southern homes, country music bound the generations together. That began to end with the coming of rock 'n' roll. At first, the music industry regarded artists such as Elvis, Carl Perkins, Jerry Lee Lewis, and the Everly Brothers as country acts who happened to have special appeal for the kids. But as these artists increasingly dominated the Top 10 country charts, pushing out the adult artists, country record promoters began to demand that the trade magazines get the young rock 'n' rollers off the country charts before they destroyed the essence of country music. By the end of 1961, Elvis and the Everly Brothers were gone from the country charts.

It's easy to say that segregating country from Southern rock 'n' roll was a terrible commercial mistake. On one hand, many Southern kids may have decided that there was nothing left for them in country music, and when they left, so did a whole lot of record sales. In the late '50s, more and more radio stations dropped or de-emphasized country music until, in 1961, there were only eighty-one full-time country stations across America. Country as a commercial genre nearly died. On the other hand, had the country music industry not fought to disconnect rock 'n' roll from country, country might have lost its distinct identity anyway, or quietly succumbed to rock 'n' roll.

From another viewpoint, the decade beginning in 1956 saw country music reach unprecedented popularity in the mainstream pop world on the strength of a rich variety of rock 'n' roll records that "crossed over" from country to pop. Nowadays the media and record industries are constantly classifying the various genres of music in an effort to concentrate on the audiences that buy each kind of music. But in the '50s, the categories were still a little vague and confused. Rock 'n' roll had begun as the selling of black music to white teenagers, yet the first of the big white rock 'n' roll stars, Bill Haley, had a definite country cast to him. To make it more confusing, Elvis was a budding country star before "Heartbreak Hotel" made him the reigning king of rock 'n' roll.

The problem was that for all the segregation of the South, the regional musical culture was integrated. If you can't hear blues and future rock 'n' roll licks in some of Hank Williams records, you're just not listening. If you can't hear country in Chuck Berry, then you don't know country. In Memphis, Sam Phillips had started by recording black artists, and when he started messing with white ones like Carl Perkins and Elvis, the switch from R&B to whatever the white guys were doing was more one of detail than of genre. That new music eventually came to be called *rockabilly*, a good choice of labels, because it was a fusion of black music, white music, black-influenced white music, and white-influenced black music.

Mostly it was simple stuff, three- and four-chord melodies with earnest emotional lyrics, usually devoid of Tin Pan Alley–style wordsmithing. What made it jump was its innovative rhythms, what Alan Freed called "the big beat." But the big beat wasn't even new to white audiences. They had heard plenty of crazy rhythm in the big bands of the thirties and the forties. After many of the big bands broke up for economic reasons, the big beat took a bit of a break, but it would soon reappear to white audiences in the form of smaller bands and gospel-tinged black vocal groups.

The music coming out of Nashville in the late '50s and early '60s sounded unique. It sounded *refreshing*. The songwriters wrote with passion. The musicians were creative, not scripted. The artists—well, the artists were *different*. Eddy Arnold was no Perry Como. Jim Reeves was no Tony Bennett. Patsy Cline was no Kay Starr.

Country music as a genre was dying. But even while Southern kids were giving up on country, even while radio stations were giving up on country—even while rabid fans were still mourning the death of Hank Williams years after his demise—country records were finding their way into the *pop* charts.

In 1956, Elvis was number one on the pop and country charts with "Heartbreak Hotel," and followed with crossover number-one smashes— "I Want You, I Need You, I Love You," "Don't Be Cruel," and "Hound Dog." Carl Perkins' "Blue Suede Shoes" was number one on the country chart and number two on the *Billboard* pop chart. Johnny Cash hit number one on the country chart and number seventeen, pop, with "I Walk the Line." Marty Robbins had the first of his many crossover hits with "Singin' the Blues" (number one, country; number seventeen, pop), and would have probably had a bigger pop hit if Mitch Miller had not put out a version of the song with Guy Mitchell.

In 1957, country music was all over the pop charts, led again by Elvis, but there was a whole lot more than Elvis. Sonny James hit with "Young Love." Ferlin Husky had a number-one country record with "Gone," which also hit the number-four slot on the *Billboard* pop chart. Marty Robbins had a major country/pop crossover with "A White Sport Coat (And a Pink Carnation)." Jim Reeves just missed having a Top 10 pop hit with his number-one country record, "Four Walls." The Everly Brothers hit the jackpot twice, country and pop, with "Bye, Bye Love" and "Wake Up, Little Susie." Bobby Helms had one of the great country classics on the pop charts, "Fraulein," followed up with "My Special Angel" (number one, country; number seven, pop), then capped off his amazing year with "Jingle Bell Rock," still a Christmas standard on pop and country stations today.

As if all that weren't enough, Jerry Lee Lewis made his spectacular debut with "Whole Lotta Shakin' Goin' On" (number one, pop; and number three, country).

Over the next few years, the Everlys, Marty Robbins, Johnny Cash, Elvis, and Jerry Lee Lewis would continue as regulars on both country and pop charts, but new names would keep the crossovers coming. Some, like Don Gibson, Patsy Cline, Skeeter Davis, and Johnny Horton, would break the pop barrier multiple times, but sometimes it seemed as if nearly every country artist would have his single moment in the glare of pop stardom. Webb Pierce, Faron Young, Stonewall Jackson, Leroy Van Dyke, Jimmy Dean, the Browns, Hank Locklin, Claude King, Bill Anderson, and others found pop glory at least once in their careers.

In addition, there were a number of artists recording in Nashville that were basically recording pop. The amazing Brenda Lee comes to mind, along with the Newbeats and Sue Thompson, two hit acts that recorded for Acuff-Rose's Hickory label.

Much of this music was coming from the newly minted Music Row, recorded in the Quonset Hut, and in RCA's beautiful new studio just a short block from the Quonset Hut.

Unlike those who built the studios in Nashville that came before, RCA was not flying by the seat of its collective pants. In 1957, when RCA began construction of its new studio on 17th Avenue South, there were other RCA studios around the country, and like the others, this one was built from the ground up *to be a studio*, using the latest technology. There were no quaint, jury-rigged pieces of homemade equipment. At least not at first.

But as the studio came on line, some of the engineers and musicians had to admit that the studio's sound wasn't all that wonderful. After years and years of recording in studios built by amateurs, experimenters, and radio engineers, the music makers of Music Row must have been beside themselves with excitement at the thought of a studio crafted by experts just for *them* to work their magic in. But alas, the sound was, just, well, *all right.*

For all the new technology today, studio design remains as much an art as a science, and that truth was even more evident back in the late '50s in the nascent days of Music Row. The studio's engineer, Bill Porter, understood what caused the muddy acoustics. He and his assistant, Tommy Strong, took a ride and bought a number of two-foot-by-four-foot acoustical tiles, and cut and assembled them into pyramid-shaped devices that they hung at various heights. They experimented with mic locations on the floor. They adjusted and they tweaked, and when they were done, the RCA studio on 17th Avenue South sounded like it was supposed to sound, a crystal-clear, neutral room, a blank page on which all sorts of wonderful music could jump from the artist and the musicians, into a mastering console, then onto a record, then out to the world.

6

Oohs and Aahs

History is very sloppy. The commercial genre we call "country music" almost perished in the late '50s and early '60s, and yet while the genre was dying, the music was exploding on pop stations all over America. Was Nashville fixing to become the next big thing in pop music? In a way, yes.

Some of country's greatest artists, including Eddy Arnold, Ray Price, and Patsy Cline, were bringing new vocal sounds to country music. Price and Arnold had modified their traditional styles to a sound more reminiscent of the pop crooners, and Cline had an unmistakable bluesy approach to many of her recordings. The instruments were changing too. For a time, the banjo nearly disappeared, the fiddle retreated, the Dobro stepped forward, the lap steel morphed into the powerfully expressive and versatile double-necked pedal steel guitar, and, most appalling to traditionalists, Nashville producers began using string sections and vocal groups to "sweeten" their productions.

The two men most responsible for this new "Nashville sound" were Owen Bradley, who had become head of Decca's Nashville office in 1958, and Chet Atkins, who was being groomed to run RCA's country music headquarters in Nashville.

Bradley's country credentials are unassailable. Early in his career as a producer, he supervised the recording sessions of Ernest Tubb, Webb Pierce, and Kitty Wells. But Bradley's musical interests were many and varied. He produced Brenda Lee's big pop hits. And he produced some of the most magnificent tracks in the history of country music, the Patsy Cline Decca sessions, which redefined country, because of Patsy's singing style and the quality songs she was getting from brilliant young songwriters like Hank Cochran, Harlan Howard, and Willie Nelson. After Brenda and Patsy, Bradley continued to be one of Nashville's top producers, guiding Conway Twitty and Loretta Lynn through most of their extremely successful careers.

Chet Atkins was one of Nashville's best session musicians. When RCA built its studio in Nashville, Atkins became its manager, and eventually he ran RCA's country music department. Even as his career as a record executive and producer progressed, a long string of successful albums made him one of the world's best-known guitar players. With the rise of rock 'n' roll and the fall of country, Chet had to find a way to bring the listeners back. Like Owen Bradley, Chet called on his varied musical knowledge, and like Bradley, he opted for records that he felt would find a wider audience. It was Atkins who was responsible for the Don Gibson and Jim Reeves hits that kept country alive while the industry identified its core audience. Other record executives, like Don Law at Columbia and West Coast–based Ken Nelson at Capitol, also tinkered with the sound of country records.

In 1957, somebody coined the term "Nashville Sound," and according to Bill Ivey in the *Encyclopedia of Country Music*, it first appeared in print in 1958 in the *Music Reporter*. Early on, it seems, the term was complimentary, used to describe the Nashville way of making music: musicians came together in Nashville studios to play and turned songs into magic. Later, the term more specifically referred to the style of production that deemphasized fiddle and banjo in favor of strings, vocal group arrangements, and sometimes even horns.

And there was a quartet of young men who were there to watch it happen. Actually, they did a whole lot more than watch. Their voices would enrich popular music over five decades in Nashville, New York, and Los Angeles. But Music Row saw most of their best work, often at the rate of four sessions a day. They were the Jordanaires.

The Jordanaires and the Anita Kerr Singers were part of the A-Team. In the early days it seemed that nearly every record out of Nashville featured one group or the other on backup. The Anita Kerr Singers were a mixed group. The Jordanaires were (and still are) four men, but for many years they frequently brought in Millie Kirkham to sing the high, haunting wails that added so much to hit records like Ferlin Husky's "Gone," Elvis's "Blue Christmas," George Jones's "He Stopped Loving Her Today," and many others.

The Jordanaires have been in business for over fifty years and continue to appear around the country, though Gordon Stoker is the sole surviving founding member of the group. According to Ray Walker, who has been the group's bass singer since 1958, in the course of their career, the Jordanaires have backed more than 2,100 recording acts. Walker has a list of these acts in alphabetical order by first name. The names near the top of the list include Andy Williams, Andy Griffith, Barbara Mandrell, Billy Ray Cyrus, Bobby Vinton, Burl Ives, Charlie Rich, and Clyde McPhatter. There were years when it would have been easier to list the hit acts that were *not* backed by the Jordanaires. Today's group of Jordanaires are Stoker, Walker, Curtis Young, and Louis Nunley, the latter two of whom have also had long and honored careers as backup singers. In country music today backup singers are still frequently used, but often just one or two of them "stacked" on multiple tracks to sound like a group. But in the '50s and '60s, sessions were done "live," that is, with all the musicians and singers doing their parts together. They had to be creative, quick, and damn good if they expected to survive, and the Jordanaires excelled in all categories.

Although they had an earlier career as a pop/country/gospel group, it is their association with Elvis beginning in the mid-'50s that launched them as America's top backup group. But their association with Elvis was almost stillborn.

Says Stoker, "The Jordanaires were called to do his first sessions [on RCA], but Chet Atkins had another idea. He had just signed the Speer Family to the RCA label—they were an organized gospel group here in town—and he wanted Ben and Brock Speer to work with me. He said, 'Elvis asked for you guys, but I really would like to use Ben and Brock Speer because they need the work.'

"I said, 'Well, I know 'em, but I never worked with them.' He said, 'Aww, it don't make any difference, just come in and do some *oohs* and *aahs*, he's just a passing fad, he ain't gonna be around long anyway.'

"The first thing Elvis asked me was, 'Where's the rest of the Jordanaires?' and I told him. Do you know he couldn't stand Chet Atkins 'til the day he died because of that? He called him a sneaky SOB is exactly what he called him. Chet didn't mean anything by it—it was just one of those things—but Elvis never liked him because of that.

"We were there, or at least I was, when 'Heartbreak Hotel' was recorded," says Stoker. But he and the Speers were never called on to do their thing because the lonesome, empty feeling of the song didn't call for backup voices. "I was just sittin' there because I was so fascinated. Ben and Brock didn't, they left, but I was fascinated by Elvis, he's just a very interesting person. He was entirely different from anybody that I had been recording with. He had a beautiful smile, was just extremely friendly, and he actually kind of seemed to want me to stay. And I respected that."

Elvis had been hearing the Jordanaires on the NBC network portion of the *Grand Ole Opry*. "We would sing a lot of country songs, but a lot of times we would sing a finger-snappin', hand-clappin' spiritual, and this is what he loved, much more than anything else." When they were backing Eddy Arnold at a show in Memphis, Elvis came backstage. "He didn't come backstage to meet Eddy Arnold, he came backstage to meet us, and he said, 'Hey, fellas, I'd like to sing a little something with you.'

"We didn't know who he was. He said, 'I'm on a small label right now, and if I ever get a major label, I want you guys to work with me.' What I remembered about him was that, in '55, a guy didn't wear a pink shirt. He had on a pink shirt with black trousers and a white stripe down the side. This was just a little unusual, and he looked unusual too, in that he had the sideburns, which nobody else had. He had his hair slicked back, which wasn't black as you know—his hair was dirty blond. But the main thing that I remembered so much about him was his beautiful smile—it's something that you just won't forget. He was very cordial to us, and I guess we weren't used to being treated that way by a young guy.

"He got a lot of his clothes at the black store on Beale Street. He loved the black people, he loved the way they sang, he loved their music, their rhythm—that's what Elvis dug. Elvis was the most concerned person I ever knew about the way he looked, about the way his hair looked, about everything about him.

"For twenty years, we did from two to four sessions a day, and that is the reason we couldn't do the Elvis movies. We did the soundtracks, we appeared in some of the movies, but *King Creole* took six weeks and we couldn't stay out there because we had so much stuff goin' on in Nashville, jingles and all that type of thing."

The earliest work the Jordanaires did on Music Row was in the little basement studio Owen and Harold built before they added the Quonset Hut. "Among the first sessions we did there was 'Young Love' with Sonny James," Stoker recalls. "We did 'Gone' with Ferlin Husky, which was a huge record, about five million. 'Gone' was the first recording that we used echo. Mort Thomasson set it up, he put a speaker under the steps comin' down, and it was closed in. He had like a concrete floor. They wall-boarded it down and all that kind of carryin' on, but he had a speaker and a microphone, and he fed it back through the board.

"Among the first sessions [at the Quonset Hut] were with Patsy Cline. We did all her hits except 'Walkin' After Midnight.' The first things we did with Patsy Cline were for 4-Star Records, 'Just a Closer Walk with Thee' and another gospel song. They were the only two religious songs that she ever did.

"We backed Patsy on 'Crazy,' 'I Fall to Pieces,' and 'She's Got You,' which was my favorite, and 'Sweet Dreams,' which I could listen to for-ever. You know, Irving Berlin said, 'I don't even like country music, but there is no one who sings my song 'Always' like Patsy Cline. Have you ever heard her sing 'Always'? Believe me, she turns you on. Patsy was a char-acter. I loved her. When Owen Bradley told her first that he was gonna bring us in, she said, 'Look, hoss, I don't want four men coverin' me up!' Owen said, 'You just relax and leave that to me.' On the first session, she wasn't too friendly to us at all, because she really didn't want us there. But then after 'I Fall to Pieces' was such a hit, she said, 'Yeah, I like those guys, keep bringin' 'em in.' And then she got very friendly with us.

"She had heart and soul in everything she sang. Those songs were her life. 'I've got these little things, but she's got you'—That's the way she felt about her love life. She always thought that some man was better lookin' than her husband. She dug good-lookin' men, and I think when she was singing, she was saying, 'That's the way I feel about you, about him, about whatever.' She and [her husband] Charlie Dick were not that close by any means, even though Charlie's a friend, I mean no disrespect, but she was always lookin' at somebody else.

"She got in a huge argument with Owen about 'Crazy.' Willie Nelson wrote it, and he had done the demo. She heard it and she wanted to do it like that, and Owen said no, and they fought and fussed for three solid hours. The only time I ever heard Owen Bradley use the language that he used—Owen was sharp as a tack, and he never used bad language. He said, 'You've got to be the meanest bitch I ever knew!' He won out, but they blew three hours on it, and she came back in, and I think the reason she did such a super job is she was about half mad on that song. She was mad!

"Patsy had her way of gettin' what she wanted. She was attractive—not particularly beautiful, but she was very attractive. She was sexy, and she had a very strong personality and very strong talk. She'd use the Lord's name in vain just as quick as she wouldn't, and she used four-letter words just as quick as she wouldn't. But you knew where you stood with her. If you said something she didn't like, she'd say, 'Look, hoss, you sonofabitch, don't give me that crap!' The people she liked, she was extremely nice to, but if she didn't like you, brother, she let you know about it."

The Jordanaires worked a lot with Jim Reeves over at RCA's Studio B, and Gentleman Jim made some vivid impressions on the group.

"Jim was like an old maid," Stoker remembers. "He looked at the clock and he wanted to get at least three numbers for every three hours. Well, you know it just didn't fall that way a lot of times. Most of the time he'd push for *four* numbers, and he didn't want anyone to make jokes, he couldn't stand if you said something funny and everybody laughed—you know, you're not givin' your one-hundred-percent attention.

"Jim was extremely nice but he always pushed, and most of the time he'd record at ten o'clock at night, and we'd have done two or three sessions before we got to him. I remember so well the last session we did with him, Buddy Harman, who was one of the most sought-after drummers of all times, had done two or three sessions already and he had an hour to relax between sessions, and he laid down on the floor and was restin' his back. Jim walked in at like ten minutes to ten. He said, 'Yeah, it's always this way, I get a bunch of broken-down musicians to do my sessions.' Buddy said, 'You're gettin' your money's worth, you're getting' about two hits a session!'"

For all the many artists they recorded with, it was always Elvis who commanded the loyalty and love of the Jordanaires. They traveled together, shared their lives, and in a world of men who were constantly trying to get something from the King, these were the guys who were always there to support him.

Elvis and the Jordanaires were preparing to do a Christmas album when RCA executive Steve Sholes told Elvis that RCA had made a deal on "Blue Christmas," so Elvis was going to have to record it. In the record business in those days, it was not uncommon for a label to ask a publisher to cut their royalty rate on a song if the publisher wanted the song to be cut by a major artist on that label.

"Elvis didn't want to do that song because Ernest Tubb had had a big record on it," remembers Stoker. Elvis objected, and Sholes insisted, and they went round and round until Elvis came up with his own way to resist.

"He said to us, 'Okay, we'll do it, but you guys come up with the most ridiculous background you can come up with." If you listen to the record you can hear the Jordanaires and Millie Kirkham bleating '*oo-hoo-hoo-hoo-oo*,' trying to please their friend by making a record so bad that RCA would not release it.

"And then, every time Elvis would step up to the mic he'd sing, 'I'll have a blue *Bdbdlistmas*, without you,' and Steve would stop it every time. He'd say, 'Elvis, we can't release it like that. People will think you're making fun of the way they talk.' And again, he'd sing 'I'll have a blue *Bdbdlistmas*, without you.' The only time that he said, 'I'll have a blue Christmas,' is the recording that you're hearing. Neal [Matthews] said something to him—'It looks like we're not gonna get out of recording this, so you're gonna have to sing it.'

"Millie says she's gonna have that lick (*ooh-hoo-hoo-hoo-oo*) engraved on her tombstone because everybody knows her by that," quips Stoker. Sometimes the Jordanaires and Millie still perform together, and when they do, even in the middle of the summer everybody wants them to sing the song because they want to hear Millie do that part.

"Elvis had fun with almost everything he did. He had the best attitude. One morning, we had to do a different version of 'Stuck on You,' and Elvis called that 'Stuck in You.' He didn't like the song. He didn't wanna do the song. The Colonel had made a deal, and he had to do the song.

"We'd always go down to Graceland right after Christmas to take him a Christmas present and a birthday present. The year after 'Teddy Bear' came out, they had stuffed teddy bears from the floor to the ceiling, all around the wall in that dining room. He said, 'I guess I'll have to call Good Will and the children's homes and everybody else to come down and get these damned teddy bears out of here!' Elvis didn't like teddy bears, and everywhere, all over the world they sent him teddy bears! That's only a song in a movie! He wasn't endorsing stuffed teddy bears. When we do Elvis impersonator shows right now, they will still throw stuffed teddy bears to the guy on the stage."

Elvis's manager, his publisher, and the movie people were constantly pressuring Elvis to cut particular songs. "And many times we'd say to Elvis, 'If you don't wanna do it, just tell 'em you don't wanna do it,' and he'd finally get worn down to the point where he'd say, 'Oh, no, man, I'd just rather do it than to argue with them.' We'd say, 'You don't have to argue with them. You're the boss!' 'Cause he was his own producer.

Steve Sholes, Chet Atkins, Felton Jarvis, these guys had their name on it as being his producer. But *Elvis* was the producer, not those guys. He knew exactly what he wanted and he knew what sounded good. He knew what *was* good. You put on an Elvis Presley record from forty years ago and it sounds like it was done yesterday."

Charlie Fach mentioned earlier that RCA originally thought of Elvis as a country act when they first signed him. "But at the same time they didn't allow him to do country songs," Stoker insists. "He didn't get to do 'I Can't Stop Loving You' 'til much later in his career. He wanted to. He loved country music. And they didn't want him to do a gospel album.

"Did you know that Elvis had tried out for two male [gospel] quartets in Memphis and didn't pass the auditions? Elvis told Ray Walker that the Lord messed up on him in two ways—He didn't make him a bass singer, and He didn't make him black."

The Jordanaires worked a lot of live dates with Elvis, but eventually they had to quit. "He wanted us to go into Vegas with him, one-week show, and four weeks, rehearsal. That was five weeks out of town. We had some thirty sessions set during that period of time with Owen Bradley. Owen said, 'Gordon, we have got to have somebody do our background, and if you guys move out, I'm gonna have to bring in another male quartet. You just make up your mind what you want to do.' And we made up our minds that we'd just quit Elvis. And I always regretted that we quit Elvis, but we had no choice. We had to do what we thought financially was best for the quartet. Had we gone to Vegas, we would have missed a Coca-Cola commercial that paid us more money than working two years with Elvis.

"What killed Elvis was, he should not have had to do two shows a night in Vegas, he should have only had to do one show a night. Elvis was a perfectionist. He was determined that the second show be as good as the first. So what did he do? He took uppers and downers. He wasn't doing anything like that before Vegas. Elvis thought that as long as a doctor prescribed it, it was okay, and of course Dr. Nick prescribed *everything*."

Stoker also had an interesting take on Elvis and the way he moved. "You know, a lot of people laughed when he said, 'I can't dance,' but all that stuff he did, that wasn't dancing, that was just movement. He said he got that movement from the church. He was brought up in the Assemblies of God, and they move when they sing. And you know, on the *Ed Sullivan* shows, when they called him vulgar? He said, 'Man, that's the farthest thing from my mind, my mama would whip me if I were vulgar.'"

One of the Jordanaires' favorite artists was Don Gibson. "We sang on all his hits except 'Sea of Heartbreak,'" says Stoker. "He was very shy and had to be pushed. We took a huge interest in him and encouraged him. When he first came to Nashville, he sounded like Jim Reeves. And RCA turned him down because they said, 'We've already got one Jim Reeves, we don't need another one. You go back to Knoxville and come back and sing like Don Gibson and we'll hire you.'"

The Jordanaires also backed up Marty Robbins on most of his records. "Marty Robbins was a character, believe me. The last record we did with him before he died was 'Some Memories Just Won't Die,' and he would dance around the studio on the turnaround, and he would stick his finger in your butt or just anywhere. He could stick it in your mouth, just anything to break you up, but then if you laughed, he'd go, 'Hey, we'll have to do that over 'coz you laughed!'"

Were they on Marty's landmark record "Don't Worry 'Bout Me,' when Nashville discovered the hit value of distortion? "Yeah, we had to *ooh* and *aah* all the way through that." There are a lot of stories about what caused Grady Martin's distorted guitar sound, but Stoker's recollection of the moment is vivid and positive. "Grady said there was a tube blown out in his amplifier. He wanted to get a different amp and Don Law [the English-born producer on the session] said, 'I like the way it sounded, old boy.' That's the way he talked. Different people have different stories on it, but we were standing there and I know it was in the amp."

They also backed Johnny Horton on his mega-hit "Battle of New Orleans."

"That was Neal's arrangement," Gordon says. "We spent two and a half hours on 'Sal's Got a Sugar Lip,' and a half hour on 'The Battle of New Orleans' and it must have sold about five or six million."

One other thing generally credited to the Jordanaires is the famous Nashville numbering system, which is the way studio musicians today keep track of what they're going to play. Back in the old days, New York and L.A. sessions were generally arranged, and the musicians read the music and played it as it was written. But Nashville sessions relied on the musicians to improvise, and in the early '50s, they'd just write down the names of the chords, e.g. C, F#, G, or they'd just keep the chords in their heads. But Neal Matthews, who generally arranged the Jordanaires' vocal parts, wrote down *numbers* instead. That way, if the producer decided to change the key they could still sing off the same chord chart.

"We used the number system for some two years before anybody else would ever use it. One day, Charlie McCoy walked over to Neal and said, 'Hey, Neal, explain that to me.' And so Neal explained it: if you were playing in the key of C, C is '1.' F, that's your '4' chord, '3 minor' would be E minor." Five decades later, the number system still rules in Music Row studios, and probably just about everywhere else in the U.S.A.

For two decades, the Jordanaires set the pace for backup groups on Music Row. Their influence in the world of pop music is incalculable. One time, Paul McCartney was recording in the Sound Shop down on Division Street when Stoker came in to visit.

"He turned around to me and said, 'You're one of the Jordanaires?'"

"I said, 'Yeah. I wanted to meet you.'"

"He said, 'I wanted to meet *you*. The Beatles learned to sing harmony by listening to you guys behind Elvis and Ricky Nelson.' He said, 'When we'd buy a record of Elvis, we never listened to Elvis. We'd listen to the Jordanaires.'"

7

SAVING COUNTRY

I n the late 1950s, country music was in the process of finding a wider audience through its crossover records, but the industry might have died anyway had it not been for a stalwart group of country professionals who formed an organization expressly to save it. That was the Country Music Association.

Lawyer Dick Frank was a part of it almost from the beginning. "The CMA was the spiritual successor to the Country Music Disc Jockeys Association," says Frank, "which had become defunct because its treasury disappeared. So a small group gathered in a hotel room down in Miami at a NARM [the National Association of Recording Merchandisers, a trade group that serves the music retailing community] convention in 1957. They decided to form a country music association to try to publicize and advance country music as an industry. Some of the people there were Wesley Rose, Connie B. Gay [a media entrepreneur], D Kilpatrick [a record executive], and Cracker Jim Booker [a Florida disc jockey].

"They came back to Tennessee, and my partner, Ward Hudgins [a former U.S. attorney who had done some local work for Acuff-Rose] volunteered me, as a new tax lawyer, to get their federal income tax exemption, in the course of which I got to know the people, got sort of involved, became fascinated by the business and the intricacies of it. I remember our first meeting was in a room on the mezzanine of the old Hermitage Hotel with the louvered windows open. It was rather hot, a little noisy, with the traffic going by. Ward had broken his leg and was sitting up there in a leg cast. That was our organizing meeting.

"The stated purpose was to advance country music commercially and as an art form. Our first annual membership meeting, if you can call it that, was down in the basement of the Andrew Jackson Hotel, which is now torn down, among folded tables leaning against the walls and things like that. We elected a board of directors, but at that time, we had no employees.

"The first several years were rough. Hubert Long was a successful publisher, manager, and booker here. He volunteered a small cubicle in the old Exchange Building on lower Church Street. He lent us a typewriter, and a light bulb, and a cubicle, and that was the first CMA office."

Another person who would play a huge role in the history of the Country Music Association was a young woman named Jo Walker, later Jo Walker-Meador.

"Radio stations were droppin' [country music] by the hundreds across the country, largely, I think, due to the advent of rock 'n' roll, probably starting in 1956 or '57. Not only rock 'n' roll but the Top 40 format." Walker-Meador says that when the Top 40 format came along, a lot of stations that had "block programming—blocks of time devoted to different kinds of shows—dropped country music in favor of shows featuring the Top 40 records in the country, regardless of genre.

"The CMA had their first organizational meeting during WSM's convention in November 1958, and I began work December 8, 1958," Walker-Meador recalls. "I came as a gal Friday. There was nobody there but me, but I knew the board's intention was to hire a man as an executive director. This was long before women's lib and I thought that's what they should do. I thought they found the perfect man, a man named Harry Stone. He had started working for WSM in 1925 and was later the manager of the Grand Ole Opry. The problem was that CMA was new and the money was not there to pay both our salaries. The board expected Harry to come up with ideas to fund the association.

"Harry had thought that the record companies and the big publishing companies were already behind CMA. It was just a misunderstanding, of who was going to be funding the association. By virtue of that, Harry was only there ten months. By mutual agreement, Harry resigned. That left me by myself until 1963."

"It was during those early years that we had a meeting in Shreveport," Frank recalls. "We tried to have board of directors meetings in different markets, at which we wouldn't just meet but we would try to have a little function for local distributors, radio station people, going out and preaching the gospel [of country music]. Bob Austin was on the board and he was the editor of *Cashbox*, an important music trade magazine at the time. Following the meeting, this headline comes out in *Cashbox*, saying, 'CMA may not survive to next board meeting.' A lot of people didn't like him after that."

But Austin wasn't that far off. The members of the CMA took to holding fund-raisers to keep the doors open and they managed to hang on by their fingernails while trying to get the word out to the radio and record industries that America still loved country music. "We entered into an agreement with one of the first telemarketers, under which if we got all the royalty-free clearances for a TV package album, he'd pay us twenty-five cents an album for all those he sold. Oddly enough, that gave us a capital nest egg. It was very successful. Next time he came around we were getting a dollar an album. This was around 1960 and that created a 'capital mass.' So we were able to concentrate on *projects* as opposed to *survival*."

The "capital mass" Frank was talking about came none too soon. CMA records show that by 1961 there were only eighty-one full-time country radio stations left in the United States. Walker-Meador says that country actually had hit the pits several years before. "It really bottomed out about '57 for sure," she says. "The first survey was made in '61. We made a mailing to the radio stations, that's how we came up with that number."

The various members of this young organization rolled up their sleeves and went to work to save their music. They created their own body of demographic research and sales kits, and gave pitches and presentations to broadcasters' and advertisers' conventions. According to Frank, "We had a luncheon for the Sales and Executive Club in New York at the Waldorf. Tex Ritter, Don Gibson, oh, about four artists were on the program. We recorded the show and sent a copy of the album to everyone who attended. The door prize was a Tennessee Walking colt, which we fitted with rubber shoes and took up in the elevator. "We were trying to break the Madison Avenue stereotypes. When you said 'country music,' they thought of bales of straw and piles of horse manure. Too many of them still do." (It makes one wonder why they thought that giving away a horse would break the stereotype, but then, Tennessee Walking horses are considered to be very elite animals.)

Walker-Meador described how the CMA sold the country format to radio: "It was done through letters, phone calls, board members giving their time to go out and talk to the people. We looked at stations' ratings. In a major market, if you've got four stations programming rock, at least one of them is gonna be sufferin'. Go for the station that's hurtin', and show him how he can make money by becoming a country music station. Bill Hudson [a noted PR executive in Nashville] did a lot of the work, and then Don Nelson, who was general manager of WIRE radio in Indianapolis and was on the board, he gave a lot of his time, not only to work with stations but also to work with sponsors, people that wouldn't normally buy time on country. Joe Allison was wonderful at that."

They were learning to use the human resources available to them. WSM executive Irving Waugh and Tree chief executive Jack Stapp had good ties to the mighty Chicago advertising agency J. Walter Thompson. They sold the idea of a country music awards show to the agency for Kraft. This powerful purveyor of cheese was a perfect choice—over the years they had sponsored classy TV drama and music shows, and they would lend a sense of dignity that would separate modern country music from the years of raggedy hillbilly costumes and gap-toothed country comedians. The first televised CMA awards show occurred in 1968 as part of the Kraft Music Hall series.

"They did the production and we got a license fee of $25,000," Frank remembers, adding that in a major TV network setting, country music received serious exposure to audiences that had been conditioned not to take country music seriously. "They attracted a demographic that we regarded as probably being the optimum demographic for the music—middle-class households. Twenty-five-to-forty-five age group, which still is the best demographic."

By 1969, there were more than 600 radio stations around the country that identified themselves as country music stations. In a very short time, country had come a long way.

"I well remember one season, within a period of months, that five radio stations in major markets like Cincinnati and Denver all changed their format to country music," says Walker-Meador. "This was a great cause for celebration and a great influence on other stations that were possibly considering such a move at the time, but were afraid to make the leap.

"We always played it that country music is an umbrella for a lot of kinds of music. It's for the modern, it's for the hillbilly, it's for the rockabilly, it's for the Cajun, it's for the bluegrass. We had to get away from 'country and western.' A lot of time was spent in board meetings in the early couple of years talking about what to call it. We had to get away from 'hillbilly,' and then, the 'western' part. It took a long time. It wasn't that we didn't include *western*, we felt that western was a part of *country*, just like these other types that I mentioned."

The major media has often seemed uncomfortable with country music and the culture it represents. Walker-Meador recalls when *Hee-Haw* was a very successful show on network TV. "That was on CBS to start with," she says. "It was my understanding that they dropped it because the wives of a lot of the executives at CBS were concerned that, 'It's gonna be known as a dang hillbilly network,' and they put so much pressure on 'em that they dropped it. Of course, the producers of *Hee-Haw* were better off syndicating it, because a lot of CBS stations wouldn't carry it anyway, so they got on a lot more stations when they syndicated it."

The Country Music Association did more than just increase country music media exposure over the years. It brought onto Music Row the attitude that music competitors could work together for the common good of their industry and rejoice in each other's triumphs. That attitude was easy to adopt in the '50s, when Music Row was so small and so new, and the CMA made it possible for the industry to sustain that attitude for many years as the industry got larger.

"It has been said that the Country Music Association is the world's most active trade association," says Robert Oermann. "And in many ways maybe they did their job too well. Now that Nashville is so identified as the country music capital, all of our other music is ignored!"

8

DANG ME!

As the Quonset Hut and RCA Studio B grew busier and busier, producers found they could not always get the A-Team guys. But the A-Team wasn't all there was. Today they may be viewed as "gods," but they were by no means divine, they were just great studio musicians, and Nashville was about to be inundated with great musicians from all over the country.

Sometimes a producer is willing to take a chance on a new guy with a new sound, and if the record hits, people up and down Music Row will be demanding to know who he is. When it happens, that musician may be on his way to a long and rewarding career. By 1962, there were a number of original-sounding session players who had embarked on that journey. One of them was a guitar picker from Shreveport, Louisiana, barely old enough to vote, but more than old enough to hold his own in the studios of Nashville, Tennessee.

For more than three decades, Jerry Kennedy was one of Nashville's premier studio musicians, as well as a successful producer, and later head of Mercury Records in Nashville. As producer and executive, he was responsible for much of the success of Tom T. Hall, the Statler Brothers, and Roger Miller, among others.

Kennedy began his career in 1950, singing at the ridiculous age of ten. "I had two or three singles at the ages of eleven or twelve," he recalls. "I recorded some sessions in Dallas, and then I came to Nashville for the last session I did." After his abbreviated recording career, Kennedy became interested in playing guitar. "I got a Fender Telecaster electric guitar and I thought it was the biggest thing that ever happened to me. That was about 1953 or '54, and my mom had to work real hard to get that done for me, but she managed to pull it off and I started playing, and didn't really care much for singing after that." Kennedy got his first guitar lessons from Tillman Franks, who would someday gain country music success as personal manager for Webb Pierce, Johnny Horton, Slim Whitman and David Houston.

By that time *The Louisiana Hayride*, a radio show that blasted across the South on 50,000 watts of AM power through KWKH, was a big thing in Shreveport. Over the years *The Hayride* featured some huge artists, including Hank Williams, Elvis, Jim Reeves, Johnny Horton, Webb Pierce, Faron Young, and Kitty Wells.

While he was still in high school, Kennedy was playing staff guitar Saturday nights on *The Hayride*. He might have never moved to Nashville but for another man from Shreveport, one of the great characters and hustlers in the history of country music, Shelby Singleton.

Texas-born Singleton was an industrial engineer for Remington Rand, who got into the music business only because his first wife, Margie, wanted to be a singer. "So I got involved in promoting her, developing her, and she became a member of *The Hayride*," says Singleton. Just a taste was all he needed. In 1957, he quit his job at Remington Rand and went to work for Mercury Records, first in record promotion, then as a southern regional representative of the label. In 1961, he moved from Shreveport to Nashville to run the Mercury office.

Charlie Fach, who by this time had left RCA and was working for Mercury, credits Singleton with much of Mercury's country success. "Mercury had been in the country business for many years," he says. "D Kilpatrick ran it at one time. But Mercury really seriously got into the country business when Shelby Singleton moved here, opened an office, and hired Jerry Kennedy."

When Kennedy came to Nashville, Mercury was in the Cumberland Lodge Building along with all the other companies who had yet to move onto Music Row. Eventually Singleton, Kennedy, and drummer Buddy Harman would buy the building next to Cedarwood and rent it to Mercury. That would be Mercury's first office on Music Row. By that time, Singleton would recall, Ampex Tape would be located in a building alongside Cedarwood, Columbia would have bought the Quonset Hut and built their new Nashville offices around it and the little house that started it all, and Hubert Long, a powerhouse in booking, management, and music publishing, would be operating out of a place built right up against the new Columbia building.

Before Singleton moved to Nashville, he was making trips here from Shreveport to produce sessions for Mercury, and when he did he would bring young Jerry Kennedy along to play on those sessions. "I did not want to move here," Kennedy remembers. "Shelby talked me into it, and against everything I believed in I came up here to try it. He told me we were gonna get rich and be famous. Shelby always had that kind of personality where he was positive about everything. I wish I had that. He kept bothering me for weeks before he moved up here. We had been doing some record sessions in New Orleans, Baton Rouge, Lake Charles, Beaumont, and I guess he liked the way we worked together."

Kennedy moved to Nashville in March 1961. "In April," he says, "Shelby hired me as his assistant. So it was up to me to find material and look for new acts. That turned out to be a big thing for me because what people don't realize, in '62, that was when the explosion happened here in Nashville.

"Shelby had a lot to do with it because Mercury was bought by Phillips. Phillips wanted to start a label called 'Phillips.' And they also wanted to do the Smash label. All of this happened in January of '62. All of a sudden there were three labels to funnel artists into."

It was not unusual for major record companies to have several labels. Columbia had Columbia, Epic, and OKeh. Decca had Coral. What made this different was that the Nashville office of Mercury/Phillips/Smash would have considerable involvement in pop production.

"It was so crazy back then, I can't remember [how many acts we were dealing with]. All of a sudden they were signing acts in Chicago that we were recording here in Nashville. Nana Mouskouri, the Springfields— Shelby was signing everybody. If he signed a steel guitar player to do an album on Mercury, he signed one for Phillips and one for Smash. So we had Don Helms on Phillips, I think, Walter Haynes on Mercury, and Pete Drake on Smash. In fact we had hits on Pete."

Kennedy was looking for songs, looking for artists, producing sessions, and playing on sessions for three related record labels, each of which was ramping up its rosters. Just two years after coming to Nashville with few prospects, he had all the work anybody could hope to handle. Sometimes that work was unbelievably instructive.

Kennedy recalls a day when he played on three huge hits. Typical session times then, as now, were 10 a.m., 2 p.m., and 6 p.m. One morning he walked into the Quonset Hut and played on Ray Stevens's pop smash,

"Ahab the Arab." That afternoon he played on Leroy Van Dyke's classic, "Walk On By," which was number-one country for nineteen weeks and was Top 5 on the pop charts. That evening, he closed his day's work by playing on Joe Dowell's pop hit "Wooden Heart." The way that session came about is indicative of the speed with which the Row could react when there was a hit record at stake.

Charlie Fach, head of newly created Smash Records, was talking to a disc jockey friend of his in Buffalo. "Guy by the name of George Lorenz, who had a record tip sheet," says Fach. "He says, 'Charlie, RCA's crazy, they got this *G.I. Blues* album out [on Elvis] and people are beggin' for 'Wooden Heart' as a single, and they refuse to put it out as a single."

"I said, 'That's all I needed to know.' I called Shelby and said, 'Find somebody that sounds like Presley and cover 'Wooden Heart' as closely as you can.' So he found Joe Dowell to do it. I put the record out on Joe Dowell and I find out there's two covers out already! Presley never did come out with it as a single, so we battled it through and we ended up with a number-one record on the thing."

Record labels were beginning to change the way they did business with their creative staff and, in May 1963, Kennedy left Mercury to open Columbia's Epic office in Nashville. In the glory years of Owen Bradley and Chet Atkins, both men reportedly were on straight salary. By Nashville standards, they must have been paid well, but considering the large rosters they supervised, and their many hits, there's no telling how much they would have made had they been paid a royalty override against their salary.

Kennedy was also on salary, and he was working very hard for that salary. Columbia offered him an override. It didn't take long for Mercury to miss Kennedy, and when they offered him a similar override to come back in October of that year, Kennedy agreed. When he left Epic, Kennedy recommended Billy Sherrill to succeed him. Sherrill would become one of the great producers of the late '60s and '70s, producing hit after hit for Tammy Wynette, George Jones, Tanya Tucker, Charlie Rich, Johnny Paycheck, Johnny Duncan, and many others.

So Kennedy was back working with three label rosters, playing on all their sessions, and playing outside sessions, too. And Mercury was not the only label jacking up its Nashville productivity. "Owen was recording twenty-five or thirty people, and so was Chet," he says. There were a lot of independent labels, too. There was Hickory [Acuff-Rose's house label, which boasted many successes in the '60s]. Harold Lipsius was coming down from Philadelphia doing some things for Jamie; Archie Bleyer was coming in doing some things with Cadence. I remember working on a Johnny Tillotson session." A lot of this music was not country at all. Kennedy played on the sessions of Perry Como, Vic Damone, Fats Domino, Duane Eddy, and the Everlys. Roy Orbison was just busting out and Kennedy played on many of his hits, including "It's Over," "Blue Bayou," "Mean Woman Blues," and "Oh, Pretty Woman."

The intro on "Oh, Pretty Woman" is one of the most famous licks in the history of pop music. "There were three guitar players on that intro," remembers Kennedy. "Me, Wayne Moss, and Billy Sanford. Roy had the lick when we all walked in. Roy was a good arranger. He knew what he wanted."

Like many Nashville musicians, Kennedy considers the '60s to be a special time on Music Row.

"I've told people so many times, we were having so much fun working so hard that we really had trouble getting to socialize with each other outside of the studio, yet we were all great friends." He says that he and the other label heads may have been in friendly competition with each other, but on the record promotion level, tough professionals made the phone calls to and fought for airplay on the radio stations. "Those guys were at each other's throats. But the guys who were in charge of the labels, it was a different situation. I can remember getting phone calls on different records that I would release, from Chet, from Billy Sherrill, saying, 'What a great record that is, congratulations.' I remember Billy Sherrill called me on 'What's Made Milwaukee Famous'—he thought that was great; and then 'Chantilly Lace,' he called me on that one, too." Both were hits by Jerry Lee Lewis on the Mercury label.

Kennedy made his biggest mark in the world of pop music with the groundbreaking hits he produced for Roger Miller in the mid-'60s.

"Roger came to me and asked if we were interested in signing him. First, I checked with Chet to make sure that everything was okay with him leaving RCA—that was the way we did it back then." Roger had had some decent chart activity on RCA but there were no signs that he was an emerging star, so Atkins gave Miller his blessing to move to Mercury.

At this point, Roger had movie-acting ambitions, but he had no money to get him to Los Angeles. "After we agreed to do a session with him he came back and wanted to know if there was any way he could get a sixteen-hundred-dollar advance, that was what it was gonna cost him to move to L.A. I called Charlie Fach. Charlie had already agreed to sign Roger, now all of a sudden we've got this request for this money. Charlie said, 'Let me get back to you,' and he got back to me and told me he would do it if Roger would give me sixteen sides at a hundred dollars a side. So he got enough money to move to L.A. and we got 'Dang Me,' 'Chug-a-Lug,' and 'Do-Wacka-Do.' I realized we had good songs there. But I didn't know that we had something that would cross over."

The song that made Roger a star was "Dang Me." How it came to be Roger's first release on Smash shows that nobody really knows what makes a hit. Kennedy tells the story: "The Friday-night session was put on one reel, and the Saturday session was put on another, a big reel, because there were twelve songs. At my house I did not have a take-up reel that would hold those twelve songs. When Smash called me and asked me for a 'single coupling' on the Roger Miller thing"—meaning what the A- and B-sides would be on Roger's first single—"I got out my tape and I listened to the first sides we did, and I listened to as much of the twelve-song tape as my take-up reel would hold, and I picked the single from there. It was a song called 'Got to Again.' I thought that would be a good song to do, and I loved everything Roger did anyway.

"That was a horrible decision on my part not to listen to the balance of that tape. One night after I had made my decision to go with 'Got to Again' and whatever the B-side was, I went by Nicholson's Hi-Fi and bought a big take-up reel, and I was playing the whole tape in my office at home. And it got to 'Dang Me.' My kids came tearing downstairs, man, they went *nuts* when they heard Roger doin' all that scat stuff right at the beginning. And I said, 'What have I done?' I called the label the next day—they were pressing 'Got to Again'—and Irv Green, bless his heart, president of Mercury, I told him I needed to change it, that I'd made a mistake. And I told him the story, and I said, 'I'm gonna admit to you what I did.' He said, 'Are you sure about this?' I said 'Yeah.' Instead of saying, 'No you can't change it now,' he went along with me. It could have been that thing where it didn't do anything and they would have dropped Roger. That's how close we came to not having 'Dang Me' as our first record.

"Charlie Fach [who was then running the Smash label] had bigger dreams for what we were doing with Roger than I did. Charlie would not have signed him if he didn't think Roger could do more than just country. Roger turned this town upside down. I can remember everybody was really pulling for him. Nobody was jealous of him. That was the way it was in those days. We all pulled for each other. In fact, I have had songs pitched to me that I took and gave to Chet because I didn't have anybody who could do them, but they were great songs, and you knew that he had somebody who could do them. He did the same thing with me. He would send writers over to me with a great song that he didn't have anybody for. It was like a big family."

"Dang Me" hit the country charts in June 1964, zoomed to the number-one spot, stayed number one for six weeks, and peaked at number seven on the pop charts. "Chug-a-Lug" was also Top 10 pop. The Following year he scored even higher with the million-selling "King of the Road." With less than perfect timing Roger had landed smack-dab in the middle of the British Invasion and one can only wonder what his sales and pop chart positions might have been if he were not competing *mano a mano* against the Beatles, the Searchers, the Dave Clark Five, and the Kinks. As it was, he collected an incredible five Grammy Awards in 1965 and earned Tree the capital to move out of the Cumberland Lodge Building and into their own two-story house on 16th Avenue South, just a block down from RCA and the Quonset Hut.

The chief beneficiaries of the Roger Miller phenomenon, outside of Roger himself, were Jack Stapp, the president of Tree, and the man who ran the daily operations of the company, Buddy Killen.

There is a famous dive on Lower Broadway in Nashville called Tootsie's, just across the alley from the Ryman Auditorium. Back in 1958, it was just another beer bar called Mom's, and one evening Buddy Killen, fresh off his "Heartbreak Hotel" triumph, was playing the pinball machine to a near empty house. It was a weekday evening and Killen was still dressed in his tailored suit. Intent on his game, Killen didn't notice the young man with the short hair and the short-sleeved, button-front shirt who walked in and bought a long-necked bottle.

The young man heard the bells ringing and walked over to the pinball machine, where the guy in the suit was jabbing at the flippers and guiding the machine with expert body English.

"You're Buddy Killen," he said.

"I am," came the response.

Roger gave Killen a quick pitch, and it must have been a good one because Buddy handed Roger a five-dollar bill and invited him to visit the Tree office in the Cumberland Lodge Building the following Monday. Tree became Roger Miller's publisher.

Sometime in '65, Joyce Bush, secretary/treasurer of Tree, sent Roger a publishing royalty check for $64,619.31, a huge sum for a country songwriter in those days.

Roger Miller was the artist that made Jerry Kennedy one of Nashville's premier producers, but it didn't happen the way he thought it would. "I had high hopes for Roger as a country artist," he recalls, "because that was what I had heard him do. 'In the Summertime' was the only 'crazy' song I'd heard up to the point of hearing all these other things."

With the making of any star, there is always the producer's story, and then there is the label executive's story. Put the two stories together and you get an idea of how record labels work. If there hadn't been a Smash record label, Roger Miller would probably never have happened.

When Shelby Singleton moved to Nashville, Mercury moved Charlie Fach out to Chicago to be national promotion manager. About a year later, Mercury was very hot. "We had nine or ten records in the Top 100 and I couldn't get stations to play any more Mercury records," says Fach. "So we had a meeting one day trying to figure out what we're gonna do and my boss says, 'Why don't we toss out another label?' They already had the name 'Smash' registered, so he said, 'Charlie, why don't you run Smash on a part-time basis?' The second record we put out was a master that Shelby picked up from New Orleans called 'I'm a Fool to Care' by Joe Berry. They said, 'Charlie, why don't you start a separate label with Smash, find other distributors [other than Mercury distributors] that are hot for a brand-new label, and we became as good a label as anybody in the business."

Another master Smash acquired was Bruce Chanel's "Hey, Baby," a big hit that is remembered today for Delbert McClinton's eloquent harmonica intro, which would later influence John Lennon's harmonica playing.

And then there was Roger Miller. "Shelby wanted me to get into the country business on Smash," recalls Fach. "I said fine. The first two country acts that we put out, I promptly destroyed their recording careers; Billy Deaton and Bob Beckham. I ran them out of the recording business. I did such a lousy job with them. But they later went on to become very successful in the music business.

"Not long after those two fiascos we were having an A&R meeting in Chicago, all three of the labels—Mercury, Phillips, and Smash—and Jerry Kennedy said, 'Roger Miller is on RCA but he's very unhappy, and he'd like to go to another label. I'd seen him on *The Tonight Show*. He had a record out called 'In the Summertime,' a really crazy thing he did on the

Carson show, but Andy Williams had covered it on Columbia, and had a number-one record on it. I said, 'Yeah, he's an interesting guy, maybe we oughta put him on Smash.' But I didn't do anything—it sorta got put in a corner for a while. A couple weeks later, we came down to Nashville for the Disc Jockey Convention.

"The first night of the convention Mr. Green, the president of Mercury, Shelby, and I were having dinner in a restaurant down in Printer's Alley. Shelby looked around and he said, 'Oh, back over there in a corner, there's Buddy Killen with Roger Miller.' He says, 'We oughta sign that guy.' I says, 'Yeah, let's sign him to Smash.' Shelby went over there and talked to them, he came back in less than a minute, says, 'Yeah, we got a deal.' Can you imagine that happening in the record business today?"

When Smash released "Dang Me," like RCA years before with "Heartbreak Hotel," they thought they would have a pretty good country hit. But the public decreed otherwise. "One day I get a call from Bill Ennis, the program director at KLIF [a big pop radio station in Texas]. I thought what the hell's he calling me about, *I* usually call these Top 40 guys. He says, 'Charlie, I'm gonna put one of your records on this weekend and I wanna make damn sure you got stock in the market [records at the local stores].' I say, 'What record?' He says, 'This "Dang Me" record by Roger Miller. This thing is *flyin'* out of the one-stops.' I say, 'I'll cover it, Bill.'

"We had an independent distributor in Chicago that had a promotion man that was as good as any that was ever in the business, guy by the name of Howard Bedno. The big pop station in Chicago was WLS, 50,000-watter that boomed down in the nighttime. So I told Howard Bedno [about KLIF] and he says, 'If that record makes it on KLIF," he says 'I'll have it on WLS the following week. Damned if he didn't!"

Within a few weeks Bedno had four big 50,000-watt pop stations booming Roger Miller into the night. "To be honest with you, I didn't even pay attention to the country play, we were getting, you know, with this premier pop play on it."

The country stations all came along anyway, as did the MOR (middle of the road) stations. "Dang Me" was huge. The follow-up was easy. "I told Jerry that all the accounts were telling us that the college kids were buying the album because of the 'Chug-a-Lug' thing, it was like a theme song at the fraternity houses. This is decades before binge drinking. I told Jerry not only do we have the college market but that record'll be in every barroom juke box in the country!"

9

CRAZY

I n the mid-'60s, the so-called British invasion, led by the Beatles, the Dave Clark 5, Gerry and the Pacemakers, and others, wiped many major American singers off the airwaves. Music Row remained a destination for successful established artists who were looking for a change, but the number of high-profile pop acts recording in Nashville declined. There were no new Elvises, Brenda Lees, Everlys, Sue Thompsons, Newbeats, or Ronnie and the Daytonas.

Jerry Kennedy suggests that Nashville's country image hurt its ability to place pop acts in L.A. or New York. "I remember thinking that we used to record some sessions that we would intentionally aim pop, rock, R&B, whatever, and I used to think that if we left off the producer's name, and where it was recorded, that it might have a better shot because it *was* Nashville." In the mid-'60s, many of the pop acts that had been coming just *stopped*. There was a huge change that took place in music during that era, and a whole generation of pop artists, including many who recorded in Nashville, lost their record deals.

"I know I enjoyed doing the country stuff more than intentionally aiming some records at the pop market," Kennedy says. And he is typical of his generation of A&R people that worked on Music Row: when much of pop music changed to a form that was not really compatible with what Music Row did, the Nashville music machine continued to do what it knew how to do best, turning out song-driven music that they could get played on country radio.

By 1975, there were more than 1,100 full-time country radio stations, nearly double what it had been just three years before. "It was something that went completely by me," he says. "I wasn't thinking about the business part of it as much as I was the music, even though by '69, Mercury had made me vice president of A&R in Nashville. All I knew was that as we moved into the '70s, Mercury was beginning to make more sense with country music than we had in the '60s," not only by remaking Jerry Lee Lewis into a country star, but with the arrival of Tom T. Hall in 1967 and the Statler Brothers in 1970.

And thanks to new technology, the way Music Row made records was changing, too. Back in the '50s and early '60s, recording was still essentially mono. Sessions were recorded live, including the strings.

Chord charts were used as a guide, but within the basic structure of a song, musicians came up with their own licks and solos. There was a lot of inspiration. But when the recording called for string sections, then the music had to be written out so that each violin, viola, and cello player knew *exactly* what he was going to play.

"I can remember that when an arranger like Bill Justis would bring his arrangements to the studio," Kennedy says, "the string parts would be written, but he'd give *me* a piece of paper that said, 'Play your heart out!' or something like that. He didn't try to pigeonhole the rhythm section. He knew that we would make any adjustments that we needed to what he had written for the strings, who couldn't make changes unless he had to go in there and rewrite, which he *did,* a lot. He would rewrite the string parts if the rhythm section came up with something good that he didn't have written for the strings.

"I went to Germany in '63 with Orbison to do some recording in Berlin, went with Fred [Foster, head of Monument Records], Bob Moore, Harold Bradley, we may have been the only musicians from here that went. That's the first time I ever saw eight-track, and when they brought that huge tape out and put it on the machine, I looked at it and said, 'If we ever get that in Nashville, that's all we'll ever need.' It was a lot of time later before we ever got it here. And when I first saw sixteen-track, I basically said the same thing."

In fact, he says, the first sixteen-track session done in Nashville was Roger Miller in 1969, when he recorded the Kris Kristofferson (and Fred Foster) classic "Me and Bobby McGee."

"It was still being written when we recorded it," says Kennedy. "Beckham and Kris came over and sung the song to Roger half finished. We agreed to record it. The second verse was not written yet. We recorded what was written and had Roger come back in and finish the song after Kris had finished writing it. When we finally finished recording Roger's part on the song, I told the engineer, Mort Thomasson, 'Let's mix it.'

"Mort had this offbeat sense of humor. He told me nothin' doin'. 'We've only got fifteen tracks recorded and we're not mixing this 'til we've filled every track.'" Kennedy shrugged his shoulders and went along. "I called Charlie McCoy, had him bring in his harmonica, and where Roger sang the line, 'I took my harpoon out of my dirty red bandanna and was blowin' sad while Bobby sang the blues.' When he sang the part about 'blowin' sad,' Charlie put in this soulful little harmonica lick, and that lick was my way of fillin' that last track for Mort."

The word got out that Nashville was a place to go for great session musicians. For a time, the A-Team had so much work that at their busiest, they scarcely slept. As more studios came on-line, places like Fred Foster's Monument Studio and Owen Bradley's Barn out in Mount Juliet, there would be numerous sessions going on simultaneously, and producers unable to get their old reliable A-Teamers would heed the recommendations of their peers, or they would inquire about the unique licks they were hearing on the song demos being pitched to them, and new guys would be fed into the mix.

Nashville session musicians pride themselves on being laid-back. When it's time to come up with the licks that will make a song a hit, somehow they are able to combine the appearance of effortless virtuosity with deadly serious concentration. But they're also good for an outrageous practical joke—when the moment is right.

"Quincy Jones had come to Nashville in 1962 or 1963 to do some sessions on Bobby Scott, who wrote 'A Taste of Honey,'" Kennedy recalls. "Bobby was a piano player and singer. He was going to do an album, and they decided that it would be best to bring him to Nashville. We used to make these decisions at A&R meetings in Chicago. Shelby sent out and got sheets and pillowcases for all the musicians—to *wear*. I still remember Quincy's face when he came in and saw all these musicians sitting with their instruments, ready to play, in white sheets and pillowcases.

"It was just a great way to break the ice, in fact for years Quincy told the story all over the place, too. I don't recall us having to make any special effort to be nice—I was one of the first people he saw when I came out from under the sheet and he cracked up."

Future songwriting great Bobby Braddock, who made his first appearance on Music Row back in 1959, moved to Nashville for good in 1964. Braddock's memories of that era and its music are very vivid.

"I got a job playing a bar out on Dickerson Road for, I think, it was forty-five dollars a week for two, three, four nights a week—it was peanuts. There was a drummer named Jimmy Stewart who had been playing on the road with Roger Miller, and he called me up one day in the latter part of '64 and he said, 'Do you want a job that could last forever?'

"I said, 'What's that?' and he said, 'Marty Robbins's piano player Joe Babcock is quitting the road.' So I went and auditioned for Marty and got the gig. A lot of the shows we played were big package shows. You'd have Marty Robbins, Ray Price, maybe Johnny Cash, Kitty Wells, the Osborne Brothers—there'd be a bunch of superstars on the same show.

"Marty started using me on sessions of other people he was cutting, and eventually he decided to use me on one of *his* sessions. He had this song written by Jeanne Pruett called 'Count Me Out,' and the session was in Studio A at Columbia. Now, I had a little style I played on the piano that was like steel guitar, but it wasn't the slip-note that Floyd Cramer used, I used my entire hand. And in all modesty, I can tell you, I have not known anybody else that does that. So I had a piano turnaround worked up for that song in the key of C. I was gonna take the lead on it. There at the session, that was *me* playing with Harold Bradley and all those guys. I played that turnaround and they said, 'Wow! Bobby that is just great! That's phenomenal! How are you doin' that?'

"Then Marty says, 'You know, that's a bit high for me, let's drop that to B-flat.' So I went from my best key to my worst key, and it was just horrible. The last two notes on it actually were *clunk, clunk*! They were talking about it not being just right and Marty said, 'Oh hell, it'll be a B-side and nobody'll hear it. The way they dealt with it was not a really good way to do it. They should have put somebody else on there or just not put it out, it was that bad.

"What they did, was they turned it down in the mix—it was on the track with the lead instruments—so when it came time for the solo, not only was it played badly, it was played not very loud, which made it sound even worse. When we were out on the road I remember one DJ came up and said, 'Was that you playin' piano on 'Count Me Out'? That thing that

Marty said was just gonna be a B-side was an A-side, and it was a hit, with my bad piano-playing on it.

"Tex Davis asked if that was me and I said, 'No, that was some guy in California.'

"In '66, I told Marty I'd like to stay in town, 'cause Marty cut a couple of my songs and I thought, well, shit, maybe I *am* a songwriter." Braddock had been writing songs for Robbins's company, and Marty agreed to return to Braddock all the songs Marty hadn't spent money demoing. "That year Tree had overtaken Acuff-Rose and Cedarwood, they were the number-one publisher. I also knew that Roger Miller had been their knight in shining armor and he had just moved to California. It's a hot company, but their big guy has moved away, and so I went and I asked for Buddy Killen on the phone.

"Buddy was adamant in making sure that I knew he didn't usually see unknown people. I played him a bunch of songs. He liked them, signed me up, and put me on a draw—something really low, even for then—I think, forty dollars a week. He said, 'When it's time for you to get a hundred-dollar-a-week draw, I'll know, you won't have to ask me.'

"Between Buddy and Curly [Putman, writer of 'Green Green Grass of Home' and many other huge hits], they started getting my songs cut left and right. Jack Barlow, Jack Scott, Little Jimmy Dickens, the Statler Brothers, and Jim Ed Brown. Yeah, I thought that Tree might be a good place. To be honest, a Ouija board told me that I should go there."

Another colorful and successful songwriter from that era, who is still productive, is Hank Cochran, who wrote or co-wrote some of Nashville's greatest standards, including "She's Got You," "Little Bitty Tear," "Make the World Go Away," and "I Fall to Pieces." His songs have become hits for Merle Haggard, George Strait, Mickey Gilley, Vern Gosdin, and many others of country's elite.

Garland Perry Cochran was born in Isola, Mississippi. "Me and my uncle, we hitchhiked into Hobbs, New Mexico, and I went to work as a roughneck when I was about twelve years old and then I went to drillin' wells when I was about thirteen.

"By then, I was makin' pretty good money, and I got me a car and went back to Mississippi to show it off. I turned it over and tore the sonofabitch all to pieces, so I hitchhiked to Mississippi and worked there 'til I got enough money to stick in my pocket, and I hitchhiked to California.

"At sixteen, I was like a grown person, and I'd been through all that other shit already, but they made me go to school. There I am, sittin' in this damn third or fourth grade with these little kids."

In the mid-'50s, Hank had joined with future rock 'n' roll legend Eddie Cochran to form a duo called the Cochran Brothers. Eventually the two split up "'cause I wanted to do country and Eddie wanted to stay rock 'n' roll. I said, 'I just can't take any more of them people grabbin' at me—I'm not into that.'"

Cochran did grow up into a genuine adult, and early on he found himself in the California music business. "This guy in California had a wife who *didn't* sing, but he thought she did, and *she* thought she did, and they would make records and put 'em out. Ralph Mooney was playin' steel guitar, he was the hot thing out there, and he asked the guy, 'Why in the hell don't you start a publishin' company and put the songs that you record in that company, and [see] what little airplay you get? If you get any at all, at least you'll get some money from it.'

"Claude Cavendish was his name. He went in to use the bathroom, and he saw a bottle of Pamper Shampoo. He comes back out and said, 'What do y'all think of Pamper Music?' and everybody said, 'Hey!' And he says, 'Anybody got any songs?'

"Ralph Mooney says, 'Me and Chuck Seals has got a song called—it's a little weird—called 'Crazy Arms.'" Cavendish says, 'Well, is it good? You think we can do it? Well let's try it.' So they cut 'Crazy Arms' on his wife, who couldn't sing, and shipped it out. And this DJ in Florida played it a little, and he got all these calls—as bad as it was, because the song was so good. Ray Price come through [the station] and this guy says, 'Hey, Ray, I've got a record that's the worst you ever heard, by a woman who sings so bad, but the song gets calls like you can't believe every time I play it.'

"Ray's got a great ear. He played it for Ray, and Ray said, 'Hell, yeah, that's a hit, son,' so Ray took the record and he come back to Nashville to record it. They got a hold of Claude Cavendish and they started a company called Pamper Music, with a guy named Hal Smith." The year was 1956. These were the humble roots of one of the most successful little music publishing companies in the history of country music.

"So I got a job with Hal Smith at Pamper Music payin' fifty dollars a week, and I was sendin' twenty-five dollars a week back to California to my family. I had a wife and three kids, which didn't leave very damn much."

Hank started hanging out at a bar down on Lower Broadway, across the alley, where there were always lots of musicians. "A place called Tootsie's, used to be Mom's. Tootsie let us have a little beer, and she's got a cook in there that makes some chili and stuff, and you can eat during the week 'til you get paid.

"And then I got to knowin' more people. I played rhythm guitar and Buddy Killen played bass on the Grand Ole Opry. It paid ten dollars for the first spot, and three dollars for every spot afterwards.

"Pamper was out on Two Mile Pike in Goodlettsville, in a little house," Cochran recalls. "My job was to write songs, find songs, and get 'em recorded." In fact, at the time, Cochran was the only writer there. "Songs would come in the mail every day," he says. "You never find anything in the mail, and all that time I spent listenin' to them songs, if I'd been writin' them, would have been a lot better."

After a while, Cochran began to forge ties with a few songwriters who deserve more than passing mention.

"Harlan [Howard] would send songs from California and I'd redemo them or take 'em like they were to people who knew songs, who could hear.

"We were sittin' up back at Tootsie's passin' the guitar, and this feller was singin' some songs and I asked, 'Whose songs are those?' And he said, 'They're mine.' I said, 'Well, who publishes 'em?' He said, 'Nobody. Nobody wants 'em.' I said, 'You won't be able to say that tomorrow. Can you get out to the office?'

"He said, 'Depends on where it is.' I told him, 'It's in Goodlettsville, it's about twelve, fifteen miles out there,' and he said, 'I can get out there if you can get me back.' He came out the next mornin' in an old green Buick. I had two dollars and I gave him one of 'em for gas.

"I went in and talked to Hal about signin' the guy. Hal said, 'We're fixin' to give you a raise of fifty dollars, and if we give it to him, you don't get your raise.'

"So I said, 'Well, give it to him, and I'll have somebody to work with, and we'll make it up somewhere down the road.' So he gave my raise to the guy, and that's how we signed Willie Nelson."

Tootsie's is where Hank and Willie caught Faron Young one night, and Willie sang "Hello Walls" to him. "Faron said, 'Boy, I'd like to cut that, would y'all bring it over to the house tomorrow?' So me and Willie took the song over there to Faron, and Faron cut it. Just about that time [country singer] Darrell McCall introduced me to Patsy Cline. I got to be friends with Patsy, so she cut 'I Fall to Pieces,' although she didn't like it. She was forced to cut it because Owen Bradley thought it was a hit. They finally made a deal. Owen said, 'You pick one and I'll pick one,' and she said okay. He said, 'We'll cut "I Fall to Pieces" first.'"

Of the three songs recorded on that session, "I Fall to Pieces" became the single, but it did not hit immediately. By Cochran's reckoning, it might have never hit if it weren't for the fact that in those days publishing companies took an active role in the promotion of a record.

"We worked on it about six months before we finally broke it. We hired two promotion men." One of them was from Cincinnati, "and he hung out at this pizza place where all the disc jockeys hung out. So we told him to take Patsy up there, and get us an order for five thousand records, 'cause I'd talked to Owen, and Owen said, 'Sell me five thousand records somewhere and we'll go to work on the record.' So they went up to Cincinnati, and one of the disc jockeys said to Patsy, 'Can you stay over a week?' Patsy said, 'Hell, yeah, if you'll put my record on.' It was the number-one pop station. He put the record on and was playin' it constantly, and pluggin' her to be at a show Saturday night, and the first order out of that distributor was five thousand.

"Owen called and said, 'Okay, we're on it!'

"I Fall to Pieces" became Patsy Cline's first number-one country hit and was a major pop hit as well.

As "I Fall to Pieces" was climbing the charts, Cline suffered serious injuries in an automobile accident. "I'd sneak into the hospital on a Sunday," says Hank, "and tell her what her record was doin'. I said, 'Patsy! We're in the pop charts, we got a damn smash. You gotta get your ass outta here!'

"She said, 'You ain't lyin' to me are you, you little bastard?'

"I said, 'No, I ain't lyin' to you. We got a pop smash!'

"In the meantime, we did a demo session, and 'Crazy' was on it. I said, 'Gosh, that'd be a great song for Patsy, and I knew Owen loved those big band things."

After Patsy came home from the hospital, Cochran and Nelson decided to take the demo of "Crazy" over to her house and play it for her. "I don't know whether they was awake or not, but I beat on the door and she come to the door. She said, 'What in the hell do you want?' I said, 'I brought you a damn hit!' and she said, 'Well, come in and play the sumbitch!'

"So I went in and I played it, and she said, 'D'you write that?'"

"I said, 'No, Willie Nelson did.'"

"She said, 'Well, where the hell's Willie?' I said, 'He's sittin' out there in the car, he's bashful, he's too bashful to come in.' She said, 'Well, I'll go get the sonofabitch. If he's too bashful to come in *my* house, I ain't gonna cut his damned song!' So she went out there and she drug Willie in, and then it got into a little party.

"After we cut it, and they worked on it for I don't know how damned long.... Then they quit. We cut it again the way Owen wanted it cut, and we went back in again and cut it, and we never could get it. So Owen went back and took that first damn cut, and that's the one that came out. And you can hear on the end—even now, with all the instruments and shit they got now—you can hear her say [very softly] 'you,' 'cause she missed it." The ghostly "you" is a bleed-in to one of the instrument mics from when she came in too early.

It seems that the relationships between Hank, Patsy, and Owen gave Hank a sort of unofficial A&R man status for her sessions. After the huge success of "Crazy," he needed to find a follow-up. "I looked every damned where. I was askin' people, huntin' her hits, you know, 'cause I wanted to keep it goin'. I went out to a little shack, a little place that we had built out of the garage, so we could have a place to go and pick and sing and write, or whatever we wanted to do. And I was sittin' out there and everybody was gone—it was about five or six at night—and I opened a drawer. There was a picture of someone I used to go with.

"It was just a picture, but I shut the drawer and thought, well, I got her picture. And that's what started it. The mind went sayin', 'He's got this, and I got her picture.' I thought, well, damn, that sounds pretty good. So I grabbed a piece of paper and just wrote it down. Zap! I made a little tape of it, and I called Patsy, 'I found the sonofabitch!'

"She said, 'What?' and I said, 'That hit we've been lookin' for.' She said, 'Well, go get a bottle of whiskey and bring the sonofabitch over here.' You had to go all the way into Nashville to get to a liquor store, 'cause back then, you couldn't buy it out there in Goodlettsville, unless you knew the bootlegger, which I did. But I couldn't find one, so I drove all the way in and got a pint—'cause the money was tight—and drove out to her house, which was in Madison or Inglewood or somethin'.

"I went over there and I set the bottle on the table and she just twisted the cap off and throwed it down, took a big drink, and handed it to me.

I took a big drink and she said, 'Now sing the sonofabitch.' So I sang it to her and she just went all to pieces, you know, and she said, 'Sing that again.'

"I took another drink, and she took another one, and I sung it again and she cried some more. Then she called [her manager] Randy Hughes and we sung it to him, and that sonofabitch was cryin' on the phone. Then we called Owen and [we sung it] and he got to cryin', you know. So we had half the town a-cryin' over that song. We went into the studio within the next day or so, the same bunch, and then I'm scared to death. She's had two smashes, and now this one's all my song, and what if it don't hit, and I'll be the one that.... But it *skyrocketed*!" "She's Got You" would be Patsy's last number-one record. A year later, in 1963, she would be dead.

It was around that time that Cochran wrote "Make the World Go Away," one of the all-time country classics. "I was at a movie with this girl, and in the movie, the guy said somethin', and then the actress said somethin', and somethin' said somethin' else to *me*. I said, 'Hot damn!' loud as I could in the theater, right there, and everybody looked around. I grabbed my girl's arm and said, 'Come on, let's go.' She said, 'The movie ain't over,' and I said, 'The hell it ain't!' We got in the car and I wrote it between there and my apartment. We got there and I told it to her and she wrote it down. I went over it—it was all there, just like it had been handed to me. Boy, I was so excited, I couldn't wait for the office to open, you know?

"So I went in that next mornin', I said, 'Hal, I got a damn smash. Oh, the Old Man upstairs has given me a big one!'

"He said, 'Well, sit down there and sing it,' so I sit down there and grabbed a guitar and sang it. He just looked at me and I said, 'What is it?' He said, 'Boy, I hate to tell you this—and you may prove me wrong—but that's the worst song that you ever wrote. *Nobody wants to make the world go away.*'

"I said, 'Where have *you* been? That'll be one of the biggest songs in this catalog, if not the biggest.' And he said, 'Well, you've proved me wrong before.' And I said, 'I will again.'

"So, I got me a piece of paper and I wrote, 'Make the World Go Away,' and put a number '1' on both ends of it, and set it on my desk where I had to see it every time I sat down, every time I answered the phone. I think it was Buddy Killen that called me and said, 'I got a girl here that's fixin' to record and she needs a hit because she just had one called 'Hurt.' The artist's name was Timi Yuro, and 'Hurt' had been a huge hit for her in 1961. I said, 'Well, I sure got one—I wrote it the other night.' I went down there and I sat down with the song and sang it to her and she just broke down and cried. She said, 'Would you sing that again?' So I sang it to her again and she said, 'Have you got a copy of it?' I said, 'No, I just wrote it.' I said, 'Buddy, do you mind if I put it down?' One publisher talkin' to another, so he said, 'Hell, no.' I put it down just me and the guitar, and give it to her, wrote the lyric down. I forget who the secretary was, she typed out the lyric and give it to her, and her and her producer said, 'We're goin' back to California tomorrow, and we'll probably cut this next week or somethin'.'

"So I was home asleep, it was about three in the mornin', and I answered the phone and they said, 'Hank?' I said, 'Who's this? What's wrong?'

"On the other end of the line was Timi Yuro. 'Nothin's wrong,' she said. 'We just cut and finished "Make the World Go Away" and I wanted you to hear it.'"

She played it for Cochran and he swore that it sounded like a hit. The following week she came to Nashville for other business and brought him a copy.

"I took it over to Ray Price. He said, 'Well, who was that?'

"I said, 'That's Timi Yuro.' He said, 'Well, I can sing it better than her.'

"And I said, 'Well, you can't or you'd have put it out.' And he said, 'I'll show you, you little ass.' He got on the phone and called [his producer] Don Law, and they set up the session. We went in, me and Ray and the whole band and strings and all of it, and cut 'Make the World Go Away.' He put it out with all the strings, just like hers, and sung it the way she sang it. It was like a number-two record for him."

It was a nice start for a song that Cochran's boss had scorned, but Hank and "Make the World Go Away" were just getting started.

"I was sittin' in the RCA office with Chet Atkins. I had cut it for an [RCA] album called *Hits from the Heart*, and it was all songs I wrote. I did it just straight, I couldn't sing the way she did it. [Eddy Arnold's producer] Bill Walker stuck his head through the door and he said, 'I'm gonna cut an album of "world" songs,' and he says, 'Has anybody got one?'"

Walker knew the song, and he was dubious. "'Oh, Eddy couldn't sing that song.' I said, 'Yeah, but I just cut it, and I did it the way that

I wrote it.' Chet was already on the phone and he said, 'Bring me a dub of Hank Cochran's 'Make the World Go Away.'

"And in a minute it was there. So we put it on and played it and Chet said, 'Oh yeah, he'll cut that. I'll make sure he cuts that.'

"Well, Eddy Arnold cut it for an album, and while he was cuttin' they come in to videotape it, because he was gonna do *The Jimmy Dean Show*, which was a network show. They said we'll go from this, with you cuttin' it live, to you on the show. I don't know how many singles he sold, ain't nobody figured it up, but he sold at least six million singles, 'cause he was number one everywhere."

Around 1967, Cochran and Willie Nelson bought Ray Price out of Pamper Music (Claude was long gone by then), with money advanced by Frances Preston at BMI. Shortly thereafter, Willie sold his interest to Hank, then, a couple of years later, Hal Smith and Cochran sold Pamper to Tree for a figure Cochran calls "more than a million dollars." Over the years, the Pamper catalog has repaid Tree's investment many times over, and today the standards that Cochran, Howard, Nelson, and others wrote continue to make millions for the catalog's present owner, Sony.

10

HOMEGROWN TALENT AND THE NASHVILLE MACHINE

"We never really got into it for money. Money never crossed our minds," says Jack Jackson, who started out as teenage rocker playing "combo parties," and who has made his living on Music Row for over forty years. "We just loved the music, especially when rock 'n' roll and rockabilly came along. It just made you feel good, it'd get you excited just listening to it. I remember the first records I heard that changed everything. I remember hearing 'Blue Suede Shoes' when I was in the fourth or fifth grade, at a field day at my grammar school. I couldn't believe it. And everybody just loved it, they kept playing it over and over."

Jackson's first ax was actually a sax, which he picked up around the age of twelve. It must have been strange for any young musician to grow up in Nashville in the '50s and '60s, playing in party bands and yet fully aware that the big time was only a few miles away on 16th Avenue.

"Me and one of my neighbors who lived up the street, Pat Patrick, decided to have a band. I didn't know how to play the saxophone at all. I had found it in the attic—it belonged to my father—and I bought a Belwin Band Builder book on how to play the saxophone. I think the first song we learned how to play was [the Billy Grammar hit] 'Gotta Travel On.' After a while, I decided that I wanted to play the guitar, so I mowed lawns and bought a little electric guitar. I think the guitar and the amp together was maybe sixty dollars.

"Pat had also gotten an electric guitar, and we started to really have a band. Back in those days, the bands would play a lot of Jimmy Reed and Chuck Berry, things that you could pick up. We would go out occasionally and listen to guys who were older than us, say in high school. You could learn more watching somebody for a couple of hours, than you could pick up on your own in a few months."

This was about 1959 or '60. "One of the first bands I ever heard was the Casuals. I just thought it was the most unbelievable thing I'd ever heard. It was at a party for kids, like sixth, seventh, and eighth grade, at Hillwood Country Club. They just sounded great. Buzz Cason sang, Richard Williams played piano and sang, Joe Watkins played the saxophone, Billy Smith played drums, and I can't remember who played bass and guitar at that time, it might have been Wayne Moss.

"That really got us all fired up because we'd never heard a live rock 'n' roll band. There were other groups that were very good, too, in the early '60s—Charlie McCoy and the Escorts, they were terrific. Charlie would play bass and harmonica at the same time, also trumpet, and sing. Kenneth Buttrey played drums, and I think Mac Gayden played with Charlie and them for a while. We took a lot of ideas from those guys."

Many of these kids that Jackson was so casually mentioning were unknowingly matriculating at the best commercial music university in the world: Buzz Cason went on to a stellar career in publishing ("Little Green Apples," "Honey"), production (Clifford Curry and "She Shot a Hole in My Soul"), songwriting ("Everlasting Love"), and recording (as Garry Miles with "Look for a Star"). Mac Gayden's career as a songwriter, producer, recording artist, and performer is long and distinguished. Charlie McCoy became known worldwide as one of the best harmonica session players ever. Wayne Moss became a major session guitar player, and Kenneth Buttrey became one of the top session drummers of his era.

"Some of the first jobs we had we weren't even old enough to drive. Our parents had to drop us off and pick us up. We'd play at Vanderbilt frat parties and that was a big experience because they were all eighteen, nineteen, twenty-one, just having a big time, and here we were, fourteen, fifteen."

By the time Jackson was sixteen, he pretty well knew that he wanted to do music for a living. "I started hangin' out at Tree Publishing," Jackson recalls. "I think it might have been about '65. By then they were in that two-story house on 16th. John Hurley, who wrote for Tree for a long time, had come to see our band." The result was a friendship that led Jackson to walk into the real music industry and start running errands. "I was just happy to be there, and they were successful. By that time, Roger Miller was breaking. And Joe Tex."

Joe Tex was the kind of success story so common on Music Row—in other words, totally *un*common. Born Joseph Arrington Jr., he was a black rhythm and blues singer who had won a talent contest in Harlem's Apollo Theater. A Tree writer named Robert Riley brought Tex to Tree, and Buddy Killen liked the songs that Tex played him, as well as the way Tex sung them. When he couldn't find a label that would be interested in having Tex, Killen and Jack Stapp started their own label, Dial Records, and Killen began to put out records on the R&B singer. After four years with no success, Tex was ready to go elsewhere, but Buddy wanted to try one more time.

By then, Muscle Shoals was gaining somewhat of a reputation for making great soul music, so Buddy and Joe made the journey south, to Rick Hall's FAME Studio (FAME stands for Florence, Alabama Music Enterprises). Almost nobody thought they had recorded anything worthwhile on the session, but Killen thought they had something, and Jerry Wexler at Atlantic Records, Dial's distributor, believed they had cut a hit.

Wexler was right. "Hold What You Got" launched Joe Tex on a career odyssey that included the smashes "I Gotcha," "Skinny Legs and All," and "Ain't Gonna Bump No More (With No Big Fat Woman)." Joe Tex was the biggest of a number of R&B successes that Killen had with Dial.

As a publishing company with its own studio and a growing staff of writers, Tree was constantly doing demos on its new songs. By being there, Jackson eventually was asked to play on a demo session. "I was scared to death. It was an evening session and when I walked in with my guitars I saw that Bobby Goldsboro was on the date, playing guitar, and Buzz Cason was on the date, playing piano." The other musicians were also well-known session players.

"There was a time there when we would go down to Memphis on the weekends and do demos at Chips Moman's place, American Studio. All that stuff kinda got me interested in studio recording, but I just couldn't really get a grip on how I was gonna go about making it work. I was having breakfast one morning, there was Buddy Killen and myself, and I think John Hurley was there, and I just asked Buddy, 'How do you make all this stuff work? How do you get these songs cut, how do you turn it into a business where you can make a living?' And his response was something to the effect of, 'Well, you just have to get up and do it every day.'

"After a few years Pat Patrick and I got back together with another buddy of mine and we played in a band called the Fairlanes. We were kind of a pop rhythm and blues band. Robert Knight [who would gain everlasting fame with a hit version of the song 'Everlasting Love'] was the singer in the band. Buzz Cason and Mac Gayden, who produced that on Robert, heard him in our band, and the record took Robert out of our band, so we had to get some other singers. We were a blue-eyed soul band and usually had a black singer.

"In those days, we played a terrific amount of black night clubs," Jackson marvels, "and we just really enjoyed the enthusiasm. Not to be *braggadocious*, but we had a pretty good kick-ass blue-eyed soul band. We had a good rhythm section, two horns, two or three guys in the band could sing backup, and Robert would come out there and do his thing and it was pretty good. We did all cover tunes, everything from James Brown to Wilson Pickett, Sam and Dave, Eddie Floyd, and I played saxophone most of the time in that band, '66, '67, '68, and the only radio station I listened to was WVOL, which was the rhythm and blues station."

In 1972, Jackson, Pat Patrick, and two other friends of theirs, Doug Yoder and Paul Whitehead, built a little studio in an old house on Division Street, maybe four blocks from the Quonset Hut, which was still ground zero on Music Row. "We got it all up and running, but nobody was coming in the door, so we started doing jingles. We'd have to go out and get the business, so, usually, myself and Doug would go to radio stations all around; we even went as far up as northern Michigan, you name it. We had a lot of radio stations [as clients] and we would do these inexpensive jingles. We all played, so we could do the stuff for almost nothing, and we'd get a few hundred dollars for them."

The name of the studio was Audio Media Recorders. It was a relatively small enterprise that would have a big influence on Music Row.

"We had a few people who started coming in and recording, 'til we got pretty busy. Then we bought the property on 19th, we bought two lots. I think Jack Clement owned them. We blew a hole in the ground and built the studio from the ground up, scared to death—I think I was the oldest of the four of us, and I was twenty-seven." At the time there was a genuine railroad caboose on the lot. "We didn't keep the caboose. Somebody came and got it, maybe it was Jack.

"We bought that property for about fifty thousand dollars, which would be like giving it away today, but it was a lot of money then. We had to have a few trees removed to do the foundation. Then we got a loan from the bank to build the building. A friend of mine who was a contractor built it for us. We had one large studio and then a smaller remix studio. We had quite a few offices on the second floor, and we were only gonna use about a third of the second floor." Before they had even built the building they had a tenant for the second floor, Warner Bros. Records. "We moved in near the end of '74, and the rent from Warner Bros. helped us out a lot.

"It's not like today where you have Pro Tools and you can make records at home that are great." State-of-the art equipment was expensive. They had to equip two studios and they barely had enough equipment for one. So these four pilgrims had to go well into debt to set themselves up in business with sixteen tracks on 19th Avenue South. But it worked.

"We had quite a few clients renting the studio from us, and then we were still doing quite a few commercials, and a lot of soundalikes of hits."

And then there were the "remakes." "Stan Shulman had Dune Records in New York way back. He'd had 'Pretty Little Angel Eyes' by Curtis Lee, and Ray Peterson's hit on 'Corina Corina.' He got into doing some projects with us in the early '70s—I guess it was Dominion Entertainment, but everybody thought of it as K-tel." They began recording what we might refer to as "vintage acts," classic pop stars from the '50s and the '60s like Frankie Laine, Little Richard, Chubby Checker—there were hundreds of them. "We did Trini Lopez—he was a lot of fun; Pat Boone; Jay Black of Jay and the Americans—what a singer; Sam and Dave; Rufus Thomas; Eddie Floyd; Paul Revere and the Raiders; Mark Dinning. I think there were probably about four or five hundred artists. I'm guessing we did about 2,500 titles, maybe 3,000. A lot of the country acts came in and redid their hits: Paycheck; Porter Wagoner; Faron Young—he was great, Don Gibson.

"I'll be fifty-eight this month," says Jackson, "and I've literally been making a living in the music business since I was thirteen or fourteen years old." Today he works for Sony/ATV, essentially the Tree Publishing Company that he worked for more than forty years ago. He licenses songs and recordings for use by other record companies, and licenses the use of recordings for TV and movies, a lucrative area known as "sync rights," meaning the synchronization of this music with the video portions of the shows.

"For a long time I didn't really care about the money, just as long as I could make enough to get by," he says. He remembers the early studio days when there was no money in the business and he supported his family by playing gigs "nights and weekends, in town or out of town, about 150 nights a year." Today, older, wiser, professional, he says, laughing quietly, "The music I like is the music that sells."

"Audio Media was just four guys that wanted to build a recording studio, who'd played in bands together since they were kids," says Pat McMakin, a veteran Music Row engineer, who today runs the studio at Sony/ATV Nashville, and who early on worked for Audio Media. "They became four businessmen who set about doing the thing that every studio owner needs to do, finding business. We would go to MIDEM [an international music trade show held annually in Cannes, France] and bring back business. Probably the biggest album done out of there was 'Mickey Mouse Disco,' which I think is probably a twenty-five-million-selling record by now. It was one of the few places in the country that had a staff band. Every day Paul Worley [guitar] would come to work, Dennis Burnside [keyboards] would come to work, Eddie Bayers [drums] would come to work, myself [engineer], Marshall Morgan [engineer], and Jack would come in to play bass.

"We had an A studio and a B studio and we ran constantly. It allowed that rhythm section to jell at a time when there was sort of one mainstream rhythm section. You know, Nashville's always talked about the A-team, and we both know that the A-team does exist but it's *fluid*. There was the Harold Bradley A-team, and then after that came the one with Reggie [Young] and Larrie Londin, Shane Keister and those guys. And right after them was Eddie Bayers and Paul Worley and them.

"The original A-team probably came from more varied backgrounds than I have any clue of. The second-generation A-team—Larrie Londin had been in a group that recorded for Motown for a period of time. Reggie did all that music in Memphis. Generationally speaking, they were coming out of the '60s and really rollin' in the '70s, whereas the Audio Media rhythm section rolled out of the '70s into the '80s pretty hard. Their influences were more rock. When we were young turks, the young bucks, we would have to do soundalikes of the Eagles, Rolling Stones, Billy Joel, and all of the contemporary acts of the time. As an engineer, it was great for me because I learned very young in life how to get those sounds that were goin' on record. What made it such a great training ground for them as musicians was, I think any musician starts out learning how to copy the masters before they begin to create on their own.

"The demo process has become sort of the staging ground for the up-and-coming musicians and producers," he continues. "John Rich [of Big and Rich] learned how to produce by doing his demos. So did Braddock. So here we have this rhythm session migrating across the street to Tree, and then those demos go out, get heard by the people that are in the established positions, and they start hearing this musicianship and they want it to be a part of what they're doing. They're looking for new talent, so they pull from the demo pool, and by the late '80s they were all double-scale musicians playin' on all the hits. I just heard the other day—it's kind of fascinating—Eddie Bayers was recently put in the top-ten list of all-time great drummers by one of the drum magazines. Somebody quoted a statistic that you might wanna look at—he played on 258 number-one singles that came off of platinum albums. That's not including the number-one singles that came off of the nonplatinum albums that he's played on.

"I've known him for twenty-three years and I'll bet he hasn't worked less than an average of two sessions a day over that period. And he's got a classical piano degree. He was in a band with Larrie Londin playing keyboards, he started getting Larrie to show him how to play, and he moved over to drums."

McMakin broaches a sore subject on Music Row: "The eighty-twenty rule is very much alive here, in my opinion, and always has been," he says. "Eighty percent of the records are made by twenty percent of the producers. I think there are six guys making eighty percent of the records. I think when you have that kind of a recording schedule, that it's very difficult to take a lot of time, and to stretch out, and to be real creative. It becomes a little bit of a machine, and certainly we have been very guilty as a community of turning out records that sound that way. Usually the most exciting records are ones like what we have going on here now, the Muzikmafia stuff, where it's somebody coming in and saying, 'We're just not gonna do it that way.'

"It's very difficult for young artists to turn their back on a guy who's an A&R person and a label head, and say, 'I'm not gonna play. I'm gonna do it the way I wanna do it.' But those almost categorically are the artists that succeed the greatest. I mean, you know, we get hits out of all the sort of factory music that gets made, but the earth-shattering, direction-changing music comes when people play by a different set of rules."

11

THE EVERLY BROTHERS AND THE BRYANTS

I f you're looking for an office to rent on Music Row, or a building to buy in the area, then Dane Bryant is your man. He is Music Row's most popular realtor—he carries a map of Music Row in his head, but he also carries a family history that cries out to songwriters today.

Dane's parents, Boudleaux and Felice Bryant, are considered Nashville's first professional *nonperforming songwriters*.

Why is that important? Because what makes Music Row unique among American commercial music centers today is that it houses a music industry built around people who spend their days writing songs *for other people to sing*.

Music Row is part of the magnificent American songwriting tradition that begins with Stephen C. Foster and embraces the songs of Jerome Kern, Richard Rodgers, the Gershwins, Irving Berlin, Billy Strayhorn, Yip Harburg, Harold Arlen, Sammy Cahn, and Cole Porter—the men who wrote the American Songbook—as well as Holland, Dozier, Holland; Leiber and Stoller; Mann and Weil; Goffin and King; Otis Blackwell; Doc Pomus and Mort Shuman; Jimmy Webb; and many other great writers responsible for fueling the Motown music machine and writing hundreds of hits for nascent rock 'n' rollers.

It's a tough business. There are many songwriters who never win at all. Many others score a little cut or two, and some get a few decent songs out, maybe even a hit. But most hits are not *classics*, not the kind of songs that live ten years later in the honky-tonks, or become hits a second and third time for different artists.

Boudleaux and Felice Bryant wrote classics. Had they only written "Bye Bye Love" and "Wake Up Little Susie," it would have been enough to insure their position as superstars in the pantheon of songwriters. Had they only written "Rocky Top," it would have been enough. But they also wrote "All I Have to Do Is Dream," "Bird Dog, "Devoted to You," "Take a Message to Mary," "Love Hurts," "Like Strangers," "Raining in My Heart," "Let's Think About Livin'," and many other songs that have remained impervious to the erosion of time. Their songs have been recorded by the Everly Brothers, Buddy Holly, Carl Smith, Roy Orbison, Jim Reeves, Leo Sayer, Tony Bennett, Charley Pride, Linda Ronstadt, Glen Campbell, Bobby Gentry, and about four hundred others, for total record sales of an estimated 300 million.

Dane Bryant remembers his parents not merely as songwriting icons but as a deeply romantic and feeling couple.

After they were married and living in Moultrie, Georgia, Boudleaux was making a living playing fiddle on a local radio station. This would be about 1948. "Mom would write a little bit," says Dane, "to keep herself amused after cleaning the apartment. And so my father started writing to keep *Mom* amused, to do something with her because, it's what she liked to do. He'd written some songs, but he had no *drive* to write.

"They continued to write until they had about eighty songs. They decided that they were pretty good, and that they ought to be doing something with them. Daddy says that they got a *Billboard* magazine and it had artists, publishers, and producers listed in it, so he wrote letters asking if they would listen to material. Most of those letters came back as 'No, they didn't listen to material'; or the letters were unopened, or they were just returned to sender.

"Fortunately he ran into a buddy of his who was also a fiddle player or violinist, who said he was gonna sing country music in Nashville—and he had met Fred Rose! And Fred Rose was gonna produce him on MGM Records. The fella says, 'Let's get together!' Daddy played him 'Country Boy.' He said, 'I like that, I'd like for Fred to hear that.' He had a little wire recorder so he made a copy of it and took it to Fred Rose, and Fred liked the song, but not for this particular artist. He thought it would be good for Jimmy Dickens. Jimmy Dickens had just had a hit with 'Old Cold Tater.'

"Fred Rose called my father, told him he was interested in the song, and wondered if my father had time to come to Nashville." Boudleaux told Rose that he had time, but he didn't have any money. So Fred Rose sent him some money, and "said it *wouldn't* be an advance against royalties. He was interested in his song. My father and Fred Rose hit it off."

Boudleaux and Felice were traveling musicians. "They did pickup jobs here, pickup jobs there. They would book themselves out as a duo. They would play schools. They would sing songs together, and then Dad might start playing the violin, play some real dry classical piece, and Mom would go out in the audience and heckle. He once got them booked on a South American cruise, a two-month cruise, and Mom said, 'Well, what are we gonna sing?'

"He said, 'Well, we know one Italian song together, we can do that, and we'll learn the rest of them on the boat. Once they pull off—they'll be stuck with us!' Mom did not go for that and they did not go on the cruise.

"My father played with a lot of little bands. He played jazz fiddle, he played country fiddle with Hank Penny's band, he'd stroll in restaurants playing the fiddle."

Boudleaux and Felice had the guts to live by their wits and the confidence to believe that somehow this strange way of living would eventually turn into something that could sustain them. They traveled from gig to gig, pulling a trailer behind them, and in 1949 they pulled their trailer into Nashville. "It was hard for them to even get into a trailer park; people looked at 'em and they looked like a couple of gypsies. And then they found out that they were musicians and that was even worse." But the two young entertainers found a place out on Dickerson Road and Trinity Lane called the Rainbow Inn. They got in the trailer park there and they wrote their songs.

"My father would go down to the Opry, and he met Chet Atkins. In fact, Chet Atkins was a fan of his from when my father was playing at WLW in Atlanta. He'd hang out with the musicians down at the Opry, and now that he'd had some success with 'Country Boy,' he really focused on writing songs for country music artists. They had a string of hits with Jimmy Dickens, with Carl Smith, Kitty Wells, Ray Price. 'Hey Joe' went pop.

"My parents revered Fred Rose so, and he helped them. They never wrote exclusively for Fred, but they would often run a song by him first to see if it was something he wanted. I think he wanted them to be exclusive writers, but at that time they weren't ready to do it. A little later on, they started their own publishing company called Showcase Music, which had 'Hey Joe,' 'Blue Boy,' 'We Could,' and had a bunch of hits. Then after Fred died, Dad still would go down there [to Acuff-Rose]. He was friendly with Wesley and they thought they would go ahead and sign up with Wesley, because running a publishing company was taking up a lot of their time."

Wesley Rose played a critical role in the Bryants' success with the Everly Brothers. In the latter half of the '50s, Archie Bleyer decided to move his Cadence record label into the country field. "The most successful country publisher of the time was Acuff-Rose, so Archie went out to Acuff-Rose, and Wesley put my father with him. There were a couple of acts that Archie Bleyer was interested in and he decided to do the Everly Brothers."

"This is 1957: we're living in a little basement house near what is now Rivergate, what was then Goodletsville or Madison. We'd moved out of the trailer. Dad went down to Nashville with his batch of songs to show to Archie Bleyer for the Everly Brothers." One of the songs that he played for them was "Bye Bye Love," which had been written for Johnny and Jack, a well-known country duo consisting of Jack Anglin and Kitty Wells's husband, Johnny Wright.

"One of the gifts that my father had was that being a trained musician, if he had access to that act, he could write for that act. I remember him talking about Eddy Arnold, how Eddy Arnold could say the word *world* better than most, and that's one reason they wrote 'How's the World Treating You,' which he and Chet Atkins wrote. My father co-wrote with just a few people. Chet Atkins was one of them. Chet would give him a melody, or they would get something started and then my dad would finish it. He usually finished it with Mom, but it would say 'Boudleaux and Atkins.'

"Mom said, 'Well, it's the good old boy world out there.' At that time, women didn't get the respect they get today. Anyway, 'Bye Bye Love' was written for Johnny and Jack, and they had turned it down. Chet Atkins took Porter Wagoner in the studio to do 'Bye Bye Love.' Dad had had a couple of good records on Porter, 'Tryin' to Forget the Blues' and 'Payday.' If you listen to those, you can hear the harmony that the Everlys did, you can almost hear the sound. But Chet didn't think 'Bye Bye Love' was strong enough—he wanted to change a chord in it. Dad and Chet were good enough buddies and Dad told Chet that if he didn't think the song was strong enough to just take it off the session."

There is little doubt that the acoustic guitar intro on "Bye Bye Love" was an integral part of the Everlys' sound. "Those rhythm guitar licks are Don's," says Dane. "Dad will tell you that Don [Everly] was playing it out in the studio. Dad didn't have that intro for 'Bye Bye Love.' He heard Don playing it on the guitar and he said, 'That works!'"

Most of the time when a songwriter is privileged enough to be invited to a session where his song is being recorded, he keeps his mouth shut unless someone asks him a question, and even then he's usually careful about his answer.

"Dad showed up on a lot of sessions, and he hauled me and Del [Dane's brother, now head of BMI] along. We were music business brats. When he showed up at the sessions he would make sure that the musicians knew the songs, knew all the chord changes. I know lots of times, when he would go into a session and there would be some place where they'd want to modulate, or there'd be some great harmony line, I'd see my father working out the lines with his hand, working his fingers not like it was a guitar, like a violin, and he'd say, 'Well, this guy should be playing such and such, then you get what you want.'"

"Bye Bye Love" hit the airwaves in the spring of 1957 and was a country smash, staying number one on the *Billboard* country singles chart for seven weeks, but it was also a huge pop hit, barely missing the number-one spot.

Cadence was known as a pop record company, Dane reminds us. "So, because it had the Cadence label, it got pop play. That was one of those flukes from heaven that helped the Everly Brothers explode.

"That tells you exactly how country is put in a little box," he says. "I've seen rock 'n' roll acts come through Nashville, everybody from Grand Funk Railroad in the '70s to the Pointer Sisters, who came to town *cloaked* so nobody would know that they had produced their session in Nashville. They did not want it to get out that they had used Nashville studios or the Nashville musicians, because suddenly it would be a country record."

Talking about record executives, Dane had this to say: "Nashville had very few people who could make absolute decisions, and they were boxed in—they couldn't make a decision outside country music. If it came out of the Nashville office, it had to be country. If it was a pop group, it moved to the Coast, East or West. You couldn't sign pop people out of this area."

"Bye Bye Love" was only the beginning of the Bryants' triumphant ride with the Everly Brothers. The follow-up, "Wake Up Little Susie," was an even bigger hit. Unlike "Bye Bye Love," "Wake Up Little Susie" was written specifically for the Everlys, says Dane, "As was 'All I Have to Do Is Dream,' 'Devoted to You,' 'Problems.'

"Dad wrote directly for them. After they took off, when he knew that they were coming to town and they were getting ready to record, he would focus on them. I remember they wrote twenty, thirty, forty songs to show the Everlys.

"Now, lots of times I will say, 'My father.' I mean Dad *and* Mom. Dad wrote 'Wake Up Little Susie' in the bedroom one morning. Mom woke up and he was working on it, and she said, 'He was slipping off trying to write songs by himself because he'd like to make more money.' She'd feel left out because she was the one that really wanted to write. Daddy *only* wrote for money. I mean, he was happy to let a sweet melody whistle through his brain and enjoy it. But he didn't really wanna have to write it down. He didn't want to have to worry about whether anybody recorded it or not. But after a while, he wanted to be remembered as a songwriter.

"A lot of people didn't think Mom wrote songs, they just thought Dad put her name on it. She helped finish 'How's the World Treating You.' She helped finish 'Midnight.' But her name's not on it. She and Roy Orbison started writing a song right after Roy came to town, because Fred Foster would hang out at our house when Roy came up from Texas. Fred laid out in our back yard by the swimming pool, fell asleep, got burned to a cinder. So Mom and Roy started writing a song together. There was a big argument in my house. I only remember a handful of arguments between my parents but there was one then, because Daddy controlled Mom to where she couldn't write with anybody.

"Mom has one very successful song she wrote by herself, called 'We Could,' which was a hit in '54, '64, and '74: first by Jimmy Dickens, then it was a pop hit by Al Martino in 1964, then it was a country hit again in 1974 by Charley Pride. And I really think it's due again.

"When she wrote it, they didn't have a whole lot of money. So when it came to Daddy's birthday, Momma wrote Daddy a song. She wrote him 'We Could,' as a surprise. And that's why his name's not on it, because if it hadn't been a secret, it would have his name on it.

"I asked Dad about their roles in the collaboration, and he said. 'Well, your Mom's the idea person.' And Mom was.

"One of my favorite stories," says Dane, "is 'Take a Message to Mary' [an Everlys classic]. Mom wrote it while she was vacuum cleaning. There was a rock stuck in the vacuum cleaner [making a *tink, tink, tink* sound]. She wrote the whole song, then called Dad on the phone after she turned the vacuum off. She didn't have a little portable tape recorder at that time, so she'd get Daddy on the phone and sing the song to him, and he'd write down the melody line so that she didn't lose it, which was another reason that his name was on all of her songs, because he would write down the melody lines. He said, 'Felice, that's not strong enough,' and he added, 'This is the story—it's sad but true,' the little pickup part that goes in the front. It got his name on the song. He wasn't even gonna show it to the Everlys. Momma made him promise to show it to them.

"There were these yellow pads that Mom would write in the front of, and Daddy would write in the back. She'd start 'em, and he'd go get 'em and he'd end up being in 'em, too. When the songs started coming together, then it would go into a ledger, or if Daddy was doing it just by himself, he'd start in the ledger. In the ledgers, you could see the melody line, and then the lyrics would be worked on. The melody line was not as it would be in a piece of sheet music, with the lyric directly under the melody line—it was a melody line for Daddy for when he got ready to show his songs. Most of his stuff, he got cut himself, and he got it cut one-on-one, showing it to artists, playing it on the guitar in the kitchen. I can remember Mom and Dad showing songs in the trailer. Mom would fix spaghetti; Dad would sit there and he would play songs; Mom would sing harmony from the stove.

"When we moved out to the lake, it was the same thing. They built a nice big kitchen with a soft chair in it, and a table and a little short couch, and then the bar with the kitchen on the other side of it so Mom could make the pasta and sing harmony while Dad showed songs to the act, who usually sat on the couch. The books were all on the big coffee table—they had seventeen books by the time they were through. Daddy would thumb through the ledgers to see what might fit Burl Ives, or what might fit Roy Orbison, or whoever was in the house listening to songs."

The early deal Boudleaux and Felice made with Wesley Rose must have seemed like great publishing for Rose. Dane says his parents brought Wesley their publishing company, Showcase Music, which had some money-making hits in it, including "Blue Boy," a Jim Reeves hit; "We Could"; "Hey Joe"; and "Hawkeye." "Wesley didn't have to give them any money for it," says Dane.

But in return, Rose gave them a ten-year reversion on all the songs in the catalog from the date of copyright. In time, "Bye Bye Love," "Wake Up Little Susie," "All I Have to Do Is Dream," and the other Boudleaux and Felice Bryant hits on the Everlys became among the most valuable copyrights in the Acuff-Rose catalog. Wesley came from an era when most songwriters had very little leverage with their publishers, and it must have been galling to see those great copyrights revert to the writers.

But he didn't lose everything. Acuff-Rose retained the international rights to Showcase Music without reversion, and given the overseas popularity of these classics, Acuff-Rose's successor company, Sony, continues to collect significant foreign royalties on these songs. According to Bryant, Wesley Rose was not happy when the reversions came due. He did what he could to hang on to the copyrights, but the Bryants prevailed, at least on the domestic front.

Score one for the songwriters.

12

A Pair of Aces

I can remember two young men, who I believe called themselves the Thompson Brothers and had no teeth. In the summertime, when the Nashville sidewalks could melt the soles of your shoes, these boys would dress up in Russian-looking fur coats and hats and walk up and down Music Row, their faces awash in perspiration.

Then there was this girl who ran naked up 16th Avenue one day. I don't recall what time or day she made her run, and I never found out what was on her mind. But at least one person I asked who saw her do it said she was attempting to attract attention from the record industry.

Hundreds of aspiring artists and songwriters ride into Nashville every year with a dream. Unlike the special cases of the toothless Thompsons and the naked girl, most take well-worn paths toward success: New songwriters want to find out how the hit-makers write their songs and get them recorded; artists seek out producers or record executives who can help them attain the coveted deal with a major label; new musicians look for veterans who can tell them how to hook up with a road band or, even better, how to become a session musician; would-be engineers walk into a studio and grab a broom, agreeing to do the most menial work in exchange for an opportunity to learn the inner-workings of the recording studio. Most have their dreams crushed before they see even a glimmer of a shot at making it.

And then there are those who took their own paths, and made Music Row much better for having done so. Ray Stevens and Charlie McCoy are true originals.

Ray Stevens was born in 1939 in Clarksdale, Georgia, took up piano at the age of six, moved to Atlanta with his family at the age of sixteen, and soon got involved with Bill Lowery, a very successful Atlanta music publisher.

Ray Stevens is unique in the history of American music. He first hit the pop charts in 1961 with one of the longest titles in the history of recorded music: "Jeremiah Peabody's Poly Unsaturated Quick Dissolving Fast Acting Pleasant Tasting Green and Purple Pills." Think of what was in this phrase alone! For one thing, it was sung against a very soulfully rendered blues lick, an odd riff to go along with a line that is essentially a goof on Madison Avenue's overstated product pitches. Stevens has an uncanny ability to grasp the oddities of American culture and fashion them into an act of humor.

Perhaps the most memorable moment of his career was "The Streak," back in 1974, which went to number three on the country charts and number one pop, and put the phrase "Don't Look, Ethel," in the American lexicon. The song took one of the silliest of all American fads and pitted it against a background of America's traditional rejection of nudity as a fashion statement. In 1980, he released "Shriners' Convention," satirizing the Shriners, who, like most of middle America, loved it.

But in January 1962, he was a twenty-two-year-old Mercury recording artist newly arrived in Nashville, with an array of talents that simply would not let him fail. Shelby Singleton put him to work in Mercury's A&R department for a small salary that he augmented with piano work on Nashville's booming session scene.

"I got to meet all the session guys," Ray remembers. "And from time to time one of the Jordanaires couldn't make it and Gordon Stoker would call me and I'd go in and fill in."

Ray came to Nashville because Singleton offered him a job and because the recording scene was further developed in Nashville than Atlanta.

"I didn't think of myself as *country*," he says. "In Atlanta I listened to WAOK all the time, which was an R&B station. Daddy Sears was either the owner, the manager, the program director, or all three—I don't know. He was on the air and he had a group of really great disc jockeys: Allie Pat the Alley Rat; Zillah Mays the Dream Girl, who was on late at night; Piano Red was a radio personality on WAOK. Anyway, I listened to all the R&B records. My hero was Ray Charles. But I came to Nashville and I quickly grew to appreciate guitars and country music.

"When I arrived, Music Row wasn't quite developed yet, but I got the feeling that it was happening. Mercury's office and Lowery's Nashville office—I still wrote for him—were down in the Cumberland Lodge Building on 7th Avenue almost to Charlotte. Tree was down there. Sun, upstairs on the top, and the Wilburn Brothers had an office—of course that building is no longer there.

"I was just a gofer at Mercury. I would rehearse artists, I would listen to demos, I would do whatever needed doing. I mean there was just tons of material submitted for all the artists. [Recall those three labels at Mercury.] We were cross-collateralized to the hilt, and of course I got to play on a lot of those sessions, I played on hundreds of sessions the first year I was here and had a ball. I played on Brook Benton's stuff, Clyde McPhatter, Patti Page.

"Music is music to me, and to most Nashville musicians," he says. "Whatever it is, fine, let's play it, let's do it. I can remember working three or four sessions every day, and boy, you're exhausted."

When "Ahab the Arab" hit in 1962, Stevens started working show dates that took him away from the grind. "But I still considered myself a studio guy, and I still worked at Mercury for a while."

After Mercury, Ray moved over to Monument Records where he produced other artists as well as continuing to record himself. "I did Jim Glaser. I did a session or two on Dolly Parton. I cut 'Happy Happy Birthday Baby' on her, the old R&B tune. I thought it was pretty good, but it didn't do anything. Times were not right.

"She was gorgeous. I remember she came out to the house, we were gonna rehearse, get ready for a session, and my wife was totally jealous. There wasn't anything going on, but just the fact that she was there with the door closed.... Oh, Penny didn't like that!"

In 1969, Stevens cut the first charted version of the great Kristofferson song "Sunday Mornin' Comin' Down." The record was unusual for Ray, not only because it was a *serious* song, but because it was written by a songwriter other than Ray, and because it marked Ray's first appearance on the country charts after years of pop hits. He worked on it for weeks and was so proud of it that he turned down the opportunity to sing "Raindrops Are Falling on My Head" for the movie *Butch Cassidy and the Sundance Kid*.

"I was afraid that recording that song might delay the release of 'Sunday Mornin' Comin' Down,' so I said, 'Thank you but I'll pass.'" It was a dumb thing to do, I realize that, but I thought that 'Sunday Mornin' Comin' Down' would just be a monster. It wasn't. And the reason it wasn't—I think I figured it out after a few years passed—was that it wasn't my image. I had too clean-cut an image to sing 'Sunday Mornin' Comin' Down.'"

Stevens did not regard his new country association as any big career change. "They don't print on the record label where it was cut," he says, "and if you've got the talent here to cut a record that's not country, go ahead." Nor was he ever aware of any trends. "I just do what I wanna do and I either get lucky or I don't."

In 1970, he got lucky. "I had just signed with Barnaby Records [Andy Williams' label] and I had also been signed to host Andy's summer show on NBC. I wanted a song that would not only be a hit for my first release on Barnaby, but that would also be used as the theme song for the TV show. So I sat down in my basement for three days trying to come up with the right song. I was leafing through a book of old Indian Hindu proverbs or something and I came across the phrase, 'Everything is beautiful in its own way.' I used the Baptist, Catholic, and Methodist massed choir, which was about twenty voices or so. Then I added three parts of falsetto myself, and doubled it, and that kinda pulled it all together. Then I got the idea to record the kids at the school singing 'Jesus Loves the Little Children.' So Charlie [the engineer] and I took a portable tape recorder out to Oak Hill School—my daughter attended out there—and recorded the second-grade class. We came back to the studio and spliced it to the front of the tape, overdubbed strings over the splice, and, *voilà!*" *Voilà* indeed. A number-one pop hit was what it was.

Many artists like to talk about their passion for their music. Ray lives it. "Even when I don't have a label deal—that hasn't happened yet—when I don't have any way to put my records out, I'm still gonna cut records, and I'm gonna take 'em home and listen to 'em, 'cause that's what I like to do. I have a studio back there," he continues, and his studio is not a little bedroom-sized Pro Tools setup. It's a commercial-quality studio and he's recorded many of his hits there. "It's a great studio. I have made records where I was the only guy on the record."

Ray also owns a video studio on 17th, which is a logical direction considering he has shot videos of his hits and sold huge numbers of them to Ray Stevens fans. Unlike many Nashville artists, he has enjoyed a lot of success in Branson, which customarily involves playing a theater continuously for weeks or months at a time.

As this book is being written, Ray Stevens is working on his new album called *Ray Stevens Sings Sinatra, Say What?* "I took some Sinatra songs and did 'em with a rock and roll band," he says mischievously. The album is a work in progress, like the artist himself.

Charlie McCoy is one of those guys who can play just about any instrument he puts his hands on. That was a considerable virtue in the creative days of the '60s in Nashville, when producers were constantly searching for a unique sound during their recording sessions. Although he became Music Row's premier harmonica virtuoso, McCoy lists a half dozen instruments in his musicians union book entry.

"I was born in Oak Hill, West Virginia, where Hank Williams was discovered dead," says McCoy, matter-of-factly. "That gas station was just two blocks from our apartment."

McCoy came to Nashville straight out of high school in Miami in 1959 and auditioned as a singer for RCA, Columbia, MGM, and Decca. "I was a Chuck Berry singer. I was playing at a barn dance called 'The Old South Jamboree,' and my job was to get up onstage for fifteen minutes each hour, and play rock 'n' roll for the young kids. Mel Tillis came in one night after a show down there and heard me and he told me if I came to Nashville, he could get me on Decca tomorrow.

"Being seventeen years old, I was eatin' up every word of it. The guy I was workin' for was the only country DJ in Miami at the time. His name was Happy Harold and he said, 'Well, I don't know about gettin' you on Decca tomorrow, but he *is* well connected.' So when I got out of high school, Happy Harold volunteered to drive me to Nashville, and when I got up here, Mel was out of town. But he had told Jim Denny about me and Jim volunteered to help, so he took me around to these auditions.

"Owen Bradley said to Denny—after Owen turned me down—'Well, you know, I'm having a session this afternoon, you think he'd like to come and watch?'

"I was so naïve I didn't even know what he was talkin' about, but I had nothin' else to do, so I said okay. So we went back to the Quonset Hut, into the studio itself, and Owen said to me, 'If you'll sit about halfway up that staircase there, you'll get a real view of what's goin' on.'

"So I walked up there and I had no idea what I was lookin' at, and all of a sudden the musicians started comin' in, and to an eighteen-year-old they all looked old to me. I'm thinkin', 'What is this? What's goin' on? And then finally Brenda Lee came in. She was thirteen. She'd never had a hit yet, so I didn't know who she was.

"These guys were millin' around, talkin' to each other, and then Owen came out with a demo and, you know, the demos were discs. He played the demo and it looked to me like none of the musicians were even payin' attention. And then I looked, and I thought, 'There's no sheet music. What's goin' on? There's no music—how can this be?'

"But when I heard the first playback, it was the best-soundin' thing I ever heard. At that moment I said to myself, to heck with bein' a singer, I wanna do this."

It was the session in which Brenda Lee recorded "Sweet Nothin's." "I was in a state of shock. I couldn't believe what I'd seen or heard. I went back to my hotel that night, I couldn't hardly sleep."

McCoy went back to Miami with visions of sugarplums dancing through his head. He entered the University of Miami as a music major, but after a year he returned to Nashville.

"The hardest thing I've ever had to do was to tell my dad [that I was going to Nashville to pursue a music career], 'cause my dad was so proud that I was goin' to college. I broke his heart, you know, but he let me go. [Songwriter] Kent Westbury came down and picked me up. We drove all night, there were no interstates then." Westbury had helped McCoy get a gig playing on the road with Johnny Ferguson, who had a pop hit at the time called "Angela Jones."

"There was a rehearsal the next day, that's why we drove all night. We walked into the rehearsal and Kent walked over to Johnny Ferguson and he said, 'Hey, here's the guy I told you about, guitar player.' And Ferguson said, 'Well, Kent, I never heard from you, I already hired somebody.'

"There was like thirty seconds of silence, which felt like a lifetime, you know, and Ferguson said, 'Well, what else can he play?' I see now, he was willin' to take his own money and pay me, so I wouldn't have to go back. I said, 'I play harmonica.'

"And he said, 'Nah, I don't need a harmonica.' And he said, 'Can you play drums?' I thought, say no and your time in Nashville is over before it starts. I said, 'Yeah, but I don't have any.'

"He said, 'No problem. We'll get you some.' And that was it. I worked for Johnny Ferguson, two weeks in Canada. I wanted to get off on the right foot in Nashville, so I came back from Toronto, took all my money, and

went down to Hewgley's and paid off the drums. We did one more booking down by Atlanta and he said, 'Well, I don't have any more bookings,
I guess we're done.' And here I was with a set of drums and no money.

"So I called my mother for money because I wouldn't let my dad know
what shape I was in. My dad and mother had split up when I was two
years old, so I called her and she sent me a few dollars.

"It was gettin' desperate. I got a call from Wayne Grey. Guitar player,
worked for many years with Tex Ritter. He's from Miami. He said, 'I'm
puttin' together a band to play some fairs this summer with Stonewall
Jackson and Red Sovine. Can you play drums?'

"I said. 'Not only can I play, I have some.'"

Eventually Jim Denny started using McCoy on some of his Cedarwood
demos. "In May of '61, I got a call from Denny," McCoy recalls, "he said,
'I just got a call from Chet. He's gonna record one of our songs. He heard
you play harmonica on a demo, he wants you to come and play exactly
what you played on the demo,' and I thought, a session, a real session!
This is great! So I went over to RCA, Denny went with me and said, 'Chet,
here's the boy that plays harmonica.' Chet said, 'I know you,' and I said,
'Yeah, about a year and a half ago I auditioned for you.'

"And he said, 'Black Gibson guitar, right? Played Chuck Berry,' and
I said, 'Yeah.' And he said, 'Boy, if you had played that harmonica we
could have *done* somethin'.'

"Anyway, the first session was Ann-Margret. I mean, I totally thought
I'd died and gone to heaven. Here was my first session with the A-team
guys, RCA Studio B, and here's Ann-Margret at eighteen. It was an out-
of-body experience. And the record was a hit, 'I Just Don't Understand,'
written by Kent [Westbury] and Marijohn Wilkin. It was like Top 20 in
the pop charts. At the end of the session Bob Moore walked over to me
and he said, 'You free Friday?'

"'Course I was free for the rest of my life, you know? He said, 'Can you
come back here at two o'clock, at this same place? I'm leadin' a session for
Roy Orbison.'

"*Roy Orbison!* You think I wasn't excited? I came back that Friday, and
the song was 'Candy Man.'"

"Candy Man" featured a lot of Charlie McCoy harmonica. "The phone
started ringin'. I couldn't spell it, but I *are* a studio musician now. For fun,
I started playin' in a rock 'n' roll band playin' bass with Wayne Moss. I'd
never really played bass before, but you know, it's the bottom four strings

of a guitar, no big deal, I picked it up pretty quick." And he played a little saxophone, a little trumpet. "I picked vibes up after I came here. I was on a session for Chet one time and we were doin' some ballad, and there was no need for harp on it and he said, 'Why don't you go hit a couple of notes on those vibes?' I said, 'I've never played vibes.' And he said, 'You can do it.'

"'Okay.' So I went over and I said, 'Man, this is fun!' I went out and bought me some mallets. Back in those days, RCA and Owen's studio, there was a set of vibes there, and so I used to come to sessions early to practice. I really got into it. I ended up playing vibes on a lot of hits, such as 'Blue Velvet' by Bobby Vinton. When Milsap had that run starting with 'Almost Like a Song,' 'Let's Take the Long Way Around the World,' 'Smoky Mountain Rain,' I played vibes on almost all of those things. And then I would play organ a lot. I played organ on 'Easy Lovin',' 'You Lay So Easy on My Mind,' 'Tie a Yellow Ribbon' [the Johnny Carver country version], on a lot of the Elvis things, and then I played baritone sax on 'Pretty Woman.' All I did was *ba-dup, ba-dup*, 'cause Boots was doin' the other part. I played bass on 'Mohair Sam,' Charlie Rich.

"I went up to New York to go to the World's Fair. [Columbia producer] Bob Johnston had told me, if I ever came to New York, to call him—he could get me Broadway theater tickets. So I called him and said, 'Okay, I'm here. How 'bout the tickets?' He said, 'Okay, no problem, but if you're free this afternoon I'm recording Bob Dylan over at the Columbia studio and I'd like you to come over and meet him.'

"So I went over and he introduced me to Bob Dylan. Dylan told me he had one of my records, which I was amazed at. And then he said, 'Hey, I'm gonna do this song, why don't you play along? There's a guitar over there.'"

The song was "Desolation Row." "After the session, I left, went about my way, and Johnston started talkin' to Dylan and sayin', 'Hey, you know, we oughta go to Nashville, you see how easy it is?' So he finally talked him into comin' here." Charlie would play with Dylan on the albums *John Wesley Harding*, *Nashville Skyline*, and *Blonde on Blonde*.

Nobody knows the mettle of studio professionals like other studio professionals. Artists often believe that their talents are what made their record a hit. Songwriters point with pride to their *songs*. Producers eye their successes, and often in their heart of hearts, credit themselves. And they're all right—sometimes. And then there are the studio regulars, the ones that created the licks that folks walk down the street humming.

"Neal [Matthews] was the secret to the sound the Jordanaires had," says McCoy. "You know, all those little silly *bop, bop, bops*. I can't imagine 'Don't Be Cruel' without those *bop, bops*. At the time, people might have thought it was silly or corny, but it was amazing, and they all came out of Neal's head."

Of course, get almost anybody talking about Elvis, and the memories begin to flow.

"You know, those Memphis Mafia guys hung around all the time," McCoy remembers. "And it was weird. While you were recording, you didn't see 'em. They were back in the halls or something, shootin' dice or whatever they did. And the minute a playback started it was like... I mean, we had just finished, and we'd walk into the control room to hear the playback, and there was hardly any room for us in there because all these guys were—they just appeared out of nowhere.

"And they would always stand around and say, 'Ahh, that's great, Elvis. That's great, Elvis.'

"You know, he would sleep all day and record all night, which was tough for a lot of us because we all had work during the daytime. I remember many days when I would leave an Elvis session at RCA, go have breakfast, and go to the next session.

"They would bring food in at midnight, every night. One time, they brought in burgers and fries and all this stuff. There was a big milk shake cup, and it was full of kosher dill slices. Jerry Carrigan was the drummer, and he started to reach for one of those pickle slices, and from out of nowhere, this hand came and *slap!* 'Those are Elvis's pickles!' And you know, Elvis would have given you every one of them."

McCoy, of course, was called for many of the pop sessions in Nashville, both before and after Dylan came, and he remembers that the music from down south didn't quite fit into what he calls "The Haight-Ashbury Era."

"You know, we had that studio band, Area Code 615, around 1970," he says. "We played at the Fillmore West and it was a strange experience. The place was—I don't know what it was, it was a warehouse or somethin'—and it had a big old stage in the middle and not much else in it. People would stand, and the stage was real high. Me bein' short helped, because about a foot above my head there was a line of marijuana smoke that hung over the place like a cloud. And guys like Mac Gayden and

Wayne Moss were right up in it. Our big claim to fame there—although I didn't think we had much of an impact—to all those young kids we looked like a bunch of insurance salesmen or something. Weldon Myrick was wearing a 'Members Only' jacket.

"After Johnston brought Dylan here, Simon and Garfunkel came. Me and Fred Carter played on 'The Boxer.' He played that guitar solo in the middle and I played the bass harmonica. That was in Columbia Studio A.

"Peter, Paul and Mary came. I played on an album with them. Manhattan Transfer came. Me and Buddy Emmons played on an album with them. It was almost like the people in the folk genre, after Dylan, they'd say, 'Oh! Why, it must be okay to go there, you know, it's not just country.'

"I'll never forget, of course, over at Quad they always had *Rolling Stone* layin' around and I read so many articles about 'Nashville sells out to commerciality.' I would think to myself, 'Hey, y'all, you know, we're in the music business here. This is not an art center, you know—it's business.'

"Like they were talkin' about, 'Aw, those studio musicians, they never do anything!' Hey, we're hired by producers. We do what we're told to do. 'Course in the old days, producers hired people they trusted and just let you go. I loved playin' for Jerry Kennedy because he always gave you freedom. He would always say, 'Fill the second verse.' He wouldn't tell you what to play.

"Owen was much more vocal than Chet. Chet was very, very quiet. But I'll tell you Owen's genius: Number one, he recognized a great song. He could take a song and flip it around, change where the verse was, or change where the chorus was—he was a genius at doin' that.

"And he would have made a great studio engineer, because, most of the great sound on those records, I'm tellin' you, it came from him. Every once in a while, we would record with a string section, and in that Quonset Hut, if you had a full rhythm section and a string section, it was crowded in there. I've seen him come out and move an overhead mic three inches—you know, an overhead mic over the strings. He'd say, 'I'm payin' for ten strings and I can only hear nine.'

In the late '70s and early '80s, McCoy moved on to a successful recording and touring career that often took him away from his studio work. Over the years McCoy has released thirty-one solo albums and as this book is being written, is still going strong.

For years he was a mainstay of Fred Foster's Monument Records. "I think it was '83 they took Chapter 11, but we all kept thinkin' that they were gonna hang on. Four years passed and finally [they went under]. I went back down Music Row to every major label here tryin' to get another deal, you know and I couldn't get one. It was too late, too far after the fact. So I made some records for Step One, and I started recording for these overseas labels. Then that led to playin' overseas. Since '88, I've been goin' to Europe at least twice every year, doin' the artist thing."

In the early '90s, McCoy says, demand for him as a studio musician began to slow down, but "I'm still probably doin' fifty sessions a year." He still has the chops, but a new generation of producers has arrived, and either they're too young to know who Charlie McCoy is, or they think he's past his time.

"When my phone stopped ringin', it was hard to take, mentally. It wasn't the money. I was doin' fine. But it's a form of rejection. Even though you understand, hey it's a changin' of the guard. There are new producers. All the people that you used to work for all the time are either retired or deceased. Even though you totally understand the reason, it still feels bad, and it took some mental adjustment on my part to deal with it. Now I'm fine with it, not a problem.

"It's a little disappointing because I know that I'm playing the best I've ever played in my life right now. All this live playin' sure helps. The great thing about Europe: They don't care about how old you are. They don't care if you're not on charts. They don't care if you have videos on CMT. If you did, they wouldn't watch 'em anyway. Hey, if I never get another session, I can't complain. I sure have had my share."

13

REBELS AND RESPECT

"One thing that makes Music Row unique in the world," says Robert Oermann, "is that it gives the Nashville music business a sense of community. Unlike Berlin, or London, or New York, or Los Angeles, we have a neighborhood that *is* the music business, and we know each other intimately because of it. We know who's screwing who, we know who's sick, we know everything about each other, and some people don't like that.

"The nation at large spat upon country music, and drove them into a 'circle the wagons mentality,' and drove them into this neighborhood that nobody cared about, that had seen better days. And it was a real good thing that happened. It helped the country music industry become strong, because to defend itself against a city that wanted to be the Athens of the South, and looked with disdain upon these drunken hillbillies, they became very insular against the larger community."

"The story of country music is the story of a fight for respect," adds Belmont University professor Don Cusic. "And it never quite succeeds. And that's why so many in Nashville are thin-skinned when it comes to country music because they don't even get respect within the Nashville *business* community. Phil Bredesen, as mayor, what he wanted was an image other than Country Music, U.S.A., so he gives away the store to get the Houston Oilers here. "Well," he says, with a laugh, "they come here to do *Monday Night Football* and what do they do? They go to Roberts' Western Wear and Tootsie's, Grand Ole Opry, and all that stuff, and they got Hank Jr. singin' the theme.""

That fight for respect continues today. In recent times, a roundabout was constructed where 16th Avenue South, Demonbreun Street, and Division Street meet, at the entrance to Music Row. There were some discussions about a large sculpture to put in the middle of that round-about. Some music people came up with the idea of a young man with a guitar, standing straight and strong as he looks down Music Row, contemplating his musical dreams.

But the high-society crowd had the power and influence. What Music Row got in 2003 was nine huge naked figures dancing with abandon, all breasts and genitalia, a tribute to pagan art totally out of sync with the country music that built so much of Music Row, out of sync with the largely Christian tourist crowds that seek out the country music shrines of Nashville, out of sync with just about everything that made Music Row *Music Row*. Across the street from this sculpture, which is known as *Musica*, is Owen Bradley Park. In Owen Bradley Park, quite close to *Musica*, is a life-sized sculpture of Owen Bradley, seated at a grand piano, right hand on the keyboard, left hand upraised, apparently directing a studio session. Though he is looking away from *Musica*, the total effect of this tableau is that poor Owen is fated to spend eternity as musical director for an orgy.

Musica does not inspire a whole lot of respect within the music industry. "Neil Young was in town a couple of weeks ago," Charlie McCoy said recently. "Couple of members of his band went out and got a bunch of cardboard, cut 'em up into guitars, and hung 'em on the sculptures.

"Last week they had a prayer vigil at *Musica*," Oermann commented while we were talking at his home off Belmont Boulevard. "A bunch of evangelicals put masks over their eyes and tape over their mouth and faced with their backs to *Musica* for several hours.

"I find it ironic that the music business settled here because Nashville is such a brown-shoe town. They don't dance here. People don't know *how* to dance in Nashville. It's so funny, because everything on the face of it, in terms of the complexion of the city is not fun, and music is *fun*. I mean, Texas is much more fun. *Pittsburgh* is more fun than Nashville! And Nashville was *dry* until 1967 or '68. How weird is that?"

By 1967, Nashville had a firmer idea than ever of its place in the music firmament. Cusic has an interesting perspective regarding the events that were influencing Music Row.

"First of all, Bakersfield was selling more country records with Buck Owens and Merle Haggard than anybody in Nashville. Yet in 1967, the Country Music Hall of Fame opened and that solidified *Nashville* as the center of country music. And in '67, Eddy Arnold releases what I think is the quintessential Nashville Sound record, "Make the World Go Away."

The "Nashville Sound" Cusic is referring to is of course the amalgam of country rhythm sections with the string section overlays that seem to drive urban critics of country music out of their minds—these critics who want so badly to keep country music barefoot and...well, barefoot, anyhow. By then, Eddy Arnold had long ago forsaken his Tennessee Plowboy image and was accustomed to performing in a tuxedo. To many country fans even more than media critics, Arnold's trip uptown constituted a defection from the kind of country music they treasured, and they resented it. The same year, Ray Price released his version of "Danny Boy," which was a step down the same road as Arnold. In some ways, Price's move was more threatening than Arnold's because in the late '50s and early '60s, when country was severely wounded, Price had stood rock-solid country with a succession of Texas shuffles that stayed true to the genre.

As the 1960s marched on, rock and pop radio were moving into alternative forms of pop like the "Motown Sound," psychedelic music, second-phase Beatles, etc., that had much less country influence than the rockabilly and pop of the pre–British Invasion days. "Although radio programming at that time was a lot broader, there wasn't room for a Nashville record on pop radio other than an occasional record," says Cusic.

As the decade moved along, a number of pop acts emerged that had a definitely country sound, like the Byrds and the Flying Burrito Brothers, but the country music industry paid them little mind. Cusic continues: "The country music industry looked at the Byrds, Gram Parsons—and even the Rolling Stones cut some country stuff—and said, 'They're not one of us.' If you remember that period of time, there was the bunch that smoked dope and had long hair, and there was the bunch that didn't. What you have in country music was the counter to the counterculture, most obvious with Merle Haggard's 'Okie from Muskogee' and 'Fightin' Side of Me.'"

By the time "Okie from Muskogee" had made its way through the charts, Capitol Records and Haggard had to know that the song had touched an ironic chord in the very audience he was dissing. But instead of pandering to them, he stayed true to his core country fans. His next release, "Fightin' Side of Me," settled any question of whose side he was on, and though few hippies ever adopted the Hag as one of their own, country fans treasure him to this day.

Johnny Cash chose a different route. Records like "The One on the Left Is on the Right," "Folsom Prison Blues," and "A Boy Named Sue" (recorded at San Quentin Prison) marked Cash as a country artist with folkie sensibilities. From 1969 through 1971, he hosted a successful network TV variety show from the Ryman Auditorium, and his 1970 recording of "What Is Truth" was a definite gift to the socially conscious young of the era.

Although moving in different directions, the music of both Cash and Haggard during this time were direct responses to the culture wars of the era that were tearing the country apart.

Another talent who heralded a new era in Nashville was Kris Kristofferson, a Rhodes scholar and army helicopter pilot who rode a short but brilliant songwriting career to recording stardom before becoming a successful film star. Think of the titles: "Me and Bobby McGee," "Sunday Mornin' Comin' Down," "Help Me Make It Through the Night," "For the Good Times." Between 1969 and 1971, these were all huge crossover hits. Kristofferson was able to craft overtly sexual songs and get away with it, and for years to come many country songs written by later writers bore the stamp of sexuality that he pioneered. Whereas many country songs with their literal portrayals of reality are ridiculed by outside critics, Kristofferson was honored. At a time when country music was more isolated than usual from the pop world, his songs helped bridge the gap between Roger Miller and Kenny Rogers in letting the outside world know that country music still had input into the pop culture. With his whiskey baritone and scruffy appearance, Kristofferson looked like "one of them," even though his music declared he was "one of us." And he had the charm and street smarts to pull it all off.

Still another iconoclast was a black singer from Sledge, Mississippi, named Charley Pride. Charley Pride is the only country star of any significant magnitude to be black, and he didn't come along in the '70s and the '80s when Jim Crow was just a nasty hangover and white folks all over the country were trying to prove to themselves and others that they had never been racist. Charley Pride had his first country hit in *1966*, at a time when legal racial discrimination was still fresh in the minds of all Southerners, white and black.

For Nashville, the first half of the '60s was filled with turmoil. Restaurants and schools painfully desegregated, and two white Nashville mayors worked with black organizations to change the city's future. There were a few bombings and street clashes, and a whole lot of new private schools came into being. Many municipal swimming pools were closed.

It was against this backdrop that one of Nashville's great mavericks, Jack Clement, took center stage of the country music industry, when he cut some demos on Charley Pride. Clement once told Cusic, "I took that tape to Chet Atkins and played it for him, and Chet said, 'Let me check with Harry Jenkins.'" Jenkins was an RCA executive in New York, and Clement, who used to work for Atkins, thought that was weird because Chet didn't need Harry Jenkins's approval to sign artists. But Chet apparently didn't want to make that decision alone. Charley Pride had his first Top 10 country record in the winter of 1966, and over the next two decades he scored twenty-nine *Billboard* number-one hits and was undeniably one of country music's superstars.

Through the years there have been a number of black country artists, including O. B. McClinton, Stoney Edwards, Big Al Downing, Cleve Francis, and Trini Triggs, an artist Mike Curb has sought to establish for several years. There were several black female country recording artists too, most notably Linda Martell and Ruby Falls. Although Edwards, Downing, McClinton, and Falls all had numerous chart records, Charley Pride is the only black country singer in the history of Music Row to really have hits.

One other spectacular black artist who influenced country music was, of course, the amazing Ray Charles. Like many great artists, Charles' tastes in music ranged far and wide. In 1960, he released "Georgia on My Mind." Written by a young Hoagy Carmichael and his Indiana University roommate Stuart Gorrell, "Georgia on My Mind" was not really a country song, but one from a long line of Tin Pan Alley songs seeking to capture the romance of the South.

Two years later came the landmark album *Modern Sounds in Country and Western Music*, featuring many of country music's most enduring standards. Although he had several huge pop hits from that album, it was not promoted as country. The lesson learned was that great country standards like "You Win Again" and "I Can't Stop Loving You" were not just country standards, they were American classics. Ray cut a volume two of *Modern Sounds*, and continued to a cut a country song from time to time throughout the '70s, but it wasn't until the '80s that he began to appear on the country charts, most notably in duets with George Jones and Willie Nelson.

There is no Charley Pride without Jack Clement, one of the more fantastic characters in any genre of popular music. Clement, called "Cowboy" by nearly everybody, is well into his seventies, with a lifetime of excess behind him, and a continuing will to create and perform music.

Born in Whitehaven, Tennessee, near Memphis, he spent four years in the Marines and two more playing music in Washington, D.C., Baltimore, Wheeling, and Boston before returning to Memphis in 1954. "I ran into this guy I had known since grammar school. He was teaching dancing at Arthur Murray's," Cowboys recalls. "I was sayin' to myself, 'What a nice deal that would be.' I couldn't dance a lick, I had never danced in my life, but I'd been on the Marine Corps drill team, which was choreography. I knew my left from my right and I'd played for a lot of dances, and I had real good rhythm. I saw an ad in the paper one day, 'Dance instructors wanted, no experience necessary, call Miss Elliot.' So I call Miss Elliot, went down to see her, and was immediately sort of smitten by her—she was really shapely...pretty. I got in this training class. Six weeks later I'm a dance instructor. I go from a nondancer to being a dance instructor—tango, samba, foxtrot, waltzes, jitterbug.

"I did that for six months. Then I went to school for two years, Memphis State. I never did intend to graduate. I wanted to have a couple of years of college. I already had about a year in the Marine Corps. I was a high school dropout, you know. Got into English literature and stuff, I even took a course in nutrition, and a course in electricity, physics, trigonometry. And on weekends, I was playing guitar and singin' in a band in Arkansas.

"In 1955, I went and auditioned for Sam Phillips. He listened to me real well. I was in there maybe an hour or so. I was singing Marty Robbins songs—I wasn't really into rock 'n' roll. I'd sing a few bluegrass songs, and he thought I was real good but it didn't quite fit, a little too smooth, too slick, you know.

"I started this little record label with a guy named Slim Wallace. I told him I'd build a little studio in his garage in my spare time. We never got to a point where we could actually cut a master there, but we could do demos and work tapes and stuff. We didn't have any echo. But we worked some stuff up with a guy named Billy Lee Riley, went down and rented a radio station and recorded some sides. That's what I took to Sam to have him master it. He heard this thing and liked it and offered to put it out on Sun Records.

"Then he said, 'What are you doing?'

"I said, 'I'd been going to Memphis State, but now I'm working at this building supply place and I don't like it very much.'

"He said, 'Well, maybe you ought to come work for me.' I said, 'Maybe I should.' And two weeks later I did. That was June the 15, 1956."

By this time, Cowboy had gotten over wanting to be a star and was really into producing records.

"I was engineer and producer," he says. "I never did consider myself an engineer—engineers are technical and I wasn't technical—but it was an easy system to run: we only had six mic inputs and there were rotary pots, no EQ or anything like that.

"To get echo, you'd have to use two mics, and you had to take up one of those pots for that second mic, to run it onto a second tape recorder." This unique sound became a signature sound for Sun's great artists, which of course included Elvis, Jerry Lee Lewis, Carl Perkins, and Johnny Cash.

"After a while, I talked Sam into getting a separate little mixing board, puttin' five pots on it so I could control the echo, and didn't have to have two mics and be tryin' to keep 'em together. But sometimes they weren't together, and sometimes that made for magic sounds. So to me, that thing was like a musical instrument. I wasn't approaching it tryin' to get *reality*. I didn't care about that, I wanted to make it sound *better*! That's what that was all about, as far as me being an engineer.

"So he showed me the basic things and then sort of turned me loose and, you know, within a few days I had that down pretty good."

Early on, Cowboy continued to work with Billy Lee Riley, who would soon have a record out on Sun. "Johnny Cash was there," he says, "but I didn't work with him for maybe a year or so. Sam kind of kept him back. He was Sam's fair-haired boy.

"Sam didn't have a [studio] band really, he had these certain guys he'd call to do sessions, and there wasn't any real structure to it. He'd get 'em in there and they'd do two, three, four sides, and he'd give 'em like fifteen bucks or something. And they seemed happy with that. I said, 'Why don't we set up some kind of an hourly rate?' He said okay and started paying them two dollars an hour. After a while I talked him into giving them a buck raise so they were making three bucks an hour when I left there.

"I'd been there since June '56, and it was September when Jerry Lee Lewis came in. I was back in the studio piddlin' around, experimenting maybe, not doing anything in particular, and Sally up front says, 'There's this guy here says he plays piano like Chet Atkins.' 'Hey,' I said, 'I wanna hear that, send him on back!' So he came back, sat down at this little spinet piano, and played 'Wildwood Flower,' sounded like Chet Atkins. And I said, 'You sing?'

"So he starts singing these George Jones songs and…he was great! But I had to tell him we don't do that here much, we're not into country. It's rock 'n' roll. Country was pretty much in the doldrums at the time. So I told him he oughta go home and get up some rock 'n' roll and come back. Well, in the meantime, I played the tape for Sam one night and he just loved it. He said, 'Get that guy in here!'

"About a week later he showed up. He'd written a song called 'End of the Road,' kind of rock 'n' roll. I said, okay, that's good enough, but better still he'd worked up an arrangement of an old Gene Autry song, 'You're the Only Star in My Blue Heaven.' I said, 'That's it, pal!' or something like that. I think it was on a Monday or Tuesday. I remember because Sam was leaving that Thursday to go to Nashville to the annual Disc Jockey Convention. So I told [Jerry Lee] to come back Thursday and I'd have some musicians there and we'd cut some tapes. So he came back, and we got in there and cut those two songs and then toward the end of the session we were about to quit when I said, 'Do you know "Crazy Arms"?'

"'I know a little of it.'

"'Well, let's do it!'

"Now, at this time, it has been a huge hit by Ray Price. So we cut it as an afterthought, and I had the thumb tacks on the piano keys. The sound that was on his first record, 'Crazy Arms,' and 'Whole Lotta Shakin'' and 'Great Balls of Fire' was a little spinet piano with thumb tacks in it. You mic it down underneath, take that piece of wood off and stick it in the bottom—I was always experimenting with stuff like that."

Clement went on to great success at Sun, not only as an engineer and producer for their great acts but as a songwriter, most notably with Johnny Cash hits like "Guess Things Happen That Way" and "Ballad of a Teenage Queen." "My role model for 'Guess Things Happen That Way' was Dean Martin's record of 'Memories Are Made of This,'" he says. "Kinda like a rumba. But Cash didn't do it that way at all. I mean, I loved the way he did it and it sold a lot of records, but when I recorded it myself, I went back to sorta the way I wrote it."

Cowboy had, and has, a strong, bigger-than-life personality. Once, when he prefaced a remark to Cash with the phrase, "In my humble opinion," Cash replied, "Cowboy, there's *nothing* humble about your opinion."

Clement came to Nashville in 1959 to work for Chet Atkins. "You see, I cut several records myself," he says. "And I didn't want to record in that funky old studio. I wanted to come to Nashville to record, so I came over here and rented RCA, and that's when I first met Chet Atkins. He was real impressed with what I did and tried to get me to come to work at RCA, but they wanted me to move to New York. I didn't want to do that. After I left Sun, I started a record label, but that didn't happen. About a year later, I'm needin' to go to work, so I called Chet and asked him if he was still interested in hiring me, and could we do it in Nashville, and he said *yes*. So I came over here and I was like his assistant for about a year and a half.

"Nothing much came of that. He let me record all the people he didn't want to fool with, like Del Wood. I did three albums with her, playin' piano. But that wasn't what I wanted to do.

"So then I decided to move to Beaumont, Texas—I had a buddy down there, Bill Hall—and he had a little studio and I had some equipment in Memphis. We moved to a new building. I went in and gutted this build-ing in down town Beaumont on the main street there. Tore out a bunch of stuff and then I built a front room, a studio, a control room, and an echo chamber—I was the head carpenter. It was a beautiful studio and it sounded great, we just never did have enough equipment in there really." That was 1961.

They called the studio Gulf Coast, and they must have been doing something right because, Cowboy says, within six or seven months they cut a million-selling record, a song called "Patches," recorded by Dickie Lee.

"Then I cut a bunch of Cajun records, did an album with Moon Mullican, did some stuff with Joe Tex one time for Buddy Killen's label. It was a rental studio, but then we did our own producing. Of course, George Jones would drop by and I'd play him a song that I published like 'She Thinks I Still Care,' and he'd go to Nashville and record it. Then I'd go and write one called 'A Girl I Used to Know,' and he'd go record that."

In fact, he says, pitching songs out of Beaumont he had three Top 5 songs in a row with George, including two that he wrote. It must have given him and Bill Hall confidence that they might be able to compete in the tough, competitive world of Nashville publishing. He was continuing to come to Nashville and pitch songs too, and in 1965, he made the deci-sion to move back to Tennessee.

Cowboy rented a house in Madison, and rented an office on the third floor of the RCA Building on 17th.

"I started doing pretty well soon after I got here. I had that 'Laurie' thing in the charts [Dickie Lee's death song hit 'Laurie (Strange Things Happen),' that he published]."

He didn't have to wait for his BMI royalties to come in because BMI executive Frances Preston had a great eye for coming publishers in Nashville and kept many of them alive with advances against future royalties from BMI. Cowboy was an easy client to take care of because he had, as they say, "money in the pipeline" from hits like "Laurie" and "The One on the Left Was on the Right," his big Cash hit of the '60s. Preston did not mind gambling on others on the basis of her belief in them, and she was often right. If Owen Bradley and Chet Atkins were fathers of Music Row, then Frances was most certainly the mother of Music Row.

"Back in those good old days, go down BMI, pick up a hundred grand, you know, something like that," Clement says, laughing.

"I'd only been here about seven or eight months when Charley Pride came along. While I was still living in Beaumont, on one of my frequent trips here, I'd met this guy named Jack Johnson, who worked as a PR man for Cedarwood Publishing. We got to be good friends, and every time I'd come up here we'd get together.

"There was this place down on Music Row called the Professional Club. The building's not there anymore, but it was right there across the street from Cedarwood. That's where all the songwriters would hang out, and music bums in general. It was also right across the street from the Quonset Hut, so a lot of people would come in there on breaks from sessions or after sessions or before sessions and just hang out. Tom T. Hall was there a lot. I was there a lot. I took Kristofferson there first time he came to town and he got so enthralled with it he resigned his Army commission and moved here in about a month.

"It was a great place. I'd go home—I was living in Brentwood at the time—I might go home and write a song and say, Well, I think I'll drive down there and play it for the boys.

"Anyway, Jack Johnson kept telling me about Charley, and then one night we'd had a couple of cocktails and I let him talk me into going across the street and listening to a tape at Cedarwood—tape he'd made when Charley came by there one day. And it sounded pretty good. It wasn't great, the recorder wasn't great, but I could tell that the guy was good, and that he was for real. So we went back across to The Professional Club, had a couple more cocktails, I said, 'Get him on in here, I'll pay for it, cut a session.' So about a month later Charley shows up. He was living in Helena, Montana, at the time, working in a smelter, but his father lived in Sledge, Mississippi, where he grew up. Anyway, he was here. I gave him five or six songs to take with him, and he drove down there to visit his daddy, came back a week later, and I had a session set up. And we went in and cut his first two sides, which were 'The Snakes Crawl at Night' and 'Atlantic Coastal Line.' And then I set about trying to get him on a label.

"I'd already told Chet Atkins I'd let him have first crack at it, which I did, but they turned it down after a while. He was interested, thought about it. But then they turned it down. Then I pitched it to the various record labels. Shelby Singleton, who was at Mercury at the time, went and played it for some R&B disc jockeys. And of course, what are they gonna think about that—it wasn't remotely R&B, it was just country, you know, redneck country.

"There was a guy named Art Talmadge, had Musicor Records, I called him in New York. I told him I had this black country singer, and he said, 'Oh, that'll never get you anywhere.'

"I said, well, the guy's really good; and then I asked him would he just give him a listen. He said okay. And he heard it and said it's real good, but he didn't know what to do. And I played it for a few other people. I had a buddy named Joe Talbot who was working for a pressing plant at that time, and he would periodically go on promotion trips. One time he was going to Texas. And he liked the record so he agreed to take it with him and play it for some disc jockeys while he was there. He came back and said they loved it, said they played the heck out of it.

"So I was right on the verge of pressing it up myself. And then I run into Chet Atkins down by the coffee machine downstairs next to the big studio [in RCA]. He said, 'What did you ever do with that colored boy?'

"I said, 'Well, I haven't done anything yet. I'm thinking of pressin' it up myself.'

"He said, 'Well, I've been thinkin' about that, and we might be passin' up another Elvis Presley.' And he told me that if I'd get him another acetate, he'd take it to L.A. next week and play it for this big A&R meeting, so I got him another acetate. He came back a week later, said, 'They went for it.'

"He did the same thing I did: I would play the tape for people, then I'd show 'em Charley's picture. And they wouldn't believe it. It was fun. He did the same thing. He played it for them out there and then passed his picture around and they said, 'No, the guy we just heard.'"

"The Snakes Crawl at Night" did well for a first record, says Cowboy. It sold six or seven or eight thousand copies, which, he adds, was not bad for a brand-new artist.

Charley's next thirteen singles were Top 10, including six number-ones in a row, five of which stayed number one for at least two weeks. His first two Top 10 hits, "Just Between You and Me" and "I Know One," were both written by Cowboy. He went on to produce Pride for six and a half years, during which time the two churned out twenty albums.

The reactions were sometimes surprising. "There were some places in Mississippi: They started playing it before they found out who he was, but then the people went for it, and they kept playing it. They were threatening to take it off when they heard he was black, but then the people wanted to hear it. Pretty soon, 'Hey, man, here's a black singer, you know?' He started in Texas of all places and Louisiana, really redneck. His first show was a place in Louisiana, not too far from the Texas line. I wasn't there, but he's told me and other people told me he walked out on stage. 'Course Charley had this real nice kind of drawl, this cowboy kind of drawl—he doesn't sound like a hillbilly, sounds like a cowboy. And then he has a great voice, he's a good-looking guy, and he walks out on the stage, and a hush falls over the crowd. And he said, 'Well, I do have this sort of permanent suntan.' From then on, man, he had them right there in the palm of his hand. Then the next night he's in Texas, and the same thing happened again. They'd love him from then on."

Charley Pride was more than a curiosity. He had twenty-nine *Billboard* number-one singles over a fourteen-year period and nearly half of those stayed number-one for two or more weeks. His sales were huge for his time, and he filled auditoriums again and again. His audience was almost exclusively white country fans, and they were out there not to prove that the civil rights movement had changed their hearts, but because they genuinely liked this country singer.

"He was just that good," says Clement, simply. "And he looked that good, and he was charming. People liked him." Was it possible that Pride was about to integrate the music that was a cultural emblem of the South?

In spite of the previously named black country artists, most of them gone, some of them lingering, there have been no other real breakthroughs. Why?

Each artist is an individual case. "I tried to cut some stuff on Stoney Edwards," Cowboy remembers. "He never really connected with the right record. Of course, he wasn't as handsome as Charley, but he was for real, he was absolutely for real." From 1971 through 1980, he had fifteen chart records on Capitol, none of which rose higher than the number-twenty slot.

But why haven't there been more black country artists signed?

When Frankie Staton is not a waitress, she is a very good piano bar singer in Nashville. She also has a mission to promote successful country singers, and to that end, she founded the Black Country Music Association. I have seen a number of her showcases, and while most of the artists are up to her high professional standards, quite a few of them are middle-of-the-road singers who realize that middle-of-the-road is a hard row to hoe these days, so they lean toward the country genre.

The country industry is extremely sensitive about people who migrate to country from other genres because they think "it's an easy place to go." Back in the '70s, a number of older songwriters with a successful New York prerock background moved to Nashville to continue their career only to find it very hard going. In the '80s and '90s, a bunch of pop writers and artists whose careers had faded moved to Middle Tennessee believing that Nashville would be easy pickings for people with their vast pop success. Most of them quickly eased their way into retirement. So it is with black artists who don't sound country.

Frankie Staton has cited studies from more than ten years back that claimed twenty-four percent of black people who listen to radio listen to country music. If that study still holds, then black listeners apparently constitute a very silent minority. New hit artists almost always come from among the young. Young black artists do sometimes come to Nashville seeking acceptance in country music, but they are not many. Country music has the reputation of being white folks' music and it stands to reason that few talented young black artists would care to try their luck.

Robert Oermann makes a great point about race in country music. "I get this from every visiting TV crew—'How come there's not another major black country star?' You know what? How come there's not a major black metal star? How come there's not a black president? But that question keeps coming to the country industry, and not to other industries. Nobody says, 'How come there's not a black boy band?' All the other genres get to be what they are. The underlying meaning is, 'You are racists because you are country music.' That infuriates me!

"The TV crews come to Fan Fair and they find the fan who's a complete wack job, who's covered in buttons and doesn't have front teeth, who's old and weird-looking—that's who they focus on. The fact that there are seventy-five nineteen-year-old chicks over here who are screaming for Kenny Chesney or whoever, they're not at Fan Fair, only that one is. Here's your 'typical' country fan and that infuriates me."

And Oermann solidly rejects the media stereotypes of country music as a right-wing dominated genre. He points out that a recent survey of bluegrass fans indicated that something like seventy percent of them described themselves as either fairly liberal, liberal, or very liberal.

"I still maintain that this is a deeply divided nation and that politics played itself out in country music. It did not play itself out in rock, or pop, or anywhere else, but in country where you have the Dixie Chicks, the Music Row Democrats, the 'Have You Forgottens,' the 'Courtesy of the Red, White, and Blues,' and all this stuff. And that says that we still have our fingertips on who America is.

"Of course, what the mainstream media would choose to focus on is 'Courtesy of the Red, White, and Blue,' but that does not speak for *all* country fans, or all country radio stations, or certainly not for Music Row. You know, it was fascinating to me that the moment we formed Music Row Democrats, it exploded. It was like there was this huge group of people that weren't being addressed.

"It's fascinating that country music continues to be the mirror of America that way, and that's a good thing."

14

GALLICO AND HIS BOYS

B y the late 1960s, Owen Bradley and Chet Atkins, the founding fathers of Music Row, were on the downhill side of their careers as star-makers. The glory years of Owen, with his huge hits on Brenda Lee and Patsy Cline, were beginning to fade, although he was still directing the recording careers of Conway Twitty and Loretta Lynn, both as solo acts and as a major country duet. Likewise, Chet Atkins was past his prime as a record executive, but with artists like Charley Pride and Waylon Jennings beginning to establish themselves, Chet's future at the top seemed solid.

Acuff-Rose was also losing ground in the industry. But their catalog of Hank Williams, Pee Wee King/Redd Stewart, the Bryants, and John D. Loudermilk songs continued to bring in big money, which made it easy for Wesley Rose to continue to run the company the way he always had. After all, why compete for the top writers in town when all the great old Acuff-Rose standards continued to get cut again and again?

By the late '60s, the vast majority of important record labels and publishing companies had either relocated to Music Row or were planning to, but Acuff-Rose remained isolated down on Franklin Road, a couple of miles—and worlds—away. They would remain in splendid isolation until after Gaylord Entertainment bought Acuff-Rose in 1985.

Around that time, Tree International was the coming publishing powerhouse. Its purchase of Pamper Music for $1.6 million in 1969 provided the company with a core of standards that looked good even next to the great early Tree standards like "Heartbreak Hotel," "Green Green Grass of Home," "Saginaw Michigan," and "King of the Road."

Two smaller publishing companies—Combine Music and Al Gallico Music—were on the upswing, and in the late '60s and early '70s, they would more or less drive the direction of country music.

In Nashville and elsewhere, successful music publishing companies do a lot more than simply sign songwriters, take their songs, and find ways to get them recorded. Publishing companies succeed by being on the inside, and the way to be on the inside is to make deals with record producers and recording artists. There is nothing evil or nefarious about this. If you are a publisher, and a young talent walks through the door who can not only write songs but sing them, you want to sign him up because singer/songwriters like to sing their own songs, and if their songs are also *your* songs, they will make you money without your having to stand in line, hat in hand, begging to have your songs recorded. Today, more than ever, record companies depend upon publishers to find talented artists and develop them to the point that they are ready for stardom.

Combine Music was founded in 1958 in Baltimore by Fred Foster, who that same year established Monument Records. Foster moved his two companies in 1960 to Hendersonville, Tennessee, just north of Nashville. By the early '60s, Foster was having great pop success on Monument with Roy Orbison, and in 1964, he guaranteed the future success of his publishing company by hiring Bob Beckham to run Combine.

Beckham was one of those rare publishers who truly loved songwriters, and he quickly established his reputation as a gruff but very supportive father figure to his staff writers. When the company moved to Music Row, it became a gathering place for not only Combine writers but writers for other companies who enjoyed the atmosphere created by this unusual man.

Al Gallico ran his company, Al Gallico Music, from New York, but his warm personality made him a very popular figure on Music Row, which he visited frequently. Gallico began his music career back in 1938 as an errand boy for the old New York publishing firm G. Schirmer. In 1953, he became the general manager of another great old New York company, Shapiro-Bernstein. Eight years later, Gallico set up Painted Desert Music, Shapiro-Bernstein's new BMI-affiliated publishing company, and hired Merle Kilgore to run the company's Nashville office. Almost immediately the company had two huge hits, "Wolverton Mountain" and "Ring of Fire."

In 1963, Gallico started his own company, funded by British capital, and again his success came early with "House of the Rising Sun." Gallico put together a small staff of talented Nashville writers and helped them find jobs in the business that put them in a position to get their songs recorded.

One of those people was Norro Wilson, who had a long, successful career as a songwriter, producer, and publishing and record executive. Wilson credits much of his success to Gallico's connections. When I asked him why he and others maintained such a long business relationship with Gallico, Wilson replied simply, "Because Al Gallico is a very nice man."

Norris D. Wilson comes from the town of Scottsville in central-south Kentucky. He started piano lessons at the age of seven or eight—"Something I kind of wanted to do, but didn't want to do because it made you a sissy." To make things worse, his piano teacher would peck at his fingers with hers to make him play the right notes. "I wanted to pop her so bad!"

Later he started taking lessons from a gospel piano player. While in high school, he got involved singing in an award-winning barbershop quartet, and these guys acquired the knack of being able to make local crowds go berserk. "That was the first smell of the greasepaint and the noise of the crowd, and I assure you, you are affected by that!" Bolstered by a scholarship, young Norris went off to what is now Western Kentucky University in Bowling Green, just a hop and a jump north of Nashville. "Great music department, big one!"

The family liked gospel music and from time to time they would head on down to Nashville on the last Friday night of the month to catch an event known as "Wally Fowler All Night Singing" at the Ryman Auditorium, then home of the Grand Ole Opry. "We would listen to the different groups and I became infatuated and thrilled by the Statesmen Quartet and the Blackwood Brothers Quartet. It wore me out, it was just the coolest thing I had ever seen. Those guys could just get up there and entertain as well or better than *anyone*, far better entertainment than most country acts in those days, because they had so much going on, four big guys workin' out, and the piano players, you know, and there was the great Jake Hess, R. W. Blackwood. I went nuts over it!"

Through the first twenty-five years of Music Row, most country singers and songwriters grew up heavily influenced by gospel music, and for many years nearly every country act carried at least one gospel tune in his or her repertoire. The writers often wrapped their reality lyrics around old gospel melodic phrases. For example, it's not hard to hear the melodic relationship of Curly Putman's timeless song "Green Green Grass of Home" to the old gospel standard "The Old Rugged Cross." And the old country anthem "Wild Side of Life" is melodically identical to the gospel song most often identified with Roy Acuff, "The Great Speckled Bird." Folks outside of country music might find it strange that great gospel melodies might re-emerge in secular songs about murder and drinking, but the relationship is taut and ever-present, and very similar to the historical tension in Southern black communities between gospel and blues. As the recording industry grew in Nashville, it became logical that gospel acts would come to Nashville to record—there were lots of good country musicians and studios there and the costs were not outrageous.

"We came down to Nashville one Friday," Norro continues, "and somewhere along about eleven o'clock at night, the piano player for a group called the Southlanders spotted me in the back of the theater, buying a snack or something. I was a typical freshman in college, with my charcoal-black slacks and pink sweater—it was the days of charcoal and pink, and I had my key chain and watch fob hangin' down. I was hot to go, or thought so. We just greeted each other and I told him how good I thought the group was, so he says, 'Well, what do you do?' And I said, 'Well, I'm in college at Western and I'm a music major and I got a scholarship and I'm a voice major.'

"'Oh, well, what do you sing?'

"I said, 'I'm a tenor,' and one thing led to another then the next thing you know they invited me down to Gallatin, Tennessee, forty miles from Scottsville, to be interviewed. And damn they loved how I sang, and all of a sudden out of no place and very quickly, I became a tenor singer for a quartet."

After a while the Southlanders decided to become a pop group, like the Four Lads or the Four Freshmen, and for a couple of years they played the nightclub circuit of the Southeast, "Which was one of the greatest thrills of my lifetime. These were wonderful nightclubs with the little lanterns or little lamps, and the women and men came in dressed up, looking like a million dollars. There would be four or five acts per show on these nightclub venues. We worked the Domino Lounge in Atlanta, we worked with Jonathan Winters, Brother Dave Gardner, Roberta Sherwood, Nelson Eddy."

Earlier they'd had a job with the Philip Morris Music Caravan, a country touring show that featured Carl Smith and Red Sovine. The people got to see the show by buying Philip Morris product and showing proof of purchase as they came through the gate. At the time Elvis and the Jordanaires were a big thing—it gave a show some class to have a good backup group. "So we were hired to do '*Ooh aah*,' as well as being featured in two or three songs. I remember one of the songs was 'That'll Be the Day.'"

During his time with the group he was living in Nashville, so when the group fell apart he decided to try his hand at the music business there. "I'm making an effort to meet more and more people all the time, and learn things like 'What is a publishing company?' and 'Who does that?' and 'Who is Jim Denny over at Cedarwood?'"

In 1962, he was part of a trio called the Omegas. "And the Omegas recorded for Owen Bradley, that was the first record I had anything to do with. I think I was singing the lead, finally at that time.

"Then I recorded for Monument, and at the same time I'm telling you this, I'm feeling a little embarrassed, because I didn't really have any success hardly at any of the labels, but I knew there was something about me they liked. I knew they thought I could do the job, and I had the looks, but what I realized later as I became a producer was that I didn't get the *songs*. I mean, I worked with the greatest. Jerry Kennedy recorded me [for Mercury]; Ray Stevens made a record on me; Owen Bradley made a record on me. George Richey made a record on me for Capitol. Bob Ferguson made a record on me for RCA." Eventually it became obvious even to Norro that if he was going to be successful in the Nashville music business, it would *not* be as a recording artist.

Around 1962, he met Boudleaux and Felice Bryant, and soon he was a regular at their house on the lake. "Felice would call me 'Neurosi'—I don't know if I was neurotic or what that means. One day Boudleaux came out with 'Norro,' and it's been Norro ever since. Then I got to hanging with Phil Everly and he and I became very goods friends. I try to tell people about success and I say, 'If you wanna see success.... I give Garth Brooks and Tim McGraw all the credit in the world, but they don't know what success is compared to what the Everlys had when they happened. They didn't just happen in the United States—they happened all over the damn world. It was unbelievable."

Through much of the 1960s, he continued to pursue a career as an artist, and although he made some good money performing in Las Vegas, he did not see his recording career going anywhere. So he turned to the music publishing business in Nashville. Norro was a champ at making friends within the business, and two of those friends were Beckham and publishing executive Henry Hurt, who helped him get a job pitching songs for Screen Gems/Columbia Music. "I did that for a year and got fired," says Norro. "Lucky for me, because then I got introduced to Al Gallico, whose office was right across the hall from me in the 812 building."

There are mainly three types of buildings on Music Row today: old houses remade into offices; a few office buildings that look as if they were actually designed by architects; and one- or two-story buildings that look as if they were thrown together overnight by an ambitious guy who brought in a truckload of concrete and cinder blocks, started slappin' them together, and by the end of the night had put up a building a bit too big for the planning commission to knock down with a small bulldozer.

The building at 812 16th Avenue South looks like one of the latter, and is located just a couple of buildings down from the Quonset Hut. "One day I see Gallico and he says [affects gravelly, *Godfather*-like voice], 'You're Norro Wilson, aren't you?'

"I said, 'Yeah.'

"'I hear you're a great guy!'

"I said, 'Well I appreciate that.'

"He said, 'Ya know? We might oughta talk. I might have ya work for me, you be my *boy* here.' Don't you love that?" Norro says, laughing.

So Norro moved across the hall from Screen Gems into Gallico's little two-room office. Norro had fallen into the situation that would make his career. He was hired to be a songplugger for what seemed like a one-man publishing company (Gallico), but Gallico had a way of finding talent and helping that talent find their place in the record industry. Billy Sherrill, who was a young up-and-coming A&R man for Epic and Columbia, wrote for Gallico, as did Glenn Sutton, Sherrill's assistant.

"So what took place," says Norro, "I'm out on the streets plugging Al Gallico songs that Billy had written, or Glenn had written, or whatever he asked me to pitch. And the next thing you know, I'm *writin'* with Billy. And then the next thing you know, Billy's saying, well, I'm gonna cut so-and-so and so-and-so. So why shouldn't we sit down and—we wrote shit overnight, man! We didn't analyze it the way they do it today; we'd just sit up there with a rhythm guitar and sing a simple demo." With very little songwriting experience, not much of which he was proud of, he had stumbled into the most powerful and prolific little production/songwriting clique in Nashville.

Both Sherrill and Sutton got so hot as producers, and the Gallico songs so often had the same names on them—usually some combination of Sherrill, Sutton, Wilson, George Richey, and a wonderful country songwriter named Carmol Taylor—that the perception grew that these guys had a tremendous advantage in getting their songs recorded.

And they did.

"We were writing songs and they were going to number one—well, you can't say much when that happens," says Wilson. Tammy Wynette, George Jones, Johnny Paycheck, Charlie Rich, David Houston, and many others from that era rode to the top of the charts on Sherrill/Sutton/Richey/Wilson/Taylor songs.

There were a few other publishing companies that shared in the Gallico/Columbia sphere of prosperity, most notably Tree and Hall-Clement, but many publishers felt shut out of the hottest recording scene in Nashville. The Gallico clique was neither the first nor the last to gain privileged access to major artists, and in fact Sherrill was considerably more open than some of the earlier and later producers on Music Row. But the Gallico gang had a high profile. Everybody wanted a Tammy Wynette cut, or a George Jones cut, or a Charlie Rich cut, and few seemed able to get one.

"Al is a gambler," Norro says, smiling at a very old memory. "He likes to win, he likes to lose. 'I love the action, Norro!' he'd say. He told us that he had given this one act five thousand dollars for a song they'd written. He played it for me and Billy, and we're looking at each other thinking, what a piece of shit. We never did say that aloud, but he could just tell we didn't get it.

"Doesn't matter whether *we* got it or not. A year later he came back to us and said, 'You know, guys, that song that I played for you, you know, you all didn't seem to respond to it too much, you know I gave five G's for it, you know?'

"We said, 'Yeah, yeah, yeah, yeah, yeah, we know.'

"'That was the Zombies,' he says. 'They gave me six songs to put in my publishing company.' Wow! That's the kind of move he could make. He had a warm heart, you know how Italians are if they like you. He rolled the dice on that song. Turns out the song itself didn't do anything, but the favor he did for them—big payoff. God knows what that one album made for him. That's a typical Al."

Norro's early hits included "Baby, Baby (I Know You're a Lady)" for David Houston, as well as "I'll See Him Through" and "My Man," two early big hits for Tammy Wynette. One of his biggest hits, though written in the late '60s, would not see the light of day for a number of years. "Rory Bourke and I wrote 'The Most Beautiful Girl'—might have been '68, '69—but the dang song laid around for seven years almost." Eventually the song, which was also co-written by Billy Sherrill, became a multi-million seller for Charlie Rich, number one, both pop and country; and the next year he had another big Charlie Rich hit with "A Very Special Love Song," which was number one, country, and number eleven, pop.

On "A Very Special Love Song," Norro was inspired by the piano licks on the theme from *Summer of '42*. He started working on the song with a very pretty piano intro. He played it for Sherrill, who turned to Norro and said, "That's very special," and Norro said, "Yes it is."

"Oh," replied Sherrill, "A very special love song."

"Happened exactly like that," says Norro. "I guess I'll always kind of cherish the fact that I got to write some things, just me and Billy Sherrill, which I thought was very special."

Eventually he began producing records, and over the years he has amassed an impressive track record that ranges from Joe Stampley to Reba McEntire to Kenny Chesney. Our conversation came not too long after he had announced his retirement. But a man like Norro Wilson, who did what he loved to do as long as he did it, will find it hard to stay retired.

Another great songwriter from this group was Royce Glenn Sutton, who grew up in a sawmill town called Chireno, Texas, just outside of Nacogdoches. Later he moved to Henderson, Texas, where one of the announcers at radio station KGRI was Jim Reeves. He started writing songs as a child, about "horses and saddles and stuff," and at the age of sixteen, "I got a fifteen-minute radio show on Saturdays. And Jim was the announcer in the booth. I'd write up requests at home, from family or somebody at school, you know. My theme song was the old Bob Wills' song 'I Bet You My Heart I Love You.'"

After a stretch in the military Glenn got involved in a band with Murray Kellum, playing clubs around Jackson, Mississippi. One night after they were through playing, Murray and Glenn drove to Memphis, got there at seven o'clock in the morning, and walked into Pepper Sound Studios.

"For $182 we cut four sides, including 'Long Tall Texan.' We came back to Jackson and pressed about two hundred records and put 'em out there in town. And a little guy at a record store in Jackson, Mississippi, played it for a salesman who came through Memphis, and *he* played it for a man at Hi Records in Memphis. They leased it as it was, the two sides. I was one side of the record, and Murray was the other. 'Long Tall Texan'—his side—went to number fifty with a bullet in the pop charts. The day President Kennedy was killed, it killed the record.

"I was working for Remington Rand cleaning electric shavers at the time. There was a show at the VFW and our band always backed everybody that came in. Bob Luman and Justin Tubb were the ones on [this] show." After the show, Sutton was talking with Tubb, who was the son of Ernest Tubb and a talented singer/songwriter. "I told him I wrote songs and that I'd like to pitch some in Nashville, how would I go about that?

"He said, 'If you'll give me a call when you're comin' in town, I'll be glad to try to help you a little bit.'

"I figured, well, that's probably bull, you know, but about a month later I came into town and I just went to a phone booth and I dialed that number. A voice on the other end said, 'Ernest Tubb Record Shop.' And I thought, *Sonofabitch, he's given me the number of the record shop, I'll never find him now.* But I said, ' Yes, I'm trying to get a hold of Justin Tubb.'

"He said, 'This is Justin.'" Sutton was speechless, his cynicism at a loss to account for this.

"Justin," Glenn said, "I don't know if you remember or not, but this is Glenn Sutton from Jackson, we played with you a month ago."

"He said, 'Oh yeah, how can I help you?' I said, 'Well, look, I brought some songs with me and I wanna see somebody, if you can help me.' He said, 'Give me about ten minutes, I'll call Tommy Hill out at Starday Records and try to get you an appointment out there.' I called back in ten minutes and he said, 'I set you up with Tommy for one o'clock.' He told me where it was at, on Dickerson Road. I drive out there, and I had a little book with about twenty songs in it. I went in and met Tommy, he set me up in a chair with a mic and a place for me to put my lyrics and stuff, turned the machine on, and said, 'Hey, I'll be back in thirty or forty minutes, just sing whatever the heck you want to and I'll listen to it later.'

"I set there and I sang all twenty of the songs in about forty minutes and he still wasn't back, so I just set there with the machine running. He came back in and I said, 'You gonna listen to them?' He said, 'I'll listen to them later and I'll be in touch with you. And I just went home and went back to work.

"I guess it was a month and a half or two months, I come home for lunch and my mother says you've got an envelope from Starday Records. I said, 'Give me that,' I'm looking at this bright yellow envelope, 'Starday Records' in the corner. I open it up and I'm lookin', wondering what this is, probably a rejection. Because I had got letters back from Wesley Rose himself turning songs down; I had got letters from Gary Walker, who was working for Painted Desert. But this time, I open it up, it's a contract for two songs. One song was called 'Gonna Buy Me a Juke Box' and the other song was called 'Credit Card.' He [Tommy Hill] said, 'I'm cutting these two songs on the Willis Brothers next week, please sign these contracts and get 'em back as soon as possible.' I signed 'em and sent 'em back and sure enough, he cut 'em on the Willis Brothers.

"I quit my job that day, I said, '*Shwwwhh*, I'm a songwriter now, babe. I'm in.' I didn't like the guy at the company I was working for anyway, I couldn't wait to tell him. I said, 'I'm probably goin' to Nashville, you know, I got some songwriting contracts and things there.' Oh, I was some big dog that day.

"So, the record came out. 'Gonna Buy Me a Jukebox' was the side of the record they were pushin' to start with, but the B-side was 'Give Me 40 Acres (To Turn This Rig Around),' which became a number-one record for the Willis Brothers! So I'm looking at a trade ad one day and I see, '280,000 and still climbing,' the sales of the Willis Brothers Record! I call Starday and I say, 'Hey, what about an advance, I see where you're sellin' pretty good,' and Tommy says, 'What are you talkin' about?' I said, 'Well, I just see the ad here you got in *Billboard* 280,000 and goin' strong.' He said, 'Don't believe all that. This record ain't sold five thousand!'"

That was Glenn Sutton's introduction to the Nashville record business of the '60s.

Music Row is about relationships, and Sutton knew Merle Kilgore, who by this time was working for Al Gallico. Kilgore soon saw enough ability in Sutton to sign him as a writer for a fifty-dollar-a-week advance, which, even in 1964, was slim money for surviving in Nashville. Before too long, he found himself about deeply in debt to his publisher.

"I couldn't live on that," Glenn says. "So to supplement my income, I went to work for Music City Recorders. Scotty Moore was the engineer there and Scotty and I became good friends." Moore, of course, was the guitar player who helped create the original Elvis sound in the old Sun Records days during the mid-'50s. So by day, Sutton was learning the publishing and songwriting world, and by night, he was absorbing the mysteries of the recording studio.

Like Norro later, Sutton's first big break involved Al Gallico. "If Merle couldn't haul him, I'd haul him, because he never rented cars—he just used the people that he had working for him. He was in the office one day and he said, 'I'm going over to see Chet Atkins and Eddy Arnold. You wanna go with me?' and I said, 'Y-yes!' I was just thrilled to death because I had never met Chet, or Eddy either, for that matter. So we go over to RCA, and they're just finishing up a session. Al introduces me to Chet, and they're talking and Chet says, 'Well, you know we're doing an album, and we want to call it *The Easy Way*, because Eddy sings so easy and nice.' And I'm sitting there listening and Gallico is saying, 'Yeah, that right?'"

Anybody from the old Gallico clique who quotes Gallico always attempts to imitate his voice, and the result is a nasally, gravelly New York sound. It's pretty funny to hear these good old boys from Kentucky, Alabama, and Mississippi sounding remarkably close to Gallico's Brooklyn bray. All of them to this day seem amazed that this outsider with the golden connections chose them to be the beneficiaries of his kindness. Atkins said to Gallico, "You reckon your new boy here can come up with a thing called 'The Easy Way'?

"I said, 'Of course, sir. Yeah, I can, if that's what you want.' So we leave there and I go home to my apartment, and that night I wrote 'The Easy Way' and another song called 'Tell 'Em Where You Got Your Blues,' and put 'em down with me and a guitar. They cut 'em both, and the title of the album was *The Easy Way*. The single came out and 'The Easy Way' was the A-side and I was ecstatic, you know, until I turned it over. You know what the back side of it was? 'Make the World Go Away.' It paid me out, got me slick, and I made about ten or fifteen thousand dollars and I've never owed a publisher a dime since that time."

In the old days, when the industry was built around two-sided 45-rpm singles, the expected hit would be designated the A-side, and that was the side that usually got played on the radio and generated the money that came to songwriters through airplay. The writers and publishers on the B-side song would only get paid for records sold, not for airplay. In country especially, A-sides were greatly desired because airplay earnings were so much smaller than sales earnings.

But every so often radio stations would start playing the B-side, turning it into a hit, much to the chagrin of the writers and publishers who had the A-side. This happened to Sutton's first two releases, and in the case of Eddy Arnold's "Make the World Go Away" was such a huge worldwide hit that his royalties on sales virtually turned Sutton's career around.

"That was the start of it," he recalls. After that the cuts came often, but Sutton is quick to point out that he was scribbling in a writer's paradise. "Back then, there weren't but about maybe ten, fifteen people writin' nearly all the songs, and we just had that kind of little community. There was Harlan [Howard], Hank [Cochran], Dallas Frazier, Curly [Putman] was around then but he was just like me, trying to get goin', and the record labels too—they were all right together. You could see Owen Bradley very easy by just picking up the phone and telling his secretary you'd like to play him a couple of songs.

"Plus, the good part about back then was I never did demos. I had one demo session that I cut for Al Gallico Music, that's it. The rest of the songs through my entire career were pitched from me and a guitar. I'd go in there and sit down play it to Owen, play it to Chet, sing it, and then just put it down if they liked it, me and a guitar. And of course, when I went to work at Columbia as a staff producer with Billy there, we just sang 'em to the artist."

In 1964, Billy Sherrill was hired to run A&R for Epic Records in Nashville. "Epic had a little one-room office in 812 16th Avenue South. The first door inside the building was Aud-Lee Booking Agency and Productions, which was [Hank Williams' ex-wife] Audrey Williams and Buddy Lee." And then the next office was SESAC, smallest of the three U.S. performing rights organizations. "Roy Drusky [singer on the Opry] and Lloyd Green [one of Nashville's top steel guitar players] ran that. The next office was Bob Neal's booking agency [Bob Neal was Elvis's manager before Colonel Tom Parker], and the next office was Al Gallico on the last door on the right.

"Across the hall from him was Johnny Cash's office, his publishing companies, Screen Gems/Columbia was the next one—Tony Moon ran that then—and the next little office was where Billy took over Epic Records."

Sherrill was just a name to Sutton at this point. "Billy and I started seeing each other in the hallways and just talkin'," remembers Glenn. "I didn't know him from Adam and he didn't know me. He and Gallico were good friends, so Gallico introduced me to him and I went to lunch with him a couple of times. There was a little club next door. The owner was Dotty Swann, and she was of 'Radio Dot and Smoky,' which was a thing in West Virginia somewhere, and they were very popular in the '30s. We started going in there for lunch. Then we started playing pinball machines together. Then we'd get to talkin' and I said, 'You wanna write something together?' He was cuttin' some acts. I had pitched him a song called 'Bluegrass Banjo' for Jim and Jesse, and he had cut it on them. So we started foolin' around with some ideas. I'd go up there and say, 'What do you think of this idea? You wanna help me on that?' And we started co-writin' like that. And then when David Houston [who in 1963 had a big country hit with 'Mountain of Love'] was coming back to cut, we started trying to write stuff for him. Then for Tammy, we were writing for all the artists on the label. I would stay up nights coming up with ideas and stuff and then go down there [to Sherrill's office]. Billy's a wonderful melody guy, I mean he can come up with stuff—'cause I can play maybe seven chords total.

"We started fooling with the 'Persuaded' idea for Charlie Walker, who was on the label. I wrote a couple of verses and we were just kickin' it around—he had the melody thing goin'. We ate dinner with Gallico, and he wanted to go with us, he wanted to *see* us write. He just sat there readin' the paper and watchin' us write. I said, 'Who does this?' It was about two o'clock in the morning, and I said, 'Well, this is pretty good like we got it, but we got no really central title to go with the bridge here.' Billy was sittin' at the piano and there was a Broadman Hymnal there. He started flippin' them pages, said, 'What about "Almost Persuaded"?'

"I said, 'Man, that's a great idea.' 'Cause we were lookin' at a gospel title, so that's what we used. You can't copyright a title, and it's nothing like that song. Years later, I got to thinkin' about that melody and it's almost 'Nearer My God to Thee.'"

Sherrill would remember that evening just a bit differently. "There's a verse in the New Testament that Paul said, 'Almost thou persuadest me to be a Christian,' and that kind of stuck with me. I don't know whether it was the Scripture or the old song. Maybe it was a little of both."

"Almost Persuaded," the Billy Sherrill–Glenn Sutton composition, not the old gospel song, came out in the middle of 1966, and it was a B-side. This time the record was flipped in Sutton's favor, "Mack Curtis was a program director at WPLO in Atlanta, which is a 50,000-watt station. He played it during drive time in Atlanta one morning. He got a hundred and something calls in thirty minutes. He called Billy and said, 'Hey, you're on the wrong side of that record,' so Billy called New York and had them reship it with 'Almost Persuaded' as the A-side. Meanwhile the publisher of the flip side, 'We Got Love,' called and said, 'Hey, what's the deal here? We ran an ad and everything else on this.' Billy said, 'Well, look at it this way, would you rather me just take you *off* of the B-side? I can do that too, and put one of *mine* on there.'

"They said, 'No, no, go ahead and let it ride.' He says, 'This thing's gonna be a monster, and you'll be happy you're on it.'"

David Houston's recording of "Almost Persuaded" was number one, country, for nine weeks and was Top 25 on the *Billboard* pop charts. "But everybody in the world started covering it and we had a lot of other versions in the charts. Patti Page cut a version of it. The artists who have cut it are phenomenal, like Louis Prima, Louis Armstrong, Harry James, Si Zentner and His Orchestra—people you couldn't imagine—Nancy Wilson, Nancy Sinatra, Wayne Newton. I can't think of another country song with that many varied people on it. I have copies of almost two hundred versions of it now, but there are so many overseas records and stuff that I'll never see."

That's the kind of success that can give a songwriter tremendous confidence that he can do it again. It certainly put some momentum into the careers of these two go-getters.

Sutton got his job with Columbia by nagging Sherrill. "I kept asking him, 'Why in hell won't you hire me here, I'm up here all the time, I go to every session, let me try cuttin' some artists?' And he said he'd ask Len Levy, who was the head of Epic at that time. So he asked Len Levy, and Len said, 'Okay, give him a job!' So they gave me a job and I think I made $7,800 a year."

One of the artists he started producing was a girl who had been having radio hits on Chart Records, a small independent label owned by a man named Slim Williamson. Her name was Lynn Anderson, and in 1968, she and Glenn became Mr. and Mrs. In 1970, she debuted on Columbia with a song Sutton wrote and produced called "Stay There 'Til I Get There." It was Top 10, a nice start on her new label, but she was about to have one of those career-making hits that most artists never even dream of.

"We were doing a session in the Quonset Hut for her next album. She had heard a song on Joe South's album *Introspect*," says Sutton. "About seven of the songs in that album became hits, like 'Birds of a Feather,' 'Games People Play,' and the one she wanted to record, 'Rose Garden.' We carried that song to three different sessions and didn't cut it. This particular night we had it just like we always did. We had cut four sides and we still had twenty minutes left. I said, 'We got twenty minutes, you wanna try the "Rose Garden" thing?'

"I had objected to it because it was a man's song and I didn't wanna do it, but she kept bringin' it with her—she loved it. So we did it in an old [straight, boring beat] and it wasn't working until Ray Edenton [one of the A-team studio veterans], a great rhythm man, said, 'Why don't we try it in eights?'"

They ran through a chorus using that rhythm and everybody liked it and they had it down by the time the twenty minutes was up. "It still wasn't gonna be a single," Glenn says. "It was just for the album. But Billy was doing strings on two things on Tammy and he didn't want to spend the whole session on that, so he said, 'You got anything you wanna put strings on?' I said, 'Yeah, put 'em on 'Snowbird' and that 'Rose Garden' thing.' So I had Cam Mullins write strings for the two.

"During the DJ Convention, Clive Davis [president of Columbia] and everybody came into town for that week, stayed at the hotel, and had meetings while we acted the fool and got drunk. While they were in, me and Lou Bradley [Columbia staff engineer] were downstairs in the Quonset Hut mixing the album, just puttin' it together. I was listening to the playback—'Rose Garden' was playin' back when Clive and his bunch came in through the back door and about halfway through the studio he just stopped and stood there and listened a little bit. He said, 'What's that?' I said, 'That's a thing we cut on Lynn, it's called "Rose Garden."'

"He said, 'Play it from the top again.' Lou Bradley run it back, and when it finished, Clive said, 'I'll talk to you in a little while, we got a meeting right now. That's her next single. Get that mixed. That's great, that's a smash.'

"The record went gold, platinum, everything," says Sutton, "And I'm still sittin' there on $7,800, no incentive. Today I woulda made two or three million dollars. The Gavin Convention was in Vegas that year [Gavin was a report sheet that tracked airplay activity] and I had asked Billy to talk to them about my salary, but he just never did, so I said, 'Hell, well, I'll just do it myself.' We were in Vegas and I saw Clive in the lobby down there walking around the crap tables. I said, 'Clive, can I have ten minutes with you later, just private?'

"He said, 'Have breakfast at my room in the morning. Be there at nine o'clock,'

"So I went to his room at nine o'clock the next morning. He had breakfast there at a little table near the window. We sat down. He said 'What's your problem?' I said, 'My problem is that I just cut a record that sold a couple million and I'm makin' $7,800 a year.'

"He said, 'Would you be happier with twenty thousand?' I said of course I would. He said, 'Well then consider it done. What else?'

"I said, 'Well, that's it for now!'"

Along with Sherrill, Sutton was a Nashville star in the eyes of Columbia's bean counters. Once at a meeting in New York, a New York producer stood up and asked why he and other producers in New York were discouraged from recording their own material on their acts. "What about Sutton and Sherrill, everything that comes out down in Nashville they've written," Sutton remembers him saying. "And Clive Davis says, 'That's different, they write hits!'"

Unlike the rest of the Gallico crew, Sutton wrote some of his biggest hits alone, and his songwriting talent launched Jerry Lee Lewis's country career, back in 1968 with two classic country songs, "Another Place, Another Time" and "What's Made Milwaukee Famous (Has Made a Loser Out of Me)."

Glenn Sutton worked for Columbia as a producer until about '76, then suddenly quit. For about a decade, he had flown about as high as a country songwriter could fly. I'm not sure he himself understands what made him leave Columbia, and once he went independent he was never again quite the Music Row force that he had been. But for a time, his production and writing successes made him one of the biggest names on Music Row.

He continued to do some independent production, including Lefty Frizzell's last session for Columbia, but never got back into the A&R game full-time. He continued to write, publishing his own songs, and every so often he'd hit a lick as a songwriter. In 1979, he scored fifteen minutes of fame as an *artist* with a novelty record on Mercury called "The Football Card," which made it to the middle of both the country and pop singles charts.

"I'm retired," he says today, flatly. "I got hobbies. I'm very happy with the career I had. Overall, writing songs was just a great way to make a living."

Then he pauses. "Maybe we might think of writin' one after the new year," he says, and damned if there isn't a bit of a young man's enthusiasm in his voice.

STRINGS AND
POWER SAWS

The second generation of great Nashville producers was led by Billy Sherrill, who in the late '60s, through the '70s, and into the '80s defined much of what was hit country music: He made stars out of Tammy Wynette and Tanya Tucker, he took a piano bar singer named Charlie Rich and made him one of the biggest-selling country artists of his time, and he brought George Jones to the peak of his career, and kept him there for a decade, turning "He Stopped Loving Her Today" into the great anthem of country music. Sherrill pushed the writers to do their best work, and he knew how to take great songs and make great records.

Perhaps the most amazing thing about Sherrill's career is the longevity of his relationships with his artists, how he could keep them at the top of the charts for so many years. He says he did it with songs. "Shakespeare said it first," he says. "The play's the thing."

Billy Sherrill was born in Phil Campbell, Alabama. His father was a traveling preacher, and Billy played piano for a multitude of tent revivals. "I guess everything I've ever learned stemmed from gospel songs." That must have included his penchant for mischief, too. When his father called for offerings and it was time for Billy to play, he played "That's Where My Money Goes." "Got my butt whipped, too," he says, with a laugh. "I played 'Bye Bye Blues' one time at a funeral," he adds. "There wasn't but about three people there and nobody recognized that one but my daddy."

Early on, Billy Sherrill, Rick Hall, and Tom Stafford started a publishing company over in Muscle Shoals. Billy called it Florence, Alabama, Music Enterprises, or FAME, and it became one of the leading publishing operations in the Muscle Shoals area.

Sherrill was also the engineer at Sam Phillips' studio at the Cumberland Lodge Building in downtown Nashville. "I was making these records and I'd play all the instruments and lease them out to this label or that label. Bob Morgan, the head of A&R for Epic, heard two or three of them." Jerry Kennedy had just left Epic to go back to Mercury and the label needed an A&R man in Nashville. "Morgan came down and we hung out, you know, and he was interviewing people, Pete Drake and all these likely people, to run it, you know. But we'd never get around to the interview. We'd go to Printer's Alley every night, go to dinner, have a few drinks, and he'd say, 'Well, we'll talk about it tomorrow.' This went on for about a week and so. Then he had to leave and go back to New York. I said, 'You know, you never interviewed me or anything about this job. What do you wanna do?'

"He said, 'I don't know, I like you, here's the keys to the building. It's your job, that's it, you got it.'" That may have come about because Kennedy recommended Sherrill. Or maybe Gallico might have. Says Billy, "We were all kind of tight back then."

Billy made his mark at Epic with David Houston and "Almost Persuaded," a song he put on the B-side to a song called "We Got Love," because he and Sutton co-wrote it, and that's what producers did in those days. He had no conception that the song deserved any better fate than that.

"Back then a country record that sold fifty thousand copies really did a lot," he says. "One day the New York office got a call from Comstock Distributors in Atlanta: 'This David Houston Record, we want twenty-five thousand of it.' That really got New York's attention. The next day Comstock called again, said, 'You better make that fifty thousand.' So I called them—and I *never* talked to a distributor—I said, 'What's going on with "We Got Love" selling fifty thousand records in two days in Atlanta?' He said, 'What the hell? "We Got Love"?' It was the other side that was sellin' the records, the side that's got that piano thing goes, *doodle-do-do-do*."

All of a sudden, Sherrill was right in the middle of the action, right along with Decca's Owen Bradley, RCA's Chet Atkins, Columbia's Don Law, and Mercury's Jerry Kennedy.

That's when Virginia Wynette Pugh walked into his office, the woman who eventually became known simply as "Tammy," the best female country singer of her time.

Sherrill had his tiny office in the flat little building at 812 16th Avenue South, less than a hundred feet from the Quonset Hut, where he would produce all his great hits. "She had called and made an appointment. I didn't want to see anybody, but she waited in the outer room, waited and waited and waited. Got to be about five o'clock in the afternoon. I got ready to leave and I walked out. She's still there and I felt crappy and I said, 'Well, why don't you come on in?'"

Billy Sherrill is a complex man, a reclusive man, an articulate man who enjoys one-on-one conversation once you get him there. He is impatient with rules, yet possessed of a conscience, care of his preacher daddy, perhaps.

"She had a tape. I said, 'You got a good voice, but I really don't think these songs are strong enough.' She left and went back to the Anchor Hotel a few blocks away, where she was staying overnight with her kids.

"At the time I was trying to pick up the master of a song called 'Apartment #9' [recorded by Bobby Austin] that had been making some noise around the country. The label called back and said, 'We are not interested in leasing this record to a big company like Epic, so just forget it.' The curtness of the way they talked sort of pissed me off, so I said to myself, 'Well, I'll just cover the sonofabitch with somebody else.'"

He had been trying to think of a guy to do it, but then Tammy popped into his head, and he called the motel. "I said, 'You wanna make a record tomorrow?'"

"She said, 'I'm really not in the mood for any jokes. Your place was the last place on my list to stop. I've seen 'em all.' And she named off a few of them. A couple of them made passes at her and all that."

We all know the image of Tammy: the frazzled housewife with kids tugging at her apron, sweating over of a sink full of hot water and dishes, irritated with her life, but standing by her man for all that. This was the Tammy that Sherrill was hearing on the phone as he hatched his plan to teach Tally Records a lesson.

"Two o'clock tomorrow afternoon we're gonna make a record," Sherrill told her.

"Are you serious?" she asked.

"I said 'Yeah. In fact, come by the office about ten, eleven o'clock in the morning and learn this song. And then we'll do it, and we'll do two or three of yours.'

"That afternoon in the studio, we did one of her songs first, to get her kind of warmed up. So I said, 'Okay, let's do 'Apartment #9.'"

"I played the Bobby Austin record two or three times for the guys, where they could learn it and get her key. She walked up to the mic, and sang, 'Just follow—the stairway,' and Jerry Kennedy [guitar] looked at Bob Moore [bass] and Bob Moore looked at Pete Drake [steel guitar] and Pete Drake looked at me—you could have heard a pin drop in that studio. God Almighty! We did the record and Kennedy came back and said, 'Boy, you got something here!' I said, 'Well, I think I do too!'"

Billy and Tammy started making records, each one doing better than the one before. "Still, they [the label] weren't really throwing a whole lot of weight behind country music," recalls Sherrill. And then they did 'D-I-V-O-R-C-E,' which seemed like a career record until the next release, 'Stand by Your Man.'

When "D-I-V-O-R-C-E" became a hit, followed by "Stand by Your Man," suddenly the housewives of the silent majority could listen to a woman singing *about* them, instead of having to be content with sequined men singing *to* them. The arrival of Tammy Wynette was a major moment in country music, and the sales proved it.

From 1968 through 1976, Sherrill cut fourteen *Billboard* number-one hits with Tammy. Many of them were written by a combination of a tight group of songwriting associates that included Sherrill, Norro Wilson, George Richey (Tammy's last husband), and Tammy. One of those was a gorgeous piece titled "Til I Can Make It On My Own."

"Tammy had the best line in the whole song, by far," Sherrill remembers. "'Til I get used to losing you, let me keep on using you.' Hah! And what galled the hell out of Richey was that while we were writin' it—I was contributing to the song—I was also watching a football game. 'Can't you turn that football game off for a minute?' I said, 'No, no, I got a nice bet on this game.'

"'We're puttin' the song together, okay?'

"'And, who you gonna get to produce it? So hush!'"

Tammy, of course, had a complex personal life that included five husbands, and it was inevitable that her personal life might occasionally bleed over into the studio. By the time she and George Jones recorded "Golden Ring," one of their classic duets, their marriage was ancient history, but Jones was still not over her. "By that time, she had dated one of the Gatlin Brothers," Sherrill remembers, "and *they* were on the session.

She was singing and telling the engineers not to put Don Chapel [her second husband] through on the phone—she wasn't gonna talk to him. I said, 'Tammy, you need to slow your love life down a little bit!'"

Sherrill and Tammy had a close professional relationship that lasted a quarter of a century, but he and Tammy did not socialize. He says he never socialized with any of his artists. But Sherrill sometimes gets a sad, wistful look in his eye when he talks about the woman with whom he spent so much time writing and recording songs. "You know what?" he says. "I don't think Tammy was ever a happy person. I think that had a lot to do with the way she sounded when she sang."

Just a couple of years after Tammy exploded on the country scene, an evening of J&B Scotch chanced Sherrill into another record deal. "We went down to the Alley," Sherrill begins. "Me and Sutton and maybe Gallico. Barbara Mandrell was playing in one of the clubs. She was singin' and playing the saxophone, her sister Louise was playing the fiddle, and Irlene was playing drums barefooted, and I thought, that's the cutest thing there ever was. Between sets they came over, and after probably three or four JBs I said, 'Hey! Ever thought about making a record?' Barbara said, 'Yeah, we think about it all the time, you know it's hard to get signed.' I said, 'Why don't you come by my office tomorrow about two o'clock. We'll do something about that.' So, the night went on, forgot all about it. Went home.

"Next afternoon I was in the office, Emily, my secretary, buzzed and said, 'Barbara Mandrell's out here.'

"I said, 'Who?'

"So she came in and she said, 'Well, what's next?'

"Things were kind of in a lull, but we had all kinds of money to spend. I said, 'Why don't we start looking for songs, and we'll cut a single, see what happens.'"

Barbara stayed on the label for about five years and had several airplay hits but, said Sherrill, she never did sell any records at Columbia. "Once a year we'd all get together [for label meetings and the New York executives would ask], 'Why are you keeping Barbara Mandrell? Why are you keeping Johnny Duncan, 'cause they're not selling anything.' Well, you get to be friends with these people and you hate to have to call them up and say, 'Hey, we're droppin' you!'"

In 1975, Barbara moved over to ABC/Dot, hooked up with producer Tom Collins, and began a decade of success culminating in CMA

Entertainer of the Year awards for 1980 and '81, and a successful Mandrell Sisters network TV weekly variety show. At the peak of country's *Urban Cowboy* boom in 1981, she would record the anthem "I Was Country When Country Wasn't Cool."

Another of Sherrill's great success stories was an aging artist who had had some rock 'n' roll success, but was basically a piano-bar-type entertainer who happened to have a classic, expressive smoky voice. Charlie Rich was such an incredible singer that early in his country career all the great writers longed for a Charlie Rich record, even though he was not scoring any hits.

"Charlie would drive into town," says Sherrill. "He had some kind of old station wagon—and we'd look for songs, and we'd record this or that. He was hittin' the cracks—he was like too country to be played pop, and too bluesy to be played country. We just had mediocre record after mediocre record. We put out 'I Take It on Home' and it did pretty good. And then we put out 'Behind Closed Doors,' which was the same kind of song, written by the same guy [Kenny O'Dell]—same tempo, same musicians—and it just went wild. Number one, country; very big pop!

"After all this, Charlie was a big star, he was making fifty thousand dollars a night on the road. In my mind I had it all figured out, I knew what was gonna be the next single—'The Most Beautiful Girl.'"

Sherrill was sitting in his office when Emily Mitchell, his secretary, walked in and told him, "Charlie and his people are out here."

"So instead of Charlie coming in the office, there's Charlie, his bodyguard, couple of roadies, his manager Seymour Rosenberg—they all came in. Charlie sat down, picked up a *Billboard*, and was lookin' at it. You ever watch the *Andy Griffith Show* where Don Knotts puffs out his chest and says, 'Well now, just listen here I'm gonna tell you'? Rosenberg said, 'We been talkin', we been thinkin' about it, doin' some research.' He had a song which was a real piece of garbage called 'Peace on You' that he published. He said, 'We think that Charlie needs a good up-tempo and we think "Peace on You" has gotta be the follow-up to "Behind Closed Doors."'

"I said, 'Seymour.... *What?*'

"He said, '"Peace on You."'

"I said, 'Let me tell you something. When we did "Behind Closed Doors," Charlie and I, it was not *we* who picked the record, *I* picked the record. And "The Most Beautiful Girl" is gonna be the next single. It's not *we*, it never has been *we*, it's *me*. I pick the record as long as I'm the record producer.' The place got deadly silent. And after about ten seconds, Charlie looked over the *Billboard*, said, 'I told you he'd say that!'"

Sherrill's long run with George Jones in the '70s and '80s is one of the great producer/artist sagas in the history of Music Row. Before Billy Sherrill, Jones had been a star for more than fifteen years, but his increasing unreliability made some feel that he had a clouded future. Working with Sherrill, he never shook his negative reputation, yet he enjoyed fifteen more years at the top, and in 1980, a quarter of a century after his first hit, he released "He Stopped Loving Her Today."

George came to Epic as a direct result of his relationship with Tammy, whom he had married in 1969. "I'd really wanted to record him," says Sherrill. "I just never did pursue it. When he signed with us, I told Tammy, 'I know George is used to having his own way.' Most of the time his producers were just there. Buddy Killen, who played bass on many of his early sessions, really produced half of them. I said, 'I'm a record producer, I'm not a yes-man, and he's gonna do things the way I ask him to do, or we'll never get along.'

"So she told him that and he mumbled something that ended in, 'Good record producer, fine with me!' And we never had any problems, ever. The first thing I knew about Jones, though, you never said, 'We've got to do this tomorrow at two o'clock.' You never pinned him down on a time, you'd say 'Sometime tomorrow when you get ready, we'll do this, if you feel like it.' He'll say, 'Okay, what about two o'clock?' 'Fine with me.' Once it's his idea, he'll show," Sherrill adds.

If Sherrill was cutting a session, and Jones was supposed to come in. Billy didn't worry. "I knew he'd come in," he says. "But on his own time. I'm the same way. Like, if you said, 'You've got to see Mayor Purcell, August the fourth at three o'clock. It's very important,' I would think about that every day until that day. I would count the days, and it'd worry me. See this here calendar? Nothing's on it. Nothing's ever on it."

So Jones started his string of hits with Sherrill, songs like "Loving You Could Never Be Better," "A Picture of Me (Without You)," "The Grand Tour," and "The Door," as well as huge duets with Tammy like "We're Gonna Hold On" and "Golden Ring." Jones's career hit new heights. But in his long hit-making career, Sherrill has been dogged by media critics who couldn't stand that Sherrill thickened the texture of his records by adding string parts—layers of violins, violas, and cellos—to his basic country rhythm tracks. They criticized his Tammy hits, they criticized his Charlie Rich hits, and they criticized his George Jones hits.

"It was not only the reviewers that did that," Sherrill says. "The first call I got on 'He Stopped Loving Her Today' was from the label: 'Why did you have to put all those damned violins swirlin' around?'

"I said, 'Because the record called for it! That's his soul going to heaven, make something out of it. I like the violins.' They were always on me, always sayin', 'Why do you have to put so many violins on records?' *Because it makes the records sound better.* Pick out an old Hank Williams record from the '50s, sounds like a bad demo even though he's a great stylist."

I asked Sherrill why he thought critics who didn't seem to like country music felt qualified to tell him how he was supposed to produce country records.

"If I could answer you that," he replied, "I could answer you what's the secret of life."

"He Stopped Loving Her Today" was a labor of love. It did not come to Sherrill all finalized and wrapped in a bright red ribbon.

"I wish I'd a saved all the rewrites, they looked like a book. I kept sendin' it back to Curly [Putman] and Bobby [Braddock]," says Sherrill.

"What's wrong with it?" They'd ask.

"You killed the guy off right up top! You don't do that! Halfway through the song—wait awhile, wait awhile. Then they'd come back. 'Okay, that's a little better, but can you wrap the story around a little better?' 'Yeah, okay, okay.'

"Several times later they had it, and it just blew me away when they finally did it."

"He Stopped Loving Her Today" was a simple song about a man who lost his woman and vowed that he would love her until he died, and he did. It was a number-one country hit for George Jones and energized a recording career that was lagging just a bit. Thanks largely to that song, George was CMA Male Vocalist of the Year in 1980 and '81. Years later, the song emerged as the best-loved country song *ever* in a number of fan polls.

One of Sherrill's biggest challenges as a producer was how to choose hit material for a thirteen-year-old girl with an enormous voice. He had found her, was floored by her talent and presence. Now what?

"I was in Las Vegas," he recalls, "and I knew this lady named Delores Fuller, and she says she's got a *girl*. I said 'Yeah, everybody's got somebody, Delores.' She says, 'No, this girl's really good.'

"I was going back to Nashville the next day, and in a few days, here comes this tape and I thought, 'Wow, I can't believe this voice is coming out of a thirteen-year-old girl. But the songs weren't worth a damn. I said, 'Man! I wish I had something to cut on her. I'm not gonna cut kid stuff on this kid.'

"That night, I went home and turned on Johnny Carson and Bette Midler sang 'Delta Dawn,' I thought, man oh man, I wonder if she's made a record of that. I called around and they said, 'Yeah, it's comin' out on Atlantic or something in a week, two weeks, and I said, 'Ain't gonna beat me out!' So I called Delores and said, 'Get Tanya, get her on the next plane. I've got the song!'

"She said, 'You sure?' I said yeah. She said, 'She'll need to learn it.' I said, 'It's real easy—she can learn it in ten minutes.'

"So they sent a demo. I gave it to Tanya. She took it and learned it, and the next day we cut it. She just floored everybody. Tanya Tucker is the only person I ever recorded who had no fear. She had more confidence than anybody I'd ever recorded, she just knew she was good. And so she stepped up to that mic and just tore it up!

"The epiphany was when I heard Bette Midler sing the song," he says. "I believe I could have pulled somebody off the street and cut a hit on it. But Tanya had this unique voice.

"Her daddy wound up managing her," Sherrill says, "and he kept pretty tight reins on her for a while, although naturally that exploded, as we all know. We got along real well, but I never really got to know her. I just respected what she could do with a song, and she gave me all the leeway to find the songs. She never found the songs. I don't think she wanted to. She just wanted to sing. But she was born with all this confidence—I never saw anything like it. Nothing fazed her. Jordanaires and all these great musicians, all legends, and she just walks into the middle of it and [imitating Tanya's vibrato], '*Okay, let's go!*'"

Once her first single hit, it was easy to find material. "Once you cut a hit on somebody, the material brought in is always better," he says. The way was paved for a long producer/artist collaboration, but it was not to be. Three short years at Epic, then she skipped off to MCA and a lucrative deal. "There's not a whole lot to talk about with Tanya," he says. "She's just Tanya. She's a diamond in the rough and the rough never came off.

"I tried to maintain my objectivity choosing songs, but...I'd hear rumors—guys that I'd have a few drinks with, they'd say, 'You know so-and-so says you cut all your own stuff.' I'll tell you what, it got to me to the point that I called Clive Davis who was the president of the company at the time, who is now I think the biggest thing to ever hit the music business. I said, 'I gotta see you.'

"He said, 'What about?' I said, 'Well, I'm gonna be in New York next week, can I see you?' and he said, 'Yeah, come on by the office.'

"And so I came by his office. He said, 'Let's have a sandwich.' I said, 'Okay.'

"So we had a sandwich. I said, 'I hear rumors goin' around that people are sayin' I'm doing my own stuff, I got my own publishing company, which is a conflict of interest, and I got a lock on things. How do you feel about that?'

"He said, 'I'm your boss, right?'

"I said, 'Yes.'

"He said, 'I can fire you right now on the spot. Do you really wanna piss me off?'

"I said, 'Not really.'

"He said, 'Okay, if you wanna keep me happy and not piss me off, you go back home, keep writing, keep publishing, and keep doin' exactly what you're doing. Now get the hell out of my office.'"

There was another maverick producer who worked at Columbia during the early years of Sherrill's tenure, whose views were passionately different from his, but who would also have a tremendous impact on the Nashville recording industry. His name was Bob Johnston.

Johnston was born in Hillsboro, Texas, and raised in Fort Worth. In his youth, he moved to New York and later to Nashville to see if he could break into the music business. "Nobody would see me," he recalls. "I waited for Owen Bradley five days one time, and when he came out [of his office], he said he was goin' fishin,' so that was the end of that. I got pissed and left. Went back to New York and went to work for Clyde Otis, who was head of Mercury Records, who did all the Brook Benton Records, Clyde McPhatter, Dinah Washington.... While I was there, I met a guy at Kapp and Clyde who helped me get a gig there, and I was their first A&R man."

Eventually he got an A&R job at Columbia Records in New York. His office, he says, was a converted broom closet. He produced records on Patti Page and Don Williams's group, the Pozo-Seco Singers. And then he became Bob Dylan's producer.

Their first meeting, apparently, went very well. "I said 'Bob?' and he says, 'Yeah.' I said, 'I'm Bob Johnston,' and he said, 'I'm Bob Dylan.' Nicest, biggest smile. Never had anything from that day on, for seven or eight years, except that smile. Whatever the fuck he wanted, I didn't care. I didn't question him."

This was becoming the pop way of doing things. A new breed of young artists had arrived with a desire to do things their way and they presented a credible threat to break up the candy store if they didn't get their way. Older record men found it difficult to adjust to the new balance of power in an industry they no longer understood, but a young man like Johnston, who had some destructive proclivities himself, understood Dylan and believed that the artists, by dint of their talent, *owned* the candy store anyway. So why *shouldn't* they get their way?

"I never questioned him or Paul Simon or anybody. Man, I figured they knew so much more than those cocksucker producers that tapped their foot out of time and whistled out of tune. I didn't give a shit what Dylan did, I was the biggest fan in the world of Dylan." And Paul Simon, who he also produced with Art Garfunkel in the course of his career with Columbia.

During his early days in Nashville, Johnston wanted to do some demos of his wife Joy's songs for Elvis. To make the demos sound right for Elvis, "I used most of Presley's band, and the Jordanaires." Johnston loved the Nashville vibe, and knew Dylan would, too. "I went up to him in the studio [in New York] one day and I said, 'You gotta go to Nashville, man. The people there are great; there's no clocks or anything.' Later, his manager, Albert Grossman, and [Columbia president] Bill Gallagher came up to me and said, 'You ever mention Nashville to Dylan again, you're fired,' and I said, 'Why?' Gallagher said, 'Because, you're doin' good here, you don't need to go to Nashville.'

"I said, 'Well, you're the boss.' Six months later, I took him to Nashville and cut *Blonde on Blonde*, which has been voted the best album in rock history."

He also cut Dylan's next two albums, *John Wesley Harding* and *Nashville Skyline*, in Nashville. *Blonde on Blonde* musicians included Charlie McCoy,

Kenny Buttrey, Henry Strzelecki, and Pig Robbins, as well as Joe South, Robbie Robertson, and Al Kooper. *John Wesley Harding* brought steel player Pete Drake into the mix, and Charlie Daniels and Norman Blake worked on *Nashville Skyline*, which was intended to sound very country. *Skyline* gave us "Lay Lady Lay," one of Dylan's biggest hits.

"CBS has the Quonset Hut down there. And then they had a big room [Studio A], with little doors to isolation rooms, where they put everybody, and the sound would be shit. And I went in there with Ed Grizzard, and I got a saw. We stripped it, took everything outside and had the fire department burn it and put the drums against the middle of the wall, and put everybody else around there, so they could walk around and see each other. I put Dylan behind glass so he wouldn't leak, but so everybody could see him."

According to Johnston, the Nashville studio people sent New York a letter detailing Johnston's idiosyncrasies and work habits, and what they intended to do about it. "So I called Bill Gallagher and he flew down, and I told him. He said, 'Well, let's go see 'em....' He says [to the Nashville people], 'The only thing I got to say is this—I'm gonna go and have lunch with Johnston, and I want to tell you that if he wants the microphone on the *ceiling* I'd advise you to get the tallest damned ladder you can find and start climbing or I'll shut this motherfucker down tomorrow!'"

In 1967, the head of the Nashville office, Don Law, retired, and in a moment of inspiration the label chose Johnston to succeed him. Johnston only lasted about a year in that position, but during that time he managed to stir the pot considerably. "I remember Johnny Cash walked in one day and he said, 'I've always wanted to cut an album in prison and nobody would let me.' I was told that I'd be fired if I did it, it would ruin his career," Johnston recalls. "We cut *Folsom Prison* and it sold millions. I got told I would be fired if I did it again. I took him to San Quentin and 'A Boy Named Sue' [off of the album recorded there] knocked the Stones out of number one."

Ask Johnston about where the hits he cut came from. He says, "I have no idea. I never cut a hit in my life." Unlike Billy Sherrill, Johnston did not look for songs for his artists. "I just let them do what the fuck they wanted to do, I figured Cash knew more than me."

Other artists Johnston worked with included Flatt and Scruggs, Marty Robbins, the Byrds, and many others, but one particular bit of studio work haunts him to this day.

"Dylan was in the studio and Cash came in. They went to eat or something, and when they came back I had the studio set up with microphones and lights and all, and they smiled and went out there and they cut about thirty songs that CBS has never released. It was the most beautiful fuckin' shit. Then I talked to one of the executives and he said, 'You can't ever use that because Cash says, 'Oh, don't do it!' and Dylan says, *'Whooaa*, don't do it!' And he said, 'They've gotta be together!' I said, 'I can't even understand what the fuck you're talkin' about! What if Cash died?' He said, 'Then it'd be worth money.' I said, 'What if Dylan died?' He said, 'It'd be worth a fortune.'"

16

LOU BRADLEY: KNIGHT OF THE CONSOLE

"I always wanted to work in the Quonset Hut," says Lou Bradley. "That was hillbilly heaven to me. They didn't realize I loved to do country, they thought they was hirin' a guy to do pop records up here. They didn't think I'd like the Quonset Hut, but I *knew* I was gonna like it.

"It just sounded good in the room," he says, "and that was, you might say, evolved by design over time. It was originally a film studio, and so when they started doing records in there, it started changing.

"The floor was not totally dead. The ceiling was the most dead thing there. The walls were maybe nine to ten feet up, and then they angled up, and they put opposing louvers going up this frame, and each panel of them was as wide as a kitchen table, maybe a little wider. Each section was pointed different, you see, so the sound would go up, and go in a different direction. That diffused it, and then they just deadened the heck out of it. The sound would go up through those louvers, and they had bought some old curtains from a theater and they had them all up there—so that sound would go up there and wouldn't come back down. The curtains were just layin' all around up there on the framework, they weren't hangin' or anything.

"They could've used fiberglass, but they had these curtains up there. Well, I came in June '69, and the console that I worked on all the time arrived the same day. They'd revamped the control room for the new console. The console was built in New York, but they used the same EQs and faders as was in the console that resided there all those years."

The reason they called the Quonset Hut "Studio B," Bradley explains, is that there were two Studio A's. The original Studio A was the old house where Music Row literally began. When the Quonset Hut was built it was natural that it would become Studio B. It was still Studio B when

Columbia built its new building around the original studio, and when they constructed the new big room next to the Quonset Hut, then that studio became Studio A.

"I was never in love with Studio A," says Bradley. "It had a floating floor and it always rumbled in the mics, and you had to deal with that. Even though they said it wasn't supposed to happen, it did."

Back to the Quonset Hut: "The walls were kinda neutral. They were just rough wood and they had it painted with a spackle-type paint, just a neutral color, but in the middle they had panels of the old-style-radio acoustic tiles, you know, with the holes. The panels were about as big as say half a double door. That contributed to a neutral sound. It wasn't just totally dead. There was *some* reflection.

"Go in a room that has nothin' in it, like in a home, say, a den, and it's all live. You put down a piece of carpet, partially cover the floor, it's gonna be less live. It's more approaching neutral, but you're still gettin' a reflection around. Then you hang some drapes, but you've still got a live ceiling, and probably three walls." *Neutral* he describes, is not totally dead but a mix of absorbed and reflected sound that makes for a natural, comfortable feel. "The musicians could really play without earphones if they wanted to," he adds, "and they did for years. That really gives you good dynamics and togetherness, and it's hard to explain that to people like the young guys, they don't know about it. They rely on cue systems and earphones and the isolation. Well, you don't have isolation, but there are some other things that happen that's just magic.

"I came in '69, and they had gutted the control room. They had to put the new console in, and all the patch bays and everything. It was a sixteen-track console. But nobody used the sixteen-track, even though we got it, they still recorded eight and four for a while, then one day I said, 'Why do we have to record on a four-track, then transfer to eight, then to sixteen [if they wanted to keep overdubbing]? Why don't we just start on the sixteen?'" And so they did.

Bradley talked about the musicians Sherrill used, ticked them off as if he could hear them playing as he spoke: Jerry Carrigan, Buddy Harman, sometimes Jimmy Isbell, Kenny Malone, and later Larrie Londin on drums; Bob Moore or Henry Strzelecki on bass and Tommy Alsup on tic-tac bass; Pete Drake on steel, sometimes Lloyd Green or Weldon Myrick. Sherrill generally used three guitars, two rhythm acoustic and one electric lead. "That was a strange deal," says Bradley. "There was a peckin' order there. And all the players who worked for him knew it. And I kind of saw this with other producers. They knew who the number-one guy was, and they knew who number two or three or four was. So if, say, Billy Sanford walked in and he saw Jerry Kennedy, he'd go get his acoustic guitar, he wouldn't have to be told. If Billy Sanford walked in and he saw all the other guitar players and he didn't see Jerry Kennedy, he'd go get his electric guitar. And then Pete Wade, one of them would be the lead, then he used Phil Baugh, and he used Reggie [Young] some, and he used Grady [Martin] occasionally. He used Pig on piano all the time. Charlie McCoy doing whatever Charlie would do. He might play vibes, he might play another guitar, but generally harmonica or percussion.

"He'd either use the Jordanaires or Hershel Wigginton's group, the Nashville Edition on background vocals. On 'Delta Dawn' [Tanya Tucker], we used both groups, and I treated them as two separate groups, not like all standin' together in a choir. They sang live into different mics.

"We [Bradley and Sherrill] worked with some great singers. By great, I mean, when they step up to the mic, it inspires the band—you know, Tammy and George, Charlie Rich.

"The two that stick out in my mind—every take they'd put a hundred and ten percent in there and you'd feel that in the band—that was Paycheck and Tanya Tucker. They would lay it in the microphone, and oh man, you could feel the energy out of the band. You feel the same thing out of Tammy, but not *every* take. See, if she didn't really know the song, she'd still sing it really good, but it wouldn't be that lightnin' bolt where you'd see the goose bumps rise up on Pete Drake's neck.

"That's somethin' a lot of singers need to realize—that if they can nail it, they can get another twenty-five percent out of the band.

"We kinda had a set way because there was a real magic spot down toward the control room where the singer always stood. Jim Williamson [Columbia engineer] would tell you it was tile thirteen—it was just a good spot in the room—Mort Thomasson found it. We put the voices down there.

"But Charlie Rich liked to be near the piano, so when we cut all his records, he was standin' right by the piano, in the middle of the band. Well, we cut 'Behind Closed Doors,' and after it came up a big hit, people would cut everybody that way."

That made it tough for Bradley because the vocals and the band, including the drums, were so close together it was hard to get a proper sound, but that's the way everybody seemed to want it from then on. Most artists seemed to care more about Charlie Rich's piano proximity than Mort Thomasson's sweet spot at tile thirteen.

Bradley recalled a time when Andy Williams came to town to record a country-flavored album, and he brought his producer, Dick Glasser, with him. "Glasser said, 'I've been working with him out in L.A. I'm here just to come along. I'm not involved at all, but would you tell me one thing? How did you get the cymbal sound on "The Most Beautiful Girl," with Charlie Rich? I worked six hours in an L.A. studio and couldn't get it.'

"So I got him a stool [near the console], I said, 'Sit right there.' And I just played the demo of the song the band was workin' on learnin'. I said, 'I'm gonna get the mics set, and I won't touch the console, and I'll show you. What spooks guys that never recorded a lot of live sessions is that it is *all in one room*, so every mic hears other things.

"I told Glasser, 'Once I get it set here, I'm not gonna touch it. When they start in a live environment, it sounds awful 'til they all lock in. What makes it sound good is when they get together.' And so they start, and it was kinda, you might say a *chordy* song, it wasn't a three-chord song, and I said, 'Just watch, I won't touch a thing.' I knew when it was gonna lock in. About the third time through, it would lock in and it was just like a big flash of light went off, and it'd come dancin' out of the speakers.

"I just kinda watched him out of the corner of my eye and you could see he had a Doubting Thomas look on his face. And about the third time through, runnin' it down, there it came. I mean, it's just like you reached over and threw a switch, it comes out of those speakers. Normally I'd be still tweakin' stuff, but I did this on purpose [without tweaking], because I knew it'd be close. And I looked back and he had the biggest grin on his face and he leaned over and he said, 'We never woulda got it.' What it was, was that live recording—it was the cymbals on Charlie's mic, it was the cymbals on the backup singer's mic, the whole thing. But when you listen to the record, you can't tell where it's coming from."

Many of Bradley's greatest moments in the studio occurred with Sherrill, who was often praised for the dynamics on his records. "I think a lot of people misunderstood how the dynamics came about," says Bradley. "He wasn't necessarily doin' the dynamics for dynamics' sake, and a lot of people that would try to make a record that sounded like him would do that.

"Tammy would have this wonderful way to sing the verses that was very quiet, and then she'd knock the wall down in the chorus. Well, he'd make the band play that way, too. You know, they'd get out of the way in the verses and kick in the choruses, and it was great.

"Piano was so important in Sherrill's records. I'd honestly say when I mixed particularly for him, everything was based off the piano. That was a great-sounding piano. A lot of people wanna put everything else in the mix; I would put the piano in there first and then everything else would have to fit the piano. If you do it the other way, you tend to wanna thin the piano out too much."

When the eight- and sixteen-track machines came in, in the late '60s, Bradley believes he used them differently from the way people record today. "You could help yourself with the multitrack," he says. "That's the way I looked at it. I tried to record with the multitrack offensively, not defensively. Now everybody wants to record defensively, have everything so they can do whatever they want to [after the tracking session], and that may be good, but the magic to me is the performance of the band and singer."

Today, many records are made by overdubbing one instrument at a time, and Bradley believes the recording loses its dynamic and energy that way. "If you took a big band, like Les Brown or Glenn Miller or any of those guys, and you set 'em all in the same room and played one of those great tunes like 'In the Mood,' where it gets loud and soft, all the dynamics and everything? If you cut just the basic rhythm, and then you overdubbed the reeds, and you overdub the trumpets, and you overdub the trombones, it wouldn't be the same as if they all played it together. It's intangible, that cohesive togetherness, bringin' it up and takin' it down, and the dynamics, which we did on all of Billy's records that were made in that room."

One of Bradley's pet stories involves Merle Haggard and a song, one of Haggard's best, and perhaps his biggest (four weeks number one, country, and number twenty-eight, pop). "We were doin' a session once, six o'clock. We done one song, it was, you know, a *good* song. Then he pulled out this *really* good song. They worked it up in fifteen minutes, cut it, and it was great. As Porter Wagoner says, there were people throwin' babies in the air!

"We started playin' it back and the tape dropped out in three places—*bang bang bang*, it dropped out. We went and checked the tape and the oxide and the backin' was off the tape. You could see right through the tape, there was a hole about the size of a quarter. Haggard went ballistic. We calmed him down and did another take, and it was even better 'cause everybody knew the song better. Before the session was over he called me aside, he said, 'I wanna apologize for going crazy a while ago.' He said, 'I had a reason.' I said, 'Yeah, I know you had a reason, but we couldn't help that—it was brand-new roll of tape, and we just never had tape problems like that.'

"He said, 'That had nothin' to do with it. Two years ago I cut that song at Bradley's Barn here and shipped it to Capitol in L.A. and it got lost. Last year I cut it at Capitol Tower and it got erased.' And he says, 'I cut it now and this happens. So I'm spooked.'

"Six months later, Fuzzy Owen—his producer, manager, you know—calls and he says, 'Lou, can we get in the Quonset Hut, Studio B there? Overdub that song again? We've cut it with the Strangers at Buck's studio and we need to get Johnny Gimble on it and mix it down.' In fact, I think he said, 'And slow it down a tick—we cut it too fast.'

"I said we can do all that if we can get in the studio. Billy Sherrill gave up the time he had booked and we mixed it.

"But all those delays delayed that record hittin' the market until 1973, about three and a half years after he first cut it. A bad recession was goin' on, things were really tough all over. It hit the market about Thanksgiving and was a big hit—'If We Make It Through December.'"

Lou Bradley cherishes the ghosts that made history those early days on Music Row. "Mort [Thomasson] told me this about a year before he died," he says. "Everybody loved old Mort. He said, one time, at the original 'A' studio—the house studio before the Quonset Hut became a studio—they had a two o'clock Patsy Cline session and she was forty-five minutes late. And Owen doesn't pass blowin' his top—he was strictly business in that sense. He was right in that he was lookin' after everybody's money 'cause they worked under budgets, you know, and they didn't waste money.

"'When she got there,' Mort says, 'I knew that the ship's gonna hit the sand, so I went outside the control room.' And she hit the studio and Owen hit the talkback, and they cussed each other like a bunch of sailors on a Saturday night. She said, 'I'm not recordin' for you SOBs today. I'm goin' home,' and stormed out of there.

"She's runnin' up through there and [Mort] said, 'Hey! You can't leave!'

"She said, 'I'm not gonna record for 'em today, they made me mad!'

"He said, 'Well you can't leave,' so she walked over and said, 'Why?'

"He said, 'You ain't hugged my neck and give me any sugar.' So she walked over and hugged his neck and kissed him on the cheek.

"He said, 'Come on and record!' She says, 'No, they made me mad, I'll not record today.'

"He said, 'Well, you do me one favor.'

"She said, 'Mort, I'll do anything for you.'

"He said, 'Will you do one take for me?' He was thinkin' if he got her in there and did one take, see, they'd get somethin' out of it.

"She said, 'Mort, I'll do one take for you,' walked back inside, cut 'Walkin' After Midnight.' She just did one take and left."

Another legendary story Bradley tells is his take on the birth of the fuzz-tone, on Marty Robbins' recording of "Don't Worry."

"Jimmy Lockart was an engineer, and he did Marty. Like a lot of other engineers, he came out of WSM. Those guys did live music all the time, so mixin' to them was a snap. He worked for Owen. But when Columbia bought the Quonset Hut, he didn't get hired into the group. Then he worked for Sam Phillips with Billy Sherrill.

"I came up here one time from Florida around 1960, and he'd just done this session. He said, 'Tell me what this is.' I said, 'Sounds like a bass guitar but....' He said, 'The preamp in the console distorted, and Grady Martin just played through it instead of fixin' it.' Everybody thinks it was in the studio. But it was the *console*. Everybody said it was a tube, but [engineer] Glen Snoddy said it was the transformer they used in the Langevin amps, shorted out from the high input level. I said, 'How did that occur?' Lockart said, 'Well, Grady was playin' electric with a mic, and then he was gonna play the tic-tac bass. So I wired him up direct and said, 'Don't hit it.' I needed to go pad it down in the control room [to control the input so it wouldn't blow up the equipment]. He waited while I walked across the studio and got in the control room, and just as I was about to pull down the control, he just ticked it.'"

Grady's inadvertent "tick" blew the transformer of the preamp. But they liked the sound of it, and they used it on Grady's solo.

But then the distinctive fuzz vanished. "It wouldn't do it anymore," says Bradley. "And they tried everything to get it back. It didn't heal," says Bradley. "It just quit."

"Finally, Glen Snoddy [also credited with wiring the first stereo console in Nashville] sat down and designed the fuzz-tone, and sold it to Gibson." The fuzz device that Snoddy invented became the Maestro Fuzztone, one of the very first commercially available guitar effects in 1964. It started a revolution of guitar sounds the very next year when the Rolling Stones used it on "Satisfaction."

Photo by Sid O'Berry, courtesy of Grand Ole Opry archives

First Music Row studio, 1955. Quonset Hut is behind the house.

Courtesy of Harold Bradley

An early Quonset Hut recording session. Harold Bradley and Jerry Reed are on guitars. That's Merle Kilgore singing at Tile 13.

This Old House Is Still Swinging

Bradley RECORDING STUDIOS, Inc.

804 16th Avenue, South
Nashville 4, Tenn.

◄ Print ad for Bradley Recording Studios.

Harold Bradley, Chet Atkins, and Grady Martin—three of Music Row's greatest session guitar players. ▼

Diagram by Lou Bradley of where they played and sang in the Quonset Hut. ▼

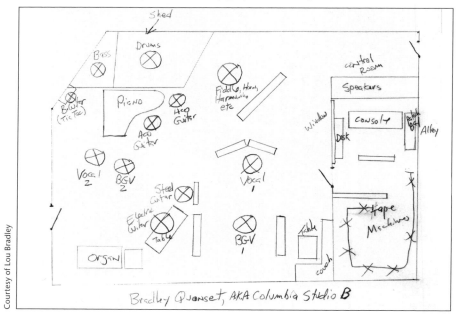

▲ RCA Studio B, also known as the musical home of Elvis, Waylon, Dolly, Charley Pride, and a thousand other hit-makers.

▲ Owen Bradley, pictured here in later years with Clint Black and Emmylou Harris. If anyone can take credit for founding Music Row, it would be Owen.

Chet Atkins, one of Music Row's founding fathers, with Mae Axton, co-writer of "Heartbreak Hotel." He didn't think Elvis would be around for long. ▼

▲ Trafco. Elvis cut "Heartbreak Hotel" here and became rock 'n' roll's greatest superstar. This photo was taken in September 2005, five months before the building was demolished to make way for a parking lot.

Frances Preston, head of BMI for many years, bankrolled many publishers and songwriters in their struggling years. ▼

▲ Ray Stevens, pictured here at the 1983 Fan Fair, has an oddball imagination and makes great records.

▲ The Jordanaires (left)—considered the greatest backup group ever, country or pop—with Ronnie McDowell, D. J. Fontana, and Scotty Moore.

▲ Jerry Kennedy (left) produced Roger Miller's greatest hits, and Fred Foster produced the Roy Orbison classics.

Tootsie's Orchid Lounge, where Hank Cochran discovered Willie Nelson. ▼

▲ Brenda Lee and Jo Walker Meador: two of Music Row's great pioneers.

▲ Charlie McCoy. A year out of high school, he headed north and became Nashville's top session harmonica player.

▲ Recent photo of the old RCA building, where Chet Atkins passed the baton to Jerry Bradley.

Photo by Alan L. Mayor

▲ Recent photo of the old Decca (MCA) building, across the street from the Quonset Hut. Owen Bradley ruled Decca like the gentleman he was.

Photo by Alan L. Mayor

◄ Bob Dylan must have found some magic in Columbia's Studio A. He recorded three albums there.

◀ Printers Alley, where Billy Sherrill discovered Barbara Mandrell and her sisters.

Norro Wilson couldn't make it as a singer, so he wrote great songs. ▼

The club where a thousand songwriters drank their troubles away, Kountry Korner coming down. ▼

◄ Five of Music Row's greatest: (from left) Bob Beckham, Billy Sherrill, Owen Bradley, Buddy Killen, and Larry Butler.

Cowboy Jack Clement with Kris Kristofferson. Kris didn't stay on Music Row for long, but he left a huge songwriting footprint. ►

◄ Loretta Lynn, Dolly Parton, and Tammy Wynette—the whole world knows these ladies.

▲ Larry Butler. His great records made superstars of Crystal Gayle and Kenny Rogers.

▲ Waylon Jennings, Jessi Colter, and Jack Clement—outlaws all.

Willie Nelson and Billy Jo Shaver. ▼

Dan Fogelberg, who made pop hits at Quadraphonic studio. ▼

▲ Nashville skyline at dusk, 1974.

Recent photo of Quadraphonic, the studio where the pop folks came to capture the magic. ▼

▲ Jimmy Bowen and Reba McEntire. Bowen told her she should produce her own recording sessions.

Mike Curb, the titan of the independent label operators. ▼

Allen Reynolds and Jimmy Bowen—a match not made in heaven. ▼

Photo by Alan L. Mayor

ASCAP and BMI Nashville, big money for songwriters and publishers.

Photo by Alan L. Mayor

◄ Bob Doyle, Garth Brooks, Pam Lewis—a team for success.

Photo by Alan L. Mayor

Garth Brooks with record executive Jim Foglesong. ►

Photo by Alan L. Mayor

Jack's Tracks, the studio where Allen Reynolds cut most of his hits on Crystal Gayle, Garth Brooks, and many others. ▼

Photo by Alan L. Mayor

▲ Columbia staff on 16th Avenue to celebrate a number-one record for Rodney Crowell. Quonset Hut is in the right rear of this building.

Big event at Bradley Park, at the top of Music Row in 1986, before the roundabout and the sculpture *Musica* graced the park. ▼

Photo by Alan L. Mayor

▲ Tim Dubois, accountant-turned-songwriter-turned–label genius.

▲ Toby Keith and songwriter Bobby Braddock celebrate their megahit, "I Wanna Talk About Me."

Musica. ▼

17

"Wesley, It's Music!"

As 1970 arrived, some nice things were happening in the world of country music. Its core audience had a growing number of radio stations on which to hear their favorite music, and on a Saturday night they could tune in to their local TV station and catch an evening of syndicated rootsy, country TV. Two of country's biggest stars, Glen Campbell and Johnny Cash, had high-profile national network TV shows and records that were regularly crossing over to the pop charts. Also, there were a slew of pop acts arising in California that were heavily influenced by country music.

And yet there might have been a vague feeling of unease along Music Row during this period. Although there was a lot of music coming out of the Row, some of the most popular-selling country acts, including Buck Owens, Merle Haggard, and Campbell, were doing their recording in California. Johnny Cash was a Nashville act, but his big albums were being produced by the distinctly anti-establishment Bob Johnston. The Row was in a state of transition—it just didn't realize it at the time.

Slowly, reluctantly, Owen Bradley and Chet Atkins were passing the torch to a new generation of music people. Billy Sherrill at Epic was an obvious power center, but never again would any country music executives mean to Music Row what Chet and Owen did in the '60s. Bradley left MCA in 1976, a move that shocked the Row. Chet hung on at RCA until 1982, but he had relinquished much of his authority before that time. Was the transition at RCA smooth? Well, the year after he left RCA as an executive, he moved his artistic talents over to Columbia, suggesting that he no longer felt comfortable at the label where he had labored for three decades.

In spite of the prominence of West Coast country acts, and the growing cultural distance between pop and country music, Music Row had grown far beyond the critical mass necessary to sustain it. Talented people all over the country knew about it, and they came there to follow their dreams. Many of them were more than music people, they were entrepreneurs, as well. This chapter deals with three of them, and shows how Music Row is constantly growing in different directions. How country was Music Row in the '70s? Sometimes very. How pop was it? You'd be surprised.

Ray Baker meant to be a publisher, and he succeeded, but he did a lot more than that. Perhaps more than any man on Music Row in his time, Baker knew where the country side of country was, and he stayed true to it throughout his career.

"I started my publishing company in 1965 based on the strength of meeting a young man in a little beer joint in Madison called the High Hat. The young man's name was Dallas Frazier.

"Dallas was working in a service station that Ferlin Husky owned, and he was writing songs. Dallas and I met over a few beers, and then he started singing me some songs he had written, and he just knocked me out."

The High Hat was a really small place. Baker remembers that "the only thing you could accommodate yourself with in the men's room was if you had to take a whizz. If you had to do something else, they couldn't afford that. It was that kind of place.

"Dallas and I were sittin' in the High Hat trying to think of a name for the company. We started off with beer names and we just kind of came up with Blue Crest as a combination of things. I actually asked Dallas if he wanted part of the company at that time and he said no, because the way he looked at it was if somebody sued, he'd have to go to court. I wound up borrowing money and started the company. I guess the biggest break we had was...I got to researchin' some of the songs he had in Ferlin's company, that he had written and nobody had ever recorded, and I found one of them called 'There Goes My Everything.' I asked Ferlin, 'Can we pitch these songs and I'll just make a handshake deal with you? If we get 'em cut, well, we'll split the publishing.' And he said, 'Sure, fine.'

"That happened to be the CMA's very first Song of the Year when they decided to have that category. The song was recorded by Jack Greene in

'66 and it propelled him from being a drummer for Ernest Tubb to being a star in his own right. Then of course, Engelbert Humperdinck, who had just had a big hit called 'Am I That Easy to Forget,' followed it up with 'There Goes My Everything,' so it was a big pop hit too.

"That really was the ground force that gave us enough sustaining power to get us into the publishing business and stay in it for a while." And soon there were other great country writers at Blue Crest. "I actually met Whitey Shafer through Doodle Owens, who was a great lyric guy, and he became a catalyst for Dallas's writing because he kind of injected some fresh ideas. He and Dallas have written a lot of great songs. I'm sure you're familiar with a lot of the Charley Pride hits: 'All I Have to Offer You (Is Me)' was a big record; then 'I Can't Believe That You've Stopped Loving Me' is another one; '(I'm So) Afraid of Losing You Again'—all three of those went number one for Charley.

"Back in those days, if you got a hit, it was maybe a year or so before you'd make any money off of it. If I'd have had the financial power, I would have signed all three of those guys [Whitey, Dallas, and Doodle], but I could only afford at that time to sign Dallas. Eventually I paid Whitey a little bit of a draw, but I couldn't pay him enough to live on, so he had a job at Sears at the time changing out mufflers. In fact, he's got a song in the catalog about that."

Now that country was surviving, did they look to the future with a glimmering feeling of optimism? "You know, we didn't look into the future much, we just—it was like a day-to-day thing. I'd go to the office on Sunday sometime and make a list of songs I wanted to have in a brief-case on Monday to go pitch. And of course Saturday night was a big night for me at the Opry, because so many of the stars played. I'd go down there with little reel-to-reel tapes in both pockets to hand out to different art-ists, because that's the way you'd plug songs, or you met 'em in the upper room at Tootsie's, which was across the alley from the back door at the Opry. That was just the way they did it. I'd been up in Tootsie's Orchid Lounge on many a Saturday night and seen Roger Miller, Justin Tubb, Harlan Howard, Hank Cochran—people like that passing the guitar, pitching songs to somebody like Patsy Cline. It was a party atmosphere. You'd drink a beer, tell a joke, have some fun, and then if there was a song around, the guy would pitch it.

"And songwriters were so helpful to each other back in those days, because if a guy was pitching a song, and the artist said, 'No, that doesn't fit what I'm doin', well, if he was out of songs [the writer] would say, 'Hey, I was over at Harlan's the other day, and he wrote a song that I bet you'd like,' and he'd get them in touch. It wasn't uncommon to have somebody like Harlan walk into a session at Columbia that was either in progress or just starting and say, 'Hey listen, you guys need to hear this,' and everybody would stop and listen. It was a mutually respectful atmosphere. And the songwriters were just as important as they ever have been. In my opinion, they were always the very seed that started the tree growing. But they didn't make a lot of money back then, and there was kind of a—I don't know how to put it—but not everybody was as respectful to writers as they are now, of course.

"An example of that was when Mel Tillis wrote a song that Webb Pierce liked, but Webb wanted Mel to give him half the song—not that he'd earned it. It was just, 'Hey, I'm in a power position to cut it.' And so I think Mel made a deal with him, well, he gave him half of 'I Ain't Never' and Webb, in addition, gave him a pair of boots. Mel tells that story about his $800,000 pair of boots.

"I remember when they used to have the old Disc Jockey Convention at the Andrew Jackson Hotel, Webb was downstairs outside the hotel and he was looking for [songwriter] Wayne Walker—they called Wayne "Fluffo" back in those days—and Webb was asking Mel where he was. Mel stutters, and he's trying to tell Webb as hard as he could and Webb says, 'Slow down and tell me,' and Mel keeps getting more and more flustered. Finally, Webb just grabbed him and said, 'Sing it, you sonofabitch, sing it!'

"He sang, 'He's up there in room thirty-nine.'

"Lefty Frizzell wasn't living here then, I think he was living in California, but he moved here in the late '60s. When Whitey and Lefty met, that was just a magical moment, because both of them were from towns in Texas that probably weren't fifty miles apart. They had that in common. And then they both liked to drink, they had *that* in common. They both had a sense of humor, and Whitey had always kind of flavored himself toward Lefty as far as his phrasing and his feel for songs. I was fortunate enough to have Whitey's publishing. Lefty wasn't signed with anybody, he had his own company, but he wasn't taking care of that part of the deal. So I'd get him to sign his part of the publishing over to me, and then I'd use my influence to go to people like Frances Preston to get him an advance, because even though Lefty was a big star and had been, he was not that careful with his money.

"Whitey and Lefty wrote a lot of great songs. 'That's the Way Love Goes' was one of the biggest things they ever wrote. And 'I Never Go Around Mirrors.' 'That's The Way Love Goes' has an interesting history—the first record on it was Johnny Rodriguez. A lot of people don't know that, but Johnny had a number-one record on it. Lefty cut it first in an album, but I don't think it was ever released as a single. And eventually when I was producing records I cut it with Merle Haggard."

It was natural that Baker go from publishing songs to producing records. "When you recorded songs for demonstration purposes back then you were really producing a record in itself, because you wound up arranging a song with the clock running. I was actually on a hunting trip in 1973, and this boy came up to my hotel room—my wife at the time, her mother worked at a company that he worked at. And you know how people know if somebody's in town who is connected to the music business.... Anyway, Moe Bandy came up to my room, introduced himself, and said that he wanted to do a session. I said, 'Well, bring me some tapes. I'm not in the record producing business, but I'll be glad to listen, see if I can help you out.' When I got back to Nashville I listened to his tapes and I liked them. I thought, 'Well, the guy sings pretty good. He's *country*.' So I called him up and I said, 'Moe, it's hard to get a deal for an unknown artist, you're probably better off to cut something on your own and try to press it up, and put it out, locally.'"

Bandy decided to take the advice, with Baker producing. The cost of the session was about nine hundred dollars in those simple days, without Baker charging for his time, and with a discount from the studio, which was located on 19th, on the edge of Music Row. "We cut two or three songs," says Baker, and one of them was 'I Just Started Hatin' Cheatin' Songs Today.' I couldn't get anyone to put it out, so I pressed it up on my own label, little ol' label called Footprint. Joe Talbot had a pressing plant here, so I went down there and paid in advance to press up a thousand or fifteen hundred records, mailed it out to the disc jockeys and we had what we called a 'turntable hit,' meaning that it was getting great airplay, but nobody was selling the record because it wasn't there to be bought.

"Based on the chart activity, I took it around to the people I'd pitched before, they still turned it down. But Wally Cochran had left RCA and went to a new label called GRC, they picked it up, and then we had a real hit."

Record companies always have their eyes open for up-and-coming producers. "I Just Started Hatin' Cheatin' Songs Today" put Baker on the radar screen, especially because Moe Bandy was so country and so many producers had gone uptown with their production techniques.

"Based on that, I got a deal to start producing Connie Smith, who had just changed from RCA to Columbia. I did some sessions on David Houston. When Moe Bandy moved over to Columbia, we had some big records there, and then Joe Stampley, and then Moe and Joe together." At a time when so many producers were trying to tailor their records for the more diverse audience they figured was now listening to country, Baker was establishing a solid reputation as a producer who could find real country songs and record real country records.

"I remember a fellow told me that Mark Wright was doing a session, he was gonna cut somebody country, and he said, 'Now give me a Ray Baker mix.' What he meant by that was, I want the voice out front, I want the rhythm guitar up a little bit, and it has to sound country.

"I didn't mean to build a reputation like that. But I enjoy country music. I was raised in South Texas and grew up listening and playing country music, and there was a certain kind of sound that I always liked. I was able to take that into the studio and apparently a lot of the people liked it because some of the records did pretty good."

As for the Haggard sessions, here's how they came about: "I did a session with Leona Williams, who was married to Merle at the time. I think she was on Mercury. We didn't have real big success with Leona, but we had some good records, and apparently Merle listened to 'em and liked 'em. He called me one day—this was like 1982 or '83—and wanted to know if I would be interested in doing a session on him, and I said, 'Yeah, I believe I would.'"

Haggard wanted Baker to do something different. Merle often recorded with his own band, and he preferred to start recording around ten at night. For this session, Baker changed all that, using Nashville musicians, and cutting at ten in the morning. "My theory was that all these guys who used to come out of the walls at midnight were asleep, and I could actually go in and not worry about" songwriters and hangers-on who would come into a session late at night, drunk or stoned, demanding a hearing for their song or otherwise disrupting a session. "We used Studio Eleven, which was Larry Butler's studio in those days, on 17th, right next to Waylon's office. If I remember, I got Mike Leech on bass, Kenny Malone on drums, Bobby Wood on piano, Reggie Young on guitar, and Red Lane on rhythm guitar.

"We went in there and we cut three number one records in two-and-a-half hours. We were just in there doin' the music while everybody else was asleep. One of the records was 'That's the Way Love Goes,' which won a Grammy for Merle."

All told, Baker recorded three number-one albums and seven number-one singles on Haggard. In the late '70s and early '80s, Baker could see country music diversifying. "I thought that was great, because guys who were cutting records that weren't anything like the ones I was cutting were having success, but at the same time I was cutting records like 'Just Good Old Boys' by Moe Bandy and Joe Stampley, and 'It's a Cheatin' Situation' with Moe Bandy by himself, and both those records went number one."

If Ray Baker represented the hard country edge of Music Row in the '70s, Norbert Putnam was a central figure for the pop side of Music Row.

Like Billy Sherrill, Buddy Killen, and a number of other important Music Row figures, Putnam was raised in the Muscle Shoals area of northern Alabama, on the Tennessee River. This area was dominated by four communities—Muscle Shoals, Florence, Sheffield, and Tuscumbia—which have since grown together into virtually one metropolitan area. In those days, there wasn't a lot to do there, and for some reason, a significant number of young white men learned to play musical instruments very well. These young white men tended to be much more interested in black R&B than in white country music.

If you can find Avalon Avenue in Muscle Shoals, you will see a large sign on a building that reads FAME Recording Studios, where it all started. This company was founded by Tom Stafford, Rick Hall, and Billy Sherrill.

Starting with Arthur Alexander's "You Better Move On," the '60s saw a stream of black pop and R&B productions flowing from Muscle Shoals, and when Atlantic Records executive Jerry Wexler started bringing his acts there, the future of Muscle Shoals as a recording center was assured, at least for a while. In time, white rock stars followed their black colleagues into the area, hoping to grab some of the magic. These acts included the Rolling Stones, Bob Seger, Paul Simon, and Rod Stewart. Putnam, a bass player, got in on some of the early sessions, along with his buddies pianist David Briggs and drummer Jerry Carrigan.

Muscle Shoals was happening, but a few hours to the north Nashville was booming. Word got back to Alabama that there was plenty of studio work for good session players, so Putnam, Briggs, and Carrigan split for Music Row.

Although Putnam had a great affinity for his Muscle Shoals R&B roots, he related well to the Nashville way of recording in the '60s and '70s, which was more about making good records and supporting the artist than seeking technical perfection. "You gotta remember," he says, "when you had Billy Sherrill producing 'Behind Closed Doors' and stuff like that, Billy would make an album in three three-hour sessions. The drummer wasn't going for a different drum sound every time. When he walked through the door, he was thinking about a crossed stick or an open snare sound and that was pretty much worked out with the engineer before he even sat down.

"And I have to tell you, Sherrill was right, and before him, Owen Bradley. They all did four songs in three hours, and the band got two ten-minute breaks on the hour. The sessions were very relaxed and a lot of fun to play. With an Owen Bradley session, Owen would come over and sit at the piano at ten o'clock, call everybody around the piano, and he would play the piano in the run-through, with, let's say, a girl singer. And while he's playing he's talking. He would literally play it all the way through once while he's talking to everybody around the piano. At the end of that he'd say, 'Does anyone have any questions about the arrangement?' And you needed to speak up if you had anything to say.

"Then we would go to our instruments. The girl would go to the mic, Owen would go to the control room and he would say, 'Let's play it down.' So we play it down once. Now the engineer has three minutes to get his balances. And Owen would say, 'Let's roll one!' And we're now playing for the second time and the red light's on. End of which, Owen would say, 'Everyone come to the control room. Let's hear it back.' And you walk into this big giant control room with the speakers blaring and loud. Owen always turned it up a bit too loud. The reason for this was he was going to go around while it was playing back and talk to all of us. He would come over and whisper in my ear, 'Hi. Bar nine, verse one, do not play the fifth. I need the note on the third beat, got it?' 'Got it, Owen.'

"He leaves me, and I see he's talking to Pete Drake, the steel player. Then he's talking to Grady Martin. By the time that first playback is finished, he has voiced his concerns to every player in the session, and we've all written down our corrections. Then he would turn and smile at the singer and say, 'Honey, I'd like to do a couple more, the band's just getting into this, and I think you're great today, this is gonna be a great record.'

"Now we go back out, he turns on the red light again, and the band plays it exactly the way Owen Bradley has heard it. He then maybe does one more take, talks to the singer, tells her how great she is, she needs to watch a few things. You look up at the clock, it's twenty-three minutes after ten, and Owen has just given us a ten-minute break."

As the number of sessions on Music Row grew, there was always a need for new session players, and Owen Bradley had his own way of finding them.

"It was 1964. I was twenty-two years old. Owen called me, he said, 'I want you to play the Belle Meade Country Club.'

"I'd never played with Owen Bradley and I said, 'What kind of music is this?'

"Owen said, 'Well, it's just gonna be my trio, it'll be acoustic bass, drums, and my piano.'

"I said, 'Well, Owen, my weakest suit is Gershwin chords. You know I'm an R&B bass player from Muscle Shoals.'

"He says, 'Well, look, I want you to come out there anyway. Bring your acoustic bass and don't worry about it.'

"So I go out to the Belle Meade Country Club very much worried—when Owen Bradley realizes that I don't know all the changes to 'Satin Doll' and 'Take the "A" Train,' he's gonna say, 'Later with you, kid!'

"'Let's start with 'Dancing on the Ceiling,' he says. I've never heard this song in my entire life. And he says, 'In E-flat.' I say, '*Great...*'

"He says, 'Don't worry, just watch my left hand.' Well, hell, his left hand was all over the keyboard—it was meaningless to watch it. So I sort of stumbled through 'Dancing on the Ceiling.' And then he called out another one, and I sort of stumbled—well, I stumbled all night. And at the end of the evening, he says, 'Well, let's stop in Belle Meade and get a corn dog.' So we stop in Belle Meade and he says, 'Kid, not bad, you found most of them.' That's what he said. He wanted to see how good my ears were. And he said, 'I'm gonna make you third bass on my sessions. If I can't get Bob Moore, and I can't get Junior Huskey, you're gonna get the call. But when you come, I need you to play like Junior or like Bob. Come over to the office tomorrow. I'll give you a stack of records. Study their styles, realize you're filling in. I don't want any of that Muscle Shoals shit. Don't bring the Fender bass. And whatever you do, don't ever play anything fancy over any of my singers.'

"Well, he laid it out for me, didn't he? And so I go over there the next day, he hands me a dozen albums. And he doesn't book me for anything. He just gives me the records. 'Study them. When I call you, when you come, that's the guy you bring.' So I go home, and I'm listening to Junior Huskey, Bobby Moore. I actually went so far as to write out, notate out some of the playing—because there was a pattern, the way Junior and Bobby would approach those songs.

"Well, two weeks later, I get a call to do one session. I think it was Loretta Lynn. That means that of the three sessions in the album, Junior couldn't do one of them. So I go over there to the Quonset Hut. I was the only outsider. There's Floyd Cramer on the piano, Buddy Harman on drums, Ray Edenton on rhythm guitar, Grady Martin, Harold Bradley. I took a deep breath and said to myself, 'Okay, this morning you're Junior Huskey.'

"So I go in there—I'm scared to death. We count it off, and we play it, and I'm pretending I'm Junior Huskey. Finally, we get to the break. I'm so scared, I don't even leave my bass. Engineer walks by. 'Hey, kid! You sound just like Bobby Moore and Junior Huskey!' Made my day!"

So Putnam had found his way into the Nashville studio session world. The money was good and the music was fun, and he was able to stretch out from basic country to artists of many stripes, including Elvis, Linda Ronstadt, the Beau Brummels, the Monkees, Manhattan Transfer, Henry Mancini, and Tony Joe White.

But he had other career ideas on his mind, and in 1970, he and his Muscle Shoals buddy David Briggs opened Quadraphonic Recording at 1802 Grand Avenue, just a block away from Ray Stevens's studio and three or four blocks from the Quonset Hut.

Once Quadraphonic opened its doors, it didn't take long for word to spread that there was a great little studio in Nashville that somehow fit into the culture of the pop world.

"We had all these outside artists from New York and L.A.," says Putnam, "and they had no real need of Nashville publishers. When Joan Baez came to Nashville, she didn't need to call up publishers for songs— she already had them."

This shook up Nashville's publishing moguls more than a little. When Dylan had recorded at Columbia, the publishers could deal with the fact that Dylan was Dylan, *the* songwriter artist. But when Quad started recording one singer after another—Baez, Neil Young, Dan Fogelberg, Jerry Jeff Walker, Jimmy Buffett, artists who came into the studio ready to go, either because they wrote their own stuff or because they found their songs elsewhere—this was a new situation for Music Row publishers, and some of them did not like it.

"When I was doing Fogelberg," Putnam recalls, "every publisher in town sent me songs. And they couldn't believe that I wouldn't look for a better song than Dan Fogelberg had, because it was so different from the way they made records. Of course, as a producer I loved it because I didn't have to listen to a bunch of songs.

"So Quad wasn't making a lot of money for the Nashville establishment. And they were worried—what if this becomes a trend? What if another complex like Quad popped up, and then another, and then another...." Putnam laughed at the thought. He was dramatizing the situation, but he did have a definite sense that to Nashville publishers, a studio that catered to artists outside the Nashville scene and artists who turned down, maybe even turned their noses *up*, at the thought of recording an album full of Nashville songs, constituted a real threat to the Music Row way of doing business.

"Back in the '70s, publishing companies barred their writers from writing with a guy in another company," remembers Putnam. "Bob Beckham was one of my best friends, and he always said, 'I will never co-publish!' Beckham is one of the guys who encouraged Jerry and David and me to move to Nashville. He was really a tremendous supporter. He and Fred Foster had Combine and Monument, and those were the accounts that supported us in the early days. And when David and I built Quad, we decided to start a publishing company. Beckham, we felt, built his company because he had free beer every day at five. Between five and six, you'd run over to Combine and there would be a party going on. There'd be eighteen people in there, and half of them worked for other publishers.

"So when David and I started our company we talked about this. And we said you know, we gotta beat Beckham! So we came up with the answer. We wouldn't have free beer between five and six. We'd have a completely stocked, open bar available twenty-four hours a day. We'll have every great writer in town in the palm of our hand!

"Anyway, Beckham hated co-publishing. And we've got Troy Seals running our company. Troy's working on a song. He has a verse and a chorus;

he's hung up on a couple of lines. Donnie Fritts walked in. Donnie writes for Combine. The song is called 'We Had It All.' Troy plays him the song and says, 'I'm hung up right here,' and Fritts gives him a couple of lines and completes the song in about two seconds."

The trouble is, Donnie Fritts writes for Bob Beckham.

"Now Dobie Gray is down the street recording,' and they're looking for songs. So Troy and Donnie run down there and play it for Dobie and [producer] Mentor Williams, they go, 'Great song. We wanna do it tomorrow.'

Seals calls Putnam and tells him that they're about to get a Dobie Gray cut, then reminds him that Beckham does not like to co-publish. "So David and I went over to talk to Beckham. He goes, 'Damn it, I'm not co-publishing! I told you, damn it, I don't do that!' He could talk to us like that. We were like little children, 'Oh, Bob, we're sorry. It was never intended to happen—he just walked in and suddenly they finished it!'

"And Beckham goes, 'Well, I'll tell you what, damn it, here's what we'll all do. You've got that one! They can write another one for me, and I've got that one!'

"'We Had It All' was later recorded by Elvis Presley. It went on to be recorded, I don't know, sixty, seventy times. And sure enough, they wrote another song, for Beckham, and I don't think anybody ever recorded it."

Over the last two decades things have radically changed. Now no publisher would *dream* of telling his writers they can't write with writers outside the company. Many writers are signed to co-publishing deals where they hold half the publishing on their own songs. Also, a significant number of hits are written by at least three writers, so it's not at all unusual for at least *six* publishing companies to hold publishing shares on one hit song.

Putnam also worked for Chet Atkins during his Nashville session days. "I don't ever remember him saying anything to a musician on one of his sessions." Putnam says. "Except, he'd walk around and go, 'Grady, that's a beautiful guitar.' And Grady would say, 'You wanna play it?'

"I don't ever remember Chet even picking up a guitar in a session he was producing and playing it. And David Briggs said to me once, 'You know, you can't do a track that's bad enough for Chet not to take it.' In other words, usually the first run-through, the first recording, Chet would say, 'That's fine.' But if you go back, look at the equation again," Putnam continues. "As musicians we knew that we could improve the track. But what Chet probably knew was that we would not improve the vocal.

I only know it now that I've been out of Nashville for twenty years, and I'm living among normal people, and when I ask them what do you hear when I play a record they say, 'Well, I hear this great voice.' And then I say, 'Well, what else do you hear?' They say, 'What do you mean?' The track is taken for granted. The average person, that's the way they hear music."

As attracted as he was to the R&B music that he was playing in Muscle Shoals, why did Putnam and his buddies leave for the mostly country streets of Music Row?

"Pure economics," Putnam answers. "We were getting tons of sessions in Muscle Shoals—we were working ten- and twelve-hour days. We would work all week on an album. Maybe fifty or sixty hours. They would turn in three sessions." That meant that for their sixty hours of work, the musicians would get paid essentially for nine of those hours. "Meanwhile, Felton Jarvis is coming down to Muscle Shoals doing Tommy Roe. And the Tams are coming up from Atlanta. And Ray Stevens is coming down writing charts. Ray was a great arranger. And Beckham would come down here. And they're all complaining about the food and the Holiday Inn, but they like the way the rhythm section plays.

"Ray Stevens took us to lunch one day and said, 'Guys, you can make it in Nashville. You can make forty-seven dollars every three hours in Nashville. You can do it three or four times a day.' He said, 'I'll hire you for every pop-rock thing I do.' And Felton Jarvis said, 'I will use you on all the ABC-Paramount stuff.' This is before he left and went to work for Chet at RCA. And Beckham said, 'Well, you're doin' all my demos, and Fred Foster will grab you [for his Monument sessions]. So the three of us had a meeting and Jerry and David said, 'We're going. You coming?' I was a little hesitant. I remember Rick Hall called me in, he said, 'Look, if you'll stay, I'll make you leader of the session, and I promise you a hundred dollars a week.' Well, then we moved up to Nashville."

During his rookie year in Nashville, Putnam says that Harold Bradley saved his career numerous times. Harold often was called to play an instrument referred to as a "bass guitar," a weapon seldom used today. It was used to add an edgy "tic-tac" sound to the bass line, so Harold was extremely familiar with the bass work of Bob Moore and Junior Huskey.

"On the first run-through, if I'd do anything stupid, he'd say, 'Look, going into that second chorus, you need to do it like this.' And he would play the line and I would say, 'That's what Junior would do or Bobby would do?'

"'Absolutely.'

"He saved me so many times. Occasionally I'd be on a record date and I'd have a very difficult bass part that would be written out. And Harold could read it. He'd play it for me. Harold Bradley and I did the Henry Mancini sessions. In the late '60s, Henry came down and did an album of country standard ballads. It's a beautiful record. Henry played piano, I played acoustic bass, and Harold Bradley played bass guitar. B. G. Cruiser played all the B-3 organ parts. Henry wrote every note that was played on the record, which was very rare in Nashville. Then he went back to L.A. and put his beautiful orchestra on it. It was a gorgeous record."

Charlie McCoy played on some of those Quad pop sessions, and he recalls that they differed a good deal from most of Nashville's country sessions. "There was a lot of horsin' around and a lot of sittin' around, and they had, obviously, bigger budgets. There never was the efficiency. Of course, a lot of those people, you know, they had it in their mind that the normal Nashville way of doing records was not artistic, and they wanted to be more artistic than that. The music was simple, it could have just as well been done the old way, but they didn't see it like that. That was okay. For the musicians, it was great because you stayed on the clock a lot longer."

Bob Beckham's name appears again and again in this book because he represents so much that is the spirit of Music Row. For twenty years, he ran Combine Music and made it one of the great independent publishing companies on Music Row because he had a talent for finding good song-writers and making them feel wanted.

In 1990, he started all over again, with Japanese backers, and formed Horipro Music.

Beckham is revered as a man with a thousand stories to tell. Holding court at his main hangout, Valentino's Ristorante, a few blocks from the Row, he talks about one of country music's great singers, and characters, Faron Young, a small, pugnacious man who, when properly juiced, would try to fight anybody, anytime.

"I had a couple of songs on Faron's 'comin'-up' session, and Jerry Kennedy called and said, 'Bob, the session is cancelled.'

"I said, 'What do you mean?'

"'Well, his wife called me this morning. Faron stayed out late last night. He came in about twelve-thirty, one o'clock. They have a carport and his wife, unbeknownst to him had bought a bunch of these hangin' baskets like with flowers and stuff, and hung them up there.' And ol' Faron, bless his heart, he comes in and he runs into one of 'em and he thinks somebody is trying to attack him. So he turns around and starts fightin' these sonofabitches. And these damn baskets beat the shit outta *him*, and cut his damn tongue, and he couldn't sing!"

A little history: In 1958, Beckham rode a train from Oklahoma City to Memphis, and a bus from Memphis to Nashville. "Paul Cohen made a record with me. What else do you want to know?"

"How many records did you actually put out?" I asked him.

"Son," he responded, "beats the shit out of me. I tell you what, Owen Bradley, one of the last things he did, he sent up to Decca—they got a vault up there someplace—and he sent me a copy of every song we tried to do. And I must have been the worst artist in the world, but Owen, bless him, he stuck with me, so I've got a whole bunch of stuff that *I* don't even remember.

Ronnie Gant is sitting next to Beckham. Ronnie is Beckham's right-hand man at Horipro. "Owen's the one that recommended you get into the publishing business, wasn't he?" he asks.

"Yes. Now thank you, son. See, I need clues like this. Owen was a frustrated builder. He loved to build things. And every time I'd come in talkin' to him about makin' a record, he'd show me a damned blueprint 'cause he knew I was a damn electrician. And he'd say, 'Well, what do you think about this?' and I'd say, 'Well, uh, what about a little song? He didn't want to tell me that I'd lost my record deal. A diplomatic man. He said, 'Bob, you know, your background is real interesting. You know, you're a singer, you're a songwriter. You ought to think about gettin' into the publishing business. I swear to God, I said, 'What in the hell is that?'

"He said, 'That's where these songs come from.'"

In 1963, Beckham went to work for Atlanta-based Bill Lowery, in the Fender Building on 17th, now Music Square West. "Upstairs was an architect that Martha Sharp worked for as a secretary. Downstairs was Lowery Music, and my writers were Ray Stevens, Jerry Reed, Joe South, and Kendall Hayes. Also in the building was Pete Drake—Window Music, Felton Jarvis, ABC [Records]....

"Wasn't that Mel Tillis who wanted you to wire his...," says one of the fellows at the table at Valentino's.

"Well, that's another story. Jesus Christ...you know what, boys? I'm just a walkin' goddamn story, ain't I? Tillis? Aww, that little wimpy bastard. Owen told me to go down to Cedarwood. Cedarwood had just done that building across from the Quonset Hut. I've been starvin' my ass off back in Oklahoma, and he gave Mel Tillis two hundred dollars to entertain me."

Remember that at this time Beckham is an artist signed to Decca, and Mel Tillis is plugging songs for Cedarwood, so Beckham is worth entertaining.

"Tillis took me downtown in the alley behind the Opry so I can see the stars comin' out, took me to some bar and bought me two beers, took me back to the motel and left me. Next day he picked me up, took me out to his house in Donelson. He said, 'I understand you're an electrician. We'll give you a good supper, b-b-but we just bought a-a-a washing machine and a dryer.' He says, 'You think you could wire that in for me?' Hey boys, I'm tellin' you the truth now. I wired the sonofabitch in. Hell, I think I wound up cuttin' one of the rotten bastard's songs!"

When Fred Foster hired Beckham to run Combine Music in 1964, the company was located in Hendersonville, a good half hour north of Music Row. "I stayed out there for about three weeks," he says, "and I'm thinkin', damn, man, if I'm gonna get into the publishing business, I gotta leave.

"I had a secretary, little old gal from Sweden, and she couldn't hardly talk English. About three or four weeks after I came out there, I said, 'Let me see the copyrights,' and she looked at me like, 'Hmmm?' She had never copyrighted anything. She was knocked up by...never mind. Went back to Sweden, and I went into Fred's office and I said, 'Fred, son, if you're gonna be in the damned music business, hell, I gotta go down to Music Row. And Fred said, 'Well, do what you gotta do!'"

Beckham inherited a small writing staff that included "A little ol' sixteen-year-old gal that Fred had sent to some kind of grooming school, name of Dolly Parton. I was faced with the problem of having to fire some of the boys. And I did, I did. I just started listening to the songs and trying to figure out if they were good enough to get something done with them." To those who complain that Music Row has consolidated too much, Beckham replies: "Believe me, my friend, back then you had Surefire, you had Tree, you had Cedarwood, Acuff-Rose—it was just as restricted as it is now. I wasn't brilliant, but I figured out that the only way I was ever gonna get any songs cut was to find writer-artists.

"I was lucky because ol' Fred had that Monument Records thing goin' there, and Fred, bless his heart, he was a good man, he put out a lot of dang records. I remember the review of 'Polk Salad Annie': 'That's a Southern record and nobody outside the South would understand what "Polk Salad Annie" is.' I hired a couple of promotion men over in North Carolina that broke that damn record, and you know what the biggest market was? Detroit!"

As Norbert Putnam mentioned earlier, Beckham made Combine so hospitable to writers that he had talent from all sorts of other publishers hanging around, including quite a few from Acuff-Rose, writers who felt isolated because Acuff-Rose was still located a good distance from Music Row.

"I remember Wesley Rose come in my office one day, 'cause we had so much goin' on there. He come walkin' in the back door and said, 'I just want to see what's going on here.'

"I said, 'Wesley, it's *music!*'"

In the '60s and '70s and beyond, Combine Music kept a small staff of writers that turned out a large list of hit songs, writers like Tony Joe White ("Polk Salad Annie," "Rainy Night in Georgia"), Kris, Larry Gatlin ("Broken Lady," "All the Gold in California," and a bunch more), Dennis Linde ("Burning Love, "Goodbye Earl," and many others), Johnny MacRae ("I'd Love to Lay You Down" and more), Bob Morrison ("Lookin' for Love" and lots more), John Scott Sherrill ("Wild and Blue" and more), and Bob DiPiero ("American Made" and other huge hits).

In 1986, Monument Records went bankrupt, leading to Combine Music's sale to SBK, a big New York organization. The great collection of Combine copyrights now resides with EMI, one of the handful of huge, bloated worldwide publishers left.

Beckham hated having to sell the company he had so lovingly built, and his crusty façade crumbles as he sums up his feelings about today's Music Row. "Yes," he says, "it was a little old hillbilly town down here, and good, *damn*, real caring people were puttin' out music they loved. They were naïve. I'm naïve, you know. All of a sudden they let these New York and West Coast bastards come in here and rape 'em. Now, we've got acts out there that sound like they were squirted out of the ass end of a goddamned computer!"

18

KNOW WHEN TO HOLD 'EM, KNOW WHEN TO FOLD 'EM

W hen Larry Butler came to United Artists Records in 1973, the label had enjoyed some Nashville success, particularly with Bobby Goldsboro and his crossover smashes like "Honey" and "Watching Scotty Grow," and with Del Reeves, who had a series of country hits in the '60s and early '70s. But, on the whole, United Artists was not the first choice for artists seeking a big-time country career—at least not until Butler arrived.

Butler came to Nashville with a talent for playing piano that was so evident that he was going to get noticed.

"I was playing in a group," he remembers, "Jerry Woodard and the Esquires, based out of Pensacola, Florida. We played the Southern circuit—Atlanta, Pensacola, we played Fort Lauderdale, and Nashville. The club we played in Nashville was the Black Poodle in Printers Alley, which at that time was kind of like a supper club. We were sort of a show band/ dinner music kind of thing, and lo and behold, the first night we played there, there was a gentleman sitting in the club by the name of Buddy Killen.

"At the first break, he called me over to his table and said he really liked my keyboard work, and he said if I ever decided I wanted to come to Nashville, to let him know, that he would endorse me and help me get started. So thirty days later, I showed up in his office and said, 'Here I am.'" The year was 1964.

"He said, 'That's kind of quick, do you have enough money to survive?'

"'No, I've got three-and-a-half dollars in my pocket and the clothes I've got on my back.' He wrote me checks to get an apartment, to lease a car, to buy some clothes. He really believed in me, and gave me the jobs to start. I immediately started working the studio. In fact, the second week I was in town I did nine sessions. Buddy got on the phone and called Chet Atkins and called Owen Bradley, he called everybody and said, 'Give this kid a chance because he really plays good.' As luck would have it, this is about the time that Floyd Cramer was pulling away from doing session work."

Music Row was still young, but it was so hot that there was plenty of session work for a variety of piano players. "It was incredible," Butler says. "There was Pig, there was Floyd, Jerry Smith, David Briggs. Briggs and I got to town, I think, thirty or forty days apart."

Butler was thrilled to be making a living as a session player so quickly, but he had dreams of being a record producer. "From the very first session I played piano on, I saw Buddy tellin' everybody what to do and I knew that's the job I wanted. I'm serious, I knew that moment. I said, 'Oh, my goodness.' What a great thrill, what an incredible thing to be able to do, is to go into the studio and put together your thoughts and your ideas, and then hear them come through the speakers."

At the time, the up-and-coming producer in town was Billy Sherrill, and Butler was determined to learn from the young master. Butler would spend his free time at Sherrill's sessions, watching and learning. Sometime later he had a plaque made up for Sherrill. "It said, 'Dear Billy, thank you for allowing me to look over your shoulder.' And it's the only thing pertaining to music in his home. I'm very proud of that. He was an incredible producer and I learned a lot from him. The main thing I learned from Billy was the emotion in a ballad—the way he treats ballads. He's the world champion," Butler says. "The simplicity of production, and his arrangements. He doesn't clutter 'em up with an awful lot of fill instruments—he lets the tone of each instrument stand on its own, and whenever there is a fill, it says something."

Although he was making a living in town right from the get-go, and production was in his future, Butler was sampling everything there was for a creative musician to sample. "I was doing a lot of demos," he recalls, "and then I decided I wanted to write some songs. Everybody around me was writin' songs and gettin' them recorded at Tree—Bill Anderson, and Roger Miller, these were my friends. And I thought, well, hell, I can write. I *thought* I could write, so I started trying to write, and every time I'd bring a song into Buddy, he'd kinda wrinkle his nose up, 'Larry, I don't know—it's just not there.' I finally got upset and I said, 'By golly, I'll go in the studio, so I went in the studio with some of my friends and demoed some of my songs, and they were horrible. But I got my feet wet as far as starting to produce.

"I did an awful lot of session work for a producer by the name of Kelso Herston. I went into Tree one day and Curly [Putman] said, 'Kelso's lookin' for a producer.' I ran out the front door and ran down the street, ran up the stairs—it was upstairs in the Buddy Lee Building. And of course, his secretary let him know I was there, and then when I walked into his office, I had to sit there and catch my breath. I said, 'I understand you're looking for a producer,' and he said, 'I've already hired one.' I said, '*Noooo!*'

"He said, 'Yes, Larry, I've already hired one.'

"I said, 'Well, I don't know who you hired, but I can promise you this: he won't do the job for you that I would.' And I left.

"He called me at seven o'clock the next morning. He said, 'Be at my office at nine o'clock.' And I went and he said, 'I couldn't sleep last night. You've got the job.'

"The first record I produced was Jean Shepard, 'Seven Lonely Days.' That was a Top 10 record. So, that was a nice way to start."

Butler had a nice run of records with Capitol, and then, "In my office, one day I got a call from Billy Sherrill. We had lunch and he offered me a job to come over to Columbia. I started working with Tommy Cash, and then I worked with Johnny Cash. I produced Lefty Frizzell. I produced the Carter Family, and then I became so involved with Johnny Cash that he asked me to come to work with him as his studio manager, his music director, his producer, and his pianist for the concerts. I worked with him for almost four years. I traveled all over the world. Had a ball. He was such a good man and my time with him was spiritually good for me."

After his time with Cash, Butler became Tree's in-house producer. Publishing companies sometimes hired an independent record producer to work with them in-house because that person would cut songs on his artists from within the publishing company. That kind of arrangement worked especially well at Tree, because it had such a strong catalog and an in-house producer could often find hit material right there.

While Butler was at Tree he recorded "Slippin' Away" on Jean Shepard, an artist who was by then considered by many to be past her prime. "Slippin' Away" was a Top 5 country hit that even penetrated the pop charts. Before long he was out in Los Angeles discussing the possibility of his running United Artists' country division.

"When I went out to interview at U.A., in my initial meeting with Mike Stewart in L.A., I said, 'We'll never even get to the salary part, 'cause you're not gonna give me what I want.'

"He said, 'What do you want?'

"I said, 'Total, complete control of the country division.' And they gave me as much or more control over the country division of that label as anybody had ever had in Nashville. I could sign anybody I wanted to sign, up to a certain amount—$250,000. Consequently, when I signed Kenny Rogers, U.A. thought that was a bad idea. I had to fight to get their approval. I had to say, 'Well, look at my contract.' And they did, and they found out I could sign anybody I wanted to sign. That's how Kenny got signed."

That was just a bit later. The first artist Butler signed was Billie Jo Spears, followed by Crystal Gayle, Dottie West, Ed Bruce, and the Kendalls, among others.

"The meeting with Crystal was really funny. We met, we talked, and I said, 'I wanna approve your contract and I wanna welcome you to the label.' And I said, 'Do you know a guy named Allen Reynolds?' She said no. I said, 'I'd like you to meet Allen, I'd like for you to work with him.' And she said, 'What?' She got tears in her eyes, she got very upset.

"And I said, 'He's a great producer, and I think your voice and his production style could give you your own place, your own world, your own identity. It's not that I don't want to produce you—I'm producing Jean Shepard, I'm producing Billie Jo Spears, I'm producing Dottie West. I think it would be a good thing for you, number one, *because* of that, and number two, if it doesn't work, then I'll produce you.'"

Butler was right on the money. Crystal's long studio relationship with Reynolds resulted in some of the best records and best-selling albums of any female up to that time. "That lonely feeling they had," Butler remembers. "Her voice has that lonely sound to it, like an emotion. It was a perfect match."

But the biggest coup was yet to come.

"Merlin Littlefield [then an ASCAP representative] called me and asked me if I liked Kenny Rogers. I said, 'God, yeah.' He said, 'Well, Kenny Rogers and the First Edition are doin' their last show.' I thought about it—I thought about 'Reuben James' and 'Ruby, Don't Take Your Love to Town'—I thought, 'Hmm, I wonder what's going on?' So I went to Montgomery, unannounced, and watched the show. I noticed that whenever Mary would sing or the other guy would sing, there was courteous applause. Whenever Kenny would sing, the people would come out of their seats, and I thought, 'Man, he's not through, it's not over for him.' So I called some friends of mine at radio stations, music directors, and said, 'If I sign Kenny Rogers, would you play his music?' They said, 'Larry, we'd love to. Every time he does something anywhere near country, we play the hell out of it.' I must have called twenty-five or thirty stations.

"Then I called Kenny. He came into town, and we made a deal in fifteen minutes. The first album was *Love Lifted Me*, a mediocre success. [After we recorded the next album] I had a meeting with [producer/publisher] Bob Montgomery and I said, 'Bob, how do you feel about Kenny Rogers?' and he said, 'Aw, he's great.' I said, 'Well, I've just done a new album with him and I'm gettin' ready to release the single. If this single doesn't work out, would you be interested in producin' him?

"He said, 'Lord, yes.'"

That's how close Butler came to giving up on producing Kenny Rogers. "But the next album was *Kenny*, and the single was 'Lucille.'"

Butler had a lot of confidence in "Lucille," but just getting Kenny to cut it was an effort.

"Roger Bowling sang me the song in my office on his guitar, and I stopped halfway through it and I said, '*Shhwwwww*, I gotta have that!' So I played it for Kenny and Kenny said, 'Larry, I agree with you, I think it's a hit song but I don't think it's for me. I just think it's too country… for me.'

"We went in the studio every night for a week, and we had twenty-somethin' songs selected. We'd cut a song and he'd say, 'What do you wanna do next?' and I'd say 'Lucille.'

"He'd say, 'Aw, no L.B. let's do this one, *blah blah blah*.' We did some sorta pop kind of stuff—'Desperado,' we did a wide range of material—and every time it was time for another song, I'd say, 'Kenny,' and he'd go, 'No man, let's do this one.'

"Friday night, we had fifteen minutes left. He said, 'We don't have enough time for another song.' And I said, 'Yes we do.'

"And he said, 'Aw, that country song.'

"'Yup.'

"So we cut it. He said, 'Larry, before we cut this, there's something that bothers me about this song. In the lyric, the guy goes to the hotel with her. I don't think he should go to the hotel with her, not after seein' her husband come in the bar and the whole bit. We oughta do somethin' like, 'I couldn't hold her,/'Cause the words that he told her,/Kept comin' back time after time.'

"And you know what, he was right. It made all the difference in the world. We played it for the band. The first take was the record. The vocal, too.

"We had I think twenty-somethin' cuts, and Chips Moman came by and we played him some. I played him 'Lucille,' and he said, 'There's your record.' Everybody that came by and listened to what we did, Kenny was playin' them the pop kind of stuff and I'd play 'em 'Lucille,' and they'd say, 'Well, there you go!'

"Hal Bynum [the co-writer of 'Lucille'] almost ruined it. He went over and played it for Waylon. Waylon cut it. Waylon called RCA and said release it and they said, 'Well, we understand Kenny Rogers has released it.' Waylon said, 'Well, I want mine out—it's a hit!' And they said, 'Well, we're gonna check tomorrow morning. If it hasn't come into the charts, we'll release it, put a three-day special on it.' We came in at number sixty-one with a bullet. That's how close I came to losin' that record."

"Lucille" went number one, country, and Top 5, pop, and Rogers was off and running on the most productive phase of his career. Eight of his next ten singles were number one on the country charts, and most got considerable pop action, but the one most remembered was the one that made Kenny Rogers a movie star.

"Merlin Littlefield walked in my office with a 45 in his hand and he threw it on my desk and said, 'There's your next number-one record for Kenny Rogers,'" Butler recalls. The "45" was not a handgun, but a seven-inch record. "I looked at it and I said, 'Oh, I've heard this. This has been a hit, hasn't it?' and he said, 'Nope.'

"I said, 'Merlin, I've heard it on the radio a lot.'

"He said, 'Nope. It died at sixty.'

The song was "The Gambler," as recorded by its writer Don Schlitz, on Capitol.

"Kenny came by about an hour later and I said, 'Man, listen to this.' And when I played it for him he said, 'Well, yeah, I've heard this.' I said, 'Well, it hasn't done that much, really.'

"He said, 'I don't know, man, you know. It's been done, it's been out on the radio.'

"I said, 'Kenny, I got a funny feelin', I got a feelin' that if you do this, *you will become The Gambler.'*"

Rogers did indeed become "The Gambler" in a series of popular made-for-TV Westerns.

In 1980, smack in the middle of the biggest winning streak of his career, Rogers decided to change direction, and left Butler for Lionel Richie. "I'll tell you this," says Butler. "I was all prepared not to like Lionel Richie or 'Lady,' until I heard it on the radio. Man, what a great, great record!" Butler's career as Kenny Rogers's producer was over, but what a run they had together.

"Do you know we sold two million a month, for two years?" Butler asks, rhetorically, an astonishing figure, particularly in an era when very few country acts were selling a million in the life of an album. "I think that was '79 and '80. And in '81—it was either '80 or '81—Kenny Rogers earned United Artists Records a hundred million dollars income, just from his records."

In the middle of his unparalleled success, Larry Butler was suddenly gone from United Artists Records.

"I was trying to get a raise for my promotion man, Jerry Seabolt, and they said no. I said, 'Well, he's the lowest-paid promotion man in the country music business and he's doing one hell of a job. He's makin' about a third of what his friends and his competitors are making. All I want to do is increase it so much.' Well, they said no, and I said, 'Well, as a matter of fact, *yes*.' And they said, 'We're not gonna do it. Hell, we'll hire somebody else.'

"I said, 'Well, gentlemen, I guess this is it.' And they said, 'What are you talkin' about?' I stood up and I said, 'I am no longer gonna be associated with this label, 'cause the deal was, I would have total control of the country division, and it looks like I just lost control.' And I walked out. It was a guy from TransAmerica. TransAmerica was the parent company, and they had a guy there representin' them, and he wasn't the nicest of people anyhow. He pissed me off and I said, 'Adios.'"

Now Butler had to take the flight home to Nashville. How did he feel about his bold stand?

"Scared to death! Whoa! *What have I done?* But Jerry Margolis put together a production deal for me which was unbelievable."

As an independent producer, Butler continued to work with Kenny Rogers until Kenny moved over to Lionel Richie. Butler also worked with John Denver, Don McLean, Mac Davis, and many others. "I even produced the Chipmunks," he says with a smile.

Butler's career as a producer and studio musician is among the most impressive in the history of Music Row, and somewhere in there he even honed his songwriting skills to the point where he and Chips Moman wrote one of the classic hits of the '70s, "(Hey Won't You Play) Another Somebody Done Somebody Wrong Song," which in 1975 was number one, both pop and country, for B. J. Thomas.

"I think I've got something like over a hundred gold records—gold and platinum albums—be it as producer, or writer, or publisher, or musician." He has two Grammys to his credit, one as producer, one as a writer.

Larry Butler is retired in Pensacola, but if a special artist came into his life, you'd find him back in one of Music Row's studios, putting together song, musicians, and artist in search of that mysterious formula we call a "hit."

"I am so proud of my involvement in music," he says. "And I feel like I've made a decent contribution. I don't feel like I'm king of the mountain, I don't feel like I need to be treated special. I never took part of a song to record it. I never had a deal with any of the writers or publishers. Everything I did was based on the merit of the song because I've always said, 'Give me a good song, I'll cut a good record. Give me a great song, I'll cut a great record. It depends on the song."

Like the man says, "Never underestimate the power of a song." Proof positive was the Kendalls' "Heaven's Just a Sin Away," an indie-label phenomenon so big that Nashville stood in awe of it, like Jonah before the whale.

It took five fiercely independent people to make it happen. Dick Shory was an ex-drummer who started Ovation Records. Headquartered in Glenview, Illinois, the label released a little folk and a little blues, sold enough product to struggle along, and tried once or twice without success to put out some country records.

Brien Fisher was a guitar player with label and production experience in Ohio and Illinois.

Royce and Jeannie Kendall were a father-daughter duo from St. Louis, Missouri, who had recorded for Pete Drake's Stop Records, Dot Records, and United Artists. They had charted but never had a real hit.

Finally, Joe Sun was a record promoter with the talent and ambition to be a country star, if he could only get on a record label.

"I had known Dick Shory," says Fisher. "One day he calls me and says, 'Hey, we're doing tax packages.' A tax package was an investment of eight to ten thousand dollars—or as much as you could get the investor to put up—that would finance a recording project, and if you had the master done before the end of the year, then it was a legal write-off for the guy who put up the money. At the time it might have been five to one." That is, a five-dollar write-off for every dollar invested.

Fisher had already recorded the Kendalls at Fred Carter's Nugget Studio in Goodlettsville, and Fisher got Shory to finish up the album as a tax package. One of the songs recorded as part of the package was a little gospel-tinged song written by Jerry Gillespie called "Heaven's Just a Sin Away."

"Now we had to put the album out. I went to Minneapolis and mastered most of the album the week after Christmas of 1976. Nashville was so busy at the time that I couldn't get into any of the mastering studios. Remember, I had to have the masters in hand before the end of the year for the tax package to be legal.

"So Ovation put out the album. And the first single was the old Jimmy Work classic, 'Making Believe.'" The single staggered up to the number-eighty position in *Billboard*, then it ran into an Emmylou Harris album cut of the same song, which eventually became a hit single for her.

There was another classic country song on the album, an old Carl Smith hit called 'Live and Let Live' that had a similar sound, so Fisher and Shory decided to make that the next single. The backside of the record would be a song written by Jeannie Kendall called "Let the Music Play," which was also the original name of the album.

"There was a disc jockey in Paducah, Kentucky, named Jay Diamond who had an evening radio show," recounts Fisher. "He called me three different times to tell me that every time he plays 'Heaven's Just a Sin Away'"—still just an album track—"on his show the phones go ape. He told me, 'I really think that's your hit,' but in those days you'd get a lot of calls like that from little stations, and maybe I didn't take him as seriously as I should have. He called Royce too, but Royce took him a lot more seriously than I did.

"We already had manufactured copies with 'Let the Music Play' on the B-side, but at the last minute, I took it off and added 'Heaven's Just a Sin Away.'"

To work the record at the radio stations, Fisher had hired a single intrepid record promoter—Joe Sun. Ovation was only paying Sun fifty bucks a week, but Fisher promised Sun that if the Kendalls became a hit act, Sun would be the next artist on the label.

Almost immediately, a couple of radio stations—that reported to *Billboard*—started playing the B-side of the record. When that happened, Fisher reshipped the single with "Heaven's Just a Sin Away" on *both* sides.

"I still credit Joe as a heck of a lot of the reason for the record's success," says Fisher. "He'd promoted for London Records, and he knew the game quite well. And I remember that Max Gardner in San Antonio and two other radio people, one in Illinois and one in Georgia, were playing the record. Joe asked the three of them to let him tape them talking about what had happened at their station when they played 'Heaven's Just a Sin Away.' Max would say stuff like, 'As soon as I'd start playing the record, the calls would start and sometimes I can't get 'em to stop calling and I have to play it again!' These were all credible disc jockeys, and once he had their comments on tape he edited them down to one minute. Now he would call St. Louis and tell the guy there, 'Hey, today instead of me telling you all this stuff, I'll take a couple of seconds to tell you what I'm doing, then I need one minute of your time and that's it.' He played that one-minute tape for lots and lots of stations, and that tape really made a lot of people pay attention."

"Heaven's Just a Sin Away" debuted on the country charts August 6, 1977, quickly zoomed to number one and hung on for four weeks. In those days, singles still sold, and Ovation sold 900,000 of them in the United States that first year, incredible sales for a country single at the time. The album was later certified gold, and the record helped earn the Kendalls a Grammy in 1978 for Best Country Duo.

Many country hits are strictly radio hits, records that climb the charts because lots of stations believe it'll sound good on the air. But "Heaven's Just a Sin Away" was one of those rare phenomena, a record so exciting that it shook listeners out of their lethargy and made them besiege the stations with phone calls. The Kendalls went on to have ten Top 10 hits, including three number ones, most of them on tiny Ovation Records.

As for Joe Sun, he did get his shot, and his first single, "Old Flames Can't Hold a Candle to You," was a Top 15 record. He continued to chart over the next seven years, and according to Charlie McCoy, Joe is still a country star in Europe.

Over the next four years Ovation had a high profile on Music Row, before it ran into money trouble and descended into the oblivion reserved for most independent labels. But at its peak, absurd rumors circulated the Row that Ovation was negotiating to buy RCA. Of course, Jonah was never going to swallow the whale, but Music Row is a small town, and people talk....

19

WANTED: JERRY BRADLEY

O f all the major labels, none has had a more consistent track record in developing artists than RCA, which today goes by the name BMG, or, sometimes, given the mysterious ways of corporate culture, RLG.

In the early days, Steve Sholes ran the RCA Nashville office, and was soon followed by Chet Atkins. For more than two decades the label was run by a genuine "music man."

In 1973, Chet handed over day-to-day operations to Jerry Bradley, son of his friend and rival, Owen Bradley. Jerry's career would span nearly the entire first fifty years of Music Row, and his record of achievement is, in its own way, as impressive as his father's.

Owen put Jerry to work early in the Quonset Hut, when they were still making films there. "I used to hold the idiot board for them to read," he says. "I had an uncle that held the boom mic. Harold was the music coordinator. Charlie, my dad's other brother, he was running some tape machines. Daddy was in charge of all of it. So he had us all working some job over there."

Owen Bradley was a highly motivated man with the rare gift of being able to take his career wherever the times demanded. In the big-band days, he led a big band. When the recording industry began to show up in Nashville, Owen was there, to play on, lead, and produce sessions. When studio facilities were at a premium, Owen was willing to learn the studio business from the bottom up, including the film studio business, which few others in Nashville thought about at all. And when there was an opportunity to run a label, Owen was there, too. In every phase he worked hard, learned fast, and was a leader of men.

His son Jerry was a very different breed of cat.

"In '56, I was hangin' around," he says, almost languidly. "My daddy worked all the time. He either had a dance band or worked at WSM, or did sessions, and he would sleep late on Saturday, he'd sleep on Sunday, and I felt like it was my duty to get the hell out of there before he woke up. So, he was out working hard and I was, quite frankly, doin' what the hell every other teenager does—I was bein' a boy. I wasn't a *real* bad boy, but I was havin' fun—I had a hot rod and stayed out late. I had the sheriff come by my house for drag racin' or something.

"Dad bought all those buildings on Music Row and he'd have me take the furniture out of this building, paint this, do that—whatever the hell he wanted me to do."

Young Bradley attended Nashville's Peabody College for three and a half years, and didn't bother to finish, did six months in the U.S. Army Reserve. When he got out in "'62 or '63," he told his dad, "I'm either gonna be a salesman, and sell something big, airplanes, or trailer trucks or something, or I'm gonna get in this damn business you're in.

"He wouldn't do anything without getting permission from Decca, so we got on the airplane and flew to New York. He asked his people, did they want to start a publishing company? If not, I was gonna start one."

Jerry started Forest Hills, perhaps named after the upscale community where the Bradleys lived, which is now a part of Nashville. The company was located in the basement of a brick house at the corner of 16th Avenue South and what is now Roy Acuff Place, almost, but not quite opposite the Bradleys' studios.

Overhead was small because he didn't have to pay any rent. "I signed a few writers and got a few cuts—Kitty Wells, Perry Como, Jack Greene, Brenda Lee." He was well connected. The primary producers on the Row were his dad and his dad's friend Chet Atkins. "Owen didn't cut the first one I brought him, he let me learn the hard way. I did that for close to ten years. In the mid-'60s, we started the Barn [Bradley's Barn, a studio a few miles east of Nashville, in Mount Juliet when that community was still rural].

"I'd work up at the Barn, engineering sessions, and then I'd come back to Nashville and do my publishing. I'd just go back and forth, about twenty-five miles each way. Sometimes I'd make the trip three or four times a day. I'd work the publishing company 'til noon, stop and grab me lunch, go to the Barn, mix a session 'til five, or 'til nine, and then come back to Music Row."

Owen had almost, but not quite, succeeded in converting his son into a workaholic.

"I'd gone to college with Harry Warner, and Harry was working at the Roesch-Patton Funeral Home [located on the Broadway edge of Music Row. These were the days when hearses doubled as ambulances in Nashville]. We were good friends, and I was raisin' hell, and I'd go out and make ambulance calls with him, deliver somebody to the hospital, pick up a wreck, just something to do. I lived up here in Lincoln Court Apartments on 17th, and Harry was right down there. He might call at midnight and say, 'I got a shootin', go with me,' and I'd jump in my car and go down there, and we'd go pick up somebody, take him to the hospital.

"Harry had a relationship with Chet and Ray Stevens and that bunch, and one day Harry said, 'I'm going to dinner with Chet today—why don't you come along?' I said, 'Ahh...no.'"

By that time Jerry's office was in the little carriage house behind his original office. On the other side of the carriage house was the RCA parking lot. "I was leavin' my office and here comes Chet and Harry gettin' ready to get in their car. Chet said, 'Why don't you come with us?' and I said, 'Ahh, nah, I don't have a coat on,' and he said, 'Ah, c'mon, go with us.'

"They were goin' down to the Carousel [in Printers Alley] to eat dinner. I jumped in the car with them, and on the way down there I told Chet, 'Hey, if you ever have a job open, keep me in mind.' He took a drag off his cigar, didn't say anything.

"To be perfectly honest, what made me say that was, I really enjoyed mixing sessions and being a part of it, but I really realized—and I owe everything in the world to him—I was just Owen's son. And if anything ever happened to him....

"Anyhow, we went down to the Carousel, ate dinner, and they were droppin' me off and I said, 'Hey, Chet, don't forget what I said—if you ever have anything, give me a holler.' He took a drag off that cigar and he said, 'Well, you might make a pretty good executive,' and I said, 'Aw, shit, I don't want to be an executive. I'd have to get a coat and tie.' I just laughed and got out of the car and left.

"Two weeks passed. I got a message and Cecile, my secretary, said, 'Chet Atkins called you.'

"Well, anybody that knew anything knew that Chet didn't call you much about songs. If he wanted to put a song on hold he had somebody else call you. I thought, 'Well, I hadn't pitched him anything. I wonder what in the world he wants.' I thought about it a minute and I called Owen and said, 'I got a leave-word from Chet.' He and Daddy were pretty good friends. 'I got a feelin', I just got a funny feelin' he's gonna offer me a job.' And he said, 'What do you want a job for? Hell, you got a job.'

"I said, 'Well, hell, I don't know.'

"He said, 'Tell him you're lookin' for an *opportunity*—you ain't lookin' for a job, hell. You got a *job.*'

"Pretty good words, I thought. So I went over and I met with Chet and he offered me a job and I reared back and said, 'I got a job. I really don't need a job. Now if you got an *opportunity* over here I might . . .'—just right out of the book, you know. He said, 'Well, I'll have Harry Jenkins give you a call.' Harry Jenkins was Chet's boss. So, Harry flew in and he talked to me. He offered me twenty grand. I said, 'I'll take it, but in two years I want to be makin' twenty-five.' Harry said, 'I'll tell you what, I'll just give you twenty-five right now.'

"At the time, Danny Davis, one of RCA's in-house producers, was leaving his job to devote full-time to his band, the Nashville Brass. They knew that, but what they didn't know was that Felton Jarvis was leaving. Me and Felton were best of friends, and he had told me that he was gonna get an independent production deal on Elvis. Of course, I was tellin' him, 'What's gonna happen if this don't work? You're gonna be out of a job.' He said, 'I know it. I'm talkin' to Elvis tonight.' And a day or two later I talked to him and asked him, 'Whatcha find out?' He said, 'Elvis says he's goin' to the mat with me. He's gonna hang in there with me and I can just quit this damn job! Bradley, don't you tell nobody.' So I didn't. When all this was happening, RCA was hirin' me—I couldn't say anything!

"Well, the minute the word got out about me being hired, Felton called me. 'Bradley!'

"'Felton, I didn't say a word. You told me not say anything, and I couldn't tell *them,* and they told me I couldn't tell that I was comin' over there, so I didn't say nothin' to nobody.' So when I moved in, Felton moved out, and I was in his office. I forget the title, somethin' executive director somethin'.

"My first record was Nat Stuckey. I cut six sides on him. I went into Chet's office and played him all six sides, three of which I liked. And he picked the other three. I walked back into my office and shut the door, buried my head in my hands, sat there and thought, you know, I really don't believe in the other three, I believe in these three. I got the opportunity, and I decided right there at that moment that I'd have to go with what I believed rather than what Chet believed. So I did, and hell, I had a pretty good run with Nat Stuckey."

Bradley also produced a number of albums on Charley Pride, and out of those albums came a considerable number of hits.

Somewhere in his early Charley Pride days, Bradley met a man named Tom Collins, who would become an important associate over the years. Collins worked with Jack Johnson, who managed Pride, and Johnson had an office near Music Row.

"Jack's office used to be quite the place to go at five o'clock and have a drink. Only thing is, I didn't drink. I used to. Back in my early publishing days out of college, I used to go over to Ireland's and I'd drink rum and Coke. You could go in there and sit with all the music publishers, and in ten minutes, they'd tell you who was cuttin', who was listenin' to songs—they'd give away all their trade secrets. You know, they'd complain, 'Sherrill's a jerk! He didn't cut one of my songs,' but they'd also tell you, 'He's listenin' tomorrow.' Or, 'You need to get your song to Gallico,' or whoever it was." Mostly, he says, he drank with the boys to get information.

"Anyhow, people would go by Jack's office, but he could be pretty much of a pain in your butt with Pride, just doin' what he should do as a manager—and me doin' what I should do runnin' a record label. He wanted me to come out there to listen to Milsap. Well, I'd already gone to Memphis to hear Milsap, and I'd gone to the King of the Road to hear Milsap."

The King of the Road was a motel on the east side of the Cumberland River, in what was known as East Nashville. It was a multistory structure that had a nightclub on the roof and Milsap was a very popular act there. Nashville music people went there regularly to see him sing and play the piano because he was that good, but it was hard for him to get a record deal because, "He was doin' that popsy stuff and I thought, damn, I don't want anybody singin' pop."

Finally, Bradley felt that he couldn't put Johnson off anymore, so he drove out to Johnson's office in Berry Hill, a mini-city within Nashville, just a couple of miles away from Music Row. For more than three decades, Berry Hill has been a place where ambitious people with a yen for low-priced property would buy a small house and turn it into a studio or an office. "Me and Jack were in the room, and Jack put on a tape that had three or four songs on it. Jack played two of them. I stopped the tape and said, 'I'll sign him.'

"'What? Right now?'

"I said, 'I'll take him. I want him.'

"'You ain't gotta call New York?'

"'No, I don't have to call New York. I want him.'

"So he says, 'Well, who do you want to produce him?'

"I said, 'Who the hell did that?'

"He says, 'Well, I got an old boy workin' for me back here named Tom Collins. You know Tom?' I said, 'Naw, I don't know Tom.'

"Tom had an office in a one-car garage that they'd knocked the end out of, and they had a receptionist out there. He was wearin' what might have been a seersucker suit—looked like a banker comin' out of there. Jack introduced me to Tom and I said, 'Hey, if you did that session, hell, you can produce Milsap.' So I gave him the money, and they went into the studio—everybody laughs about it now—but back then you'd make a deal with an artist and you'd say, 'I'll give you four singles,' and you'd have an option to do twelve sides. And if you got something stirred up, you'd either do another four, and then you'd do the album. But you didn't have to commit to the album."

In those days, Jerry says, you could do an album for $25,000, so a four-side deal was a very small investment. This gave the label executive the ability to take risks. No record man really knows what he's got until the record goes out and the public makes its decision.

By 1976, Jerry Bradley was well established as an A&R executive at RCA, independent of his father. That was the year the West Coast delivered a major blow to the easy self-assurance of Music Row: Decca Records was now called MCA, and it was MCA head Mike Maitland out in California who decided it was time to get rid of Owen Bradley.

When MCA decided to get rid of Owen, he was about sixty-one years old. Jerry recalls that it was about time for the contract negotiations between Owen and the label that would probably have taken him through to retirement. "But those negotiations never happened," he says. "In my opinion, they didn't respect him, and they were gonna do things their way."

When Owen left, the label did not tap an established Music Row A&R professional to run the Nashville office. The message was clear. Major A&R decisions would be made in California for the foreseeable future.

"They didn't know shit from shinola," says Jerry with typical directness. "And they didn't have a whole lot of success." Eventually the MCA situation would return to normal, but the departure of Owen Bradley gave Nashville a taste of the future. The following year, Jimmy Bowen, who had been a successful California record executive, would arrive in Nashville determined to bend Music Row to his will.

Meanwhile, Jerry soldiered on. And in 1980, a major musical force arrived at RCA.

"Here's the story on Alabama," says Bradley. "I used to put all the stuff that I really liked on the floor, leaning up against my desk. I had Alabama and Ricky Skaggs. And I was gonna sign one of them. But I was looking for a *group*, because radio was playin' a male, a female, or a duet, an occasional instrumental—and the Oak Ridge Boys or the Statler Brothers. And I said, 'I want a band.' My feeling was that the disc jockeys were getting younger and younger and that they were comin' from pop and jumpin' into country.

"They used to have what I'd call 'bell ringers.' Guy'd ring a bell and he'd say, 'Ahh, git up in the mornin', time to milk the cows, we got Porter Wagoner singin' such-and-such....' Well, those days were gone, because you had a more sophisticated disc jockey in there. I put the word on the street and Beckham brought me a group, but I didn't really like 'em, and I said, 'Bob, this isn't what I'm lookin' for,' and he kind of got mad at me.

"I was drivin' home and I heard Alabama singing on the radio 'My Home's in Alabama.' I was just about at the WSM tower when I heard' em singin' that, and I said, 'I'm gonna sign them when I get back tomorrow.' Joe Galante put in a good word for 'em, Shelia Shipley put a good word in for 'em, and Tony Brown put a good word in for 'em." These were three key RCA staffers, and Jerry felt he was on solid ground. "I had the appointment with Harold Shedd [who had sent in the demo]. Harold Shedd came in, he sat down, he showed me a god-awful album cover, a Rand-McNally map that had Birmingham and a star on it and I think it had 'Randy Owen and Alabama' on it. He showed me that and we sat down and we talked, and I told him that I'd give him $25,000 for the album that they'd already cut. We had to work quick because 'My Home's in Alabama' was already headed up the charts on a little label.

"That was like a Thursday or Friday. Monday morning comes, Harold Shedd calls me. He says, 'Jerry, I need to bring over my partner, a guy from Texas named McBride. I need to bring him over and meet you.'

"'Eh, don't make any difference. Come on over.' So they came over and in walks this guy with white hair, white shirt, white suit, white belt, white breeches, white shoes—drippin' in gold. He commenced to tell us what we were gonna do. I told him, 'Man, you should have been here Friday. Me and Harold made the deal Friday. I'm not renegotiatin'.' And so, he got to meet me. That's about all that came of that meeting."

Alabama became, simply, the biggest group in the history of country music. Between 1980 and 1995, Alabama sold more than 57 million albums, had forty-one number-one singles, and was the CMA's Entertainer of the Year for three straight years. When the rest of the industry slumped, Alabama was the one country act that chugged on until the next wave of prosperity.

In the '70s, Bradley, Collins, and Pride went into the publishing business together. Because Bradley was a record company executive at the time, the relationship raised some eyebrows. Similar events have occurred over the years in the industry. In fact, to a degree, it was a reprise of his father's Forest Hills venture at Decca. Jerry described how it happened.

"Charley and Jack Johnson were having some problems, and they had a publishing company together called Pi-Gem. All of a sudden, one day out of a clear blue sky, I got a call from Tom Collins, saying he and Charley wanted to see me. So I met with them and they said that Charley was buying Jack out, and Tom was gonna be a partner, and they wanted me to be a partner. I said, 'You gotta be kiddin' me.' I guess if you asked them, they thought the position I was in would help their company, but what they didn't know, was I wasn't gonna abuse my job for songs. I'd seen that happen through my dad's eyes and others.

"They said, 'Well, we don't really care if I was gonna shove things down the artists' throat—they knew I wasn't gonna do that.' I said, 'RCA isn't gonna let me do this.' I remembered my daddy puttin' me on an airplane to New York to tell his company that we were gonna start a publishing company. So I called my mentor and boss in New York, Mel Ilberman, and I said, 'Tell me what I need to do to make this happen.' Mel said, 'Write me a letter tellin' me what you've been offered and I will okay it,' and I said, 'Mel, I ain't got enough damn sense to write that letter, would you write it for me?'

"I was pretty much a silent partner. Tom called me one day and said, 'How come you never cut any of our songs?' I said, ' 'Cause, you're giving me the crap and you're cuttin' the good songs I never had the opportunity to hear,' and I named a half a dozen songs. Well then, the good songs from Pi-Gem started comin' my way.

"I had the same conversation with Bill Hall. Bill Hall got a hold of me one day. He said, 'You never cut any of my songs. Foster and Rice, they won twenty-three awards.'

"I said, 'Bill, you gettin' them out of the wrong drawer. I never had the opportunity to hear any one of those twenty-three, you give me the opportunity to turn down one of those hits and then we can have this conversation.'"

Hall had a great writing staff, led by Bob McDill, who wrote such classics as "Amanda" (a hit for both Don Williams and Waylon Jennings), "Rednecks, White Socks, and Blue Ribbon Beer" (with Johnny Russell and Waylon Holyfield, a hit for Russell), "Good Ole Boys Like Me" (for Don Williams), "Baby's Got Her Blue Jeans On" (for Mel McDaniel), "Nobody Likes Sad Songs" (for Ronnie Milsap), "Everything That Glitters (Is Not Gold)" (for Dan Seals), "Don't Close Your Eyes" (for Keith Whitley), and "Gone Country" (for Alan Jackson), plus innumerable other hits.

McDill was an admirer of Hall, his sense of humor, and his steely determination to get his writers' songs cut. "One time Jerry Bradley was gonna record somebody big—I forget who it was—and Bill kept on Jerry, 'You gotta hear this song I got.' 'Yeah, yeah, I'll hear it, Bill.' 'You gotta hear this song, it's perfect for him, you gotta get me on this date.' Bradley put him off for a week, and then he got so he wouldn't take Bill's phone calls. If you remember, on the third floor of RCA facing the back parking lot there was a door—a fire escape door where the fire escape had never been completed, or something—just a damn door there, in a wall, on the third floor overlooking *nothing*. If you stepped out there, you'd *kill* yourself. [It was actually a door for delivering heavy equipment to RCA Studio A.]

"Bill has coordinated [with somebody over at RCA] that Bradley will somehow be in a specific spot at a specific time—to the second—as if the watches all over town had been synchronized. Bradley's been manipulated into the hall, he's walking down the hall of the third floor, and here's a damn knock on this door and he says, 'Gee, who the hell can be out there knockin' on this. There's nothin' out there. Hey! Get the janitor! Give me the key!'

"Bradley gets the key from the janitor, opens the door, and there's Bill in one of those damn cherry pickers, three stories up! There's a tape in his hand. 'You're gonna love this song!'"

Tom Collins became a very successful producer, supervising major hits for Ronnie Milsap, Barbara Mandrell, Sylvia, and Steve Wariner. Both Collins and Bradley benefited from their publishing association, and when Pi-Gem was eventually sold to the burgeoning Welk organization, the friendship outlived their business partnership.

They expressed this friendship in an unusual manner.

"In the '70s, we all worked, but we all played hard," says Bradley. One of the ways they "played hard" was through practical jokes. "Tom did something to me and one thing led to another.... If I got ready to throw something away, I'd just throw it in Tom's yard." In later years, Tom's yard was quite convenient. His office was right across the street from the RCA offices on 17th Avenue South (now Music Square West).

"I had a friend named Bobby Gropp who worked at RCA, and he had to change all the commode lids in one of the RCA buildings. He changed them all and hung the old ones in Tom's trees over there. One time we had a bathtub, and rather than throwin' it away, me and Bobby went to this cement place out in Brentwood and told the guy we had a gag, would he fill the tub up with cement? We took a stick and stuck it in the cement, hung a bucket on it and took two tennis shoes and stuck 'em in it, and drove around town for about an hour lettin' the cement set. Got a flyin' start over here at Tom's and hit the brake, and the tub dropped *pow!* right at his front door. I don't know how Tom ever got it up."

Collins must have finally had enough. "One day he went and got a pickup truck full of manure and threw it in front of RCA. It had a stake in it that said 'Jerry Bradley's office' or something. Me and Connie [Bradley's wife, head of ASCAP in Nashville] had taken an RCA guy from Sweden to dinner. We were drivin' him down the row showin' him where RCA was, and I did a double take. I put the car in reverse and backed it up and I said, 'Damn, I can't believe this.'

"I rode to the back of the studio [RCA's Studio B] and I saw Tom's car back there, he was doin' a session. I told Connie, 'You take our guest back to the hotel. Meanwhile, I went over to Forest Hills and I called my friend Bobby Gropp and said, 'Bobby, get me some shovels and your pickup truck and come on down here. Then I called another friend of mine and had him call a policeman friend of mine named Carl Dollarhide. It was about eleven o'clock and he'd got off from work. I said, 'Tom Collins is cuttin' Steve Wariner in the studio and I want you to go in there and tell him he's under arrest.'

"So he went in there and the session's goin' on.'

"'Mr. Collins?'

"'Yeah, I'm Mr, Collins.'

"'I've gotta take you downtown for vandalizing property.' And you know how Tom laughs at everything. *Hahahaha.'*

"Carl didn't crack a smile. He said, 'I've got a warrant, you're gonna have to go down to the judge.'

"'Let me call my lawyer.' So he calls Dick Frank, it's about 11:30 by that time, and Dick was asleep. Dick tried to explain to the policeman that everything would be all right, and we all was just friends, and Carl said, 'Mr. Frank, I appreciate you're a lawyer, sir, but this man's going down to jail with me and he's goin' before the judge.' So he took him with him and when he did, I got in my car and followed. Dollarhide pulled in by Universal Tire [on Demonbreun Street, just a few blocks down from Music Row] there just to wait, and I pulled up next to him. So we're all parked in front of Universal Tire, and I pull up next to Carl's car and I say, 'Tom, what the hell are you doin' down here?'

"'Ohh, you sonofabitch! You this-that!'

"'Come on, get in my car, I'll take you back to the office.' If he'd a got in my car I was gonna take him to Chattanooga. But he wouldn't get in my car. So Dollarhide took him back to the studio. The session was ruined because Conrad [David Conrad, Tom's assistant] and all the musicians, they jump in the car, go downtown to get Tom out of jail. Well, he never made it to jail. Meantime, me and Bobby Gropp have taken the hubcaps off Tom's Mercedes.

"So Tom, he's all distressed and he goes home, everybody goes home. Me and Bobby get his pickup truck, back it up to RCA, shovel all the stuff into the pickup, take it down to Tom's office [the old one, several blocks away on 16th], back up over the sidewalk. It's about two o'clock in the morning by now and there's a bunch of homeless guys or guys on the move in this old building, and they're on the front porch next door hollerin', 'Whatch'all doin'?'

"'Aw, we're just playin' a joke on somebody, he had all this delivered to our place and we're throwin' it on his porch.' And they yelled, 'All right!' We said, 'Y'all got anything up there you wanna throw away?'

"'Yeah, old Bernie moved out the other day—he ain't comin' back. We'll get his stuff,' and they went and got this guy's stuff and we had it hangin' on nails all over the front. I got home about three o'clock in the mornin'.

"I woke up and turned Gerry House on." Gerry House is a talented radio personality and songwriter. For many years he has kept Nashville country listeners and Music Row workers in stitches with his hip morning commentary.

"House is sayin', 'There's a traffic jam on Music Row, on 16th Avenue South, seems as though somebody has taken a load of manure and threw it on Tom Collins's front steps.'

"All right, that got my adrenaline goin'. I got up and I drive down around there, and then to work. Tom finally winds up down there about noon; he can't get in the front door because the manure's all up there, he had to go in the back door. He called me and said, 'Where are my hubcaps?' I said, 'They're in the bottom of the manure!'"

There must be a dozen versions of how the "outlaw movement" got started, and no doubt they're all true in their own fashion. Here is Jerry Bradley's version.

By the mid-'70s, the term "outlaw" was floating around the country culture. Many say it was first used by Hazel Smith, a Nashville publicist and journalist blessed with the gift of creativity.

But the outlaw movement itself was kicked off with the release of the RCA album *Wanted! The Outlaws* in 1976.

"We weren't selling but about 150,000 albums on Waylon," says Bradley. "Me and Joe [RCA executive Joe Galante] would have meetings— we couldn't bust 250,000. Three hundred thousand albums, maybe."

Sales figures of 150,000–300,000 were not bad in country in the mid-'70s, but country was on the upswing, and some country artists that had not sold on RCA were doing considerably better on other labels. "Willie Nelson had sold millions on CBS. Jessi Colter had sold a million on Capitol. We had a meeting, and I'm sittin' there thinkin' that all these people had back catalog on RCA." Bradley called the RCA office in New York to find out if he had the legal authority to put out a compilation album using old catalog material.

"Yeah. I didn't need nobody's permission, I don't have to ask Willie, I don't have to ask Jessi, I don't have to ask anybody. Neil Reshen [Waylon's manager] comes in, I sit there with Neil, and I said, 'Neil, we're gonna put an album out. It's gonna be Waylon, Jessi, and Willie. I'm gonna call it *The Outlaws.*

"'You can't do that.'

"I said, 'I can do that.' This is the conversation—'What kind of money'd y'all make last year, three million?'

"'Yeah.'

"I said, 'Guess what, I made fifty thousand. I put this album out, it sells 250,000, I'm a hero, and I get my job one more year. That's what's in it for me. We got the right to put it out. The sonofabitch is comin' out.'

"I'll get back to you," Reshen tells Bradley, not sweetly, and he goes back to New York. "He could talk to whoever he wanted to. I done checked the traps to find out if I could do it, so he called and he said, 'Uhmm, uhh, Waylon wants you to do one thing, he wants you to put Tompall Glaser in there.'

"'Ah, Hell, I don't wanna put Tompall in there,' and he said, 'Well....' Whatever Reshen said or didn't say must have been persuasive.

"I said, 'You know what? I'll put him in there.' I said, 'It's all a compromise anyhow, and if that'll make Waylon happy....'"

What inspired Bradley to put this album together? "Hell, to keep my job! They *were* a bunch of outlaws, and they were bookin' out as *outlaws.* They were getting' everybody pissed off everywhere they went—I didn't know there was another group called the Outlaws.

"I go down to my friend Herb Burnette [album cover designer]. I had Time-Life books of the Old West, I took a Time-Life book over to Herb, flipped a page up, I said I wanted an outlaw poster and I wanna put Waylon's picture bigger...." After Burnette created the design, Bradley took it over to Waylon's office. "Waylon looked at it. He started passin' it around the room. I didn't go over there to get fourteen different people's opinion, I went over there for him to look at it, and he's passin' it around the room, and there ain't no way fourteen people are gonna like it....

"He sees me glowin' red—I'm sure I'm about on fire—and he goes down to about the third person. I said, 'Give me that back!' He says, 'Your idea. Whatever you like, do it.' I said, 'Thank you, have a good day,' and I left. Never got anybody else's approval. But Tompall wouldn't give me the contract back...."

The deadline for manufacturing the album cover was getting close. "Back then, you're doin' album covers, you have to be way out front. So I call Tompall and I said, 'Tompall, this is Bradley.' I said, 'I got an album cover over here with your picture on it, and one without. And if you don't get that contract over to me in ten minutes, I'm sendin' the one without to New York. In about six minutes, he's knockin' on the door—'Here it is, here it is, hoss. Didn't mean to make you mad.' I didn't really have the one without his picture—I could have got it—but that's the length you had to go to deal with *The Outlaws.*"

Wanted: The Outlaws became country's first album to be certified platinum. It ushered in new, higher expectations for country music.

Bradley says he was determined not to put out another "outlaw" album, but he and Waylon did agree that there should be a "Waylon and Willie" album, and both Bradley and Waylon were excited about another Western-motif cover concept.

RCA still had some old Willie sessions in the can. "We got the right to put the Willie tapes out," Bradley told Waylon. "We don't have to call nobody. You go down and you sing with [the tapes of] Willie, we can make a duet, and we can go.

"So he went over to the studio, he got the Willie tapes out, and he tried to sing with them. Next day he called me back and he said, 'Hoss, it just don't work. I can't sing harmony with him—he's gotta sing with me.' Neil Reshen called me a week later or so and said, 'Waylon told me about that album cover. What would you say if I could get CBS to let Willie cut three duets with Waylon?'

"I said, 'That'd be great.'

"'Well, CBS wants the right to re-record ten songs of Willie's that're on RCA.'

"I said, 'What ten songs are they?' and he named them. I called up New York and asked, 'When does Willie have the right to re-record those songs?'" The answer was in about three months. "So I called Neil back and said, 'I'll tell you what, I'll let 'em re-record those songs they want to do, if they let Waylon and Willie record the three new songs.'

"They never looked at any contract to see when Willie could re-record 'em, so they traded me three duets for ten songs they could have re-recorded within three months anyway."

But wait. There's more. "So Waylon goes and records three duets with Willie, and he brings 'em in and plays them for me. They're all *inside* songs—drugs and stuff—and when he got through he said, 'Hoss, you don't act like you're excited.'

"I said, 'Well, Waylon, we might sell half-a-million of them, but I just don't have the single and I can't lie to you about it. I'm sittin' behind the desk and he's standin' just a little ways away and he said, 'What about this one?' He starts singin' 'Mamas Don't Let Your Babies Grow Up to Be Cowboys.' And I got up from behind the desk and I grabbed him and I said, 'Go cut this song, this is a damned hit, go cut this song, can you do it tonight?'

"'Yeah, we can do it tonight.'

"'I'm tellin' you, Waylon, this is the song. And by the way, shred one of those other songs, 'cause you've only got the right to do three.'

"Mamas Don't Let Your Babies Grow Up to Be Cowboys" became one of the biggest hits of 1978 and a signature song of the outlaw era.

It was during the Bradley era that Dolly Parton became a pop star—an emotional turn of events for many country fans, who historically have felt betrayed when their artists moved into other genres. For instance, when Eddy Arnold and Ray Price exchanged their country images for tuxedos and orchestras, many of their fans took it personally.

In Dolly's case, the feelings of rejection by her fans may have been even more painful, because Dolly had such a strong country-girl image. She was the real thing. But she wanted to expand her musical reach, and not only was she successful at going pop, but when she wanted to come back to country, she did that, too, effortlessly.

Much has been written about Dolly's "Star Is Born" split with her mentor, Porter Wagoner, but then maybe, not enough. Here is Jerry Bradley's point of view.

"It was after Fan Fair '74 or '75," says Bradley, speaking of the annual CMA festival in Nashville. "She called me and said, 'Porter's goin' fishin', would you have a meeting with me?'

"She came over. I sat here, she sat over there, crossed her legs. She was just bubblin', sayin', 'I really need to get away, I got ideas and I wanna do this, I wanna do that....' My secretary rings in, says, 'Porter's here, he's on his way up here.'

"I said, 'Dolly, Porter's here. He's on his way up here.' Suddenly she looked like a different person. The door flew open, Porter came in, and he said, 'What the hell are you doin' up here?' went over and grabbed her like she was a little girl. I'm sittin' there and I said, 'I beg your pardon, she's an artist signed to me. I can talk to her any time I want to.' Anyhow, we have that conversation and he grabs her and takes her out.

"Chet calls down and says, 'Dolly and Porter want a meetin' with us in the morning at nine o'clock.' I said, 'Fine, let me tell you what happened.'

"The next morning about ten minutes to nine, Dolly called me. She said, 'Jerry, this is Dolly. Everything I'm gonna say is a lie. Bye.'

"Hmm.... So I called Chet and I said, 'Okay, here's the call I got.' Then they come in, and we all go upstairs, and Dolly says how much she loves Porter and if we all need anything, we should call him—exactly the opposite of where the other meeting was going. We said, 'Fine, have a good day,' and they left.

"Several months later, Mel Ilberman called me and says, 'I got a meeting with Sandy Gallin [a well-connected talent manager] and Dolly here in New York, you know what that's about?' I told him what I knew—nobody ever talked to me about anything." Not long after the New York meeting, Bradley recalls, "Dolly was coming in to a national convention for us at Opryland Hotel. Porter walks in with a lawyer and they're sitting there and I figure that I better tell Dolly that Porter's there because this was when things were real rough, so I go up to see her and Carl Dollarhide, the policeman, is up there taking care of Dolly at the time. I told Dolly, 'Appreciate your comin' and all, but Porter's downstairs.'

"She said, 'I can't go down there,' and she wouldn't go. And she said, 'He doesn't like you, either. He thinks you started all of this.'

"That was pretty much it for me and them, but time has probably taken care of these relationships. She seems to love him, and I love everybody. Once she got hooked up with Sandy Gallin—I kinda let Joe Galante run with Dolly's career, as I ran with Waylon's career. He could put up with the Sandy Gallins. And then, for the CMA show and bringin' her back to make an appearance in country and keeping those roots there, I was on the CMA board and I'd have discussions with Joe. I really never worked with Sandy or the L.A. people. Joe did, and he did a good job of it, milkin' it and makin' it last as long as it did, but I was probably too dumb.

"We knew how important it was [that she not lose her country core audience]. I think Sandy and everybody out there would have liked her to quit doing country stuff, but deep down, Dolly wanted those appearances, and if Joe wanted them, we just talked to Dolly. Our philosophy was the artist is signed with us, not Sandy Gallin or any manager."

During this era, it would appear that Jerry Bradley, the son of Chet's friend Owen, has taken over a lot of responsibility at RCA. But what of Chet Atkins?

"It was about five o'clock in the afternoon one day when I walked into Chet's office. Chet was there and Waylon was there. Chet had just had a violent argument with Waylon about drugs and so forth. And Chet just right out of the blue said, 'You know what, Waylon? That ain't gonna matter 'cause I'm quittin' tomorrow.'

"I looked at him, and Waylon kinda got quiet and looked at him, and he said, 'Well, who's gonna run it?' And Chet looked at me and he said, 'He is.' Waylon said, 'Well, hell, I want off the label then.' I didn't say anything. So next day, I was recordin' somebody in the studio and I call [RCA president] Rocco Laginestra and I left word with his secretary that when Rocco comes in, you tell him to call me, *before* he calls Chet, 'cause he's gonna see a message to call Chet.

"About 2:30 Rocco called. I said, 'Have you talked to Chet?' Rocco said no. 'Chet wants to quit and I think he's serious.' And I went through the conversation with Waylon and all that.

"Rocco said, 'What do you think we oughta do?'

"I said, 'Well, he's like our Nipper [RCA's trademark dog], I don't wanna let him go. I think he's really serious, but he did tell me that he might stay on as a consultant if he had an office like the one that he has on the second floor, and just a little bit of a salary, but he didn't want to do the day by day anymore.

"So Rocco called him. At 3:30 the door opened to the studio where I was mixin' a session." It was Chet. "I said, 'What happened?' He said, 'Well, I talked to Rocco, I'm gonna be a consultant and they're gonna build me another office upstairs just like the one I got.' And I said, 'Well, that's what you wanted, wasn't it?' and he said, 'Yeah.' Chet never knew the whole story to the day he died, I never did tell him."

So Chet moved upstairs. Perhaps he envisioned himself with an office and an opportunity to do a project or two without the pressures of outlaws and corporate goals. He still had his career as an award-winning, revered guitarist.

"But instrumentals weren't as popular," says Bradley. "Promotion, sales—everybody begins to take you for granted, and he wasn't really happy. Chet had a way of callin' you. 'Why don't you come on up?' He might ask you ten thousand questions, but he only had one that he really wanted the answer to. I would go up and he'd talk and talk and then one day he told me, said, 'You know I'd really like to leave....'

"And I said, 'Well Chet I've been tellin' everybody that you're the 'Nipper of Country Music' and you're very important to us. Let me leave it with you this way: if you really wanna leave, I'll help you get that accomplished, but I don't want you to tell me you want to leave today. I want you to go home, I want you to think about what you're gettin' ready to do.'"

Months went by, then came the call. "'Jerry, you come up?'

"I went up there. He said, 'I really wanna leave.'"

And he did.

Bradley's turn to go came in the early '80s. "Everything was going great," he recalls. Great country stars like Charley Pride, Dolly Parton, Waylon Jennings, Ronnie Milsap, and Alabama had kept RCA at the top of the industry year after year, but as country got bigger, the corporate world was closing in on Music Row, putting a lid on the freewheeling culture that nurtured the world of Chet Atkins, the Bradleys, Billy Sherrill, Jack Clement, and the others who had built Music Row by going with their gut, knowing that there was always another day.

"I must have had ten or twelve different bosses," Bradley recalls. "You'd fly up to New York and eat lunch and," he adds with touching sadness, "I wasn't having a good time."

"I was at a meeting [in New York]. Jack Crago—he was one of my bosses—was there. They had rhythm and blues, pop, they had everybody in there, and they were tryin' to put together a budget."

By the early 1980s, the Outlaw movement and the Urban Cowboy era had kind of burned out, and although Alabama was red-hot, country's next big trend had not yet arrived. "I kept tellin' them that this year, country was gonna be flat, and they kept tellin' me how it was gonna grow. I was sittin' there and they kept on and on, and I'm just sittin' there, and finally they said, 'Well, what are you gonna do in March?' And Crago chimed in, 'We're gonna sign a new act.'

"'And how many is it gonna sell?'"

"'Gonna sell a million.' He didn't know who it was gonna be, he was answering the questions for me.

"So then we went on, talked about somethin' else and somethin' else. He probably put in six or eight million dollars worth of stuff we were gonna do, and when he got through, I just reached over and patted him on the knee and said, 'Buddy, I wanna wish you luck.'

"I came back to Nashville and decided that I was gonna leave. I just didn't like it anymore. I didn't like flyin' to lunch. Anyhow, I had ten or twelve bosses, and I had some good ones—Ken Glancy, Mel Ilberman, Bob Summer—but it was like you weren't appreciated. In fact, I had one guy, he called me and he started lyin' to me and carryin' on, and I said, 'Now where do you want me to send these bricks?'

"He said, 'What bricks?'

"I said, 'You're tearin' the foundation right out from what we're tryin' to build down here.' He hung up in my face. I figured he was gonna fire me. It was just a whole bunch of corporate BS and I got tired of it. I had a year left on my contract. So I called them and told them that I'd had enough, that I wanted to move on, and they sent down a guy called Paul Altman."

Altman sat down with Bradley and tried to figure out what kinds of perks Jerry would demand for leaving his position. He thought Bradley wanted a label of his own to run.

"'No, I'm gonna go over to that little building behind Studio B,' which is the little carriage house where my office was," said Bradley. "'I'm gonna go over there and I'm gonna find me an act and I'm gonna come over here and run him up y'all's asses like everybody else in town does.'"

So they discussed the idea of Bradley being paid to find acts for the label, a sort of "talent scout."

"So I called my accountant, Joe Kraft, and I said, 'Joe, I need you to call New York, RCA wants to give me—at that time it was about $375,000—a year to be their consultant.'

"He says, 'Why?'

"I said, 'I don't know why. The guy just came down here, told me this was what he wanted to do.' And I took it to heart. I had to give them a picture, a bio, and a tape of each act. I had to give 'em three a year, and they paid me $375,000 a year for three years to do that.

"Well, nothin' ever happened. I'd take one over to RCA. If I gave it to them at lunch, by the time I got back from lunch it was on my desk, they'd passed."

Bradley's guru still was Mel Ilberman, who had been one of his good New York bosses at RCA for many years and now was working for CBS, running their publishing. "I called Mel and I said, 'Mel, I'm really frustrated.'

"He said, 'Send me a copy of your contract.' So I sent it up there and he said, 'Jerry, they just wanted to buy you out of the marketplace for three years. Don't be upset, just do what it says, they'll do what they say, and have a good time.' Hearing it from him, I didn't have a problem digesting it." And so Jerry Bradley, the second generation of Bradleys to make it big on Music Row, passed from the major label scene.

The music business is a very strange business. Bob Johnston, the ultimate Music Row outsider, and Jerry Bradley, the anointed Music Row insider, experienced the same frustrations when it came to dealing with music executives higher up the food chain.

But Bradley was not through with Music Row, not by a long shot. Soon after Bradley left RCA, a company called the Gaylord Broadcasting Company bought Acuff-Rose. He was tapped to head Acuff-Rose, along with a brand-new record company called 16th Avenue. The record company had limited success. Bradley's Acuff-Rose tenure was another story. Before its sale to Sony in 2002, Bradley and his protégé Troy Tomlinson had returned Acuff-Rose to its former glory as one of the top music publishing companies in Nashville.

NASHVILLE, BEFORE AND AFTER BOWEN

I n 1977, the same year that the Kendalls and Ovation Records proved that people will buy a great record no matter who puts it out, Jimmy Bowen arrived in Nashville. There were no brass bands to greet him. He didn't even have a job.

But Bowen had something few on Music Row had—wild success on the West Coast and powerful friends in the offices of the major labels there. With the help of those friendships, a strong knowledge of how record labels work, and supreme confidence, he single-handedly changed the face of Music Row. The history of modern country music is now divided into two separate eras, B.B. and A.B.: *Before Bowen* and *After Bowen*.

Jimmy Bowen was born in 1937 in Santa Rita, New Mexico, and grew up in Dumas, Texas. At the age of eighteen, he played bass for the Rhythm Orchids, a band that boasted two lead singers, Bowen and Buddy Knox. Knox had a huge pop hit in 1957 with "Party Doll," and Bowen had a moderate hit with "I'm Stickin' with You." In the '60s, he made a name for himself with the Reprise label, bringing Dean Martin back with "Everybody Loves Somebody Sometime," and producing fifteen gold albums for the revived Rat Packer. He was also responsible for Sinatra's Reprise classics "Strangers in the Night" and "That's Life." During his nearly two decades in California, he got to know many of the men who controlled the labels there.

When Bowen moved to Nashville, country had barely grown to the point that West Coast executives felt that it was just too big to be run by *hillbillies*. MCA had kicked Owen Bradley into retirement, and for a time virtually controlled the country A&R department from L.A. And then, suddenly, one of their own had actually *moved* to Tennessee.

Bowen lives in Arizona now, but there will be rumors about Bowen coming back to Nashville until the day he dies. "I'm not startin' those!" he protests with a laugh. It is a well-known fact that he would plant rumors in the trade magazines about things he was or was not going to do, just to keep the pot boiling.

"Any time I was changing labels," he said, "I always started the rumors because I wanted to be in control of them, you know? Music Row is good at spreadin' rumors, but they're not worth a shit at comin' up with them. If you give 'em the right rumor, it's really marvelous how quick it moves."

When asked if he would ever be coming back to Nashville, he says, "Well, I don't know, usually, when I leave somewhere, I pretty well leave it. I'm doin' a Merle Haggard album while in retirement," he concedes. "It's like the mafia...it's kinda hard to get out."

In the B.B. era, Music Row was a place where busy producers and musicians had a lot of fun making lots of records pretty much on the cheap. Promotion, too, was on the cheap, and very often records made money on relatively small sales because they cost so little to make. Bowen changed that model, probably forever.

"Before I went to Nashville the [country] music business was in its infancy. There was only about 250 or 300 country radio stations. Country record sales were so small that everybody involved had to be involved in everything to make any real money—everybody owned their own studios, the producers had their own publishing companies. It was an unhealthy atmosphere for growth because everything was too clamped down, the artists were completely controlled and surrounded.

"One of the things that we did, those of us who moved there in the late '70s, we started to free that up and spread it out. In order for Nashville to grow, the studios had to be in competition with each other, so that they would have to bring in all the new technology and get in on the cutting edge of the technical side of the business.

"You had to find people of a like mind. Glenn Meadows [of Masterfonics Studios] was. He believed that Nashville could catch up with everybody else technically. Also the people at Sound Stage and Emerald. Before we started to make the change, the dollars in country music were so small that the studios couldn't buy all the latest gear, like the New York and L.A. studios. They'd sell a hundred thousand albums, they'd throw a party. And where I came from in pop music, a hundred thousand albums, even then, was looked down on as a failure. So everything had to be changed to sell *millions*."

With all the success he'd been having in L.A., what made him come to Nashville in the first place?'

"When I was doing Martin, Sinatra, all those sessions with fifty-piece orchestras, it was great fun, of course. And then when the heavy metal came in, and the groups took over, I just didn't have the patience to sit in the studio for two months to get an eight-bar intro. I wanted to go in and cut songs. I said, 'This isn't gonna work for me, so what do I do?'

"I went to Nashville and visited, I looked at it, and I looked at Seattle, Santa Fe, and in doing that process I realized that there were millions of people in America who no longer had a music to listen to. They were no longer in their teens and early twenties, and they weren't gonna connect with what was coming in, And I said, 'My God, Nashville, it's an adult music. If it's modernized, if it has a cutting edge again, then I think you could sell millions down there.' As I was lookin' around and thinkin' what to do with my life, I saw that, plus it already had a young industry there, and a lot of talented people. The songwriting thing in Nashville always intrigued me, 'cause nowhere else did that exist except in New York City, in the Brill Building, and a couple of other places in the '50s and '40s.

"Nashville had all the things necessary to pull this thing off. And it had a half-a-dozen people there that I had known for fifteen, twenty years that I thought were bright, intelligent people, that I believed would participate and help make the changes. Frances Preston [at BMI], what a bright, intelligent person she was, and of course still is. Old Bob Beckham, he knew there was a world outside of country music. I just felt that this whole thing could happen if the music gets on the right path. It's so strong, you can't stop it once you get it started in the right way. That's how rock 'n' roll took over.

"L.A. and New York always looked at Nashville as *hillbillies*—they don't know anything about business, they don't know what the hell they're doin'. When I went down there the first time, Mike Maitland was runnin' MCA in L.A., then at Elektra it was Joe Smith and Steve Wax, and then Warner Bros. was Moe Ostin, and back at MCA it was Irving Azoff, and Joe Smith again at Capitol. So in each case it was people I had grown up with, I had worked with, that I had a one-on-one relationship with. What I explained to all of them was that we can make great profits down here, but you're gonna have to let me do it 'cause you don't know how. They thought they knew what to do in Nashville from L.A. and New York, and of course that doesn't work.... Each one of them said *do it!*

"I remember Joe Smith said, 'Do you need me to come down for this? Do you need me to come down for that?' and I said, 'Well, *hell no*, I don't need you, stay out there!'

"He said, 'Why?' and I said, 'I don't need you comin' here and showing these people I'm not the boss.' You know, *leave me alone.*"

Bowen was hired to run MCA, but he only stayed there for a short time before he moved on to Elektra. Such quick job-jumping was a mystery in Music City, and made people wonder what was up with Bowen.

"I was only at MCA about three months. Mike Maitland had come on down for CMA week, and Mike had really started to show the signs of Alzheimer's. Back then, very few of us knew what the hell it was. It really got bad, and rather than dealing with it in a gentlemanly way, they gave him an office out there with no windows, to end it, because obviously he couldn't run the company. I thought that was cruel, and I just said I don't wanna be around these people. About two days later, Steve Wax and Joe Smith called me for the Elektra thing.

"Running a record company, I never cared for that," says Bowen. "It was just something I had to do. The studio is what I loved. I did enjoy the initial stages of putting together a company, and I always tried to put together a good record company, and tried to mix and match people based on who was available. So if I said to an artist, 'I want you to be with us,' I could honestly say, 'These people will take good care of your music.' But once I got it goin' and rollin', I hardly ever went to the office. I was in the studio. I'd go by once a week maybe for staff meetings. If you had people that did everything real good, there's no need for me to be there. It got to that point where it was really a good machine and it knew what it was doing, and that coupled with the fact of the overall growth of Nashville and the whole country music business, to fix another session was better for the overall picture, and more fun for me.

"You notice when I left Elektra, which became Warner Bros., I left the crew I put together. I never took key people, because the artists that I put there, I'd be hurtin' *them*. So I always left the labels intact. If you look at that Warner operation, it's been there for years, the MCA operation was there for years. I'm kinda proud of those things, and it was fun to put them together."

When he came to a label and hired a new staff, Bowen would sequester his key people for the first thirty days. "We'd have lunch in, dinner in, whatever it took, until they were a *team*. For some people, it took longer.

"I had to bring a lot of people from out of town. There were never really labels in Nashville until we started all this. They were just outposts, they were branches, they were country *divisions*. They were not in charge of their own marketing dollars."

When Bowen left Nashville in 1995, he left scores of people in place at record companies all over Music Row and out on West End Avenue, where he had relocated Capitol Records in order to break up what he thought could be an incestuous environment.

After he left Nashville he moved to Hawaii, and spent time recuperating from a thyroid malignancy and playing a lot of golf. "I didn't keep any interest in the business side," he says, "about who's the biggest and who's selling what—just the music side. And friends—I had half-a-dozen people who were real friends of mine, and I always kept contact with them. The reason I moved to Hawaii was, you can't just *kinda* quit the music business, you know. You just have to get so damned far away that it leaves *you*. Somebody's always tryin' to draw you back in to do something. So while I was in Hawaii, people like Herky Williams [of ASCAP] would come over and play golf, and I kept in contact that way. I lived six and a half years in Hawaii and never listened to country music, 'cause they didn't have any over there. And then I moved to Arizona, and I tried to listen for a while, and quite honestly, it bored me. I heard the same fifteen records over and over. Commercial radio today, I'm sittin', listenin' for thirty minutes; they've told me who they are twenty times, you know, with their little jingles; they told what time it is thirty times. They tell me what the temperature is, they tell me everything except the name of the artist and the name of the song. The music's just filler between their commercials, and if they don't be careful, just like cable did to television, satellite radio's gonna just knock the shit out of all of them! That's all I listen to now, satellite radio, because they play what I wanna hear.

"About a year ago, when I decided to do this Haggard album, then of course I had to start listenin' to country radio every time I'm in the car. I'm watchin' CMT, tryin' to see in ten years where it went technically, what it's done musically, where is it? I got an infusion of where it is in the last seven or eight months, and there's a few acts I like. My favorite kid out there is Toby Keith—he reminds me of the Hank Williams Jr. era [Bowen produced many of Hank Jr.'s most successful albums], when you had a relatively free spirit doing his music. And I've always liked Shania.

"I've only seen one video on Big and Rich, and it's kinda like a rock-bar band with country influence. But at least it's not that same thing over and over and over and over and over. You look at the whole country setup, and so few are sellin' a lot of product, and I think it's because it's made *on purpose*, it's not really the artist's music.

"Country music got so powerful corporate-wise, and became so meaningful to the bottom line of these major corporations, and when that happens, the pressure gets on them to succeed. When you have a good year, they want seven percent more the next year, like you were raisin' wheat or buildin' apartments. And when that happens, it gets so tight, coupled with the fact that half the people in the business are gone now, because of economics. Everybody's making what they hear on the radio, and when you do that, the music stands still and just gets slicker and slicker, like you're spinnin' in a wet rut with your wheels."

Bowen inspired extreme emotions on Music Row. Musicians loved him because he paid his favorites double scale. Some of his subordinates loved him because of the excitement he brought to the label. Others hated him because of the pressure that came with that excitement. When he took over a new label, he could be merciless about cleaning house and bringing in his own people. Music Row before Bowen was a very civil place. Billy Sherrill, who himself had plenty of detractors on Music Row, sometimes hung on to a borderline act for a while because dropping the act from the label was too painful. Executives had kind words even while they were greasing the skids that would slide you out of your job and into oblivion.

There were many on the Row who could not help but be charmed by Bowen and enjoyed his company, but were very uneasy about the changes he brought. He loved the studio much more than an executive office, and he spent most of his working hours in front of a control-room console. It was not uncommon for him to be running one label and producing many of its acts, while also producing top acts for another label. And he recorded so many artists that his business was an enormous revenue stream to the studios of Nashville. That gave him the power to create change.

When Bowen was beginning to move and shake in Nashville, the recording industry was undergoing a technological revolution. The old traditional tape system, known as "analog," was being replaced by digital technology, and Bowen was fervent in his belief that digital was superior to analog. In those early days of the new technology, there was debate whether Bowen was on the right track.

While digital recording was crisp and decidedly devoid of tape hiss and distortion, some found early digital records to have a "cold" sound, as opposed to the "warm" sound of magnetic tape. Today, thanks to constantly improved technology, digital rules the day.

One of Nashville's leading studio men in Nashville when Bowen came to town was Glenn Meadows, who ran Masterfonics, just across Music Circle from Columbia Records and the Quonset Hut. Masterfonics was best known for its prowess in mastering, that magical process that puts the final polish on mixed recording tracks and makes them ready for the actual record. But Masterfonics also built great tracking rooms, the acoustically gorgeous rooms, where music is recorded.

Meadows came from Atlanta, where he worked at Sound Pit Studios for GRC Records, home of Sammy Johns, early Moe Bandy, and late Lonzo and Oscar.

"I got very frustrated with the music industry in Atlanta claiming it was gonna be the next big thing," says Meadows. "In '74, all of the major record labels had their investments in offices in Nashville. And since everybody was trekking to Nashville from Atlanta to do work, if I was gonna be successful in the industry, Nashville was the place I needed to be, not Atlanta.

"I moved to Nashville in March 1975 and started working for Masterfonics," says Glenn. "Mack Evans and a couple a local physicians were the partners in the company. Masterfonics was a pioneering, independent mastering facility in Nashville. Most of the mastering at that time was done by the majors. CBS had their own mastering studios, RCA had their own mastering studios. Mack had been able to convince Commerce Union to invest the exorbitant sum of $100,000 in a Neumann mastering system.

"We had the same quality gear and capabilities as Sterling, Masterdisk [in New York], and the Mastering Lab on the West Coast, and we were competing for those products. We never attracted a lot of business from outside of Nashville, but I did a lot of the mastering on the pop product that came out of Nashville—Dan Fogelberg, all of Norbert Putnam's work, Jimmy Buffett, England Dan and John Ford Coley, Lynyrd Skynyrd, a couple of projects on the Allman Brothers, so it covered a wide swath of stuff. The bulk of the work was country, there's no two ways about that. There was a point in time when the facility and myself had done fifty-four of the Top 100 singles on the *Billboard* country charts."

Meadows believed that middle Tennessee had the capacity to do a whole lot more.

"I think part of the stigma of this town was created by the moniker that RCA put on their records—'The Nashville Sound.' For example, Lee Hazen had a studio out in Hendersonville called 'Studio by the Pond.' Dr. Hook recorded out there. Kyle Lehning did all of his early work out there on Dan Seals, and England Dan and John Ford Coley, and the credits on the album said, 'Studio by the Pond, Hendersonville, Tennessee,' not Nashville. The key in many respects to getting credibility for the record was to remove the word 'Nashville.'

"It was all a matter of perception as to what was actually going on. Masterfonics built a reputation for doing high-quality work and good work for the money and we had a lotta business.

"I don't remember what year Bowen came to town, but I think the first project he ever did in Nashville was a mix for Mel Tillis, when Mel was on Elektra. He came in and kinda started to shake things up in the way he wanted to work. He brought a lot of the West Coast style and ethic, taking more time with the project to make the project better. I think the first record he made with Mel he got Mel to go back to the label and double the budget.

"As I understand it, a lot of the artist contracts at that time said, 'Whatever you don't spend on the record [out of their recording advance], you get as a check.' So the mentality was, *Let's get this done, let's get this over because I don't want to waste any money on it.* And so the quality of the records compared to the rest of the industry in the late '70s was really poor, from a sonic standpoint and a technical standpoint. One of the things that Mr. Bowen brought to town was, *Let's put the money into the music and make the records better so they'll sell more, so you'll make more money on the back side.* He was able to convince Mel to spend that kind of money on the record, and it was a resounding success."

According to Meadows, it was not until 1985 or so, after Warner Bros. had merged the Warner and Elektra operations under Bowen, that Bowen began his campaign to upgrade the studio facilities in Nashville. "We built the Masterfonics mix room in the summer of '86. That was when, if you remember, there were three, four studios under construction all at once. Emerald was rebuilding their Studio A and putting an SSL console in, Mike Poston was building 16th Avenue Sound, putting an SSL in. Sound Stage was building that Front Stage room for Bowen that had no wall in it, and they put an SSL in. Those three rooms—Emerald, Sound Stage, and the mix room at Masterfonics—were all Tom Hidley designs, and they were all brought up together and put on line under the promise of work from Bowen."

Tom Hidley is a world-renowned studio designer, and Nashville's wholesale use of Hidley and his people signaled the intent of these studios to follow Bowen's lead and make Nashville studios competitive with those in Los Angeles and New York.

"So Bowen basically came to me and Ron Kerr [at Sound Stage] and Dale Moore at Emerald and said, 'Look, I'm willing to book X number of days per year in your rooms at very reasonable rates, because I know you guys have to pay for this stuff, but I wanna have three compatible rooms that I can move projects between. I want them similarly equipped with a base style of outboard gear'—meaning a basic complement of gear so he could move from studio to studio and bring the mixes back up, and basically be where he was when he left off at the other studio.

"All three of us were working together to provide him the production facilities that he needed. He'd come in and he'd book us six, seven, eight months in advance. He probably booked between two hundred and two hundred and ten days a year at card rate. It was not like, *I want it on the cheap.* It was, *I'm gonna have the budgets to do this, I want a guaranteed day rate. You tell me what you need to continue in business, and if we agree on a number, that's the number you'll get for every session, be it one day, be it thirty days.*"

This was a tremendous boon for these studios in a business where payment of fees can be uncertain. While the major labels are generally reliable in their payments, many studios are forced to rely on independent and custom sessions from people who are slow, or no pay.

But not everybody loved Bowen, and rumors eventually began to circulate that Bowen dealt for this studio time then resold it to the labels—really the artists—at a higher rate, pocketing the difference. "If he was doing that," says Meadows, "it was unbeknownst to me, because our invoices went straight to MCA, and we got paid on that. We were criticized and accused of providing kickbacks, payoffs for the work, including all of the mastering. I mastered virtually every record that Bowen put out during the time he was here for all of those years, and I offered anybody a ten-thousand-dollar payment—and I would open my books for them to come in and do an audit, and see if there were any under-the-table payments or anything else going on. He was not a partner in the studio. He was not an owner. He was not on the board of directors. He was not anywhere. He was a client. We provided him good service and good-quality work, and he stuck with the people who did that for him.

"I tell people this when Bowen's name comes up. There have always been two camps—the people who understood what he was trying to do for the industry and bought into it, and there were those who despised what he was doing and were always attacking him. And there was a big canyon between the two, and you were on one side or the other. I knew very few people who were ambivalent about the subject of Jimmy Bowen and the way he ran the record labels, the way he dictated stuff.

"He had success. He sold a lot of records. He built a lot of people's careers in this town. He taught a lot of artists what goes on and how things should be done. He insisted that when he produced an artist, for at least the first two or three records, that they be involved in every phase of the project. They went around with Don Lanier and various other people to pick songs. They had the songs pitched to them. They would come back and sell Bowen on the songs *they* wanted to record and tell him *why*. So they're getting music that means something to them. They go in the studio, they were involved every day in the production. They were there for every day of the tracks, they were there for every day of the overdubs, they were involved in the mixing for at least the first two or three albums, so that they could learn what could be done and what couldn't be done. So somebody couldn't tell them, 'Oh, we can deal with that later, we can fix that later.' The artist would be able to say, 'No, I know you can't. Let's fix that now.' So Bowen was involved in educating artists because he felt that an educated artist was a better performer and a better artist.

"And look at the length of the careers of these people. Look at the length of the career of George Strait. Look at Hank Jr. Look at Reba. I don't know if he told you the story on Reba. When he first came to MCA, she was involved with another producer on a record. Bowen came in and wanted to hear what was goin' on. He sat and talked with her and she said, 'I'm really frustrated—they're not doing what the record needs to be, they're doin' this and doin' that....' He made a phone call to the producer and said, 'You're no longer producing the record.' He gave the record to her and said, 'Here, you go over to the studio over here—it was Ronnie Milsap's studio—you go to Milsap's. You have total control—do what you wanna do to the record.'"

Bowen was involved in an enormous amount of production, and sometimes it was almost in an "executive" capacity. "He had people on staff that oversaw a lot of the intermediate portions of the record. He was not there all the time on every session in every studio.

"He respected the abilities of his engineers. He gave them direction. *This is what I want.* He'd walk in when they're mixing or tracking, and kind of change the sound and tailor it in the direction he wanted it to go. So each artist had a unique sound. And once he had that direction set, he expected the engineer to keep it going in that direction. He would always take creative input from the engineers as to what they thought. He may accept it; he may say, 'No, that's not what I want, *here's* what I want.' And once you've done that, you've offered up your two bits—if he wants to go in another direction, that's the direction you'd go. You didn't fight him."

There is no question in Meadows's mind that Bowen revolutionized the industry in Nashville. "When he came to town there was no digital. It didn't exist in the market. CDs weren't even out."

Bowen was keeping abreast of technology through his friends in Los Angeles and other people he knew. "The first commercial country record that he did digitally, the first I was aware of that anybody had done, was a Tompall Glaser and the Glaser Brothers single that we mixed to a digital two-track that we rented from JVC and brought in from California. The difference in the sound that we captured versus going to analog two-track was amazing.

"Digital had the ability to capture what was coming out of the back of the console more accurately and freeze it in time. Analog tape tends to deteriorate, tends to get worse. Even in the first thirty minutes after it's recorded, it'll lose its sparkle and its luster. What some people would describe as the 'warmth' of analog recording, I'd describe that as more of the distortion of analog tape. It has its own distortion characteristics, its own overload characteristics, where if you drive the tape harder it gets fatter sounding, more muddy 'cause you're doing a little bit of self-erasure of the top end as you drive it too hard. In digital, it captures all of that up to the point it 'clips.' Digital is great up until you hit the zero point, and when you hit zero, it tends to distort real bad."

In the latter half of the '80s, as the studio quality in Nashville went way up, so did the sales of country records, leading the way to country's biggest boom. There were many reasons why country exploded in the '90s, but Glenn Meadows believes one of the main reasons was the music Bowen produced. He saw Bowen as a successor to Owen Bradley and Chet Atkins, changing the sound of country music to broaden its appeal.

"He was 'contemporizing' the music. Making it appeal to a wider audience, which spurred more sales. The music was more friendly to the ears. In many respects, it became like early '70s rock 'n' roll with a country flavor to it, with more acoustic guitars and steel guitar added, but it featured more of the drums, it featured a more up-front sound than a lot of the sparse, small-type productions that country had used for years and years. That in turn spurred a lot of other producers to get on the bandwagon.

"He started using mixed-in drum samples to fatten up the drum sound...stuff out of the Wendel drum machine and various other drum machines added to the actual acoustic drums that were recorded during the session. They spent a lot of time building up that layering of the drum sound. It was very poppish."

A great baseball pitcher once said, "I'd rather be lucky than good." Glenn Meadows was more good then lucky. In the early '90s, he built a large studio off Division Street called the Tracking Room, a versatile place that employed all the latest technology and knowledge and gave a producer multiple choices for sonic environment. But at least two other brand-new facilities, Ocean Way and Reba McEntire's studio, also came on line and with lots of cash behind them. "With the downturn in the industry in '94 and '95, the rate wars that got started, and if you can't charge what it costs to run the business, you run out of steam." Glenn Meadows had to fight to survive.

Today an ambitious studio wonk can take a computer-based setup like Pro Tools and create a decent-enough-sounding studio in his or her basement. Meadows is concerned that "if all of the great studios go away, there's not gonna be any place to record the stuff." He believes that a great acoustical sound requires large physical spaces.

"The question is always: Does great sound affect the consumers in what they buy and what they don't? Nobody knows the answer to that.

Nashville's motto is, 'It all starts with a song.' But part of what sells the song is the *emotion*. And the emotion is many times captured by the environment that the music's played in, mistakes and warts and all. What's happening right now is that every record we put out is perfect, and it becomes boring.

"From the top down has got to come the attitude, 'Just because we *can* doesn't mean we *should.*' Just because you can make a vocal perfect or you can tweak the timing of the track doesn't mean that you should. You know part of the magic that always inspires people on a live-tracking date is that *feel* that happens right then. And then within two weeks they've all forgotten that feel and we're into massive manipulation. They come on at full tilt, full blast, full level, as loud as can be on the intro, and they have nowhere to go but smaller."

"MAN, THERE'S ONLY THREE CHORDS!"

When John Travolta, formerly the poster child for disco, hit the big screen in 1980's *Urban Cowboy*, country music became an instant fad. Filmed in Gilley's in Pasadena, Texas, *Urban Cowboy* featured mechanical bulls, cowboy clothes, line dancing, and a slick country soundtrack that made temporary, Johnny-come-lately fans out of people who did not normally pay attention to country music.

When country music becomes a fad, Music Row gets a short-term financial benefit, but it pays a price. As the industry creates new stars and watches record sales climb, labels attempt to bottle their newfound success by finding more artists similar to those that are selling, and lots of songs just like the ones that have spurred sales. Creativity is replaced by formula. A few years after *Urban Cowboy*, many of the big country stars of the '70s were on the way down.

In 1984 came the crunch, underscored by an article written by Robert Palmer for the *New York Times*.

The "fabled Nashville Sound," he wrote, "...may soon sound as dated as the ukulele." He chronicled fading record sales, and stated, less than kindly, that the Nashville Sound had evolved in the 1950s when "many Nashville producers began to smother [the rhythm tracks] under sticky-sweet orchestral arrangements and mooing vocal choruses."

To be fair, Palmer also noted that new talent was arising from the ashes of the old, "new traditionalists" that might save country music, such as "Ricky Skaggs and George Strait, who are going back to the roots of country music and making simple, soulful records without the strings and vocal choruses and other commercial clutter so typical of today's Nashville Sound." But the national media that picked up on Palmer's piece—and many did—put enthusiastic emphasis on the coming death of country, and sometimes used graphics of weeping guitars and the like to underscore their point.

Naturally, Music Row set out to do something about the slump and the perceived "death of country."

One man who would be a force in the country resurgence was Bob Saporiti, a native-Bostonian-turned–San Francisco folksinger who came to Nashville as a record promotion man and would rise to a senior vice presidency at Warner Bros. Records.

Saporiti's office is a house on Villa Street that he refers to as his "Villa villa," located a block off Music Row. It is like a museum. Nearly every room is filled with items so diverse and unrelated that it's impossible to make sense of any of it. There are toys, clocks, old photographs, a busty manikin bust in military attire, musical instruments, and dozens of globes. And in the cacophony there is great charm and energy.

Saporiti strokes his gray beard as he talks about his folk influences: "Kingston Trio begat Peter, Paul and Mary, who begat Bob Dylan, who we then learned was really Woody Guthrie, and then all the rest...."

"Got turned on to country music thanks to watching Porter Wagoner, Jim Ed Brown, and all those people on Saturday night. They were like a half an hour apiece—they'd run 'em in blocks. Navy," he adds, simply, to say where he was when he was seeing all those shows.

After the Navy, he spent a short time in Los Angeles, followed by a decade in San Francisco, where he performed folk and jazz music and owned a small but productive recording studio. In the late '70s, he started coming to Nashville on a regular basis to do some production for a small West Coast label. When that label went out of business, "I sold my house, took my cat Bessie Smith, two guitars, some jeans, and my little Datsun B-210, and on August 8, 1980, [took the long route] to Nashville. It took me about two weeks."

He got a "non-job" in promotion in Hendersonville that gave him no money but provided him with an office, a phone, and the right to bring in his own work when he wasn't promoting the records of the company that had "hired" him. His job was to call radio stations that reported to the trade magazines and persuade enough of those stations to play the record—or at least *say* they were playing the record—to earn the record a slot on the country charts.

"In those days, it took about seven stations to chart a record in the Top 100," Saporiti remembers, "and that's all people really wanted 'cause a lot of the stuff was tax dodges back then. Doctors would get together and chip in a hundred thousand dollars apiece and get a record in the charts, and they'd each get a five-hundred-thousand-dollar write-off for a hundred-thousand-dollar investment. Meanwhile, my employer was gettin' rich. It ended with the IRS camping in his office for about a year, 'cause they just couldn't catch 'em. That was the tax dodge days, in the early '80s, before they closed the loophole.

"I still had an undying belief that I could make music myself as a producer, or at least be involved in good music as a promoter, so I started going to Music Row. I hit all the little independent record companies and I'd promote their records. One of my biggest breaks was a group called the Capitals on Ridgetop Records, Alice Raleigh's company." The record was called "A Little Ground in Texas," and Saporiti helped take the record to Top 10. To promote the record Saporiti gave out "little bags of dirt to the radio people. I got noticed by the major labels for that promotion, so I opened my own office in Hendersonville. My wife was my secretary. She didn't know anything—she was Vietnamese and grew up in Paris—she didn't even know who Willie Nelson was."

Saporiti soon had a thriving promotion business. "I'd always tell people the truth, whether I thought I could get stations to play their record or not. That turned out to be an unconscious gimmick, 'cause I was probably the only person actually doing that. I found that if I could say no, even though in the short run I didn't make as much money, in the long run I was able to cherry-pick the best music. My track record got really good 'cause everything I took on was successful."

Good record promoters learn how to talk to radio people. "I had fun with the radio people, I really worked at it like a science. I like people, I find people fascinating. As I learned my job, I consciously lost my Boston accent so I could communicate more directly with people and not put them off. It's my theory that when you go into a bank for a loan, wear a suit. Don't spend a half an hour trying to convince them you're a normal person in your leather outfit. I tried to get into their world as much as I could. I took copious notes about people's families. I had a dossier on every single radio guy. At the time, I think that there was only about seventy-five stations that reported to the trades. And I called every single one of them twice a week. So I was making 150 to 200 phone calls a week.

I started calling the East Coast at seven o'clock in the morning and I went across the country every day.

"Through conversation, I'd find out what they were into. If it was motorcycles or fly fishing or baseball, I'd make a little note, and I'd go to the library and I'd become an instant expert on whatever that was, and I'd subtly throw that into each conversation. I think the reason I did well with these people was I didn't bullshit 'em, I would tell them the truth. If a record wasn't going to happen, I'd let 'em know that. My line was, 'Listen, if you think this record is good for your market, then you play it, but I'm lettin' you know that nationally it's not happening and therefore the promotion's gonna be backed off. And if you wanna play that game and only play the hits, then this is not gonna be a hit.' And I would tell the client that I would tell them that—I mean, this was all totally up front."

Eventually he made enough money promoting independent records that he was able to buy a house in West Meade, one of the greenest sections of Nashville. "I made the garage into an office and was the first promotion man in Nashville to actually have a computer program that would dial the phone for me and put up the call letters of the station, the playlist, the whole thing. Kind of ironic, I don't even have a computer now. I was from California and I wore a fedora hat at the time, so my little logo was an old dial telephone with a hat on it. Around the end of '82, the major labels started bringing me on as an adjunct. At that time, the major labels didn't have regional staffs to speak of. They basically had two people in town, and then they would hire independents.

"So I finally got into that world. I worked for all the major labels. I remember working Kathy Mattea's 'Street Talk,' her first Top 10. It just kinda grew, and I started having as many records as I could actually promote honestly, 'cause there's only so much time in one phone call. During that time, I worked the Bellamy Brothers, David Allen Coe, the Kendalls. Dolly Parton records, Willie Nelson records. Crystal Gayle. I think we had five number-ones in a row with her.

"In '84, the world changed for the record labels. It was one of those payola times when they stopped allowing record labels to hire independent promoters for a little bit. So everyone's kind of panicking. And the labels didn't know what to do. So that's when they started beefin' up their regional staffs. They started cherry-picking the independent promoters, hiring them, and putting them in different parts of the country. That's when I was asked to come to Warner Bros. as the national promotion director.

"I started January 1, 1985. I just came to the right place at the right time. I started working with Neil Spielberg in the sales department. We started travelin' around, gettin' on planes, meetin' all the other Warner Bros. people. Now I had all this money to visit radio stations, and I was really into it 24/7. I did promotion for the label from '85 until '89, and during that period I was the *Billboard* Promotion Man of the Year three times in four years. I was the *Gavin* Promotion Man of the Year twice, I think.

"So we had great success. That first year when I got there, Bowen had left and Jim Ed Norman took over, and we took all these chances because Jim Ed was that kind of guy. I loved working with Jim Ed—he's a real music guy. Quality's the most important thing, he doesn't care about the game as much. We signed Randy Travis. We signed Dwight Yoakam. We signed the Forester Sisters. We signed Highway 101. We just went crazy, and went from a company that was losing money—the first year we were there, we made like, I think, a thousand dollars—the next year we made like forty-four million."

This sharp upswing in profits at Warner Bros. was just the opening act for the biggest boom in the history of country music. Martha Sharp, head of Warner's A&R, had asked Saporiti to see Randy Travis at the Nashville Palace. "I went in and I asked Lib [Hatcher, his manager] where he was, and she said, 'In the kitchen.' I went in the kitchen and here's this guy peelin' potatoes. I said, 'I'm here to see Randy Travis,' and he said, 'I'm Randy Travis.' I said, 'Well, Randy Travis the *entertainer*.' He goes, 'Well, as soon as I finish these spuds, I'm gonna go play.' So he played, blew me away of course, 'cause he was *Randy Travis*. Afterwards, he was back in the kitchen cleanin' the pots.

"You know the story," he says. Randy Travis's first year on Warner Bros. is the stuff of legend. "We went out with 'On the Other Hand,' and we were gettin' our ass kicked. However, where we could get it played, it was a smash. We knew we had a hit, and then when it got to sixty-seven on the charts, we lost the bullet. We could have gone back, we had enough substance for the people that would play it, but the rest of the people thought it was too country. Nick [Hunter, Saporiti's boss] decided to forget this record. So Nick and I and the gang came up with a strategy. We put out this other record called '1982' that was a little less stone country. And what we did was we parlayed our base, and we told all the stations that knew we had a hit on 'On the Other Hand.' They were pissed that we wouldn't keep working it, but we brought them into our plan.

"We said, 'Here's the deal, we're gonna put this record out, and we want you all to add it [to your playlists]—high up in the chart the first day, 'cause that momentum will get the other stations to go on it.' Our plan was to re-release 'On the Other Hand' later, and we told them that, too. So we took '1982' to number five, and as soon as that peaked, we put out 'On the Other Hand' again, and it became Song of the Year for two years in a row. It started Randy Travis's career, it made him a Hall of Famer, the whole thing. My tracking charts on those first three records are actually in the Hall of Fame.

"We had to do it that way because 'On the Other Hand' was too country. Everyone was trying to be hip, kinda like they are now. Why are they goin' to New York to have the fuckin' CMA Awards?

"In 1960, there were eighty-one country radio stations. By the mid-'80s, it got to over two thousand. Where did all those radio stations come from? A lot of them came from the adult-contemporary format. This was what I consider the second big wave of country radio growth. It started with Randy Travis—the 'new tradition,' which was a term that I invented personally, I can take credit for that. It was so funny: we were sitting around the old conference room, there was only eleven people at the office in those days, and suddenly there it was, *hello, duh,* 'the new tradition.' So all our advertising was *Randy Travis: The New Tradition,* and I'm very proud of that term because it's still here today. We actually had a poster made saying 'Warner Bros. Nashville, Home of the New Tradition.' We had Emmylou Harris, we had Hank Jr., we had the Forester Sisters, we had Southern Pacific, Dwight, and Randy, so it kind of fit our whole roster.

"The next wave was Alan Jackson, Travis Tritt, Clint Black. Then of course Garth came along in the '90s and totally changed everything 'cause it made it into a marketing game. We made a lot of money, but we lost our soul.

"I quit being a promotion man in 1990. I burned out on it. It's a young man's game. I was in my early to mid-forties and I'm thinking, you know, there's nothing sadder than an old promo guy calling up an old radio guy talking about the kids and really not into the job. To be a great promotion man, to be Promotion Man of the Year nationally, you have to have some fire in your belly. And I'd lost the fire, so I went to Jim Ed and said, 'Jim Ed, I don't wanna do this anymore. I quit.'

"He says, 'Well, I don't want you to quit. What do you want to do?'

"'I don't know. I think I've had it.'

"So he says, 'Well, why don't you take a year off and be our Warner Bros. public relations guy, between the industry and the city.' At the time, they were starting the 'Nashville 2000' campaign, and they were trying to get Music Row and the bankers together, trying to get flights to London at the airport, and they were making Nashville into the millennium city. I became head of marketing for that government committee that was being put together to market Nashville.

"This was 1990, it was like my year off... kinda. I was working for Warner Bros., but I was basically doing community service. Only Jim Ed would come up with something like this. He didn't want to lose me and I didn't know what I wanted to do. And we were making a fortune—at one time, we had seven platinum acts at the same time.

"The next year I said, 'Jim Ed, this charity stuff's not for me.' There's so much corruption in that, and having to go to these functions with people I don't even like, you know, this is not music. So I was gonna quit again.

"So he said, 'Well, what do you wanna do?' So I said, 'Well, I'll tell you what I would like to do. I'd like to open the first-ever international department by a major label in Nashville, Tennessee.' Every international department had always come out of either the L.A. or the New York office. I'd traveled a lot to Europe because my wife's from Paris, and my family on her side lives over there. I love traveling. I've been traveling overseas my whole life. I have a globe collection, you notice.

"I thought, 'Well, this is great. It was such virgin territory. I'd be the only one out there. And we had some real allies in England, a guy named Paul Conroy, who was a real country fan, and he put a lot of money into promoting Randy Travis.

"We had the brick building at 19th and Division Street, the old Sarah Crittenden Home for Unwed Mothers. I said to Jim Ed, 'Let me open up an international department here.'

"He said, 'Well, you can open up the department, Bob, but there's no office space available there.' So I said, 'Well, there's the third-floor bathroom, right in the front of the building. No one's in there. I took the sink out and put a desk in. In the shower, I put a little computer, and I hired a girl from Tokyo and put her in that shower. My motto was 'It's better to start off in the bathroom than to end up in the toilet.'

"From there, I just started getting on planes and traveling around the world, visiting the Warner Bros. offices, and trying to educate them about country music. The reason I wanted to open my own department and deal directly was the international department out of Los Angeles was supposed to handle it, but they didn't like country music. It was worse than not promoting it at all. They'd kinda make fun of it with the guys in England, and they'd all sit around and laugh at it, so nothing ever got done.

"I'd hear stuff like, 'Well, that was my father's music,' and I'd say, 'Well, it's *changed*.' So part of it was an education process—I'm tryin' to educate them to people like Faith Hill and Travis Tritt. I'm pitchin' all the more pop stuff. Dwight, certainly, Emmylou.... I had a blast, went to Australia, went to New Zealand, went to Brazil, all over the world, and did that exclusively for about three years. Then they called me back and made me senior VP of marketing for the whole company here *and* there. Eventually they made me general manager. That's when it started gettin' to be no fun.

In 1995, the company moved into a vast new building on 16th, or Music Square East, one block down from Music Row's ground zero, the old Quonset Hut. That was the first of a number of changes that left the company in the hands of suits.

"It used to be run by music guys. I mean, everybody at Warner's played an instrument, just about, and then the bean counters started comin' in. That's also when Time merged with Warner. And so it became more corporate. We used to be like a really wild record company. That's all we did. Warner Bros. was just music and movies and Bugs Bunny attitude, and it was great. Then corporate came in, and there was more checks and balances, and more corporation stuff.

"It's like bringing in a consultant to a restaurant who doesn't know anything about the restaurant business, and he looks at the salad bar, and he goes, 'Well, if we just get rid of the lettuce, we can save fifteen dollars.' If you're gonna bring in a consultant in the record business, bring in a record guy. But they don't, they bring in these guys who are *consultants*, which is really not a job.

"The music will never go away," he says, "because as much as a corporation can fuck it up, someone who is truly musical will come up with something so good it can't be denied. And it will find a way to get through to the kids, whether it's a band playing live or.... I've always told people that to be a great marketing person—all you need is to have great product.

"I've always gotten into these discussions with radio people, as they went on to consolidation and started using shorter playlists...all this research stuff. Research, by definition, is always *after* the fact. Music is an art form that is always ahead of the times. So by putting music into a world of research, it's like oil and water—it doesn't work. We're not selling corn flakes here, as Clive Davis once said."

Saporiti was always fascinated by the differences between the lives of local radio personalities and major label promotion people.

"Radio has all the power," he says, "and record companies have all the money. When you're in say Wichita, Kansas, you're taking that music director out to dinner, and you're stayin' in the suite, and you're orderin' hundred-dollar bottles of wine. This guy is makin' $12,000 a year and livin' in a mobile home. And he's a big shot in town. He's got all the power to play or not play your music. You have to know how to use your wealth to get him to use his power, and at the same time not flaunt your wealth. It's a tricky thing to get on an even level with him when you're makin' six figures and this guy's barely gettin' by. And yet you need him.

"And then, half the radio guys wanted to be in the record business. You know, they see a guy pull into town, flyin' in, he's got this expense account, and he takes 'em out, and they're talkin' records, and they go to these shows, and he takes 'em to a strip club, whatever. Actually, it's a pretty shitty life if you live it."

Saporiti's glamour days with Warner Bros. dwindled down to a precious few as the corporate world engulfed Music Row like a giant amoeba. "The Time Warner merger was one thing—things started gettin' funky. It really got bad when AOL merged with Time Warner. And as soon as they merged—like the next day—I found out through the newspaper that I didn't have a job. Well, I had one if I wanted one, because they couldn't *fire* me. What they did was—and I think that because AOL was a computer company, experience meant nothing to them—they came out right away and said, 'Okay, everyone over fifty, we're gonna offer early retirement.' Well, *wink-wink, nod-nod*, you didn't have to take it, because they couldn't fire everyone over fifty, they'd have a big age-discrimination lawsuit on their hands. I think there were forty-three people in the United States that were on this level—senior vice president, over fifty—and every single person took the package, because we all knew that if we stayed there, our lives would have been miserable. Because they didn't want us. They wanted their own people—youth and that stuff.

"That was 2001 when that happened, and it totally changed Warner Bros. It's not even owned by the same people anymore, they sold it. And if you look at the major labels now, there's very few of them—they've merged. There's hardly any companies left. Less people working in the major labels. Less slots on the radio. Less records. So it's changed dramatically. I'm glad I'm not part of that. I don't like that. It's not me. It wasn't fun anymore. It was miserable being at that label at the end: that last year, pins and needles, I spent most of my time going to New York going to corporate meetings where they'd hoodwink you, you know, Levin and those guys are sittin' in these meetings. Levin, the guy who was the head of Time Warner, and the other guy from AOL [Steve Case], these guys are in the ivory tower, talkin' about stuff that we have no idea about, buying and selling corporations. Meanwhile, just to keep us busy, they got us doin' all the synergy stuff—they got all the magazine people and the record people and the movie people in these rooms talkin' about how to work together and stuff like that—and they know they're gonna blow us all out. So they were just feedin' us steak and drinkin' champagne. You know, you're up in New York and you go to these meetings and you'd brainstorm, but it was like they were just keepin' you busy because *they had a bigger plan*. It had so little to do with music anymore. You couldn't sign an act that was cool. Unless it was gonna be Garth Brooks level, you couldn't make enough money. The overhead was out of control."

Music Row can transform talented people. This is the story of Kyle Lehning, a rock 'n' roll refugee turned studio broom-handler turned hit-making producer.

Kyle Lehning was born in the near South: Cairo, Illinois, where the Ohio River meets the Mississippi. He was one of the lucky few who found his calling early.

"I went into my first recording studio in Illinois in '67 with my high school rock 'n' roll band and fell in love with it," he says. "The smell of the studio, the look of it, the knobs, the buttons, the microphones—the whole thing." In '67, he started coming to Nashville carrying tapes of his band. "One thing led to another, just banging on doors. I was very lucky. I had a friend of the family whose name was Ray Butts, who was an engineer for RCA Records. He was a sort of a protégé of Chet Atkins, on the technical side. Ray had lived in Cairo, where he invented an amplifier with a built-in tape delay, called the Echosonic. Scotty Moore and Chet both played one.

"Chet convinced Ray to move to Nashville, and I brought Ray those tapes from Paducah, Kentucky, where we went into the studio, and he introduced me to Felton Jarvis and Billy Sherrill, who were both extremely kind to me. I was seventeen, maybe."

Lehning majored in music at Milliken University in Decatur, then moved to Nashville in 1971. "At first I thought I might be a session guy, until I saw Pig Robbins playing, and then I realized I'd better find another way. So I started concentrating on engineering. I hung around the Glaser studio and swept the place, but I couldn't really get a job."

In 1972, he spent a few months down in Jackson, Mississippi, learning his craft in a well-equipped studio. "There was a songwriter who lived in a school bus behind the recording studio, and literally had an extension chord that ran from inside the studio into the school bus. His name was Parker McGee, and he and I became good friends.

"He would write his songs, and I would help him demo them. He would beat me up about my sounds and about my producing, and I would beat him up about his second verse." Lehning got word that the Glaser studio needed an engineer, so he returned to Nashville, and McGee moved up to Nashville shortly thereafter.

"We continued beating each other up in the studio," Lehning says with a laugh. "One day he came into the studio after a couple of years of writing songs and demoing them, all this sort of Bob Dylan–influenced, spacey pop-folky ethereal stuff, he walked in and said, 'I'm tired of this. I wanna write some hit records.' He had a list of things every hit record needs. One of them was that you need to get to the chorus in the first minute. So he wrote 'I'd Really Love to See You Tonight' and 'Nights Are Forever Without You' [both hits for England Dan and John Ford Coley], a song called 'You Keep Me Running' that Gene Cotton had a hit with, and another song called 'Good-bye Old Buddies' that Seals and Crofts recorded. I mean, he had this *great* run of recordings."

Lehning was working as an engineer in the Glaser studio in 1974, twelve to eighteen hours a day on weekdays, recording demos and masters, plus weekends working on his own projects. He did some engineering for famed songwriter/artist/cartoonist Shel Silverstein, and to show his appreciation for Lehning's work, Shel sent him out to California to

236 How Nashville Became Music City, U.S.A.

hang out with one of Lehning's heroes, world-renowned studio engineer Roy Hallee.

"He was at the CBS studios in San Francisco," recalls Lehning. "I walked in the door and I heard this *krrrkrk!* like a gunshot goin' off. And I thought, wow, that's weird—what is that? And I realized it was coming from the control room down the hall. It happened that a guy I knew from Nashville was second-engineering for Roy.

"I said to him, 'Man, what have you...'

"'Ah, I've been up workin'.' And he had these dark circles under his eyes. *krrrkrk!* The sounds goin' off in the background. And he said, 'You hear that? This is day five.' Roy's been working on that moment in this song on this record for five days.

"I said, 'How can that be possible?'

"He says, 'Because he's got this thing in his head and he hasn't heard it come out of the speakers yet.'

"I didn't have to hear anything else, because the image I had of listening to his records, what it meant to be a genius, was that you knew how to do these things. The fact that he had the kind of stamina, the kind of courage, the vision to keep plowin' at it until he got something that really felt right.

"I came back from that trip a different guy. I had a different sense of things, of how things could and should sound, and I was able to put it to work pretty quickly.

"We were working with Waylon. Waylon came into the studio. Back in those days, RCA and Columbia had their own studios, and they had a union. And in order to get any kind of work done in an independent studio, you had to have one of their engineers on the session. I remember doing projects for Columbia at the Glaser studio. The union would have one engineer sitting there reading the paper making twenty-five bucks an hour while the session was going on.

"Waylon was a great spirit in the studio. As intense as it would get, he never lost his sense of humor. He always was able to back up from the madness and find something funny in what was going on. The first time I met him, I was sittin' in the studio playing a Wurlitzer electric piano through a wah-wah pedal into a guitar amplifier. They just said, 'Waylon's comin' in at six,' and they didn't tell me anything else. And he walks in and he's got his whole band with him, and I'm makin' all those wah-wah noises on the Wurlitzer and he walks up to me and says, 'I hate those things!' He's pointin' at the Wurlitzer.

"I'm thinkin', 'Oooh, this is not gettin' off to a good start,' so I turned it off and said, 'Sorry about that.' So the guys came in and set up, and they cut a J. J. Cale thing called 'Louisiana Ladies,' very cool groove. It just fit Waylon like a glove, and he came into the control room to listen. While they were listening, I went back into the studio, turned the Wurlitzer back on, and the guitar amp, and started playing the wah-wah along with the track, just 'cause I thought it was kinda cool. Waylon walks out—at which point I thought, 'Oh-oh, this is it for me!'—and he walks over to me and he says, 'Hey! Show me how to run this board, and put that on this record!' So I ended up playing piano and organ on his first number-one record, a song called 'This Time.'

"I played B-3 [organ] on that record, but I also had a bunch of my instruments there, including a Fender electric twelve-string, and after we cut the original tracks, I handed it to him, I said, 'Here, why don't you put this on there.' And he did.

"One other great Waylon story: He and Tompall and Jessi went out on the road together. Tompall said, 'Waylon wants you to play electric piano behind Jessi. So here's the record, learn the tunes and do it.'

"So I learned Jessi's show. Waylon's band backed her up, and I played a Rhodes [Fender electric piano] and an ARP [synthesizer] string ensemble. She finished her set and she was walkin' off the stage, and I was walkin' off behind her. The band stayed out there and Waylon was in the wings gettin' ready to come on, 'cause there was not going to be a break. It was like, boom, Jessi's done, here comes Waylon. So I'm walkin' off behind Jessi and Waylon says, 'Hoss, where you goin'?'

"I said, 'Well, I'm done with the set,' and Waylon says, 'No, you're gonna play with us now.' And I said, 'Waylon, I don't know the tunes!'

"He said, 'Man, there's only three chords.'

"And he knew I played guitar, but he would not show me his hands, so I was just up there like, *dink! dink!*, tryin' to find the key. And he was right, his songs only had three chords in 'em, but he put them in the most *interesting* places."

In March 1976, in Lee Hazen's basement studio in Hendersonville, Lehning produced 'I'd Really Love to See You Tonight' for England Dan and John Ford Coley.

"I was on my way to Copenhagen to work with Ronnie Hafkind as an engineer on a Dr. Hook recording he was doing out there. When we stopped in New York I called Doug Morris [who ran Big Tree Records, which had signed England Dan and John Ford Coley] to see how the record was doing. He said, it's goin' *nuts*.

"I said, 'What does that mean?' and he said, 'It means it's selling thirty thousand copies a day.' I was twenty-six years old. I ended up making a number of records on England Dan, and Doug actually hired me as a staff producer."

From '77 through '79, Lehning worked for the California-based Big Tree Records, producing pop records in Hendersonville, Tennessee. "Doug Morris didn't care if you were in L.A. or Elephant Breath, Ohio—if the record was good." Lehning recorded some more hits on England Dan, then got involved producing the pop group Firefall. "Some serious drugs going on there, but I was never into it. My dad was a pharmacist and he convinced me that they were for medicinal purposes, not recreational."

After England Dan, things cooled off for Kyle as a producer, but he continued to be in demand as an engineer. "At one point I had toyed with moving to L.A., but it just didn't feel like the right thing to do even though I really connected with a lot of guys in the pop music world. I made a lot of trips out there, but by 1980, it had started to not feel so good. In the early '70s, it felt like a series of small towns connected by the best highway on the planet, and by 1980, you couldn't get anywhere. It was amazing how fast it had started to strangle. So I decided to commit to Nashville and stay.

"Dan Seals decided to pack in the L.A. thing too, and he moved his family here. We got a chance to make some records at Capitol and had a little success." He also did some engineering for Ronnie Milsap, whose knowledge and taste are so good that he gets very involved in the kinds of decisions that most artists and producers leave solely to the engineer. "I loved talking to Ronnie about the process. He would say, 'Well, why are you doin' that?' I learned from him and I think he learned from me. It was during that period, around 1984, that I produced a record for Epic on Keith Stegall. And while I was producing the record, Keith brought me a cassette tape and he said, 'I'm makin' a live album of this catfish cook, out at the Nashville Palace.' I put the cassette in and I listened to it for thirty seconds, and I said, 'You've got to be kiddin' me. How old is this guy?'

"He said, 'He's about twenty-four.' I said, 'Now I know you're kiddin' me.'

Lehning drove out to the Nashville Palace to see the catfish cook play. His name was Randy Traywick, but performing under the name Randy Ray. Eventually he would settle on Randy Travis.

Music veteran Charlie Monk suggested that Lehning call Martha Sharp, head of A&R at Warner Bros. "I called Martha up and said, 'Who knows, but I really like this guy, and if you wanna do like a single or four sides, I'd be very happy to cut some sides on him.'"

At the time, there were some people at Warner Bros. Nashville who did not believe that Martha Sharp belonged at the head of the A&R department, and though Martha Sharp was thoroughly taken by Randy, she did not yet feel secure enough in her job to go to war with her co-workers for him.

Not until Kyle Lehning called her. Then, suddenly she had the ammunition to fight for Randy. If Randy was good enough for Kyle Lehning, he was good enough for Warner Bros. Martha Sharp had her boy, and Music Row would soon have the guy who would lead country music forward into its most successful era yet.

Stegall and Lehning coproduced the first of Travis's Warner Bros. sides. "Keith was in the middle of a difficult time," Lehning remembers. "He was trying to write songs, he was trying to be an artist in his own right, and he was trying to produce. The first single was 'On the Other Hand,' and it didn't happen the first time." Stegall bowed out of the project and Lehning stayed.

The best measure of a record's popularity is not the chart position of the single, but rather the sales that single stimulates, and back then, sales of singles still mattered. "When I was working with Doug Morris," says Lehning, "Doug told me that the record business in those days was determined by tertiary and secondary markets, and if you could find a record that was selling in a small market, you could probably count on it sellin' in a big market—so you could smell a hit as it was building.

"Paul [Davis, a Mississippi songwriter] had told me that 'On the Other Hand' had gone to number one in Meridian, Mississippi, his hometown. He said, 'People are going crazy!' So I went to the sales department at Warners. They were getting orders for ten thousand singles a week, but Nick Hunter couldn't get it past sixty-three on the panel at radio. But the lesson from the Doug Morris school is that that's a hit record. When it came time to pick another single, I went to Martha and I told her that [based on sales reports] the record did not look like a stiff.

"She said, 'Yeah, I know it,' and I said, 'I'll tell you what, if you'll re-release it, I'll let you recoup the promotion costs out of my royalties—that's how strongly I feel about it.'

"She said, 'Well, we won't do that, but I appreciate your confidence.'" As Saporiti stated, they did re-release the record after "1982" and the second time around it got to number one.

Around the same time Randy was breaking, Lehning was producing his old friend Dan Seals, and again lightning struck with the song "Bop," which won a CMA award and spawned a platinum album for Seals. As country as Randy Travis was with "On the Other Hand," that's how uncountry was "Bop." It should be noted that many adult country fans of the '80s had been pop and rock 'n' roll fans in the '50s and '60s, so nostalgia records like Ronnie Milsap's "Lost in the Fifties Tonight" resonated with them, even if they didn't sound very much like country records. "Bop" was one of those rare records that just made people feel good to hear it, and that was more than enough.

After Travis had finished the first album, he and Lehning were sitting in the control room listening to it from top to bottom. By that time, "On the Other Hand" had disappeared from the charts (the first time) and "1982" was just beginning to gather a little steam. "And I said to Randy, 'You know, if this album sells like forty thousand units, that might be enough for them to make another record. And he said, 'Yeah, that'd be good, wouldn't it?' I said, 'That'd be great to get to make another record together.' And he literally walked out of the studio and went to fry catfish at the Nashville Palace." The album did sell forty thousand, plus another three or four million, and launched the biggest country boom in the history of Music Row.

Lehning remembers the mid-'80s as a real fun time in country music, a time when Music Row was stretching its creative imagination with acts like Randy, Rosanne Cash, the O'Kanes, K. T. Oslin, k. d. lang, Rodney Crowell—"A really rich variety of stuff," he recalls.

Around 1989, a couple of record labels approached Lehning to work "in-house" for them. At the time he wasn't ready. One day he went to lunch with Jim Ed Norman, head of Warner Bros. in Nashville, "He said, 'You know, they're gonna keep asking you. If you're not interested, maybe you should decide that you're just not interested.' And I said, 'Well, it really isn't that—I just haven't found the right situation, you know. Call me stupid, but if I'm gonna do this, I'd rather do it from scratch.'

"Anyway, Steve Ralbovsky, the A&R guy at Elektra was sent on a head-hunting mission, and I met with him. He had me come up to New York to meet Bob Krasnow, chairman of Elektra Entertainment, which had a phenomenal roster, everything from Metallica to Linda Ronstadt. We went to dinner and hit it off. I could talk to him about George Jones or Randy Travis, and I could talk to him about Miles Davis. He hired me to start Asylum." Asylum was an old, respected label name being revived as another Warner/Elektra imprint to take advantage of country music's popularity.

Lehning accumulated a collection of fine artists at Asylum, including Bryan White, Lila McCann, and Mandy Barnett, and he ran the label for six years. In 2003, his production talents helped bring Randy Travis back with the landmark record "Three Wooden Crosses."

During his early years as a producer, Lehning was thought of as "the pop guy" on Music Row. When he guided Randy Travis to stardom, the Row began to think of him as "the country guy." But Kyle Lehning is neither. Like Owen Bradley, Chet Atkins, and Billy Sherrill, he is "a music guy."

"I'M GONNA CUT THIS SONG AND I REALLY CAN'T TELL YOU WHY"

S ome of Nashville's pioneers and heroes are so revered that statues have been erected in their honor: Owen Bradley plays the piano in bronze at the head of Music Row in a park that bears his name, while Chet Atkins picks his guitar downtown in front of a bank building. And then there are other names that are immortalized in books and articles and other tributes and homages over the years. Billy Sherrill comes to mind. And Buddy Killen. And Jimmy Bowen.

And then there are those who amass incredible achievements over the years, but without so much fanfare. Maybe, as Jimmy Bowen would say, these guys never had the right public relations person working for them. Or perhaps they never sought the spotlight. Not everyone in Nashville does.

Jerry Crutchfield is one of those quiet guys. After college, he came to Nashville as part of a pop vocal group to record for RCA. The group never had a hit, but it did get him involved in the Nashville music business. In the early '60s, he made his living pitching songs for Tree and singing backup vocals. But as his career evolved he realized what he wanted to do more than anything else was produce records. Eventually he produced huge country hits on Barbara Fairchild, Tanya Tucker, Lee Greenwood, and Tracy Byrd, and made some first-class records with Brenda Lee, Anne Murray, Tammy Wynette, Chris Ledoux, the Gatlins, Buck Owens, Lisa Brokop, and many others, including the pop classic "Please Come to Boston" by David Loggins. In his heyday, he was a key record executive for MCA Records and Capitol, and built MCA Music into a major publishing force in Nashville. Today he owns and works a small but successful music publishing company on 17th Avenue South, one of the few of

Music Row's old guard to remain active after more than four decades on the Row.

Crutchfield believes that the balancing point of creativity and marketing in Nashville was achieved in the '80s. "You can have natural explosions because of all the right reasons, such as the Garth Brooks thing," he says. "No one said, 'Oh wait, here's a guy from Oklahoma and I have an idea, let's develop his image to be so-and-so, and we'll go to the radio and tell this story and see what happens. I've always felt ambivalent about market research because all my experiences with that validate its real ineffectiveness. I did an album with Tracy Byrd—I think it was in '93—and I know the label had some focus groups and did some research and so on, and from what I'm told, the report came back that the album didn't research very well.

"Well, of the four singles we had three number-ones, the other one was a Top 5 single, and the album now has sold in excess of three million copies. So it really makes you wonder. I remember several years ago when, I think it was General Motors and some of the major corporations said, 'We're very good at conducting research, but once we get it we're not really sure how to handle it.' And I think in the music industry, with the advent of consultants telling radio what they should and should not play, and what the public response to it is and so on, it totally negates that natural dynamic that can result from music that, we don't know why, but it just seems to work.

"In my opinion, a very courageous A&R person would say, 'I'm gonna cut this song, I'm gonna put out this record, and I really can't tell you why. It's just something I feel. It's something I'm passionate about.' Now, when's the last time you've heard anyone say that? Not only does that not happen, but in many instances, as we very well know, the people who work in A&R within our labels, even if they had the ability to do this, are not given that option because you still have label heads who second-guess, and make the ultimate decision as to what is going on. And if you're dealing with numbers, and making numbers, and so on, can you really make this thing work? Yes, but we can also do the same thing with Hula Hoops and computers. It does not necessarily reflect creativity. So we need to be honest about what it is we're doing.

"I had the opportunity to participate in the Nashville music arena when the cream had a way of rising to the top. When I was first exposed to Lee Greenwood, he was working in the lounges in Las Vegas, and evidently when the country acts would go to Las Vegas to play, many of them would go to the lounge to hear Greenwood because they thought he was such a great singer. Ultimately, Lee was brought to me by Lamar Fike. And Lamar, who has a flair for exaggerating, to say the least, and is a wonderful guy and a good friend of mine, he brought a tape to me on Lee. He said, 'This is the greatest singer I've ever heard,' and I'm thinking, 'Okay, okay, *okay*.' Well, I listened to the tape, and immediately I knew two things: number one, I knew he wasn't a country singer *per se*; and number two, I was beginning to agree with Lamar, this guy is one of the greatest vocalists. So I started working with Lee and initially took him to Los Angeles, and did four sides with him there, but I really didn't know what he was about.

"I went to Jim Foglesong [the head of MCA Records at that time] and I said, 'Here's a guy, all I know is he is a great artist and I think I can cut a record to make it work for country radio.' And so I played what I had done on Lee in Los Angeles, which was four songs that he wrote, and they were obviously not very country and certainly not suited for country radio. And Jim said, 'I think I agree with you, the guy's great, go do it and see what happens.' In looking for songs, I found this tremendous song that my brother Jan wrote called 'It Turns Me Inside Out.'

"I was firmly convinced that this could be a career song. To be honest, we encountered a lot of resistance. Much of radio said, 'Ah, this guy's not really country.' But for the first time in the history of *Billboard* magazine, that record actually lost and regained the bullet three times. It just wouldn't go away, it was so compelling.

"In the '60s, I recorded a young artist named Barbara Fairchild, when Kapp Records had decided that they were gonna be in the country music business. After they phased out their country division, I took her to Billy Sherrill at Columbia Records. Billy signed her and did an album with her, and not much happened. At that time, it was very difficult to be an independent producer, because the labels themselves were headed up by producers. I mean, some of those guys were doing as much as thirty acts each. But I went to Billy and I said, 'Would you let me try to do a record with Barbara?'

"He said, 'Okay, do it.' We put out the first single, which was doing okay, and then I got a phone call from Joe Casey, who later moved to Nashville to become the national head of promotion for CBS Records, but at that time, he was at the Atlanta branch. So he called me one day and he said, 'I just wanted to tell you that you have a smash hit record. It's on Barbara Fairchild.' Well, I was thinking about the single that we had out at the time. He said, 'When WPLO played the 'Teddy Bear Song' [off the album], the switchboard locked up completely with phone calls.' Now, that's what we miss today, the opportunity for that to happen—it's not gonna happen because of the standardized approach of selecting material for the albums." As big as the "Teddy Bear Song" was in 1973, (number one, country; number thirty-two, pop) it might have been considerably bigger, had there not been resistance from the pop stations because the record was "country."

"I talked to people at CBS Records who said to me, 'You know what? This is really, legitimately, a number-one pop record, but we have got people....' For example, there was a huge radio station, and their response was, and this is exactly the quote, 'We could play that record and it would be highly successful in our market, but we refuse to play it because it's not compatible with what we want our music to be about.'

"I mentioned the Tracy Byrd album. At that time, the album had sold a couple of million copies. Now I'm working on the second album—it's 1994. I would think that if I were heading up a record label, and a guy just cut an album for me that sold two million, he could pretty much do whatever he wanted to do. Well, I get a compilation tape from the label with songs for Tracy's next album. I sat with Tracy and we listened to them. I think there were eight songs, maybe. And he and I concurred, that we don't really hear anything on here that we think can live up to whatever we've established with the first album. So I proceed to cut some other songs, only to find out that when I was sent those songs, it wasn't necessarily to listen and consider, it was, *These are the songs you will record on the next album.*

"I never cut albums like that in my life. In twelve or thirteen albums with Tanya, I picked every song we ever did because I felt that I'm really plugged into her artistry, I know what she's capable of, I try to stay on top of what's going on at radio, and I think I'm plugged into the great 'out there.' Consequently, I was fired from doing the follow-up to this album with Tracy. Record labels don't need people like me doing records, 'cause if they're picking the songs, and you're using basically the same studios, the same players, who are all fantastic, then you just need somebody who can kind of do more of those records that sound very similar."

In 2005, Jim Foglesong was elected to the Country Music Hall of Fame, a rare honor for a Music Row executive. A graduate of the renowned Eastman School of Music in Rochester, New York, he moved to New York City and, in the early '50s, got a job with Columbia Records. At the time, the record album industry was reformatting from 78-rpm records to the LP format that became the industry standard for four decades. His job was to find a way to make those "albums" of 78s—often four separate records of one long-playing piece like a symphony—fit together on a two-sided LP.

Later he worked for Epic and RCA in New York, producing some of the bigger pop acts of the era. But New York was beginning to lose its preeminent status as a pop center to Los Angeles, and Foglesong had friends in New York who believed he would thrive in Nashville. One of them was the ubiquitous Al Gallico, who talked to Foglesong when Jim was still working for the Columbia organization.

"Gallico was working for Shapiro Bernstein, and he had hired Merle Kilgore to represent the company's Painted Desert Music down in Nashville," Foglesong remembers. "Al used to bring me songs that he had picked up down here, and he said, 'Jimmy, you ought to go to Nashville, boy, you know, you're from West Virginia. They'd love you down there. You know they hate Mitch Miller's guts, he comes on too strong. Mitch went down there one time and....' Well, Mitch is one of my heroes, but I understood, because he was very abrupt. Things he said that upset 'em down here I know he didn't mean 'em that way at all, but that's just the way it came out."

So Foglesong decided to pay Nashville a visit. Don Law, who ran Columbia's Nashville division and tended to a roster competitive with those of Owen Bradley's Decca roster and Chet Atkins' RCA operation, welcomed Jim as a guest. "I'd just like to come down and be a fly on the wall," he told Law.

Foglesong flew in and Law introduced him to Owen Bradley, just before a session. "He said, 'I'm just doing this little square dance album right now, but if you wanna come over, you're welcome. We don't sell a whole lot but we make money on these.' So that was the very first Nashville session I observed, and the second session was a Johnny Horton session that Don produced. I was totally taken and surprised by the much more relaxed attitude of Nashville, coming from New York and having done some work in L.A., where the union was so much more strict about its regulations. The Johnny Horton session, which was supposed to start at two o'clock in the afternoon I think, got under way around two thirty. Well, in New York the clock would have started right on time, but at the Johnny Horton session there wasn't a musician in the room at two o'clock. They'd gone overtime at RCA, I think. It was the A-team—Buddy Harman, Grady Martin, Harold Bradley, Ray Edenton, Floyd Cramer, and those people—so they finished at RCA and came running over to the Quonset Hut. But they were quick to explain to me that here the clock wasn't running until everybody's in the room ready to go. The other thing that scared me to death was that there wasn't a piece of [sheet] music on the session. By now I was a full-fledged producer with an artist roster to take care of, and I'm a pretty good musician, I read music, and in New York everything was written out. To go in there with nothing but a lyric sheet—I'll never forget, particularly Johnny Horton. This was right after 'The Battle of New Orleans.' The musicians are sauntering in and talking, and start doodling with their instruments. Finally, Grady Martin says, 'Johnny, what are we doin' today?' At which point Johnny picks up a guitar and sings them a song, and they all write down the chords. This was so foreign to me my mouth was gaping. I'm pretty sure the Jordanaires were on that date. After three hours, they had four songs done. Just like in New York, we tried to get four songs in three hours, and we almost always did, but there it was written out, and people knew where to go right from the word go.

"My first impression of Nashville: not very good food. Being from West Virginia, I liked the 'meat and threes' and all that, but they didn't sell liquor by the drink at the time, and there were a couple of clubs in town where the best food was. There was a club called the 329, I think, and then there was a downtown club where gambling was permitted and all that, but with the exception of that I wasn't too pleased, particularly coming from New York, the greatest city in the world for food."

A while later, Foglesong began producing a country artist named Bobby Sykes, and he came down for the annual Disc Jockey Convention. "I remember Owen Bradley and I sitting in the Andrew Jackson Hotel and counting all the really bad hairpieces going in and out, really bad ones, like red hair and the sideburns are brown, or vice versa, or put on crooked. But I loved the feel of the place, and it wasn't long before I made this town a regular stop looking for songs. I had remembered Gallico saying, 'Jimmy, they got a lot of great writers down there, it's not just country stuff, you oughta go down and just look for songs for your artists.' I was with Columbia 'til '64, when I went over to RCA in New York, and I was there from '64 'til I joined Dot on December 1, 1970."

Dot Records had been started in 1950 by Randy Wood, who owned a record shop in Gallatin, Tennessee, a town close to Hendersonville. Wood had a vision of a young white rock 'n' roller, a fresh-faced kid who was more or less a crooner but who sang sanitized versions of black R&B songs to woo the kids. As the owner of a record store, Wood was in a good place to spot coming R&B records and cover them. His main vehicle was Pat Boone, but he did the same with a group called the Fontane Sisters, and even with his hit-making pop male group the Hilltoppers, as well as other artists on the label. In 1957, Wood moved to Hollywood and eventually sold his label.

Later the parent company moved Dot to Nashville. Meanwhile, Foglesong's positive Nashville experience had led him to bring some of his RCA acts down to Music Row to record, including the Ames Brothers and Al Hirt. "I got along great with the musicians—Grady Martin, Harold Bradley, and I were really good friends." In New York at that point, things were not going Foglesong's way at RCA. He was doing well with Ed Ames, but he felt he was typecast into that middle-of-the-road adult music that was rapidly losing ground to the raucous youth music of the late '60s.

"I didn't think I was going to get an opportunity to try something different," he says. "In the meantime, the people who had now taken over at RCA brought in a couple of fellas who really had no experience in A&R, and they were getting all the plums. I wasn't looking for a new job—when I have a job I plan on staying there the rest of my life and always working things out. But when the people from Famous Music, the parent company of Dot, talked to me and offered the gig to take over Dot Records in Nashville, I took it.

"I was told in New York that Dot had sixteen acts on the label. By the time we uncovered all the production deals, the number of acts was well into the twenties, and the only one who was selling records was Roy Clark. They were doing a little pop product on Dot, but one of the first things I said was I think we should establish Dot as a country label. I felt it was very important we make the statement to Nashville that we're only interested in country product."

In those days, successful country acts sold their records fifty thousand at a time, and if a label head was really lucky, something special would walk into his office and cut a breakout record that would take the pressure off him for a while. "The biggest thing that happened to Dot was Bill Walker, the arranger, called me one day and said, 'Jim, there's a fella named Stan Silver that's gonna be calling you for an appointment. We did a session last night. This girl's name is Donna Fargo, I really think we cut a hit, and I hope you'll see him.'"

At the time the major labels in Nashville did not want to pick up any independently produced masters. When Foglesong heard that he said, "I love it. I wanna hear every master that I can hear because that's one of the great creative sources of our industry. Well, sure enough, Stan brings in the Donna Fargo session and he says, 'You know, I couldn't get an appointment at MCA and Capitol. I did play it for another person at another label and he said he'd like to play the song for one of his female artists, but I told him this is a package.'

"Well, I heard the thing, and I was determined not to let him out of the office until we had a deal. 'Happiest Girl in the Whole USA' sold over a million singles. We put out an album, sold over a million copies. The second single, 'Funny Face,' actually outsold 'Happiest Girl' by a hundred thousand or so. The company had, I don't know, five, six, seven different labels—jazz, pop, and so forth—and they were all pretty much floundering. Suddenly we're turning things around and bringin' in numbers, and of course 'Happiest Girl' and 'Funny Face' were both crossovers, so we got the pop promotion people involved. Donna was the darling of the whole company.

"In 1974, ABC bought us. That was very traumatic for me, to find that we were up for sale. What had happened was that Gulf + Western Industries [which owned Famous] was spending a lot of money trying to rock 'n' roll, and in the meantime, we were a profit center. Supposedly, Motown was looking at us, and they had twenty-four boxes of files they were studying.

"The artists were calling me, and the staff was asking, 'What are you gonna do?' I said, 'I know nothing.' The girls in the office were living from paycheck to paycheck, and I wasn't much beyond that myself. 'All I know is we just need to keep our heads down, work the product, keep putting out the best product, and whatever happens will happen, hopefully people will notice.'

"I heard our fate was decided at a cocktail party in New York on Friday, and by Tuesday the next week ABC bought us." ABC had had several labels in Nashville, and in fact had opened an office a year or two before, headed by Don Gant with Ron Chancey in charge of A&R.

"I was in a recording session with Brian Collins in the old Clement recording studio, now the Sound Emporium, when a phone call came in.

"'Jim Foglesong, this is Jay.'

"'Jay who?'

"'Jay Lasker. I just bought you guys! I want you out here Monday, can you bring Donna Fargo with you? We got all the sales people coming in and I wanna announce the purchase and I want you here, and anybody else. Can you bring Donna?'

"Frankly, I wasn't worried. We were hot. By now we were in the process of signing Don Williams, buying his whole catalog [from JMI, Jack Clement's label]. However, when I got out there, there's Chancey, there's Gant, and the more I thought about it the more I realized that there's no way they're gonna keep two labels in Nashville. There were people planting rumors on the street, and for a while it got a little bit ugly. There was some animosity coming down from somewhere."

ABC wound up putting Foglesong in charge of ABC/Dot, and Gant wound up as creative director at Tree, where he sparked a period of great prosperity at that company.

"I had really gotten into Ron Chancey as a producer," Foglesong says. "I barely knew him, but I loved his Crash Craddock records and I decided to keep him in the A&R position. I made sure we honored the contracts [of all the people who lost their jobs through the merger].

"Instead of going to New York, my headquarters were now in L.A., and I thought I had great communications with Jay Lasker, and then suddenly they decided to replace him [as label head]. But we had signed Don Williams. I had picked up a master on Freddy Fender called 'Before the Next Teardrop Falls,' which was a million-seller. It was the Donna Fargo story all over again, because Freddy's next single, 'Wasted Days and Wasted Nights' went over a million.

"We were smokin'. Shortly thereafter, we signed the Oak Ridge Boys."

For many years, the category of singing *groups* had been pretty much a wasteland in country music. The only really successful country group in the '60s and early '70s was the Statler Brothers. When the Gatlins started putting out records on Monument, they resisted the group identity for a long time. Their first four charted singles were under the name "Larry Gatlin," then they scored some hits under the name "Larry Gatlin with

Family & Friends," and one under "Larry Gatlin with Brothers & Friends." They went back to "Larry Gatlin" for three more singles before finally settling on "Larry Gatlin & the Gatlin Brothers Band" for several years.

The Oak Ridge Boys had evolved from a gospel group founded in 1945 called the Oak Ridge Quartet. Between 1965 and 1973, William Golden, Duane Allen, Richard Sterban, and Joe Bonsall all joined the group. The group won numerous Dove Awards as well as a Grammy in the gospel category, but they had dreams of broader audiences, so they signed with Columbia Records' country division in the early '70s. They bombed on Columbia, and their foray in the country industry had probably torpedoed their status as gospel stars.

But they had a great asset down in Oklahoma, Tulsa-based Jim Halsey, one of country music's most powerful promoters, bookers, and talent managers.

"I've always loved male quartets," says Foglesong, who at times in his life has sung in a male quartet. "And I know the public loves that four-part harmony from male voices. I witnessed it in my church back in West Virginia. The Oak Ridge Boys went to Jim Halsey and they said, 'We've won every award we can win in gospel music, and we're starving. We are really having trouble keeping our doors open.'

"Jim started pitching them to me, and I'd say in that year he made sure I saw them at least four times. He used to have an annual festival in Tulsa, and he'd have all his acts perform, and he would invite in the talent buyers from the big rooms in Vegas and Tahoe, and the fair buyers, and people from Nashville. I was sitting on the ground when the Oaks came on, and they just blew me away.

"That was on a weekend, and we have a staff meeting every Monday morning with Larry Baunach [head of promotion] and Ron Chancey and myself. I just walked into my office and Larry Baunach says, 'Did you sign the Oak Ridge Boys?' I said, 'This just happened on Saturday, and this is Monday! Ron says, 'Did you sign the Oak Ridge Boys?' Well, the short answer was 'yes.' I said, 'Ron, my next question to you is, if you're not doing anything, will you fly out to Oklahoma City? They're performing Thursday night and I want you to take a look at them and meet with them and see if you'd be interested in producing them, 'cause I think that you'd be perfect.' I don't think anybody believed too much in my decision. But they hadn't seen the Oaks and they hadn't heard what I'd heard. It just all came together."

Now the ball was in Chancey's court. "They were opening for Jimmy Dean," Chancey says. "They came out and did their set and they had everybody in the whole place standin' up, and clappin', stompin', and they really impressed me. I came back and said, 'Jim, I think we ought to sign these guys. If we can get that on record in a country song, we'll have something,' The very first thing we cut was a song Bill Hall had given me, 'Y'all Come Back Saloon.' We had to change a couple of things in it. First of all, it was about a saloon, which they were a little leery of, comin' right out of gospel. It said, 'The all-night benediction,' and they didn't want to sing that line.'" But there was no way around it and it stayed in the song. "But we changed a couple of other things. I called Hall, and he said fine, and *boom!*"

"Y'all Come Back Saloon" set the tone for their future success. "This probably sounds corny," says Chancey "but every time we'd go in the studio we just *knew* we were gonna cut a hit. Everything was just perfect, everybody got along and loved each other. In all the years I cut the Oak Ridge Boys, all the albums we had, we never had one cross word, not even anything close to a cross word. Remember when Golden and Duane [Allen] were havin' that terrible relationship? When we would get in the studio, that would all go away. When we'd get out, I guess it all came back...."

"The unique thing about them, we had a number-one record with *every one of them singin' lead.* You sign a group now, they'll say you can't do that: you gotta have one person to focus on—we gotta build his image. Back then, I didn't really know whether to do that or not, but we tried it. Funny thing is, you know how great a singer Duane Allen is, he actually is the lead singer, but the three biggest things we ever had, Joe Bonsall sang lead on—'Elvira,' 'Bobby Sue,' and 'I Guess It Never Hurts to Hurt Sometime,' I think that was our third biggest."

The Oak Ridge Boys projected enthusiasm more than precision on their records, kind of like the Rolling Stones do on their best rock 'n' roll records. An up-tempo Oaks hit sounded like a party.

"Yeah, everything wasn't always right in tune," Chancey agrees. "These days, if somebody would record 'em, they'd tune 'em up and stuff, but I think really they were so raw and good. Well, I'll give you an example. When Duane and William Lee had their fallin' out, and William Lee was kinda let go from the group—which was done by the other two partners also, not just Duane—they got Steve Sanders to sing in his place. Steve was an excellent singer, maybe too good—it lost that raw quality and that soulful quality that William Lee has, and to me, they just didn't sound like the Oak Ridge Boys anymore.

"We had the most fun time cuttin' all that stuff. I found that with almost everything I ever done [in the studio], if you're havin' a good time and not forcin' it, you'll generally cut a good record."

All the early Oak Ridge Boys hits were on ABC. "In the true sense of the word, we were an independent label," says Foglesong, "Because we used independent distribution. Then Curb came along, and you know, Curb is distributed by Warner Bros. As a true independent, we may have been the biggest around. We only had fourteen acts, but we had Barbara Mandrell by then, we had Don Williams, we had John Conlee, the Oak Ridge Boys, Freddy Fender."

So it was inevitable that a major label would become interested in ABC, and that label was MCA, the former Decca operation that Owen Bradley had built so well.

"Well, the same thing was happening at ABC that happened at other places," says Foglesong. "They were spending a fortune [on the pop business] and bombing out. But the people at MCA, from the president of the whole corporation down, knew that it was the Nashville operation that they were really interested in when they looked at the numbers and decided to make the purchase.

"I was more prepared for the MCA deal because I knew ABC had put us up for sale, and I was a lot more relaxed this time because I'd been through it once before. It was still very painful, because again you're talkin' to your staff, you're talking to people who are concerned about their next rent payment or mortgage payment, and they're working hard and the company's doing great, and they don't know if they have a job.

"Around 1981, the head of distribution came to me and said. 'Do you realize that your division is contributing well over fifty percent of our total income for contemporary product?'" Foglesong remembers.

"Well, I haven't figured it out like that, but I knew that pop was hurting to some degree. With the Oaks, Don Williams, Barbara Mandrell had her TV show and was doing well, Roy Clark continued going ahead, with John Conlee, we did very well.... Then the industry kind a went into a slump and everybody's numbers started to suffer. What normally causes that is when everything starts to sound alike. There have always been a lot more followers than leaders, and everybody's guilty—the songwriter, the publisher, the artist, the producer, they get into something very comfortable. They start writing formula, they don't want to take chances. They say, well, this doesn't sound like what's happening. I gotta tell you, the promotion people didn't call the shots at my label, they had a lot of input and I certainly respected them, but I went against their wishes lots of times. They're not the ones who make the product. Why do you hire a producer? Because he's got a track record. You believe in his or her talent. I'm not much into committees and I'm much more prone to go with the creative people. That's why they're hired."

A constant refrain heard around the industry is that when you let the promotion staff choose the singles, you get radio hits that don't sell records. Perhaps in the '60s and the early '70s, Nashville label heads could lull the home offices with number-one singles and CMA-award-winning acts. But by 1981, label heads were counting on country record sales to help make their bottom lines look good, and they were much harder to convince. Foglesong wanted to make it clear that he had never played the radio game, that he believed in putting out records that would appeal to the people, and that the way to find a hit was through a *producer's* gut rather than a record *promoter's* idea of what would please radio.

"I've heard a lot of records produced by radio people," says Foglesong. "Most of them are pretty bad, yet they're always telling us what's a hit. When things go bad, I always look at A&R. I just think that if the product's there, we're gonna sell. I guess it's my Baptist guilt, I feel like it's my fault. I'm not about to point a finger at promotion or marketing, it's not that everybody doesn't have to do their job, but it's amazing how easy it is when you've got the right product.

Foglesong continued to de well at MCA after the ABC sale, but the wheel was spinning in California, and when it stopped, Jimmy Bowen would be running the label again, not Foglesong. "MCA offered me a deal to stay. They wanted me to start an 'associated labels' thing out of Nashville. My first client would be Mike Curb and some acts he was pitching at MCA," says Foglesong. Curb has had Curb Records for over forty years, and the label had always been distributed by one or more major labels.

"They offered me an independent production contract on top of the existing contract, which is the best contract I ever had. I made more money there than I ever did. But I was going to have to work with Jimmy and his team, I was gonna have to work through their system to some degree. And I didn't like the way things had come down. I wasn't being told the truth."

If all this sounds a bit familiar, consider Jerry Bradley's independent production offer from RCA, and you'll see how labels function: If the label is scheming to get rid of an executive with a great track record, rather than fire the guy—which means not only controversy in the press but means an expensive contract settlement—they might try to switch him to a job that is so humiliating and degrading that the guy will either resign or settle for a less expensive severance package.

Foglesong's successor, Jimmy Bowen, had some very successful years at MCA—his two biggest artists at that time were George Strait and Reba McEntire, both of whom were signed by Foglesong during his tenure at MCA.

This does not mean that Bowen simply profited from the groundwork Foglesong laid, or that Bowen was the indispensable guy who made superstars out of George and Reba. A fact of life in the industry is that the executive on whose watch the artist breaks big gets the credit for it. That's life. The important thing about this scenario with Foglesong and Bowen is that it would be repeated just a few years later with country's biggest star.

"While all this is going on, a friend from L.A. calls me and says, 'Look, I'm not even asking your permission, I'm just telling you that I'm gonna call Bhaskar Menon, my dear friend over at Capitol Records, and tell him that I think he ought to hire you.' He says, 'Capitol hasn't meant anything in Nashville for a long time, and I think he can really use you, and I think you two would just get along famously.'"

It's a measure of the respect Foglesong commands in the industry that he would have a friend volunteering to do such a thing, but it also indicated that the inner workings of MCA were an open secret in L.A. "People out there who shouldn't have known how much money I made, knew how much money I was making. Stuff was being talked about openly. In the meantime, we're back here in the dark, which bothers me, you know, I can get along with most anybody, but when lying gets involved and you're two thousand miles away, how do you deal with that? I'm not really good at that. I hired a high-profile lawyer in L.A. This is one time I thought I felt I really needed somebody in L.A. There are great lawyers here, but there's a game that's played out there between the top people.

They love to play the games, but they all know what each other's doing, they even have their own jargon.

"[So I hired a lawyer there] to look at my contract and just get some input from. Well, the lawyer calls me and he said, 'Bhaskar Menon called me and said he wants to meet with you.' I flew out there on a weekend at my own expense and had a lovely meeting with him in his office. He had his own chef who fixed a very nice lunch, and I felt very good about it, not really knowing how I was gonna make out."

After his meeting with Menon, Foglesong called his attorney. "I told him, 'I wanna leave MCA, get me the best possible [deal]. I don't think I can win here, so let's do that.' Almost within minutes, Capitol calls and they wanna make an offer. I didn't want to listen to their offer until I was totally settled with MCA. I wanted to take a month off, 'cause I'd been through a long, very stressful period of time and I knew I wasn't being told all the truth.

"Well, it so happens that, that weekend, Capitol was having all their international people in L.A., and Monday night, they were having a big reception in Bhaskar Menon's home in Beverly Hills, and he wanted both me and my wife there to introduce me to the people I didn't already know. So that's what we did. My last day at MCA was Friday and my first day at Capitol was the following Monday. I actually took a pretty good cut in salary to go to Capitol, but I made the right choice. I loved my stay at Capitol, particularly the first team of Menon and Don Zimmerman and Jim Mazza."

But before too very long, Bhaskar Menon was replaced by Joe Smith. "I knew Joe, to some extent. I admired his work. But I never felt completely comfortable with him—I never felt that he cared a whole lot for me. I don't know if he thought I was too old." It was maybe Foglesong's fourth year at Capitol when Smith came in and he had only kept two artists from the previous regime, Anne Murray and Mel McDaniel. They had a long way to go. But there was progress.

"We signed Sawyer Brown and Tanya, Suzy Bogguss [and Garth Brooks]. The expression that I used to Joe Smith was, 'Joe, I think we finally stepped in excrement with this kid Garth Brooks that we signed. I wasn't sure that he even heard what I said, I just got the feeling that the die was cast. He was not into what I was doing and we weren't communicating. We knew we were just coming into our own. I remember talking about Garth with Joe Mansfield, who at that time was in distribution. He said, 'Aw, Garth Brooks is great,' and I said, 'We got at least gold, right? And he says, 'Oh yeah, man.' I'm just beaming about that, and of course that's when the hammer comes down and it's over."

Foglesong wasn't fired—his contract ran out. After more than four decades of doing work he loved with Columbia, RCA, Dot, ABC, MCA, and Capitol, there were no more record labels for Foglesong to run.

Music Row is a tough place for record executives. Foglesong spent nearly two full decades running record labels on Music Row and he survived everything the business threw at him. Everything except Jimmy Bowen.

THE MEN OF GARTH

In the early days of Music Row, everybody rejoiced in the success of their colleagues. There were only a self-chosen few on the Row in those days—a few producers, a few songwriters, a few publishers, a few of everything—and there was enough success to go around. But by 1989, Music Row was *big time*, with all the competitiveness, jealousy, and fear of failure that success brings.

There were now several generations of songwriters, artists, and label staffers who had seen their day pass. Some had given up, and some were still struggling for another shot.

When you are a winner on Music Row, the thrill is electric. You turn on your car radio every morning when you drive into work, you hear the hits you helped make, and you know that all over the country more than two thousand radio stations are playing *your music*. You get invited to all the parties and celebration dinners. Your calls are returned. People up and down the Row respect you.

But when you lose your job on the Row, or you lose your record deal, or the years fly by without anybody recording your songs, then Music Row can be a very hungry place.

So when a guy like Garth Brooks appears on the scene, seemingly out of nowhere, with record-shattering hits, it seems to those outside-look-ing-in lifers that somebody jumped in line in front of them, and grabbed the food right off their tray. And that's when the bitterness prevails: "He can't sing." "He looks like an idiot." "He cuts lousy songs."

Not that Music Row has turned into a purely vicious pack of nasty, backbiting, grumbling grouches. Far from it. Many of the younger art-ists and songwriters look up to the new hit makers and hope they can follow suit. Still, there were some nasty rumblings heard around the Row when Garth Brooks jumped to the front of the food line and showed the country music world what could happen when great music meets great marketing.

Bob Doyle was the catalyst for country's biggest superstar.

Doyle came to Nashville from St. Louis in December 1976 and, early on, worked in A&R at Warner Bros. Records. Around the Row he was known as a steady presence, a man who took his job very seriously and would give your song a good listen. Eventually he moved over to ASCAP, where he worked with songwriters, nurturing new talent when possible.

"I first heard Garth on a tape from his landlady," Doyle says. "Her name was Stephanie Brown and she was a writer who lived in East Nashville.

"I liked the tape and said I'd love to meet him, so he came by and I encouraged him to join ASCAP. I was always pretty capable of getting people introductions and publishing deals or record deals while I worked at ASCAP as a membership rep, but I couldn't seem to get him placed. But I really believed in what he was doing. It touched me. I connected with the music and connected with the way he communicated it, and I thought, I get his point of view. If you go back and listen to Garth's material, there's a lot more to his vocal ability than people realize. I think we took it for granted because, one, he is a very astute businessman, and two, he is a great performer as well. I was recently at a Hall of Fame induction ceremony for Jim Foglesong and Kris Kristofferson, and Garth sang 'If Tomorrow Never Comes' as part of Jim's portion of the show. Afterward, Kristofferson walked up to Garth and myself and said, 'You know, you made me cry.' He said, 'I had you in the context of this other type of person, but I didn't realize that you were the singer/songwriter that you are.'

"Garth was very focused. He was an athlete in school, and he knew about the discipline of building a foundation, but he also always had a goal in mind. I remember once asking him, 'What is your artistic point of view?' And it was kinda mom, apple pie, and putting the American flag back on the front porch." These values were not lost on Doyle, who at the time was a major in the Air Force Reserve and would rise to the rank of colonel.

"There was a very strong sense of who he was and what he wanted to say in those three minutes he had to say it. I really feel that in any artistic endeavor there has to be that point of view. I mean you can look good, you can sing great, but if you don't know what you're wanting to say and how to use your medium to say it, I don't think it'll last very long."

At the beginning of an artist's career, the manager is always the person with the experience, the one who is supposed to know what moves to make, the one to command the respect.

"I remember me having that conversation with him very directly. I said I have the ability to open the doors, I have the ability to get us in credibly, but at the end of the day, it was really his vision that we were trying to execute.

"He was the boss. Because he played sports, he's always conscious of how a team works. There's always a leader on a team, but everybody has to do his job no matter how good you are. If somebody's not blocking or somebody's not catching the ball or somebody's not playing defense, you're not gonna win."

At the beginning the team was small: Garth, Doyle, and Pam Lewis, a public relations whiz that Doyle took on as a management partner. "We were pretty well universally rejected," Doyle says. "I guess there were maybe six labels in town. We did get a second meeting at Warners. We did get a second meeting at Capitol, but it was sort of another situation that really resulted in the signing at Capitol. I got an appointment with Jim [Foglesong], played him the demos that I'd made on Garth and he liked it, and said he'd like to set up another meeting. We went back and met with Terry Choate, Lynn Shults, and Jim. I don't think Terry and Lynn reacted the way Jim did. Garth physically played for them—and then we went on with our search for a record deal."

They decided to do a showcase at the Bluebird, a café in Green Hills, one of the more affluent sections of Nashville. Since 1982, the Bluebird has become the place to go to hear great country and acoustic songs. The emphasis is on the songwriter as performer and writer of his or her own material, and unlike many club owners, Amy Kurland is highly aware of emerging talent. The Bluebird is a place where songwriters go to hear songwriters, constant evidence that there is still a core of mutual respect left in Nashville from the days when Music Row was "all for one, one for all."

"Lynn was there, and Garth did what he does with a crowd, he just sort of mesmerized them. Lynn came up to me after the show and said, 'Where did we leave this?' I mean, I wasn't gonna say, 'You passed,' so I just said, 'Hey, you said you'd get back to us.' Then he said, 'Well, I wanna talk to you guys in the morning.' Then I guess he went back and talked to Jim and I guess in some way they assured each other that they had something here that they both believed in, 'cause it wouldn't happen without Jim saying yes, too.

"The thing that's fascinating about our business is that when things are sometimes just a little outside the box, it takes a little vision. It's easy to say no. I think there's a lot of really talented folks, that if they aren't befriended in some way by somebody who really has access, they will never get that opportunity. Who knows how many hundreds of kids really had great ability and great talent, but never could make the connection that gave them access to the decision-makers, that never got the shot?

"You don't quit, you continue building those relationships to get to that next level of acceptance. That's what it is really about. If you pick up the phone and call me, I'll probably listen to something. I was an instructor pilot and I always thought that flying was ninety percent self-confidence and ten percent skill. I think it's true in our business."

Doyle is also convinced that one of the things that made Garth Brooks a success was his ability to understand all the aspects of the music industry, rather than being dependent upon the knowledge of his team. "If you're gonna be in this business," says Doyle, "you'd better understand how the media works, you'd better understand how radio works, you'd better understand how the touring business works, and how promoters control their markets. Garth was very conscious of why are we doing this or what is the reason for that—he took nothing for granted. He tried to think it all through. It's not about ability, it's about choices."

"I remember the first album intimately, because a lot of the songs were the demos that we'd done from the time that we signed as writer/publisher until we got the deal to start to make the album. One of the concerns I had as the manager was, Are we cuttin' the best songs? There were three or four songs of Garth's that were gonna make the album, and I just wanted to make sure. I trust Allen [Reynolds, the producer of all of Garth's albums], I think he's one of the greatest song men in the business, so I asked Allen, and he said, 'Let me reassure you that we're cuttin' these songs because I believe in them, too.'

"'Much Too Young (To Feel This Damn Old)' was one of the first songs I heard on Garth, and it got me the first time I heard it. That song had an interesting life in itself because it was his first single. It came out and there were major radio stations coming on it right out of the box. They were playing it, and it was like, 'How do we get this under control?'

When a single comes out it has a life in each of the markets in which it's playing. If the label is not coordinating the life of the record in all of the important markets, then there is a danger that some stations may be going off the record just as others are going on it, and then the record may never climb as high on the national charts as it would have if the record were climbing the local charts more or less simultaneously.

"I'd hired three different independents [independent record promoters] and they were telling me, 'This is a hit record.' But the record company was havin' a hard time with that. While it was in the Top 40, they came off the record."

But the independents, which included veteran promoter Stan Byrd, came to Doyle and said, "This record's not over."

"We went and talked to the label, they started workin' it again. It then went on up to Top 10, it was number eight, and I really think they quit on it again too soon, because the song stayed up there two weeks, three weeks, before it fell out of the Top 10. If the bar is high enough, and everybody's really trying to do it, it's amazing what you can accomplish."

Clint Black had started about the same time, and he was moving further faster. He was a good measuring stick for Garth. "Garth's attitude was, 'If we're gonna do this, we're gonna have to work a little bit harder.' He talked to Joe Harris, who was our booking agent at the time, and he said, 'Look, I'll work as much as we can.' And he took it upon himself over the next year and a half to work every club, every county fair, every event that we could do, to begin to get out there on a grassroots level and support these records, and I think it paid off, I really do.

"He had a band that was willing to work. They started out in a van, worked their way up to an RV, then to a really cheap bus, then a more expensive bus."

And the Garth career began to build. His next single was "Not Counting You." "He wrote that song for a young lady that we were sort of working with at the time, he never intended it for himself. We never demoed it, either. It was just a song he wrote, he played it for me, he played it for Allen, and they went in and cut it."

Although "Not Counting You" was a number-one record, the early sales of Garth's first album were steady, but not great for the boom times of 1990. "It was sort of an interesting thing," recalls Doyle. "It was building. It went gold about the time the second album went platinum."

At this point, Garth Brooks was still not *Garth Brooks*. The magic that made it happen was the first song on the second album, "Friends in Low Places."

"Garth loved the song. He demoed the song for Dewayne [Blackwell] and Bud [Lee]. After we finished the first record, we were working so much we realized that we had a dearth of fun songs. He really adapted that song and arranged it, and that was what they were playin' on the road, and when he came back in and recorded it, it was covered by Mark Chesnutt, and it was kinda like, who was gonna get it out there first!"

Bob is a very low-key guy, more into focus than excitement. "We were very busy. Pam, from day one, started promoting from a publicity stand-point, talking to her friends, developing those relationships with her media people. It was a hard sell. He was a *hat* act. It wasn't a hip, cool thing. She had worked with Steve Earle, and she'd worked on a couple of other things that were really interesting to people, but this was pretty meat and potatoes. *What's the story? What's the hook?*

"I felt this publicity push was gonna be critical, because at the time labels were about what they are now, you know, all the resources, like in-house publicity, had gone away. We weren't there six months when there was a whole turnover at the label."

Doyle is talking about the coup in which Jimmy Bowen had been hired by Joe Smith to replace Jim Foglesong as head of Capitol in Nashville.

"I'm thinking maybe we were into the second single when he took over. I remember Bowen coming up to Cookville and seeing the show—we were opening for the Statler Brothers—and Garth did a great job. And Jimmy came back and kind of grabbed us and laughed, and said, 'You lucky SOBs.' I think he realized that this was a great kid, and a smart kid, and I think he was ready to work with us and make the most of what was there."

But Bowen and Brooks were not going to be a match made in heaven. They are both powerful personalities. Bowen may have been used to get-ting things done his own way, but Garth Brooks was determined that if there were going to be mistakes made in his career, they were going to be *his* mistakes.

"Garth's real direct. There were issues," says Doyle. "Just like any relationship, you kinda feel each other out. You know, we'd always had independent promotion people working the songs, and there was an issue with that. It was an issue of having control. We had our differences with

Bowen, and I think it came down to a level of, well, we'll trust each other when we reach a point that we can trust each other.

"And then Joe Mansfield came in, and that was the critical piece. Joe's background in sales, and having come out of the world of rock and pop in New York, really brought a sense of scale to it. He felt that if the potential for moving these records is *here*, then I'm gonna put that number of units into that marketplace so that can be achieved. He worked with his customers. I don't know if any other person would have positioned the product as well as Joe Mansfield did."

The country boom of the late '80s and early '90s meant multiplatinum records for stars like Travis and Strait, Alan Jackson, and Brooks and Dunn, but the Garth Brooks explosion was like nothing in country or almost anyplace else. Garth's second album began selling and selling and selling...ultimately sales stood at *seventeen million copies*.

"When we got started in this thing," says Doyle, "I had specific goals that I wanted to achieve, but I would never have anticipated this success." Who could have? The follow-up album did fifteen million. "Garth always set the bar high. But it wasn't 'Let's move a million units.' It was like, 'Let's move as many units as we can move.'

"I remember watching some early Elvis stuff and some early Beatles stuff, and I had never seen anything quite like what we saw in the clubs with Garth. People would come, and they'd just push up to the stage, they were just jammed, all standing at the stage, screamin'—that's when I started to think, 'Whoa, these people are reactin' to this in a really interesting way.' It made you realize that something's going on here that is bigger than life.

"Then Garth decided, 'Let's try the arenas.' We maybe did one or two runs where we did three-thousand-seaters, and then immediately the decision was made—let's go up, take the next step. Kelly Brooks, Garth's brother, had come on and become sort of the tour manager. He and Garth came up with a touring philosophy and—based on the markets that we had played, the markets we needed to play, and the markets that we needed to repeat into—they basically began to set up a tour, using the major arenas in the country."

When a person hears a song on the radio, and even if he likes the record he hears, he is not necessarily *involved*. But fans willing to spend twenty to sixty dollars for a ticket to see an artist are generally willing to spend fifteen dollars or more for an album. In the case of Garth, this involvement was magnified by the tremendous effort he made to entertain his audiences. Garth was able to export the excitement Lynn Shults saw at the Bluebird Café to the fifteen- and twenty-thousand-seat venues he began to fill as his fame grew, and his records took off.

There was one more cog missing to the machine, and that was the means to inform the public and the industry that something truly unprecedented was going on.

"It was during the third album," says Doyle, "that SoundScan started." SoundScan is an instantaneous, highly accurate electronic information system that uses bar-coding to track sales of music from sales outlets to a central collection point. Before SoundScan, companies would call retailers and ask questions like, 'What are your best-selling albums this week?' The employee at the store would often give an answer off the top of his or her head, based upon high-profile titles. Because many stores did not focus on country titles as big-selling items, a lot of country acts were underreported.

The SoundScan system came on line right after Garth's third album, *Ropin' the Wind*, hit the street

"I think we would have been number one [on the *Billboard* pop album chart] the week after the album was released, but because the old [pre-SoundScan] system was still in place, there was a transition period, so we came in at a much lower position." The following week, with SoundScan in place, Garth *was* number one on the pop album chart. Both at the labels and record retailers, people were forced to notice that country music sales were considerably more important than they had conceded. Garth Brooks was the first country artist to reap huge benefits from SoundScan."

Another manager, Bob Titley, who guided Brooks and Dunn through much of their success, has a succinct way of summing up the Garth explosion. "It became news that a country album was at the top of the pop charts. And because he was number one, he was the vehicle for that news, and he had a very aggressive press agent, he worked his ass off, and he was everywhere. That was at a time when rap was coming in, and so people were looking for other alternatives. Millions and millions of people went and sampled country music, and they sampled it through Garth Brooks because he's who they saw as the picture of country music.

"I'd be riding in New York, with a cabdriver from Croatia, and I'd say I was in country music, and he'd say, 'Oh, I kind of like country.' I'd say,

'Really? What albums do you have?' and he'd say, 'Oh, I have a Garth Brooks album.'"

Garth was the center of the perfect storm.

Another thing that benefited Garth, Doyle points out, is that in those days hits went up and down the charts much faster than they do today. Sometime in the '90s, the consolidating radio industry made a conscious decision to slow down the ascent and descent of country singles—in 1990, for example, a hit single might stay on the charts for fifteen to twenty weeks. Today hits will have a chart life of anywhere from twenty-five to forty weeks. Doyle believes that a shorter chart life for singles benefits sales. "There's more exposure to the whole *album*. I think that when things are happening, and people are excited about it, they wanna consume it. They can't get enough."

That the radio and record industries do not have the same interests is obvious, but it seems logical that it is in country radio's best interest to build stars that sell records. Big-selling artists should bring listeners flocking to radio, hungering to hear their newest single. But radio does not care about the *intensity* of their listeners, they care about the quantity, especially in certain demographics. The labels strive to attract a younger demographic because that's where the record sales are.

In today's consolidated radio landscape, where one company might own seven stations in a market, they don't necessarily care if a single fourteen-year-old is listening to country music. The various pop genres cover that kid. Country and talk radio is supposed to cover the thirty-five-to-fifty-four-year-old demographic.

How does that affect country music? Well, for example, Big and Rich can boast record sales far out of proportion to the airplay of their singles. Somehow younger listeners find Big and Rich, and buy their records. But there are big radio ownerships that make corporate decisions to play less Big and Rich, because they believe that Big and Rich does not appeal to their older, target demographic.

Decisions made by people who do not understand country music have always been a detriment to the country music industry. As long as the suits are allowed to decide that country music is not for the young, then country will be hurt both financially and creatively. The '80s and '90s proved conclusively that young record buyers will home in on country music—if they get to hear it.

Ropin' the Wind shipped to orders of more than four million and things kept on getting better. Three years into Garth's recording career, he had sold more than thirty million albums. By the time he released his sixth album, that number would swell to almost sixty million.

Garth was fortunate to have Allen Reynolds staring at him from the other side of the soundproof glass. Even before Garth, Reynolds was one of the most important producers in the history of Music Row. His first major success was Don Williams, for whom Reynolds evolved a compelling studio sound. And where Williams was warm and comfortable, Crystal Gayle was dramatic. But Reynolds knew what to do with her in the studio, and lifted her to stardom. Two other singers, Kathy Mattea and Hal Ketchum, were more boutique artists, with folk sensibilities and a strong sense of style. Reynolds's productions helped launch successful recording and touring careers for both of them. And then there were those nine glorious Garth Brooks albums.

Early in his career, Arkansas-born Allen Reynolds spent a lot of time with Jack Clement in Memphis when Clement was engineering and producing for Sam Phillips's Sun Records. "I was in school then," Reynolds says. "I thought I'd like to learn to play bass, maybe get some gigs, and that'd be fun and I'd make a little money. I had a friend who played and I had gone to his house for some instruction. He said, 'I'm playin' with a little band and they're rehearsin'—why don't you go sit in for me?'

"I said, 'I don't know enough to do that,' and he said, 'That's how you learn.'" The friend was Dickie Lee, and the two began to hang out together. "Dickie was the first human being I ever met that wrote songs, and it was great 'cause I always had melodies goin' around in my head, and thought about writing, but I thought you had to know a lot more music than I knew. Then I realized you *don't*, so we got to writin' songs."

In the years that followed, while Clement fooled with his little Memphis studio and served as an out-of-town assistant to Chet Atkins, Reynolds finished college, had a record deal at RCA, and did some time with the Air Force. When Clement left for Beaumont to start his studio with Bill Hall, he asked Reynolds and Lee to move down to Beaumont, and eventually they did.

"We spent a couple of years there," says Reynolds. "Then I moved back to Memphis for about five years. I worked in a bank and moonlighted in music. Dickie and I wrote a song called 'I Saw Linda Yesterday' that was a

Top 10 pop record. But I had a family, I had a child, and I had to feed us, so I was working for the bank and that was good discipline for me, as it turned out.

"I was dying [at my day job], but during that time I started doing some producing, hustling, trying to get some things going. Meanwhile, I had written a song called 'Five O'Clock World' that was a real big success, and I would go from my desk at the bank down to the newsstand and buy a *Billboard* every week to see how I was doin'. That gave me another taste and some confidence. I really liked Memphis, and I liked the music scene there. Nashville sessions seemed a little too hurried. A Memphis session was basically five or six hours long, you just kinda looked for a *thing*—it was a different approach. But after Martin Luther King was assassinated, it changed things so drastically there—I don't know, it just began to feel like I wasn't gonna go anyplace down there. I woke up one morning and thought, this place is always kinda gonna be the boondocks—I need to look elsewhere. That weekend I went to Nashville to visit Jack. While I was visiting, I went to a party. There were a bunch of songwriters there, and a couple of them were talkin' to me saying, 'Man, you oughta come up here. This is a great town for songwriters!' I thought, that's the attitude I'm lookin' for. So, within a couple of months, I had left my job at the bank and started commuting here. That was the beginning of 1970, and I waited 'til the end of the school year to move the family up, but meanwhile Dickie and I commuted. I was putting my energy into writin' songs, trying to make a place for myself here.

"Once I got my feet wet producing, I really liked it. It was a puzzle that I liked working on. But my primary focus was as a writer because Jack had signed me and was paying me an advance, and I never wanted him to be out any money on my account. I wanted to do a good job, I wanted to prove myself.

"I got started right away in production because Dickie and I got a contract for him at RCA as an artist, and we were producing his records. I was doing a couple of other little things. Bill Hall got me to do some work with Albert Collins and I just loved it, he's a blues legend, but I gave my big energy to writin' songs at first.

"But then a couple of years later, Jack said he wanted to start JMI Records. I loved what he wanted to do. He was inspired by Sam Phillips, always. Jack, as I recall, wanted to do two things: he wanted to be a bigger publisher than Acuff-Rose, and he wanted to start a record label that had a *sound*. He wanted to find a hit sound, not just a hit record. At that time, if you were recordin' in Nashville, they were so quick, they were attuned to gettin' three, four songs in three hours, which was too quick for me. People were playin' along before they even heard the song through one time. That bothered me and it bothered Jack a lot, and we wanted to find a new group of musicians who would listen to the song first and take a little slower approach.

"Jack had those nice studios down there, and he started commandeering one of them for a whole day, one day a week, and he would hire different musicians, just looking for this band. That's where I first met Kenny Malone, Charles Cochran, and Joe Allen, and Jimmy Colvard and Lloyd Green, Buddy Spicher…this wonderful little group of players"— all respected session musicians who happened to share Reynolds's and Clement's vision—"that came together and formed the nucleus of [our house band]. Jack had asked me to run the record label, and I had naïvely stepped up and said *sure*, not knowing anything really about running a record label.

"I wanted to work with Susan Taylor [who sang in the Pozo-Seco Singers, along with Don Williams] and pursued her until she finally consented. As we worked on her album for Jack's label, she kept saying, 'You and Don Williams would like each other. I'd love for you to meet him sometime.' Don had moved to Texas to go into the furniture business with his father-in-law. One time Don was comin' up for a visit—he was not happy bein' in the furniture business—and we got together. He was talkin' like six months or so ahead, and I said, 'Well, if you do decide to move up here, come see me and I'll try to work something out.'

"Within a month he was here. I signed him as a writer for Jack's company, and told him we would produce him. The band was coming together and it provided the sound that became Don Williams's sound, a real acoustic kind of approach—pretty laid-back and gentle, really sweet, really nice.

"For me, it was *Don Williams, Volume One*. I remember lyin' on the floor listenin' to that when it was done and feelin' good, and thinkin', 'I *can* do this!' And thinkin' that album was something I would love twenty years from now as much as I did at that moment, and feelin' real happy about it."

The second single off the album, "The Shelter of Your Eyes," was a Top 15 record, a very good showing for a new artist on a new label.

"The next one was 'Come Early Morning,' with 'Amanda' on the back,'" Reynolds recalls. "That was all classic stuff for Don."

"Amanda," one of the greatest songs in the great songwriting career of Bob McDill, quickly became a classic even though Williams's record only made it to number thirty-three on the *Billboard* charts in 1973. Six years later, Waylon Jennings would have a huge number-one hit with it, and on both records the haunting harmony would be provided by studio engineer Garth Fundis.

"JMI Records didn't last but a couple of years," Reynolds continues. "It was a wonderful experience, and a great musical experiment, but it's very difficult to start a label and keep it going." One of the problems was that Clement severely reduced his cash assets by making a movie titled *Dear Dead Delilah*. The movie was a serious effort, starring such notables as Agnes Moorehead, Will Geer, and Michael Ansara. "He spent many times more dollars in that venture than he thought he would," Reynolds recalls. New record labels need time to gain credibility with their distributors, and with radio. It is tempting to believe that, considering they had a great artist right off the bat, if Clement had conserved his cash more carefully, JMI Records might have become a prime force in country music. But if Jack Clement had conserved his cash, he wouldn't have been Jack Clement. In 1976, Reynolds purchased one of Clement's studios, Jack's Tracks, on 16th Avenue South, several blocks down from the Quonset Hut.

Although he had produced memorable and successful music for Don Williams's two JMI albums, his phone was not ringing off the hook. "The one phone call I got was from Larry Butler [Nashville head of United Artists Records], who said, 'I like what you've been doin' and I'd like you to do something for us.' He offered me three artists. One was a Texas group called Callico. One was Slim Whitman, but I would have to go to England to produce Slim. And the other was Crystal Gayle. I said no to Slim Whitman 'cause I just didn't think I had the depth and the background to pull that off at the time. I said yes to Callico and Crystal Gayle. My assignment was to cut an album with Callico. With Crystal Gayle, I was to cut a single because she was new to them. It was a Top 5 single for her." The song was a Reynolds composition, "Wrong Road Again."

Crystal and Allen worked together for about nine years, recording some of the biggest and best records of the late '70s, including "I'll Get Over You," "Ready for the Times to Get Better," "Talking in Your Sleep," "When I Dream," and one of the great Music Row standards of all time,

Richard Leigh's "Don't It Make My Brown Eyes Blue," which was number one, country, and number two on the pop charts.

Leigh had written "I'll Get Over You," Crystal's first number-one hit, but didn't have an awful lot happening for him immediately thereafter. "He was renting from Sandy Mason [a talented songwriter who wrote for Reynolds], who owned a duplex, and she was saying to me, 'You need to come by and visit Richard. He's been a little down in the dumps lately because nothing much is happening.' I went out to cheer Richard up, and we were sittin' on the floor in Sandy's apartment, singing songs to one another. He mentioned a song he had written that his publisher was gonna get to Shirley Bassey, a big European singer [best known in the United States for singing the theme from the James Bond movie *Goldfinger*]. He sang it for me, 'Don't It Make My Brown Eyes Blue.' I said, 'Shirley Bassey my ass, I want that song!'

"I was really excited about it and when I played it for Crystal she was just as excited as I was. When we cut it, it was just one of those charmed sessions. I had been meanin' to hire Pig Robbins. I worked all the time with Charles Cochran [on keyboards], but Charles had had a mini-stroke and still had a little numbness in his hands. I said, 'Are you gonna be okay, buddy?' and he said, 'I think I'll be all right.' But just because I didn't want him to feel too pressured, I hired Hargus [Pig Robbins's real first name] too. So I had two keyboard players, and it was magic. We presented that song to the musicians and right off Hargus hit that *ba-dap, ba-da-da, ba-dap, ba-da-da*, and it just jelled. It was about the third time running that song that we ran tape, and the first time we ran tape, there was a recording. Charles played the horn parts on the Wurlitzer, and Hargus played the acoustic piano, including that identity lick that became part of the song.

"She sang it wonderfully. It came so fast that she wasn't sure she had done her best job. I had to let her try to sing it again on two or three different occasions until she was comfortable with the original, and that's what we went with. Everything on that recording was the original take as it went down, except the string section I added later. When you have a song that feels that exciting to you, sometimes magic can happen.

"It was so much fun working with her," Reynolds says. "The town was so different then. The music community was sweet, but so much smaller. You really had the freedom to make the kind of music that felt right, and the marketing was locally based. In fact, I think CBS was the first outfit to move in here with a major investment in marketing. At the time, I was glad to see it. Later I wasn't sure how good a thing it was, 'cause it did change the nature of things a lot."

With Don Williams and Crystal Gayle under his belt, one would have thought that the record labels would be begging Allen Reynolds to produce their acts, but it didn't happen. "Record labels have rarely come calling," Reynolds says, dryly. "I don't understand—I tried real hard. Somewhere about 1980, 1982, somewhere in there, Crystal and I quit working together. I was pretty unhappy with the business at that time. Jimmy Bowen was here, running his mouth a whole lot, and I just thought [the industry] had less to do with music than it should. For me, it's always been about music. It seemed to me, it still seems to me, that this town just can't get goin' with a good country act five minutes before they wanna take it pop, or makin' it into something else instead of just leavin' it the hell alone, and then nurturing it to be the best whatever-it-is that it can be.

"And this is true not just of record labels, but of artists themselves, and I don't know why. The one artist who was almost militantly not that way was Garth Brooks. His opinion was, 'We've got the franchise, what in the world do we wanna go over and try to climb on somebody else's franchise for? Let them come to us!' And he would not let his record label even promote or blink at any other format than country for him."

In the period '82 to '89, Reynolds says, "I was twiddlin' my thumbs and debating whether or not to sell this place and get out of production and go back to being a songwriter. My thought was, what independent producers did was develop artists and take them to labels, but I didn't find the labels very welcoming when I tried that. The last time I tried was in the early '80s with an artist named Colleen Peterson, who I thought was just wonderful. I spent months, and a lot of time, and a lot of my money recording sides on Colleen so that I could present her to the labels. When I was ready to present her—there were about six record labels in Nashville then—three of them didn't even want to listen. And I thought, *wow*, this has really changed. Then Jim Foglesong said yes [at MCA], and was gonna sign her, but before the contracts could get back from L.A., he got fired, so that fell through. I just was thinkin', you know, maybe I just don't wanna do this anymore, and maybe I'll just go back to songwriting.

"And then I went through a mental change. One day, I thought, nobody can move me off this corner but me, and I'm gonna stay here and make the best music I can make whether anybody wants it or not. And that was sort of a turning point for me—I just decided to change my attitude. I made a vow that I was gonna stay as far away from record labels as I could, I wouldn't go near them unless I was summoned. And that's a vow I've kept, I'm happy to say."

Reynolds did a number of projects that were creatively "nourishing" to him, as he puts it. It was during that period that Kathy Mattea came along. "She had a deal with the sleepiest label in town at that time, Mercury Records, and didn't have much of a budget to work with. She was a lovely person. She said to me when we were having our get-acquainted talks that she didn't want to sit on the fence, she wanted to be a country artist, and that appealed to me. At the same time, she was a folky kind of voice, with a bluegrass folk kind of background, so that's where we focused her music. She did very well and that got me going again."

By the late '80s, he was getting a lot more work, mostly from artists, not the labels. "For the first time ever, I had all the work I wanted, and it was all work I wanted to say yes to.

"Bob Doyle called me one day and said, 'I'm working with an artist/ writer I really believe in. I don't know if you're lookin' for any new acts....'

"I said, 'Well, I'm not lookin', but I'm open.'

"So he and I got together and talked about Garth. He played me demo tapes that he had. I liked Garth's voice, and I liked what Bob had to say about Garth, so I suggested that the three of us get together. I liked Garth. I said to him what I've always said to artists that I was interested in, 'Let's try a little work together. We'll do everything to prepare; we'll do a couple of recording sessions and see how we work together.'

"We cut two sessions and never looked back. The first session we cut 'If Tomorrow Never Comes,' 'Not Counting You,' and some of the hits from that first album. That turned out to be the best collaboration I ever had.

"By the time we got through with the first album, I thought really highly of Garth and I thought the album was gonna do well. In fact, I got Garth up here [at my office in Jack's Tracks] and talked to him. I sounded like a Dutch uncle. I said, 'I think this album's gonna get you way down the road.' I talked to him about handling his career, and remembering that it was *his* career, and that there would be lots of people wantin' to give input, but that *he* should manage it.

"Garth is always a good listener. He's a very bright guy. I don't know if he even needed to be told that once.

"I don't always understand what his image is, but I think he's always been in charge of his career. He's a wonderful collaborator. I never felt like I had to hammer him or shout to get his attention, and I never felt like he didn't listen to me. He didn't always do everything I would suggest, but I never asked that."

Producers often get excellent royalty deals on the albums that they produce, and these days almost everybody thinks about the money first. Allen Reynolds is a different breed of cat.

"The first thing you feel is happiness that you're working with somebody who can take the music that far, 'cause I've made records with other people that I've valued as much on a musical level as I did the work that I did with Garth. But he had the personality, the work ethic, and the commitment to take it out there. He was enormously popular, and that is a kick in the ass to have somebody who can take it out there to the public and not get stopped by label politics or any other thing.

"Plus, he's a guy who knows *who he is*. As big as he got, it never threw him off balance. Every time we got together to work on the next piece of music, he was the same guy that I worked with the last time. I was never having to dance with this giant ego. Garth comes from a big family and I remember him saying to me early on that he could never get the big head because his family would beat him up."

Every producer hopes to cut a song that's a classic, and Reynolds felt that the very first album he and Garth did together snagged one.

"'The Dance' was such a song," he says. Garth had been gathering songs before their first session, some written by him and some written by others. "I said, 'If you ever want me to listen to any of that stuff you've been gatherin', I'll be glad to.' Well, the next time he came in with a box about this big, and it was mounded up with cassettes. He said, 'You told me you wouldn't mind listenin' and here they are. So I went home and I was listenin' through, and here was this song called 'The Dance.' I listened to the song, and I listened again, and I listened again.... Here was this economic little poem, this beautiful song that had different levels of meaning. The next time we got together I said, 'What about that song, 'The Dance'—what do you think of that?' And he said, 'I love it.' But he wasn't sure. He loved it, but he wasn't sure that it was country.

"I said, 'Country people don't live in a vacuum, you know? Go drive through the country and see how many satellite dishes you see. They're listening to the same commercials and everything else. That song is for anybody.' So we cut it, and it blew me away. I remember from that session Bobby Woods startin' that little piano thing and Garth saying, 'Bobby, that thing you're doin', keep doin' it.' That's another one that just kinda fell together pretty quickly. And then Bowen came to the label mid-album and wanted to ditch that album [after the first couple of singles] and do another album within a month and a half. I said, 'Jimmy, we can't give you another album that quick that'll be up to our standards. Before you go past this album, I would like for you to go back and listen to 'The Dance,' because I know Garth would like to have that for a single. He's doin' it out on the road and you can hear a pin drop.

"To his credit Bowen listened to it and agreed, and said, 'Can you have me an album by June,' which was six months away. I said, 'That we can do.' So we went on and put two more singles out, the last one of which was 'The Dance.' Garth directed the video that was so effective at presenting that song, and it became one of his biggest pieces, you know."

As Garth's career exploded, the artist and his team had to focus on the multiple aspects of an artist's career, including the process of developing the show and booking it, the publicity side, and the many business details, but, says Reynolds, no matter how much Garth's career changed, his job as producer remained constant.

"As I've told you," he says, "for me, it's always about the music. I consider myself an entertainer even though I don't take the stage. I wanna try to cut songs that move people, and that have some enduring qualities. I like to feel like I've cut an album that I will like as much ten years from now as I do now, and an album that presents good value to the customer. I've bought albums in my past that pissed me off because all I would get was the single that drew me to the album, and then the album would be filled with inferior product that the artist wrote or published, and that would just make me so angry, 'cause I think the public deserves more than that. My attitude has always been, 'Look, this is your show for the coming year or year and a half—you can't compromise even one song. If it's only ten songs, then one song is ten percent of your show. Every song has to be the best you can find.

"The other thing I try to do," adds Reynolds, "Is to make it be like a show, so that if you took the stage and performed the album from cut number one to cut number ten, it would flow, and you wouldn't lose the audience's attention. It would be like a show, with surprises. I hate albums that sound like all they were trying to do was cut the next radio hit, and everything else got dumped into the album. I think this cheats the artist, and it cheats the audience for sure."

Allen Reynolds has said that he is retired. But he doesn't sound as if he's retired. He still cares too much. As he sits in his office at Jack's Tracks and watches Music Row go by, has he really called it quits?

"I haven't sold this place yet," he says. "But I am trying to be retired from production, and I'll tell you why. One, I am a little tired of being confined indoors, and I am enjoying bein' out and playing more golf. Producing for me is fairly intensive work and involves listening to all the songs that I get. When you work with a high-profile artist like Garth, you get so many songs, you wouldn't believe it. Another thing, the further you go with an artist, the harder it gets to find songs for him because you're always trying to find something fresh. It just gets harder and harder.

"The last time Garth and I worked together, it was not only hard for those normal reasons. I just wasn't hearing songs that I liked, that would give me bumps whether they were the right song for the project or not. It's because people are too damn busy trying to write radio singles and there are too many damn committees operating instead of songwriters. Now I don't mind co-writing. I did co-writing and I did individual writing, and the one would drive me to the other.

"When I came here, co-writing was discouraged unless you were co-writing with somebody within the publishing company. Publishers didn't wanna split copyrights and the money was too small anyway. I'm glad those things went by the boards, but I became aware in recent years, speaking to workshops for writers and all, that songwriters are coming to town going, 'How do I get with co-writers?' instead of coming to town saying, 'I'm a writer,' because they have the impression that this is how it's done. And I'm saying, 'Beware!'"

Today on Music Row, many established songwriters in search of co-writers, want to write not with writers whose skills complement theirs but with writers who are hot, or writers who write for a hot producer, or, naturally, writers who are artists. For these writers, the song is not the thing, the *cut* is the thing. Publishers book their hot writers with other hot writers, or with new, or if possible, hot writer/artists.

"I think this is so corrupt!" says Reynolds. "I stayed out of the publishing business most of my career because I didn't want any conflict of interest. I had Richard Leigh as a writer and I published 'I'll Get Over You.' Meanwhile, I was sending Richard to other publishers. I said to him, 'I don't want to do this, I don't want to wear both hats, so let me help you find a publisher.' So I cut 'I'll Get Over You,' and the day I cut it, it just happened that Jimmy Gilmer with United Artists Publishing happened to wander into the control room as we were listening to the playback and he goes, 'Who wrote that song?'

"I said, 'A guy named Richard Leigh and I've been trying to help him find a publishing deal. You wanna talk to him?'

Richard happened to be around the studio at the time. He went off with Gilmer and they cut a deal.

"Record companies, bless their ignorant hearts, say, 'Oh, I know what we'll do, let's get this artist to write with this great writer.' Bob McDill told me a story one day about sittin' down to write with one of these artists who was not a songwriter, and I will not name the artist. Bob said, 'We sat there and started working, and about fifteen minutes into it, the artist said, "Whew, boy, this is hard, isn't it?" About another fifteen minutes goes by and he goes, "Whew, you always work this hard?" And that was kind of the tone of their writing session, 'cause this ignorant twit didn't know anything about writing songs, and had no business being there.' I looked at Bob when he told me this and I said, 'Well, why the hell are you doing this? Why don't you tell him you've got plenty of songs!' And if you have to put his name on one, he should just be honest and say, 'Well, I like that song *you've* written, why don't you let me put my name on it!'"

Allen Reynolds is a mild-mannered man, a gentle soul who truly loves music and loves committing it to posterity in the studio. He is an artist and a craftsman respected by commercial and artsy songwriters alike. He is one of the most commercially successful producers in the history of Nashville, and has proved his ability to produce great music on an unusual variety of acts. But he can see the industry for what it is and is not afraid of telling the truth.

"Cowboy [Jack Clement] said one time, 'There ain't a righteous record label.' And I believe that. They're as corrupt as corrupt gets. Why did I want to retire? That's the main reason—those record labels. They're worse than ever now.

"It's every label in town. I'd have to take material in to young music school graduates who have never entertained, never written, never played an instrument, have never been onstage, never done *anything*, and they're gonna evaluate my material and tell me whether it's radio-worthy? They can kiss my ass! I'm through. I'm retired!"

If these were the rantings of a wannabe, a never-was, or an old grouch who once produced a hit in the '60s, then one could dismiss him with perhaps a small tear or two. But Allen Reynolds is one of the best record producers Music Row has ever known, and his talent and energy are such that he should still be making hit records today. If there is no room on Music Row for Allen Reynolds, is there still room on Music Row for music?

24

FROM THE
ALLEYWAY TO MCA

While strip malls and subdivisions are eating up the countryside like huge herds of kudzu monsters, there are still plenty of country folk in the hills and on the back roads of the South. Marty Brown is as country as grits—and the media loves him for it. He is also a solid singer and a fine songwriter.

"I always dreamed of comin' to Nashville, but I was always scared," he says. "I couldn't get here 'cause I lived up in Kentucky about two and a half hours away. My very first trip to Nashville, when I turned sixteen, I didn't know there was such a thing called Music Row back in 1981. I was just greener than a gourd. I remember I come up over the horizon and I seen that big city, and I'm like, 'Oh my God, I'm gonna get lost tryin' to find these places.' I remember there used to be a bunch of gift shops up there across from Shoney's [Restaurant and Inn], and I didn't realize that I was a block away from the nerve center of the music business. I spent the whole day stargazin' and lookin' through museums, but I brought home some brochures and stuff and I found out."

Once he'd heard about Music Row, Brown started driving down regularly to learn what he could. "I wasn't like a bum," he declares. "I wasn't a bum because I had a job back home cuttin' tobacco, but there was this little old restaurant called the Slice of Life, it's got a brick wall that goes around it, and a space in between the wall and the restaurant. I'd sleep up in there because I couldn't afford a motel room.

"During the day, I'd try to get people to listen to my stuff, just go up to whoever, but I just couldn't really get anything. Then I'd go to sleep there in this alley. One night it was rainin', and I'd seen a door that was cracked open. I seen the light on inside and I peeked my head in there and it was the Oak Ridge Boys in there recordin'. And they invited me in. One time,

I come in [to Fireside Studio] and Mel Tillis was propped up on the couch, he had them long legs. It was during his 'Coca-Cola Cowboy' years, and he looked me up and down and he said, 'Well, are you a singer or a songwriter?' I said, 'I'm a songwriter,' and that got his attention and he reared back and he said, 'Well, everything's gonna leave you, your house and your dog and your wife, and your car's gonna leave you, but your songs will never leave you.' And I remembered that. Eventually somebody did listen to me, over at BMI, Kurt Denny.

"The night before it happened, I got laid off. I had set my music aside and was concentratin' on this plumbin' company, and then I got laid off, me and twenty other guys, and I was kinda brokenhearted. I remember I got home and I gave my wife my check and I left her the car—we had a little old Cavalier station wagon. I called my cousin Big Joe. He had a huge beard and he's big and husky, he looked like a big bear, and I told him, 'We gotta go to Nashville, I can feel it.' I was about twenty-two then and I'd been comin' back and forth ever since I was sixteen. I made him shave his beard, 'cause with his size alone, I thought, 'Well, shoot, you'll scare 'em to death, nobody'll ever listen to us.' So he shaved his beard, and in the middle of the night, this guy give us a lift down here from the Longhorn Saloon back in Kentucky—'I'll run you down for twenty bucks'—so he dropped us off. I knew where Music Row was at that point, and we slept in the little alley behind the Slice of Life. I remember we got up the next mornin' and I looked at him, and you know, if you had an old beard on for a long time, and you shaved, you got a lot of dried skin all over your face? Well, he had that, and I said, 'Hey, man, you look like you got leprosy or somethin'—that's worse than the beard!'

"He growled, 'Aw, don't worry about it!' I remember we walked from this alley over to Mrs. Winner's Chicken. We took the rest of the money we had and bought biscuits and gravy. And I remember over breakfast I kept after him, I said, 'I can't believe that that dried skin is all over you, you're just gonna have to wait outside."

"'I ain't waitin' outside!'

"So we come back over to Music Row, and there's that BP gas station that sits over there. Well, he reached down in the bottom of a trash can and pulled one of them plastic oil jugs out and he cut it with his knife. And you know how there's some leftover oil down at the bottom of it? He rubbed that motor oil all over his face.

"So we was walkin' and I said, 'Well, let's just try this BMI buildin' over here. I went in, and from that moment on, it was a charmed life. Little lady there named Colleen, says, 'Sure, come on, we'll get you a Coke and somebody'll listen to you.' Kurt Denny came out, and after all those years of tryin' to get somebody to listen.... I remember we must have looked like bums. You know, my guitar didn't have a case and Joe's face was shinin' with motor oil, but I said, what the heck, and I sat down and I rattled off about five songs in a row. Finally, he stopped me and said, 'You got somethin' there!' I remember he tried to make a couple of phone calls—it was late in the day—and he said, 'Well, come on with me.' And he put me in his car and took me down to the bank teller and gave me a hundred dollar bill. He drove me up to Shoney's and put me and Joe up in a room. Well, in one night we went from sleepin' in the alley to havin' a pool and cable TV. It was Friday and he said, 'Now, come Monday, you come back over and you see me. Don't you leave here, you stay.' I think he called a couple of times checkin' to make sure I was still there during the weekend.

"But we had a hotel and we thought we was in heaven. I called my mom, and my dad was gripin', 'Well, you just got laid off from the plumbin' outfit. There's tobacco to cut back home, you better get home.' But I didn't go. Joe left in the middle of the night 'cause he heard my dad was comin' down and he and Dad didn't get along too good.

"On Sunday, my mom and dad they loaded up and made the drive down here. My mom, she brought all her cooking utensils and a hot plate and stuff and brought 'em up into Shoney's. I remember thinkin', 'Please let him [Kurt Denny] be there in the morning.'

"My mom says, 'See, Vincent, he does have a hotel room.' You know, when you're a country person, you don't trust people a lot, and my dad was standoffish. He said, 'Well, anybody can get a hotel room!' My dad was worried about the work that had to be done back home.

"Monday mornin'—I remember it like it was yesterday—I woke up to the smell of my mama's breakfast bein' cooked in the hotel room. We ate breakfast, and we come over to BMI, and there was Colleen and she said, 'Come on in here. Kurt's waitin' on you.' They got to meet my mom and my dad. Kurt said, 'Mr. Brown, here's the keys to my car.' He'd been workin' all weekend, callin' people. The tape that I'd left him was a tape I'd made in the bathroom back home, and he was passin' it around. So he gave his car keys to my dad, and my dad drove me around to all these places. I met with Tony Brown [MCA], Tim DuBois [Arista]—I met with them and I played for these people. At the end of that day, we went back to BMI, and Kurt Denny asked me, 'How'd you do?' I said, 'I go in and I play for them, but they just don't say nothin'.' He said, 'Well, I've heard from all of them today,' he said. 'They all wanna talk to you and want copies of that tape.'

"We stayed there all that week. The next day, they got me a manager, I mean, it literally happened like that. I remember it was Friday."

The reason he remembers it was Friday was that it was the day of the Harlan Howard Birthday Bash, an annual Music Row celebration to honor the man generally considered the greatest of all Nashville songwriters. "At the time, I didn't have a clue who he was. They said, 'We're gonna go to a birthday party, would you like to come?' My mama knew who he was. So me and Kurt and Tony Brown, and my new manager, Mike Robertson, go to this birthday bash, and they start introducin' me to people and they introduced me to Harlan.... Then it was time to go home, and I didn't want to go home.

"*48 Hours* [the TV show] had heard about me, and they wanted to do an interview with me before we went home. The funniest thing was to see my dad change, because all of a sudden my dad—I remember after the first day, when they treated him like a king, gave him the keys to the car, and he seen what was gettin' ready to happen—well, we went back to Shoney's, and *that night* he changed his tune. He says, 'I'll be back in a little bit,' and about fifteen minutes later, Mom is cookin' supper in the room, and he comes in, had him a brand-new cowboy hat on and a string tie. Mom says, 'Who are you? You think you're Johnny Cash or somethin?'

"He says, 'Well, I just might get *me* one of them record deals.'

"*48 Hours* interviewed me in the manager's office, and we all started loadin' up, it was time to go home. Well, I didn't want to go home. I'd just had the week of my life, and there was no way I wanted to leave all that! I said to Kurt Denny, 'I don't wanna leave,' and he says, 'You're gonna have to leave, because *48 Hours* is goin' to your hometown.'

"So we left Harlan Howard's birthday party, back to my home town with *48 Hours* in tow. And we no more got there—and I did the interview with *48 Hours*—I went back to work in the tobacco field. I didn't have to work long, though. It was about one o'clock on Saturday, and my sister pulls up in that white Thunderbird she used to have and she says, 'Marty, they want you back in Nashville!'

"'Throw 'em down, boys. We gotta go!' We took off, and it was Steve Buckingham. Well, he had got a hold of my bathroom tape, and he was mad because they didn't take me to see him. So we piled up and come back to Nashville. I remember we pulled up there at CBS/Sony Records and we went in, and I had my guitar and my old cowboy hat on, Mom and Dad was with me. I went in there by myself while they gave my Mom and Dad a tour of the record company. I walked in and he was sittin' down, and he had this old beagle dog up in the office. 'I've heard a lot about you. Let me hear you.' There's a song of mine called 'High and Dry' that became the title of my first album, and so I lit off on it and it's got this real high part. And when I hit that high part that dog started howlin', and I said, 'Oh God, I've set the dogs out!' He said, 'That's all right. Don't pay no attention to him. Go ahead and go again.' I tried it again, and the dog started howlin' again. I said, 'I know you don't wanna sign me.' He says, 'Well, give me a minute,' and he takes the dog and sits him out in the hallway and comes back in. And I sang again, and that dog's out there scratchin' on the door howlin'. The whole time I'm singin' he's over writin' on a piece of paper, and when I got finished, he slid that piece of paper over to me. My mama's still got that piece of paper. It had George Jones's name on it, it had Willie Nelson's name on it, it had Dolly Parton's name on—all these big names that was on their label, and he had my name written at the end of it.

"And then I had to go back home."

But Marty Brown did not sign with CBS Records. About a month later, he got a deal to write for MCA Music, and then a recording deal with MCA Records.

"I had never been out of the state of Kentucky [except to come to Nashville]. I had never had Mexican food in my life," Brown says with wonder. "Maybe a frozen burrito or somethin'. But I had never been to a Mexican restaurant. I had never been to a Chinese restaurant. I had never seen the ocean. I had never flown on a plane. All of a sudden my dreams got to come true."

If this had been a movie, Marty Brown would have become a star. He did not. "I went on a radio tour for my first single," he recalls. "We shot my first video in my hometown. We were just gettin' over *48 Hours* bein' there, and a month later we shot a video, and it was great.

But the media had found Marty Brown. "I don't know, it's like Loretta Lynn," he says. "I put myself in that category. It gives people something to read, and something to cling to. Hey, there is hope that somebody can come from the hills of Kentucky and make it, literally, overnight like that."

There might have been a rags-to-riches element in many of the media's stories about Marty, but there was also a lot about "Marty Brown, an authentic country voice," the subtext being that much of what passes for country music today is unauthentic.

By the time, Brown came along, at the beginning of the '90s, record labels usually did not stay long with country artists who didn't have hits. But MCA cut four albums on Marty Brown before they let him go.

"After my fourth album, I shot my last video. I kind of knew that it was probably gonna be my last video, but through it all I kept rememberin' Mel Tillis's advice: *write*. And that's what I did, I wrote and I wrote and I wrote. A tree don't always grow straight. A tree's gonna branch out. By me losin' the record deal, it was a branch, and I branched out. It's up to you to decide, 'Okay, which way do I go?' So I took off for about a year...."

Was he disappointed that his record deal did not break the bank? "Here's the deal. To me, I *was* breakin' the bank! Because I'd never seen anything like that in my life." Touring around the country in a car or a bus is a grind, and at Marty's level, the pay wasn't huge, but it sure beat working in a tobacco field.

"I won't say that we were poor people," he says, "because my daddy always worked. I always had shoes on my feet and clothes on my back. Of course we didn't have no money to be goin' to no restaurants. We ate at home, and Mom, she's a black belt when it comes to cookin'. She had three boys and three girls she had to feed...my mama when she cooked chicken and dumplin's, she cooked kettles of it and we ate on it for weeks. Lookin' back, I've lived a charmed life."

So when he lost his record deal after six years on MCA, he just didn't see the loss as a tragedy.

"Here's the deal. I had created such a buzz, I mean, I'm hangin' with Alan Jackson, out there with Garth Brooks. Of course they went on to be great superstars—I'm proud of them—and great songwriters, and I was right there with 'em. It was fun. Man, the '90s were a complete whirlwind. I remember I was at my manager's office and he says, 'You know, you're not gonna get renewed at MCA.' I think I seen it comin' anyway, I think I was ready to do something else, but still, it was like an earthquake. But I was able to tour for four more years and live comfortably. I had a solid eleven years as an artist—really, a solid fifteen," because as his singing career waned, his songwriting picked up with major cuts on artists like Tracy Byrd and Brooks and Dunn.

"I didn't realize at the time," he says, "that all of this press, newspapers, *People* magazine, *48 Hours*, I did not know that all of that—I was layin' ground work to be a songwriter. Because I'm gonna tell you, man, I see a lot of these songwriters. They remind me of me when I was sixteen—they have no face, no identity, no credibility. I mean, here I was a sixteen-year-old kid with a floppy cowboy hat on and a guitar with no case, who'd been sleepin' in an alley over here. You know, is this kid gonna be any good? He's got dirt on his pants, he's got oil on his hands from where he'd stayed up all night long puttin' a starter on a car underneath a carport light just to get down to Nashville."

Marty Brown views his career very clearly: He has been able to make a decent living doing what he loves to do, and he cannot for the life of him pause for even a moment to regret that he had not reached the heights of Alan Jackson or Garth Brooks. "Remember, I told you I took a year off," he says. "I went back home, and bought a horse, and I did nothin' but ride that horse and fish, write songs, and hang out with my son. That's when I wrote 'I'm from the Country and I Like It That Way.' During that period I took off, I was able to see myself as an old man, and I didn't want to be one of these people who was dyein' their hair black, or gettin' a toupee, and havin' rhinestones all over me. There's nothin' sadder than that."

The vast majority of songwriters that come to Music Row want to hear their songs played on the radio, and they will do whatever it takes to get a hit. They've studied the big records and think they understand the elements of a hit song. They hang around the bars that feature "writers nights," and by day, they hustle and do what they think they must to get a foot in the door at the publishing companies.

But among the many songwriters who come to Nashville every year, there are always a few who refuse to compress themselves into the commercial writer's mold. Most of them have a great sense of their own style and they are determined to write *their* songs, hoping against hope that every so often the industry will reach down and pluck one of their artistic gems and cut a hit on it. These writers tend to hang together. They play here and there for tips, and sit in their kitchens passing the guitar around and digging each other's songs. Some of them become artists in a genre called "Americana," a slightly folky, slightly country, slightly rockin' little format carried by a handful of stations around the country. They tend to feel alienated from the Nashville mainstream, but every so often one of them gets a hit, and once in a great while one of them becomes very successful. Don Schlitz was once one of these writers. Even after his song "The Gambler" became a classic, it took him quite a while to make the transition into country's mainstream, where he thrived with hits like "On the Other Hand" and "Forever and Ever Amen." Even then, many of his songs maintained the uniqueness and feeling of a songwriter who looks to his gut rather than to his bank account for inspiration.

More recently, Darrell Scott's unique songs jumped out of his catalog and onto the CDs of artists like Tim McGraw, Garth Brooks, Brad Paisley, Diamond Rio, the Dixie Chicks, Travis Tritt, and Patty Loveless. Scott sounds like a man following his muse when he says, "When I'm writing, I try to go where the song wants to go." But then he says, "I grew up listening to commercial radio. I know what a chorus is. I know what a turnaround is. If the song I'm working on is a groove thing, I go there." But Scott has the sensibilities of an *art writer*. He mostly writes alone, and he selects his co-writers for what they can bring to the song, not for the artists they can access.

The king of the art writers in Nashville is Guy Clark. Other art writers seek him out. They want to be like him. Clark doesn't get a hit very often, and yet he usually has a publishing deal because he commands so much respect. Over the years, a number of his songs have made their journey from his imagination to the top of the charts, including "She's Crazy for Leavin'" (Rodney Crowell), "Oklahoma Borderline" (Vince Gill), "Heartbroke" (Ricky Skaggs), "Baby I'm Yours," (Steve Wariner), and "The Carpenter" (John Conlee). "Desperados Waitin' for a Train," a solid chart record for Waylon, Willie, Johnny, and Kris, is one of those special tunes that is considered a great classic even without achieving the blockbuster hit status that most songs need to achieve that status.

Guy Clark makes much of his living on the road. He doesn't travel with a band, he travels with Verlon Thompson, a guitar player, singer, and co-writer. These two guys can fill a small club with great sound, and

Clark lures his audience into his world with his whiskey voice and charismatic personality.

When Clark gets back to Music City, he builds guitars, beautiful guitars, in the basement of his West Nashville home. Over the past half dozen or so years, he's built eleven of them. They are stunning to look at, and they possess a profoundly memorable tone. It seems that whatever Guy Clark chooses to create, he is a master.

But even if Clark doesn't spend much time on Music Row, which is only about twenty minutes from his house, he is a part of it. Guy Clark is about songs.

"My approach is, write the best you can," he says. "And I joke about it, you know, I'd sell out if I could, but I can do better than that. I can write better than that. The reality is that if you're tryin' to write it for a radio audience, you get to about the lowest common denominator in the world. And I don't get a buzz from writin' like that. Sure, I'd love to have the money, but it doesn't do anything for me, and that's the reason I write. Because it does somethin' for me."

Clark does not see an unbridgeable divide between *great* songwriting and *hit* songwriting. "I believe that good songs can be hits. It's not a total black-and-white situation. I've written some songs that were hits, like 'Heartbroke,' which was a number-one hit, and it's an okay song. It's not a song I would write today, but I liked it at the time. Townes Van Zandt's 'Pancho and Lefty,' who would ever have thought that would be a hit song? Nobody. So I've just had this kind of Pollyanna faith that good will win out—maybe not in the proportions you would like, but good shit if it's really good will get heard, if you make any sort of effort."

Guy Clark's songs get heard today largely because he is a performing songwriter. Over the years, painstakingly, he has assembled a fairly large number of fans scattered around the country. His songs are personal to them—they revel in the fact that the whole world doesn't go around singing them, and they delight in Clark's ability to tell a story and evoke deep emotion.

"I have no reason to write songs unless I'm gonna go play 'em for the folks, and I have no reason to go play for the folks unless I got new songs." That way of thinking implies a special relationship, almost a covenant, between Clark and his fans. He has an ample catalog—many of his songs are so good and time-tested that the folks would come out for them again and again—but he will not stand still. There is always a new song.

Over the last few years, he says, he has averaged between eighty and a hundred performing dates a year. Although that may not seem like a lot compared with the two-hundred-plus dates a year Ernest Tubb would log fifty years ago, that's actually quite a grind.

"It's a lot," he says, "because I automatically go the day before. I don't like cramming all that into one day, flyin' all morning, getting there, checking into a hotel, sound check, come back to the hotel, get cleaned up, go to the gig and play—and that takes the fun out of it. I make it as easy on myself as possible."

Many touring artists are retailers as much as they are singers, selling merchandise at every show. They hit the road with an impressive array of T-shirts, CDs, and every other form of "merch" imaginable, and at the end of the year, their on-the-road sales can represent a lot of the profit they've made during the year. Guy Clark refuses to push product on the road. He doesn't even sell his CDs.

"I'm not a peddler," he says. "It's somethin' else to keep up with. If somebody else wants to go do it, do it. I have a web site, which sells albums, but I don't hawk albums from the stage. It's not what I do, and it's a kinda snooty attitude. But the last thing I wanna do is get off a stage after doin' a good *or* a bad show, and go piddle with whoever was sellin', then count albums and make sure all the money's square and on and on. That's not my idea of any kind of fun. Heck, that's why they have music stores, go to a music store and leave me alone! Sometimes there's a guy who does go around on his own. I don't take any part, I just consider it like a travelin' music store."

As much as he is an independent artist and for all the time spent on the road, Clark remains tuned in to the Nashville song machine. He writes for EMI, one of the largest song publishers in the world. "It's just business, you know. They fulfill a need that I have, and I fulfill a need that they have. They're in the business of getting good songs, and I want somebody to get mine out there."

Like most songwriters, Clark doesn't see the business of music as one of the joys of his life, but that doesn't mean he hasn't sought to understand it. "Every once in a while, over the period of time I've been here, I've gotten really into it, and studied it. I can read contracts—my father was a lawyer and I know how that works." Like other songwriters, he pays attention to pitch sheets, those neatly printed schedules that tell publishers who is coming up to record and what they are looking for.

"I've got one right here," he says. "I don't have any chip on my shoulder about the business. For example, I look at that pitch sheet—every time I go down to the office I pick one up and bring it home. They come out once a week, so I don't do it all the time, but if I have a song that I think has some sort of outside chance of being recorded by Brooks and Dunn...'Hey! Send them a copy of this song!' But I don't hold my breath. If you do that, that's just a waste of time and energy, full of angst and bad vibes."

Though he puts a tremendous amount of effort into writing his songs, people who want to record his songs can have their way with them, he says. It's part of the folk tradition for songs to evolve and for the singer to make them their own. "You can do anything you want with my songs as long as you don't want part of the writer's credit. I don't care. Make it a waltz! But I know people who just get *livid* if somebody even presumes to change one little word.

"Ricky Skaggs had played on my record of 'Heartbroke.' He said, 'If I ever get a record deal, I'm gonna cut this song,' and I said, great—you know, the more the merrier. So when he got ready to record he came up to me and said, 'Look, I hope you understand, I had to change the words a little bit.' One of the lines is 'Pride is a bitch and a bore when you're lonely.' He said, 'I just couldn't stand it if Mom and Daddy heard me say that on the radio.' I completely understand. It bothered me not one bit that he changed it to something he could live with, 'cause I could always do it exactly the way it goes. And I do."

"Oh, everybody gets all excited," when an artist chooses your song. "Trace Adkins put one of my songs on hold"—a *hold* is something that happens when an artist likes a song well enough to say he's considering recording it—"Trace got it cut, finished the whole thing, mixed it, and then it didn't make the album. After a while, you kind of wait to get excited until you know that something's gonna happen."

On Music Row, all professional songwriters go through this ritual, including the desire to insulate themselves from the disappointment that is the daily diet of most songwriters.

Clark does not see himself unique as a writer—he sees a number of other writers who approach their music as he does. "Verlon, of course," he says. "Jamie Hartford, I like Shawn Camp. I like John Prine. Rodney Crowell, just old friends—and a hundred more."

For all his independence and hard work, Clark has received the highest form of respect from the establishment: a Lifetime Achievement Award from ASCAP, and he is a member of the Nashville Songwriters Hall of Fame.

So how does he feel about Music Row?

"I like chairs and tables" he says. "I hate couches, I just hate 'em, and it seems like every studio that you walk in has got a couch behind the control board. But for whatever there is wrong with [Music Row], there's a lot right. I mean, there's like the best players in the world, the best songwriters in the world. This is it! It's like Paris in the '20s."

Guy Clark writes great songs without living in the constant shadow of the commercial marketplace. Bob McDill spent his years writing for the record industry—but was also able to maintain the highest standards of the songwriter's art.

His long list of hits include country classics like "Amanda," "Baby's Got Her Blue Jeans On," "Gone Country," "Catfish John," "Rednecks, White Socks and Blue Ribbon Beer," "Nobody Likes Sad Songs," "Don't Close Your Eyes," and the courageous Don Williams tour de force "Good Ole Boys Like Me."

Guy Clark spends his spare time building guitars. McDill, who like his longtime colleague Allen Reynolds aggressively claims to be retired, owns a house next to the governor's mansion that he has been renovating with great patience, just the way he wrote hit songs for three decades.

And both Clark and McDill are Texans—Clark from a West Texas town called Monahans, and McDill from a little place south of Beaumont called Walden. "It had a little store, a café, little cluster of houses, and on the other side of the highway by the railroad tracks, there was a platform to get on the train. It was all truck farms, egg farms, stuff like that. Nice place to grow up."

McDill, like Clark, is a "thinking man's writer." What he writes about he cares about, and no song came from deeper in McDill's gut than "Good Ole Boys Like Me."

"'But I was smarter than most, and I could choose, / Learned to talk like the man on the six o'clock news.' That line addresses the Southerner's love-hate relationship with himself and his culture and his history. He changes his accent, just like kids are still doing today as soon as they're able to imitate someone on television and in the movies," says McDill.

"Some of it is autobiographical. On the other hand, I had just read Robert Penn Warren's *A Place to Come To*, which made a tremendous impression on me, and I wanted to write the quintessential song about growin' up *Southern*. That was my aim."

Then there was "Gone Country," a much bigger hit in a boom country era. Bob McDill has an acerbic side, and in 1994, this song spoke for hundreds of country songwriters and artists, and millions of fans, who could tell the real thing from the opportunists trying to get in on country music's popularity.

"I kept meeting these people who had come here from New York, L.A., Las Vegas, and they were...the truth was their careers were in the tank, but the mental gymnastics they'd do as to why they'd moved to Nashville, it was just wonderful. You know, 'L.A.'s no place for kids, we wanted a better place to raise our children....' Just grasping for straws. I kept hearing these people over and over and finally that all just sort of metastasized: 'Gone Country, / Look at them boots, / Gone country, back to her roots....'"

McDill began writing songs when he was fifteen or sixteen years old, and played in a skiffle band at Lamar University, where he ran into the kind of luck reserved for just a fortunate few. Jack Clement had his Gulf Coast Recording Studio in Beaumont, and he happened to hear the group singing in a local bar around 1963.

"Allen Reynolds was working there, and Dickie Lee, and they heard us. Bill Hall was there too. They were recording hits, 'Patches' by Dickie Lee, and 'Running Bear' by Johnny Preston, early Johnny and Edgar Winter stuff." McDill went into the Navy but some of his songs stayed in Beaumont, and "Hall and Clement got a couple of them recorded—Perry Como, Sam the Sham and the Pharoahs. Anyway, I got out of the navy and went to Memphis to join Alan and Dickie, and when they all moved to Nashville in 1970, I came with them.

"When Jack Clement's organization started falling apart, Dickie Lee had already gone over with Bill [Hall], and he talked me into comin' over, too. I was thinking about going to Tree, and Dickie said, 'Hey, McDill, Hall will make you rich, man,' and I thought, hmmm, that sounds pretty good. Bill cared about his writers. When I started with Bill, he had Foster and Rice. Foster had a Rolls-Royce and Rice had a new Cadillac, and Bill used to tell other publishers in town, 'My writers drive Rolls-Royces and Cadillacs....'

"Bill was great. You know, get you a lawyer, financial adviser, get you in the mainstream, buy you steak dinners, get you recordings—he could get your damn career going. One of the ways he stayed in close relationship with all the producers, and a lot of the artists, was gambling. Everybody gambled in those days—this was in the mid-'70s—and Bill was the middleman between the record producers and the bookie. I guess maybe some of those people didn't wanna have a personal relationship with a bookie, but they could have one with Bill. Bill took all the bets, he'd be there all day taking football bets, and talking about the 'push' and the 'spread' and the this and that. All the producers, everybody, gambled with Bill. And then they had these card games. They'd get together at CBS in Billy Sherrill's office at a big table—thirty thousand bucks would change hands in an afternoon over there."

Dedicated as Bill Hall was to the success of his writers and his publishing company, McDill recalls a dark side that his writers had to watch out for, lest they be emotionally blindsided by him.

"Bill would get in his cups and take you down a notch," says McDill. "He took everybody down a notch. He could be insulting, but I knew that from the old days. If he got a little too inebriated and he thought you were talking about your success a little bit too much, or your hopes for success or whatever, he'd look at you and say, 'Can I tell you somethin'?'

"You'd say, 'What Bill,' and he'd say, 'You ain't shit! You ain't shit!' He told most of the people in town at least once, 'You ain't shit!' Everybody from Sherrill to Bradley. He wouldn't say that if he was sober.

"Bill wasn't mean," McDill emphasized. "He was too little to be mean. Nobody could ever be intimidated by him or take him seriously."

When McDill came to town around 1970, the counterculture had not yet hit Music Row. Aside from alcohol, pills were the drugs of choice. "The Professional Club—where was that darn thing, sort of across the street from the Kountry Korner [close to South Street and 16th Avenue South]. It was an old house that had been remodeled, and inside, the barroom looked just like the set of *The Iceman Cometh*. It was creepy. Nineteen-foot ceiling in that bar over there, this ancient old woodwork... everybody went there. There was a lot of amphetamines. Nashville was a big amphetamine town at the time. In fact, my friend Jim Dickinson in Memphis, I told him I was gonna move to Nashville, and he growled, 'Hey, McDill, don't move up there. Everybody up there takes that truck driver dope!' When I got to town, it was true, the whole town was wired on amphetamines."

How did McDill consider his songs different from the many hacks around Music Row whose songs would have their fifteen minutes and then disappear?

"I did a lot of hacking myself—I'm not exempt from that," he declares. "I wrote a lot of garbage, hundreds of songs that were garbage. Thank God, nobody remembers any of them. ASCAP doesn't even remember 'em. You can look on my ASCAP statement, not a one of those crappy little hack ditties is on there. It's just like they never existed. The things that are on my ASCAP statement now are things that I wrote because I wanted to say something, or because it was really fun. 'Baby's Got Her Blue Jeans On' still plays like a hit. It was really different. You know, there's no giants killed in there, it's not saying anything except, 'This gal's got a great behind,' but it was not a hack piece. 'Song of the South,' 'Good Ole Boys Like Me,' 'Don't Close Your Eyes,' 'Gone Country,' those things still play. 'Everything That Glitters.' It's because they were different. They were written from the heart. Conviction."

When the musical trends changed, McDill stuck by his trade. "I always rolled with it," he recalls. "When cheating songs ran, I wrote cheating songs. And what I did was do my hack work week after week after week until a really good idea came along. Then I could really indulge myself and do a little bit of art, and then, when that idea was gone, I didn't wait for another good idea to come. I did hack work, I wrote junk.

"But I don't know," he says. "In the '90s, it got so difficult to get a record. Got so that when you got a recording, it could only be described as a miracle. Everybody in town competing for a handful of slots."

So McDill decided to retire. "Tired of the business," he says. "Had nothing left to say. And once you leave, and once you allow yourself to look at the music business as it is, you can never go back, reason being, in the big picture, none of it really matters. And you know, while you're in songwriting, you've got to convince yourself that this matters. That this has meaning. That somebody is listening."

25

TEXAS AND OKLAHOMA SONG DOGS

To some, it's a cold day in hell when a "suit" can cross over to the creative side of the business and play at being creative, a "music guy." We've all seen what happens when corporate gets overly involved—all too often the bottom line is paid more attention than the quality of the songs, and talented people get cut loose or go missing. But sometimes, beneath the suit beats a truly creative heart. And then, usually, the suit gets replaced by a pair of jeans.

Now meet Tim DuBois. An accountant, and one with serious credentials. He worked as a staff auditor for Arthur Andersen, then as a senior financial analyst for the Federal Reserve Bank of Dallas. Somehow this led to an outstanding career in the music industry, as a producer, an executive, *and* a songwriter.

"In '74, I left the Federal Reserve Bank of Dallas," he says. "And moved back to Oklahoma to work on a PhD in accounting. I was teaching and working on my doctorate at Oklahoma State University when I first started coming to Nashville with my songs. I was out here on spring break of '77 and walked in to the University of Tennessee–Nashville, just walked in off the street and asked to talk to somebody in the accounting department, and wound up talking to the department head. I told him that I was going to be doing my dissertation, and I would be looking for some place to teach. He had an opening starting that summer. So I just kind of lucked into that. I ended up taking a two-year leave of absence from my PhD program. I was gonna become the next Kris Kristofferson—or I was gonna go back to Oklahoma and finish my doctorate."

He didn't become the next Kristofferson, but by 1982, he had scored three number-one hits. Eventually he helped put together a group called Restless Heart, and produced and managed them to considerable success.

In 1992, he collected the CMA and ACM Song of the Year awards for the classic he wrote with Vince Gill, "When I Call Your Name."

But by the late '80s, DuBois was already working magic as an executive after Clive Davis tapped him for the Arista organization.

"The way Clive tells the story is, he just thought that the world had become very producer-driven, and with all of the explosion of rap and metal, he felt like there was going to be a turning back toward the song and the songwriter. He had been in charge of CBS when Billy Sherrill was running their Nashville office, and he felt like the South was getting ready to have their own explosion, so he tapped me to start a division here.

"As it turned out he was dead on. We opened the doors in '89, and by 1990, when we put our first albums out, Garth had exploded. The first album we put out was Alan Jackson, and that was a great way to start a record label. We had a platinum album. We had Alan, Brooks and Dunn, Pam Tillis, and Diamond Rio all within an eighteen-month period. It was a magical time. We only signed twenty-some artists during the entire eleven years that I was there at Arista, and over half of them went on to have gold or platinum albums. You just couldn't do that in today's world—it's just not possible thanks to consolidation, the slowing down of the charts.... Not only did we break those acts in that eighteen-month period, but they all went on to have three or four number-one singles within about a year. Back then, it was three or four singles a year as opposed to one or two that we have now, so those acts were not only able to break at radio, but were able to have careers that didn't have to be supported by the label in tour support. They were actually able to go out there and work."

DuBois had hit the jackpot. He had managed to launch a label smack in the middle of the biggest country boom ever, signed the right artists, and saw that they released the right material. Given its newness and its smallish staff, Arista was the most astounding of many success stories during this time of unbelievable prosperity on Music Row.

Then the Federal Communications Commission changed the rules and allowed the radio industry to consolidate. Soon just three companies controlled over two thousand stations.

"One of my radio friends explained it the best way I ever heard," DuBois says. "'We program not to offend.' So radio tends to avoid records that draw negatives from their audiences, even though huge numbers love the records. They'd rather play records that almost everybody can tolerate. The last thing they want is for somebody to push that button and go to the next station.... Big and Rich right now is a good example. They haven't been able to deliver number-one records on those guys, but obviously there's a huge audience out there, they're still sellin' thirty thousand units a week. But because they are high-passion records and there are a lot of negatives there, some stations don't stay with the record very long."

If they can sell millions without the record getting to number one, then maybe it doesn't matter if it gets that high on the singles charts.

"Well, it never has mattered to the record label, other than to the promotion department, because we don't make anything off of airplay, we only make it off of sales. If someone is motivated to get off their hiney and go to the store and plunk down their credit card, that's when we make money."

In January 2002, DuBois and former MCA Records–Nashville president Tony Brown started Universal South Records. At the time, country had not yet begun its next resurgence, and sales were much harder to come by. But artists and their publicists like number-one records, even if they don't necessarily generate large cash-register receipts. It makes for good sound bites when somebody can say that he's had twenty number-one hits over the last ten years. So what if the albums didn't sell squat?

"I've actually had to say to some artists, 'You know, we can keep this record alive for another five weeks, but look at what you're sellin'. It's time to throw dirt on this and move on.' And then some of the acts that we've signed understand, a good example being Cross Canadian Ragweed. From the beginning, I've said to them, 'I don't know that we can have huge radio records on you guys, but we can get airplay in the markets where you work, and we'll micromarket the dog out of it in those markets. We'll help you expand your touring base, and that was our agreement going in, that and they just don't want us to mess with their music at all. They don't want us to force them into a box, and it's been a great thing for both of us."

DuBois understands that not all good artists are destined to be mainstream acts. Unlike many record executives, he is willing to sign an act that is not tailor-made for radio.

"Shooter Jennings is an example. We're gonna make a mainstream radio push on Shooter, but there's an act there that's gonna be critically acclaimed and gonna tour and is gonna have an impact beyond radio. If we have a big radio hit, that will help throw gasoline on the fire, but there's enough stuff there to be excited about. It's one of those things that you do not do because you think you can have *number-one* records, but because you think there's a career there and you can *sell* a lot of records.

"The Louvin Brothers album that we put out in 2003 was the same kind of thing. We didn't think there was stuff there that would be Top 5 at radio, but we won a Grammy and we sold over a hundred thousand units. It's a success for everybody involved, and it was pretty much done without radio support."

DuBois is a throwback to the early days of Owen, Chet, and Jerry Kennedy, a more wide open time in country music. It is fine that country stars today can sell three million or more copies, but to concentrate entirely on mass sales from mass radio play is to miss much of the freshest music in the industry. DuBois knows that you can make a good record for reasonable cost and sell enough albums without radio to make a profit. He also knows that sometimes an act can pop out of the small world with one great record, the way Allison Krauss did.

Before DuBois and Tony Brown started Universal South Records, DuBois had a brief tenure with the Gaylord Entertainment Company. Gaylord had failed before in the record business, and DuBois was supposed to be the man who could lead them to success. He was hired with great fanfare, and his departure was sudden and unexpected. Some say that he left because he found out that Gaylord would not give him the kind of commitment he thought he needed to establish a new label.

"When I left Gaylord and went into what I call my gainfully self-unemployed period, I didn't know exactly what I wanted to do. I knew I didn't wanna come back on a major label because I could see that that was gonna be a lot of pain and a lot of blood for the next few years. The industry had already started into the downward spiral, the downsizing and the consolidation. Going into a major label and having to be the turnaround guy is not the fun that starting something new is—from scratch, where you're getting to offer new opportunities instead of firing people. It just never appealed to me.

"I wasn't feeling the financial pressure to do anything quickly, and then Tony called me up one day and said, 'Would you be interested in starting a new label?'"

Tony Brown and Tim DuBois had been strong competitors in the '90s when MCA was the number-one label in town and Arista was at times number two. As happens on the Row, their careers had crossed many times, when Brown was signing artists and DuBois was writing hits or managing acts. Their mutual respect was enormous, so Brown's proposition was too big a temptation to turn down. "I have such total respect for him as a music person and as a human being, and because of my checkered past as a business person, I have some tools maybe that he doesn't have. But we both are bonded by the fact that we just absolutely love artists and love songs. So—in the worst of times—he went to New York and presented the idea to Doug Morris, the head of Universal, and Doug said, 'Yeah, let's try it,' and actually flew down here a week later and met with us. We started the ball rolling in early 2000 and it took a long time to get it done. We went through 9/11, and we went through continuing bad results at the record labels, and there were those times I'll admit when I didn't know if it was ever gonna get done."

Brown and DuBois have an unusual situation. "We've been able to build a company that is a joint venture with Universal–Motown out of New York, but we're kind of in a bubble over here. We're protected from what happens across the street over at MCA and Mercury, which has been a very tumultuous time with Bruce Hinton leaving and Luke Lewis comin' in, and then Dreamworks merging into it, and a whole lot of staff reductions and things like that. We've been unaffected.

"We don't report to them. It doesn't feel like we report to anybody—we're just kind of a business down here. It feels like a small, independent record label, but yet we're still attached to the biggest, baddest machine in the business, 'cause we're distributed by Universal and we get a lot of help from them. The whole Universal South is only twenty people, seventeen people in the record company and three people involved in our new management division."

Universal South is moving forward slowly, with some sales success and considerable radio exposure. It is still very new, but DuBois is very encouraged by the country music resurgence of 2004. "Last year was a wonderful year for the mood in this town. I described it in Las Vegas terms, you know, that there'd been a lot of people standin' at this table for a long time and nobody had rolled a seven. We had not broken a multiplatinum act since the Dixie Chicks. With consolidation and the costs of doing business and breaking new artists, it began to weigh on people that maybe we couldn't do it again, that our format had become marginalized to the point that we weren't gonna be able to break that multiplatinum person out, and with Gretchen Wilson and Big and Rich poppin' through, both of them last year, whether you like the music or not, it made you smile because it showed it could still be done. I think that picked the whole mood of the town up at every level—you know, you didn't have people marchin' up and down the street singin' 'Happy Days Are Here Again,' but it at least showed us that it was possible."

Country music's biggest challenge continues to be dealing with the consolidated radio industry, whose interests seem divorced from those of the music industry.

"Their view of us is we provide them a commodity that they need to fill up the space between their commercials, and we provide that to them for free. Sometimes it feels like that they couldn't care less whether or not we break any new artists. They're not all that shortsighted, but at the same time, breaking new artists for our format is not real high on their priority list."

In the '90s, Congress and the FCC, both bent on deregulating radio, threw out the old model of radio stations as locally-owned businesses serving a local public. The result was that a small handful of companies like Cumulus, Infinity, and especially Clear Channel Communications spent huge amounts of money buying up huge numbers of radio stations.

"Stop and think about it just in common-sense terms," says DuBois the accountant. "The amount of revenue that they can generate is dictated by the fact that there's only twenty-four hours in the day, and the public will only bear so many minutes of commercials per hour. That's not growing. And if the pressure is there, because of debt service or whatever, it is to raise the bottom line when you can't raise that top. You can't sell any more than you're already sellin', so it has to come out of the middle. You have to start reducin' expenses, and one of the easiest things to reduce is your promotion costs. So you get the record labels to step up and provide you with those free artist shows, and free CDs, and all that kind of stuff that goes on to reduce costs.

"And because you have six and seven radio stations owned by the same chain in a metropolitan area, they don't cross-promote. They don't attempt to bring people over from other formats nearly as aggressively as they used to, because you'd be bringin' them over from their own stations. It's what's called a 'cluster mentality,' where they attempt to increase the time spent listening within that cluster, and they do that by trying to figure out who their core audience is, and *super-serving* that core to increase their time spent listening. Now that's an oversimplification, of the whole deal," he says, "but it's a good, concise explanation of the problems country music faces in radio today."

It takes a lot of money to break a record these days. Can little Universal South compete with the big guys in that area?

"I can spend money just as fast as any of these suckers in town," says DuBois. "We've had our heart broken a few times. We've rolled that dice with a million dollars on the table and walked away with nothing on a few things. Joe Nichols sold over a million records for us in his first two releases, that by far is our biggest success. But where we've been able to make our numbers is kind of the stuff that's off the radar screen. Matthew West is our contemporary Christian artist who's done well for us—we have a partnership with EMI on that. The Louvin Brothers record. Cherry Bombs—a hundred thousand records, just barely finding its way to radio. Cross-Canadian Ragweed, between two albums we're gettin' close to two hundred thousand albums. We've got a lot of really good stuff coming into this year: the George Canyon record is settin' up real nice for us; we've got Katrina Elam, who's an amazing talent out of Oklahoma, on her second single right now; Amanda Wilkinson, who's a little girl out of the Wilkinsons, she's dynamite...."

"We're starting our fourth year. This is the year we're scheduled to go to black ink, and Lord willin' and the creek don't rise, I think we will."

One of the most spectacularly successful Arista acts is Brooks and Dunn, who came together under DuBois's sage stewardship.

But the man behind this duo, the guy who was with them from the beginning, was another of the long line of Texans who have provided a creative force in this industry. His name is Don Cook.

Cook was born in San Antonio, lived all over Texas as a kid, went to college at the University of Texas, and, three days after graduation, moved to Nashville.

Not too long after Cook arrived in 1971, WSM built Opryland. Opryland was a theme park built around country music, and it was an immediate success. It was a beautiful place, a gorgeous park on the Cumberland River with lots of music and rides. It became a cornerstone of Nashville's tourist industry, and the city spent a lot of money on roads and other amenities to make Opryland accessible and welcoming to the public.

In the '90s, when country music was on the decline, Opryland revenues began to flatten out, and the strategists at Gaylord Entertainment, the successor owner of WSM and all the things its people had built, decided to replace this unique place with a mall. They announced it as a done deal, without a shred of consideration for the city that had nurtured it. Suddenly, a quarter of a century after its inspired creation, Opryland was over.

But while it existed, it was a great place for young musicians to work. Opryland featured bands for all of its various shows, and if playing in those bands didn't pay a fortune, it did provide a living for many of Nashville's future studio musicians, songwriters, and stars. One of the earliest of Opryland's musicians was bass player Don Cook.

After a few years at the brand-new Opryland he found a creative home at Audio Media, the studio on 19th Avenue South founded by Jack Jackson and friends. "Those were really fun times," he says. "I met some of the musicians that I still work with, like Eddie Bayers. In fact, at night at the studio after they'd shut down, Eddie and I would go over there and put on headphones and practice, bass and drums, just to build our chops a little bit. That was my first real studio experience here in Nashville.

"Back then, I was sort of mystified by everything, and I didn't have any idea of where I fit in, or whether what I brought to the table had any value whatsoever. But I was really determined to be a writer. I was doing a lot of writing and not very much connecting.

"In '76, I met a guy named Bobby Bond who was a writer over at Acuff-Rose, and Bobby heard my first demo that I did at Audio Media. He took me over to Acuff-Rose and Don Gant heard my songs and signed me.

"And that was the beginning of a really important relationship for me. Don Gant was my mentor in my early days. He was sort of the head creative at Acuff-Rose." Gant was a music wunderkind who came up through the professional music business ranks. He was a studio singer in his teens, and worked with Norro Wilson in a gospel group until, as Wilson loves to say, "God called us out of it."

"Don did a little bit of everything, and he was one of the greatest publisher-motivators. He was the guy that really helped me gain a sense of self-esteem about being a writer. He was very critical, very hard on his protégés, but in a very loving way, and really pushed the people that he chose to help. He made me believe I was a songwriter before I really was, and he kept that belief alive in me long enough for me to actually do something. Later at Tree he did the same with Sonny Throckmorton and

Rafe Van Hoy, and helped Bobby Braddock reestablish himself." All these writers wound up writing country standards in the '70s and '80s.

"My first hit at Tree was in 1977," Cook recalls. "It was a song called 'Tonight' that Barbara Mandrell did. My first year at Tree I got ten or eleven cuts, and that was due to the power that Don Gant had to push his writers." Then the hits really began to come for Cook. His first number one was "Lady Lay Down," recorded by John Conlee in '78. Other hits included "Cryin' Again" (Oak Ridge Boys), "Somebody's Gonna Love You" (Lee Greenwood), and "I Wish That I Could Hurt That Way Again," which was cut thirty-one times before it became a hit. "The way my career has gone, I've usually had a hit or two every year," he says.

Some songwriters long to produce records because it often seems as if the producers have all the power when it comes to deciding what songs will get recorded. But Cook did not dream of producing records. "I was sort of dragged into production kicking and screaming by Kix Brooks," he says. "In the late '80s, Kix and I were spending a lot of time writing together, and we had a couple of hits. Kix had an unsuccessful run at a record deal in the late '80s, and it left him very dissatisfied and very frustrated. So Kix asked me if I would help him try to get a record deal and I said sure. I didn't do it because I was an aspiring producer, I did it because he was my buddy, and because we just work well in the studio together. So we cut I think four or five sides, we got the money from Tree to do it, and Paul Worley [then an executive at Tree] took it to Tim DuBois at Arista.

"And Tim said, 'I really love this and I wanna sign Kix, but think about the idea of a duo.' He said, 'You know, it'd really be great to have a duo. It would be a great awards category slot and a new thing to find material for, an interesting approach. So he suggested that we go find a partner.

"We asked Tim Mensy, and Tim didn't wanna do it because he was pursuing a solo career. Tim DuBois said, 'I've got this other guy, Ronnie Dunn, that I'm lookin' at. Why don't you get together with him, see if you like him.' So Ronnie came over to my house and he and Kix and I wrote a song together. We had a great time. The song ended up being Brooks and Dunn's second number-one, 'Workin' on My Next Broken Heart.' So we kinda hit it off, and we decided, well, let's spend some time writing together and recording, see if we can't come up with something that really sounds great to us. We spent a year working together, writing, hangin' out, we went duck hunting, we wrote fifteen or sixteen songs. Got 'em all together, played 'em for Tim, and he said, 'Go do an album.'

"He asked me to produce it, and then he said, 'Since you haven't done a record before, why don't I put Scott Hendricks with you? He's workin' with Alan Jackson and kinda knows the ropes.' I said, 'Sure. Great!'"

Cook was still not positive that he hungered to be a producer. "Tim DuBois said to me at one point, 'Look, if you don't like production, you can always quit. You don't have to do the next album. Of course, the first album sold six million copies, so I was sort of motivated to try it again.

"After the first album, I called Tim and said, 'Well, you've ruined my life, I used to play golf, I used to fish, used to spend time with my family—that's all over now, thank you very much!'"

The first Brooks and Dunn album came out in 1991. It was the first of six albums that Cook produced on the duo. He co-wrote twenty-three songs for those albums, including "Only in America," "Whiskey Under the Bridge," and "That Ain't No Way to Go."

"Many times in the past I'd felt a little resentment for producers who did their own songs rather than doing my songs," says Cook. "And then all of a sudden I'm that guy. And I took a little bit of solace in the fact that I had been on the other side of the fence for so many years. Maybe it was okay for me to have that access for a little while."

The power was far from absolute, he emphasizes, because Arista had strong input concerning which songs would be recorded, but he was writing *with* Brooks and Dunn, and the three of them certainly had a good feel for where their music was going.

"I think there were a lot of people who were angry that I didn't cut their songs on Brooks and Dunn, and I'd been in their position, so I understood how they felt. At the same time, I knew that if they had a more appropriate song for what was going to happen, it would have been cut. Not because *I* would have made it so, but because the whole structure we had in place would have mandated it."

Cook could have spared himself the angst. Success justifies the process. Many of the songs Cook co-wrote were hugely successful. If you are a producer whose song becomes a number-one hit and helps push the album to double platinum, can an outside writer complain that if it had been his song, the album would have been, say, *triple* platinum?

Cook has a good insight on the difficulty of pitching a song from outside the loop. "A lot of times when you're playing songs for an artist, the only frame of reference you have is what they've already done," he says. "And that's really not a good target, because most artists are insulted that you would expect them to do the same thing again." On the other hand, if the writer or songplugger plays the artist something that's too far afield, then the artist might say, "Haven't you ever listened to my records?" So it's a thin line the outsider walks when he or she pitches a song to an artist. An insider, on the other hand, can be as bold as he pleases. He has time to prepare the artist for his strange pitch, and if the artist finds it to be ridiculous, he and the writer can just laugh it off together.

"There is a structure to every recording process," Cook adds, "and nobody in the structure, including the artist, has nearly as much power as everybody seems to think they do. An artist might desperately want something to happen, but without the support of a majority of the rest of the organization, it ain't gonna happen. I saw times when Kix or Ronnie would passionately want something to happen, and they just couldn't get the support to do it, and they would have to let it go. You would think, well, they're the artists, they oughta be able to do exactly what they want, well, they can't because they're accountable to other people, you know. 'My Maria' was an example of a song that almost didn't get done because Ronnie didn't want to do it. That was a case where the structure pushed to the point that he finally gave in and let it happen. The result was one of Brooks and Dunn's biggest singles of their career."

Brooks and Dunn's manager for many years was Bob Titley, who has also managed Kathy Mattea, Terri Gibbs, and Asleep at the Wheel. Titley, like Cook, is a Texan, and Dunn is from Oklahoma, so early in their career it wasn't hard for Titley to think in terms of Brooks and Dunn as a success-ful Texas-type act. "I realized that this was gonna be *huge* in Texas," he says. "They'll sell gold records out of Texas, they'll do the honky-tonks down there, it'll be like old times with Asleep at the Wheel for me. It'll be fun. I just thought it would be a successful project, you know, they'd have gold records, and we'd have fun playing honky-tonks.

"We put it out the first Brooks and Dunn album, *Brand New Man*, and it was like we put our surfboard in the water right as that enormous '90s wave came along. They didn't explode immediately out of the box—the first single, 'Brand New Man,' went out, it was a number-one record and the album sold a quarter of a million units. But the second single didn't sell. The third single was 'Neon Moon' and sales started increasing again, and then right after 'Neon Moon' was 'Boot Scootin' Boogie,' and those two back to back just drove album sales through the roof.

"Ronnie really wanted 'Boot Scoot' to be out there 'cause he'd played it in the clubs and he saw the reaction it got down in Oklahoma. He wanted to put it out earlier but the label was afraid of it: Will Boston play it? Will Cleveland play it? You know, it was a South Texas record and we might have needed some momentum to get them to play it." The momentum came from "Neon Moon," a country classic any way you look at it.

"The other thing about Brooks and Dunn's early history," says Titley, "is we labored and labored talking about the name of the act. We thought their names sounded too much like Brooks Brothers or a law firm. "We had all these ideas... *Oklahoma Song Dogs.* We had fifty names we were goin' through. And finally, out of exhaustion, we just said 'Brooks and Dunn.' None of us—none of the brilliant marketing people at the label, or myself, or anybody—stopped to think that by making it Brooks and Dunn it put us in the record bins right next to Garth Brooks. I really believe that that helped to drive some of the early sales. We were right there, and anybody who was going for a Garth Brooks album would see us. I can't prove that that's true but I suspect it is.

"And just the way they came together was an interesting confluence of circumstances. Tim DuBois saw the Judds going away and he saw an opportunity there because you had the CMA award show, and if you could make a good duo, they could win an award pretty easily and help drive visibility and sales."

Over the years Brooks and Dunn have appealed to a variety of age groups and backgrounds. Titley has an interesting insight on how mass culture has changed country audiences forever.

"I was out on the road with Terri Gibbs in '80 and '81," he recalls. "I think that '81 was the year that MTV was introduced. I'd go out to these fairs in Iowa and the Midwest that we were playing, and I'd wander around the fairgrounds between the sound check and the show. I'd go by the animal pens where the 4-H kids were, and from one year to the next, from '80 to '81, or '81 to '82, they'd be dressed in coveralls and hats. And the very next year they'd be dressed like Duran Duran.

"The impact of satellite dishes and MTV was instantly felt in these rural areas. It was amazing, the transformation occurred so rapidly. I think the one thing that's happened is that country music always was associated with this rural lifestyle, whether it's Appalachia or Texas honky-tonk, and that lifestyle doesn't exist anymore. I think there was this article in *American Heritage* that talked about country music being *suburban* music. So, really, we've evolved to a place now that I think country music isn't about a lifestyle or even a style of music—it's a marketing system, because if you look at the variety of musical content, what is there that says *country music*, specifically?"

THE KING OF THE INDEPENDENTS

"When people argue about what is country and what isn't, I always say, 'Hey, they were arguing about what was country back when the Carter Family were recording in the 1920s.' I tell people if country radio plays it, if country music fans buy it, it's country."

So says Mike Curb, founder and guiding light of Curb Records, a Music Row indie that has been releasing records for four decades. Curb has built his label into a company that is generally thought of as "a major," but he rejects that classification.

Major record labels today rumble along, operating by committee. Curb, with its star-studded roster headed by Tim McGraw, Jo Dee Messina, and LeAnn Rimes, has department heads like any other label, but the man at the top who makes the final decisions has nobody to answer to except himself.

Mike Curb has an astonishing story: he was born in Savannah, Georgia, raised in L.A., became president of MGM Records at the age of twenty-three, and was lieutenant governor of California in his early thirties.

In the early days of Curb Records, the label had a strong presence in pop, but after Curb moved to Nashville, he put much more emphasis on the country side of the label. Today he is one of the most influential men on Music Row.

He is amused that some people are constantly questioning the country credentials of songs and artists.

"I don't really worry so much about what editorial people say about records. What I care about is what people like. I listen to everything that's submitted to the company. Everything. I take it home and I listen to it at night, every night, and, if I wake up the next morning, and I'm humming something.... I mean, those great records that we loved in the '50s—whether they were pop records, whether they were R&B crossover records, or whether they were the phenomenal Music Row crossover records—you could hum every riff. I remember every riff in 'Last Date' by Floyd Cramer. I remember every riff in 'Battle of New Orleans.' I remember every part of the guitar work on 'El Paso.' We can remember these things fifty years later! Every hook you could remember, every piano part. How many records are we making today that we'll remember in fifty years, and have to think about every time we go into the studio?

"I'll tell you, when I hear a record like 'My Give a Damn's Busted,' this current record that's number one, that record's gonna be around a long time because it captures a *feeling*. Byron Gallimore produced it—that's the most magical thing he's done since he did 'Indian Outlaw,' which was the launching record for Tim McGraw on our label."

In the early '80s, CBS decided to remake the Quonset Hut and Columbia Studio A into office space. Never mind the historical significance of these two magnificent studios. They were now home to graphic designers and administrators in the CBS record empire.

More recently, Sony, which owns the Columbia family of record labels, and Bertelsmann (BMG), the German company that owns RCA, decided to merge their record operations. Since RCA already owns a large building on Music Row, it was expected that the CBS staffers would eventually move in with the RCA people. Curb saw an opportunity, and bought the Sony Music building on 16th, the ground zero of Music Row. It is Curb's intention to restore the Quonset Hut as close as possible to its original state, both visually and sonically.

"The builders who came in and actually built the building around the Quonset Hut have agreed to give us a list of all the things that need to be done to restore it exactly as it was before they made their changes. But where it comes to the acoustic side of it, I think we'd need Harold and Jerry Bradley, and musicians who played there, and producers like Jerry Kennedy."

Music Row, before it is anything else, is real estate. In the '60s, when Owen Bradley and Chet Atkins were important factors in the growth of Music Row, both had substantial investments in key buildings, including the RCA offices, the Decca offices, and numerous other buildings. Today, we see Mike Curb's influences up and down Music Row and the institutions that surround it. It is one thing to continue building the company that bears your name. It is another to get yourself thoroughly involved in the institutions significant to the Row but not relevant to the bottom line of your business. Curb is one more force in the continuum of Music Row. Like Owen Bradley, Chet Atkins, Buddy Killen, Frances Preston, Billy Sherrill, Jimmy Bowen, Jerry Bradley, Joe Galante, and so many more, he has stepped onto the stage and left some big footprints.

Curb was involved in the purchase and preservation of RCA Studio B, which is presently Music Row's foremost tourist destination. "With RCA Studio B," he says, "we were fortunate because the Maddox Foundation and the Country Music Hall of Fame had been very careful [with the building]. Even the cabinet that Elvis Presley had kicked in when he was recording 'It's Now or Never' is just like it was."

Curb's involvement with historical preservation on the Row is only part of the impact he's made in Nashville, beyond his record company.

"Music Row is anchored by Belmont University on the one side, where we have the Curb College of Music Business and Entertainment, and on the other side to some degree, it's anchored by Vanderbilt University. We have the Curb Center at Vanderbilt. The Curb Center concentrates on issues that affect the industry. Bill Ivey operates the Curb Center."

There is an old church at the corner of Edge Hill and 17th Avenue South, three or four blocks from the Quonset Hut, that was lovingly altered into a beautiful studio complex called Ocean Way. "We were going to build more studios for the Curb College," he says, "and we made a decision that we would take part of the grant that I gave to Belmont, and use that to buy Ocean Way, which Belmont operates as a commercial enterprise. But in the down time, you have that for students to learn. So, there's Belmont and Ocean Way, with the highest tech studios. Then as you go down Music Row to RCA Studio B, and then to Columbia Studio A, and the Quonset Hut, and then of course we have our own buildings in between that, Curb Records and Curb Publishing, and we have our studio, and I guess that studio has some history, too. . . ."

"When Curb Records started in 1964," says Curb, "we couldn't even get the name, so we used *Sidewalk* 'cause it was similar to *Curb*.

"Eddie Ray, who wrote 'Hearts of Stone' [a major R&B hit in the early days of rock 'n' roll] when he became a VP at Capitol, agreed to distribute my record label when I was a teenager, when I was just starting it. I said, 'How do I get a record pressed?' He said, 'You go down to Allied, and get it pressed.'"

Ray introduced Curb to a young lawyer in Capitol Records' legal department named Dick Whitehouse. "We talked and he worked on a distribution agreement. A year later, he was with Curb Records. What if Ray had said no? There are people who give you a chance. You can't do it by yourself.

"Curb had a five-year distribution deal with Capitol, and that deal ran out at the end of 1969. MGM was a New York–based company, but they had suffered severe losses and Edgar Bronfman Sr. had just sold the company to Kirk Kerkorian. They installed Jim Aubrey, the former president of CBS, as the president of MGM.

"By then, Curb had the Osmond Brothers, and we had produced all these soundtracks like 'The Wild Angels' and 'Killers Three' with Merle Haggard. We had the Electric Flag and we had the Stone Poneys. Jim Aubrey wanted to turn MGM around, so he said, 'Mike, you've got an independent—you've been operating for five years. Would you be willing to merge your company with MGM?' I said yes.

Curb began having all kinds of success on MGM with the Osmond Brothers and Marie Osmond, as well as Hank Williams Jr.'s first number-one hit, a song co-written by Curb called "All for the Love of Sunshine."

"My relationship with Music Row started then," he recalls. "This would have been right at the end of 1969." The MGM–Curb venture lasted about five years until Kerkorian sold it to Polygram. "Then I got back the Curb assets and continued on with Curb Records. What I learned by working with Hank Williams Jr. on Music Row was that all those records that I had loved by Don Gibson, Floyd Cramer, Jim Reeves, Johnny Horton, Marty Robbins, those records were not accidents. They were made by the greatest musicians that ever lived, and the greatest producers and the greatest artists in the greatest studios.

"As time went on and I realized that all the records I loved—whether it was the Everly Brothers or Roy Orbison or Eddy Arnold—all these records were cut in essentially three studios—the Quonset Hut, RCA Studio B, and Columbia A.

"As our company has grown, I've decided that I wanted to do everything I can to preserve Music Row. What we're doing at Belmont with over a thousand students is part of that—we've got student interns all over Music Row. We have twenty of them in our company. There's twenty-five of them in Columbia right now. They turn into executives, and they become recording artists like Brad Paisley and Trisha Yearwood and Selah, the gospel group that graduated from Belmont.

"When I started coming to Nashville in the late '60s and early '70s, I realized what Nashville had figured out. The great producers and the great artists and the great musicians of Nashville understood something that literally no one else understood and that was, *music is music*. And good music is good music and great music is great music. They didn't try to make *country* records with Don Gibson—they made *great* records with Don Gibson. Many people have said, 'How did your company end up with the Judds? How was it Curb/RCA with the Judds, why was it Curb/Warner on Hank Williams Jr., or Curb/Capitol with Sawyer Brown, or Curb/MCA with Lyle Lovett, or the Desert Rose Band? The Bellamy Brothers on Warner/Curb. How did this happen?' I can tell you it's because we put out the best records we could put out.

"People would say, 'How can you be in California and sign the Judds?' Well, first of all, we had spectacular people in our company like Dick Whitehouse. The saddest day in my life was when he retired ten years ago. And if there's anything we tried to do, we just said, 'We're gonna put out music.' So when 'Let Your Love Flow' came along by the Bellamy Brothers, we didn't worry about whether it was gonna be pop or country, we put it out, and it was a pop hit and a country hit. When Exile came along—and even Debbie Boone with 'You Light Up My Life'—we signed Exile for country, but their first hit record, 'Kiss You All Over,' went all the way to number one on the pop charts.

"Music Row impacted rock 'n' roll far beyond what Music Row's ever given credit for," he says. "I mean, if you go through the history of studios here, and the artists who have made classic recordings here, and the artists who have come here to get a new sound.... Right from the beginning, starting with 'Heartbreak Hotel' by Elvis Presley, and then the records that he later made at RCA Studio B, right up through 'It's Now or Never.' The impact of the Everly Brothers on the Beatles? The music that came from RCA Studio B, and the Quonset Hut, and Columbia A was a huge part of the start of rock 'n' roll, a huge part of the world music impact ten years later by the Beatles. Everybody from Bob Dylan to you-name-it has come here to do something great."

Why then, did so much of the media insist on putting a very narrow interpretation on the music coming out of Nashville?

"Well, first of all," he responded, "in the '50s, '60s, and '70s, Top 40 radio was truly Top 40 radio. They would play the hits whether they were R&B, whether they were country—you could hear Marty Robbins right next to a Motown record. As FM radio took over, you had niches, and when you have niches, then you have people protecting their proprietary areas. You have a station playing Americana music and then you have a station down the street playing country, and a station down the street playing R&B, and a station down the street playing mainstream Top 40. And they're all doing concerts, and [if] the country artist does a concert for the pop station, that artist has made an enemy of the country station. Plus the fact that as you got into the '90s, country radio became very powerful—artists that were selling two, three, four, five million. At that point, country radio was in a position to say, 'Hey, we want our core artists to be supporting *country* radio.' And of course the CMA, which was founded to protect country music, obviously carried that message even beyond radio. By 1996 and '97, we had a record called 'How Do I Live' by LeAnn Rimes, and Trisha Yearwood cut the same song. Trisha's manager at the time went out and told the world that LeAnn's song was too pop. Trisha's record ended up becoming the country hit, so much so that we actually took LeAnn's record, which I had coproduced in Nashville, at the Starstruck Studio, when everybody had told her she was too country. Here we are one year later and they're telling her she's too pop. So we said, we're gonna promote it pop—and the record became the longest-running record in the history of the *Billboard* pop chart. 'How Do I Live' by LeAnn Rimes—sixty-nine weeks on the Hot 100 pop chart—holds the record to this day as a single, a record that was recorded in Nashville, Tennessee. It was intended to be just a great record, but certainly we thought it would be played country. But in that particular time frame, the tension was so great between pop and country radio, that and the fact that Trisha's record had been a country hit and LeAnn's had not, put us in a position where we could actually promote LeAnn's record pop, because it *hadn't* been a country record."

Independent labels headed by one committed individual can be more agile than their major label competitors. On the other hand, they might not have the corporate resources to sustain in a competitive marketplace. Today, the marketplace is not nearly as competitive as it once was. The number of majors has shrunk to four, with very few added imprints within those majors. In the meantime, no plethora of aggressive independents has arisen to fill the void. Furthermore, major—and independent rosters—are much smaller than they once were.

"You have radio consolidation, record company consolidation, retail consolidation.... Who would ever have dreamed that one company, Wal-Mart, would be selling forty percent of the country records? Now my company is forty-two years old, Music Row is fifty years old. But the music that Music Row made in the eight years before I was in the record business probably made more impact on me than anything else in terms of making records.... Music Row is where the music starts and ends. Songs are written here, in little houses and people's bedrooms and dens, they're published here, they're recorded here, they're mastered here, and the world hears them. It hasn't stopped for fifty years.

"As great as the music is for Music Row, Music Row is still subject to the ups and downs of the world record industry, subject to the mergers. I mean, if someone had said to me a few years ago that they would lift the limit on owning radio stations and that one company would own twelve hundred radio stations, or that Columbia and RCA would be merged, I would never have believed it.

"I think the time is right for more independent companies. When I started my company, there were lots of independents, and then they sort of all went away. Now, with the consolidation there are more opportunities....

"It isn't clear yet whether the majors are gonna continue cutting their roster the way they have the past year," says Curb, "but certainly as they cut their roster there are more opportunities. Having said that, because of their huge volume, there's a tendency for them to want to go after what is already successful, and because they have such large volume, they can afford to make mistakes. So if an independent has a successful artist that's selling, you know in the seven figures, the majors can come to that artist and offer that artist a large amount of money to leave. And even if they fail with that artist, they're so big that the amount that they lost is not as significant as it used to be.

"The reason most independents have failed over the years is because their major artists have been taken away.

"We haven't lost artists...yet," he says. Still, after forty years of survival, he looks at his productive roster concerned that they could slip into the hands of incredibly well-endowed music conglomerates.

"But the life of a great artist can be long if the artist continues in the right environment," he insists, and his experience pretty much bears him out. "Majors, often times, when they sign a great artist from an independent, change the direction of the artist, or enter into a contract where the artist has so much control that the artist does whatever he wants. You know, you'd be stunned at how many artists, when they become successful, say, 'I don't care if this record's commercial, I wanna do this for me or my wife or because I believe it's creatively right.' And when an artist says that, it's almost impossible to make them change their mind.

"Our successful artists are so important to us, that if radio is really telling us something different from what the artist wants, we can go to the artist and maybe win the argument. Whereas with a major, there's someone in New York that the artist can get to that they can convince to tell the guy in Nashville to back off.

"Whatever agreement I reach with an artist, we don't have to get it ratified. So if I can convince an artist to put out a certain record, I don't have to worry about someone in New York or Los Angeles or Japan or Germany or wherever comin' in and changin' it.

"No one wants to be in an argument with an artist. I mean, a lot of people in Nashville have enjoyed the fact that when there was bad news to deliver, they could say, 'Well, New York told me....' Jimmy Bowen, when it was good news, he called me. When it was bad news, he would say, 'New York made me do it!' I can't do that.

"Hank Williams Jr. has re-signed with our company probably six times. He's been with our company thirty-five years." That's especially impressive considering that Hank has always been a rebel determined to do it his way. Evidently, he and Curb have experienced a considerable amount of agreement over the validity of "his way."

"Tim McGraw has re-signed a couple of times. Now that doesn't mean that he agrees with everything we do, but if you're a good parent, you may have disagreed occasionally with other members of the family. You know, if you're a good executive in any business, chances are you've disagreed with what other executives were doing. And maybe there were a few days that weren't the best. But I'll tell you one thing I've learned is, everybody I know who has left the industry is really happy for about three, four, five, six months, and then they start to miss it. And I think that the reason for that is that while the music theory stays the same—great song, great music, no limits—the rest of it is an ever-changing ball. I mean, one minute it's e-commerce, now it's m-commerce, this mobile phone. And I'm not talking just about ringtones, I'm talkin' about—this is something I have always thought would happen—kids can download on their phones. I know many kids don't have credit cards, so they can't use the iTunes and that, but *everybody* has a cell phone. Even the grade school kids have cell phones now. When you can download three to five thousand songs on your cell phone, and play that cell phone back on your car speaker, your home speaker, digitally...or on little external speakers this big that you can put in your pocket....

"We're going to continue licensing directly. We don't use any middlemen. We made our deal with iTunes. It took us longer, but we made a very good arrangement and we did it directly."

After four decades in the music industry, one of the things that still fascinates Curb is the mysterious series of "accidents" that often serves to grab an anonymous performer and dub him/her recording royalty.

"It isn't one of those things—'Come here, kid. I'm gonna make you a star.' It doesn't work that way.

"A person in Texas said to my nephew, Benson, 'I saw a girl sing the national anthem at the Dallas Cowboys game who was really great. That person sent a tape to Benson, who gave it to my secretary for me to listen to. I played it in the car with my daughters when we were on our way up to the Smoky Mountains for the weekend, and we couldn't stop playing it. It was 'Blue.'

"Now, I don't know the name of that person who talked to Benson— I should—but that person could say she discovered LeAnn Rimes. So could my nephew, and so could my secretary who handed me the tape. I'm not trying to discount in any way what others do, what I'm trying to do is maybe discount a little bit what those of us who run record companies do. At the end of the day, it's not *who* gives you the tape. Are you more apt to listen to a tape if a major manager brings it to you? Of course, if you have lunch with a major manager.

"If you had a tape you could hand it to me right now, you don't need to go give it to five other people to get it to me, you know? But if you had said to me, 'I was at a restaurant and a young kid gave me a tape that they wanted you to hear, I would listen to that tape tonight.'

"And I would put all the tapes in a row, and I wouldn't look to see which one was Sony/Tree, and which one was the kid that walked in from the street. 'Cause to me, if you only look at what has already been, then you're only gonna go where the past has been, which is not where the next superstar is going to come from. The next superstar is somebody walkin' up and down the street here, and I just hope that I cross his or her path.

"The idea that we create the star is wrong. Are there things we've learned? Certainly in the years of doing this we've learned some short-cuts—how do we master it the best way, what's the right timing, do we consider editing the record? How do we make the record sound as loud as possible on the CD Pro that's going to radio stations, how do we pro-mote the record effectively? I mean, there are certainly tons of things that we've learned where I think we can put the odds in our favor.

"But I would not want to take personal responsibility for saying I cre-ated this star or that star. I will say that there are things our company does, but we work as a team. You know darn well that on Jo Dee Messina, we haven't had a new single out in four years, well, if I coulda written 'My Give a Damn's Busted,' I would have done it four years ago. Fortunately, Tom Shapiro, Tony Martin, and Joe Diffie wrote it; fortunately Donna Hilley called it to our attention; and fortunately Byron Gallimore was willing to cut it; and fortunately Jo Dee compromised and cut it, 'cause it wasn't her favorite song when she heard it.

"I told her that because she went along with us on that, that the next single choice would be hers.

"I always worry, 'What do we do next?' The people who are gonna suc-ceed tomorrow are the people who are gonna do something differently than what we're doing today."

GALANTE AND TOMLINSON: KEEPIN' IT REAL

J immy Bowen may have been the major force in transforming the economics and technology of making records on Music Row, but many believe the man who taught Nashville to *sell* records was a transplanted New Yorker named Joe Galante.

In 1971, Galante graduated from Fordham University in the Bronx with a degree in finance and marketing. He went to work for RCA in New York as a budget analyst and, two years later, became manager of administration in the company's Nashville office. At the time, Music Row was dominated by Southern men, especially on the music side of the business. As Galante moved up in the RCA Nashville hierarchy, he began to get more and more involved with the creative side.

By 1980, Galante was a vice president, and his primary associate was the man who ran the Nashville office, Jerry Bradley. The two of them should have been like a train wreck. Bradley was a quintessential Southern boy who drag-raced his hot rod on Highway 100 in the middle of the night, rode in ambulances for the sheer joy of it, turned the Music Row practical joke into high art, and, like most other Music Row leaders, flew by the seat of his pants. Galante understood *systems*. He's a type-A wonk who seldom smiles but loves the business.

Furthermore, Bradley was Music Row *royalty*. Galante, on the other hand, was a stranger in a strange land, a man who came down from the Big City with a big degree and a name that ended with a vowel that was not "y." Different cultures. Different personalities. Yet there they were, strapped into the cockpit, and not only did they learn to fly together, they took off for the stratosphere.

Galante explained, "Jerry's a practical joker, but he also wants to get business done. We worked really well on that, and we enjoyed each other's company. I thought it was the oddest couple in so many ways, 'cause when we first met we didn't hit it off. But we respected each other and then we really grew to like one another. I enjoyed his sense of humor. I'm a smart-ass, but he was always better at it than I was. I'm not the joker that he is 'cause he'd lie awake at night thinkin' about that stuff! It was a great relationship. It was one plus one equals three.

"I learned a lot about the format and the business through him. There were certain things that I did that he couldn't do in terms of organizing the company and working with the New York office, helping to build the various departments that we had. And all those crossover things, that wasn't a thing that really happened out of Nashville before I got here. We had *so* many hits during that period of time, on Milsap and Dolly, on Jerry Reed and Alabama, and Sylvia.... I developed a relationship with all those guys in New York and worked them. And before we never had that."

When people talk about the great sales boom in country music during the late '80s and '90s, the name Garth Brooks always comes up, but Bob Titley remembers that "we began having that platinum-level sales prior to Garth Brooks. Clint Black and Garth came out at about the same time, and Garth bubbled around for a year or so. But Clint, everywhere you went, you'd see Clint Black posters and Clint Black displays. Wal-Mart was just hammered with Clint Black, and something that drove a lot of it was Joe Galante's ability to put records in the face of the consumer. Probably [the start of the big sales boom of the '80s was] Alabama, and Alabama was Bradley and Galante." The sixty-million-plus in sales from that group were a revolutionary leap from what had come before.

Although the Nashville metropolitan area is well above a million today, the city and its surrounding counties still sport a considerable amount of green space, and in certain ways, it still maintains the feeling of a smaller city than it is. Back in 1974, when Galante arrived off the streets of New York City, he was in for a profound shock.

"Ah! There's nobody in this town who could understand the culture shock," says Galante. "It was so small a community. It was ludicrous considering [its place in the music business]. Coming out of New York, you moved at a hundred miles an hour and everybody else moved at forty. And people were suspicious. For the longest period of time, I didn't realize all this stuff about, you know, 'You're down here to spy on us from the New York office.' I was sent down here to help the operation grow, and to learn. I mean, nobody said 'spy.' We were doin' a couple million dollars a year—what was there to spy on? But that was seriously what people thought I was here for.

"It was one of those times when it was difficult to make friends and everything, but I loved what I did.

"It took about four years...yeah, four years, to get comfortable."

Early friends included BMI head Frances Preston and WSM executive Irving Waugh, as well as several RCA artists. "Waylon, Dolly, and Milsap," he says. "They became my friends. I spent more time with them on the road than I did with my family. I was with them all the time and I absolutely loved doin' it. I mean, I coulda been gone for weeks and been happy with them."

How much did he know about country music before he moved to Nashville? "I was ignorant of the format," he confesses. "If it came on WABC in New York, which meant it was a Top 40 hit—'Ring of Fire,' 'The End of the World,'—then I knew what it was. Other than that I had no clue. I didn't know what the Grand Ole Opry was. I'd heard of George Jones, but I'd never heard his music."

Nor did he particularly like it when he was finally exposed to it. "I couldn't wait to get out of here. I came down here and the more music I heard, the worse it felt to me. I grew up on rock 'n' roll and R&B. I wasn't feeling it at all. And then, it all changed for me when I went over to the studio with Paul Randall. He said, 'You wanna go over and listen to Waylon?' We went over and listened to Waylon at the Glaser Brothers' studio and it just changed for me. At that moment, it absolutely changed. Then at the same time, I stumbled onto Dolly and Milsap. Jerry started taking me over to the King of the Road Hotel [where Milsap was a performing fixture before he became a recording star], and then I would go down to Memphis with Milsap.

"And then I got into Charley Pride. I went out and saw Milsap open up for Charley Pride and realized that this guy's a good singer, 'Kiss an Angel Good Morning.' 'Kawliga'—oh, okay, this is Hank—this is what it's about. And Patsy Cline. How could you not know about Patsy Cline? Then I discovered George Jones, and then I began to understand the elements of bluegrass. It was a journey for me for years, to get through that process, but then I really became a fan.

"People would say, 'Well, do you really listen to that stuff?'

"Yeah! Yeah! More so than somethin' else. And I think the thing was always the honesty and the soulfulness. All the people that I was fortunate enough to be involved with in my career early on were honest people. They were really good musicians in terms of caring what they did, and they were great singers or they were great stylists."

With major stars like Alabama and Clint Black, Galante's RCA was right in the middle of country's huge upswing of the late '80s and early '90s. What goes up must come down, but even he was shocked by what happened to the industry then.

"I think it was the nature of us to believe that when you come out of these things [the level of sales] is higher than it was goin' into it, so even when you come down, you're still doin' all right. But obviously when we came out of the upturn, in the middle '90s, it was . . . *severe*. And it lasted for a long period of time, much longer than anybody thought. Your company expects you to do better every year. Nobody expects you to do worse. They don't pay you to do worse.

"I made presentations to the CMA, trying to tell everybody that this is not cyclical. This is not gonna come back in two years. And everybody kept goin', 'Aw, it'll come back in '98,' 'It'll come back in '99,' 'It'll come back in 2000.' And we didn't come back 'til 2004. Pretty much from '94 or '95 on, we were either down or flat year over year, and we really didn't have any pickups.

"There's always been a solid base here. I was never concerned that we would go to hell in a handbasket and go from, say, seventy million units down to fifty million. I didn't see that happening, especially with the ability to cross over on records—you could always get the numbers up. I was just concerned about the health of the format *artistically.*

"It still troubles me that people can have hit records and not be able to entertain, that we've gotten so far in our studio process that sometimes we forget about singing, and what it really is. I think the reason people are able to achieve greatest hits and catalog sales over the course of time is because they truly have a show—they truly do entertain. Dolly Parton has been around for forty years because she's a *star*. She's not just a singer, she's a *star*!

"What do these folks really stand for? Just their latest hit single? How do you define your music? Someone like Kenny Chesney's done a magnificent job of going from 'Here I am this honky-tonk singer' to 'Here I am, I can relate to this audience that's young because I still remember everything that happened from the time I was sixteen years old to the time I'm thirty-five—and I can give you those songs to relate to.'

"There's a *brand* there. People understand what to expect when you go to a Kenny show, and what to expect from a Kenny record. That's true of Martina McBride, that's true of Tim McGraw—the name, the songs, the idea of what the guy looks like. But there are other people that you kinda go, 'Ohh, I don't know what that means, really.' It doesn't mean that you can't sell records—it just means that you don't sell tickets, and you don't really have a longevity. Today we get excited because people sold a platinum record. You gotta realize that fourteen, fifteen million units later, that's when you really have achieved something. I've got a lot of people I've worked with that have sold three, four, five million records over their career, but they're not household names."

After two decades in Nashville, Galante was brought back to New York as president of RCA Records Label–U.S. Although he was successful there, his years in Nashville had given him a special feeling about Music Row.

"First of all," he says, "it really is the fact of geography. You've got ten or fifteen blocks and you can walk to places. You run into people in the restaurants, and you're on boards together, and you work together on projects—it is a community. When I moved back to New York and I tried to establish that with a lot of people I worked with, it was a complete and total failure. People didn't want to have a sense of community. You'd pick up the phone and call somebody and say, 'Hey, let's go to lunch,' and they'd say, 'Why?'

"'To get to know you. I mean, *we're in the same business!*'

"It was funny, 'cause when I moved down here everybody said to me, 'Boy, you really aren't from here—where are you from? You got an accent.' After they made me president in New York, the second lunch I had in New York, I had lunch with Alan Grubman [one of the most successful attorneys in the record business]. Alan said, 'Look, I got some advice for you, kid,' he said, 'I think you need to lose the accent.'

"I said, 'Alan, I'm from New York. What the hell are you talkin' about?'

"He said, 'You're from New York?'

"I said, 'Yeah, I met you,' and I told him about when I met him the first time with Hall & Oates in Mel Ilberman's office.

"He said, 'You were there?'"

On Music Row, Galante may have continued to be thought of as 'the New York guy,' but he fit like a piece in a jigsaw puzzle. In 1994, he returned to RCA Nashville as chairman of RLG/Nashville. Over the next decade, he weathered country's modern Great Depression, and today RCA is a lead dog in country's latest surge forward. In 2004, RCA Label Group Nashville became the first SoundScan-era label group to have three country albums reach number one on *Billboard*'s pop sales chart in the same year. Since 2000, Arista has been part of the RCA organization, and today it is a vital part of an RCA Group lineup that includes Alan Jackson, Kenny Chesney, Martina McBride, Jimmy Buffet, Brad Paisley, Brooks & Dunn, and Sara Evans.

Galante has his finger on the pulse of the industry as much as anybody in the country music business, and he does not see the Internet as a fatal threat to the business.

"You're dealing in an adult format," he reminds us, "as much as people wanna keep changin' this thing and how we do it. I went to a show last night in Cleveland: It was Phil Vassar at the House of Blues, and you got all these people out there, and it's still the greatest feeling in the world to think that somebody gets up there and all these people sing along. But they're adults. They work their asses off. They're not sitting there at two o'clock in the morning downloading the latest technology. They listen to the radio, they learn songs, they borrow CDs. They may know how to burn a CD, but they buy CDs the old-fashioned way. Country music has always been on the back side of technology, because we're not early adopters. The adults aren't; they take care of their kids first. Their kids are early adopters. So I continue to see this as a disc format for quite a number of years, and I continue to see this as a live format where people go to shows, and really how big we get depends upon the talent."

Does he see the kids as they grow up morphing into the country fans their parents are.

"Sure. We become our parents. We want to deny it. We don't wanna be that 'Cat's in the Cradle' bullshit!" (But we are.)

During much of the time when Galante was building RCA in New York and Nashville, a youngster named Troy Tomlinson was working his way up the music publishing ladder to eventually become senior vice president at Acuff-Rose. When Sony/ATV Tree bought Acuff-Rose in 2002, he moved with the company, and at the beginning of 2006, he was appointed head of Sony/ATV in Nashville.

As Galante traces the success of the recording industry in the '80s and '90s, Tomlinson looks at it from the writer's perspective.

"I felt like in the early '80s, a lot of people were just really tryin' to *hold on*; that if a writer got enough cuts on albums, whether they got the single or not, they could eke out a real modest living. In the late '80s and early '90s, if you had a hit single, particularly if you were on a good album, you weren't just making a modest living as a writer, you could actually begin to build *wealth*. I think that might have been for the very first time ever in Nashville.

"Writers began to see that money could be made simply being on an album. Whether you got the single or not, if it sold two or three or four million records, the publisher was gonna make some money and they were gonna make some money. Once they *got* that, then we started to see more high draws. In '84, an okay draw [a draw is like a salary, money paid in advance of royalties] was thirty thousand dollars. And in the late '80s, as we started really selling some records and having good performances, a lot of folks were handin' out fifty- and sixty- and seventy-thousand-dollar co-pubs without even battin' an eye."

Co-pubs are co-publishing deals whereby the writer participates in the publishing income as well as all his writing income. Deals in the more modest early '80s, Tomlinson points out, rarely included co-publishing for the writer.

"Songwriters are more astute at business these days. It's not that they're any brighter than they used to be, but the access to information and the understanding of the business by writers is so much better today than it was years ago. The days of the publisher taking advantage of a songwriter are pretty much past. People are gonna have to cut good, fair deals with writers in order to keep them. Because if they're not willin' to, the guy down the street is."

Songwriters think of Tomlinson as a *songwriter's publisher* because they know he cares about them. Songwriters are a sensitive, vulnerable lot. Many of them have careers that always seem on the verge of crashing, and they need to feel needed.

"One thing's not changed," says Tomlinson, "and that is the need for a songwriter to feel like they have at least one person at their publishing company who listens to their music even when they don't have to. When I'm listening to a new demo in the car goin' home and I'm moved by it, and I call that writer at 6:30 and say I just heard your demo and I love it, that seems to mean more to that writer than if I'm at the office in the course of a day, and I hear a demo, and they're walkin' by and I say, 'Hey, we heard your new demo and it really sounded great.' That's an encouragement, but there's something about them knowing that their plugger is not even on the clock and he's listening to their music. I've done that over twenty years now."

Over the past twenty years or more, many of the great old independent publishing companies have been gobbled up by the handful of major worldwide publishers that control the business. But unlike independent record labels, which find profitability on Music Row to be very elusive, music publishing is still a business that a knowledgeable individual can step into without a lot of money and create a good business, just as Al Gallico Music, Combine, Tree, Acuff-Rose, Surefire Music, Bill Hall, and many others did before them.

New publishing companies have come along and carved a nice niche in the industry. Troy reels off the names of some of the best little companies: "Big Yellow Dog, Kerry O'Neil's company; Jody Williams Music; 1010 Management [Barry Coburn's company]—I would call these folks an independent. Horipro, Island Bound Music, Roger Murrah Music, Teracel, Windswept, Wrensong, FAME, and then, to a certain degree, Peer." The majors, he says counting them off on his fingers, are Sony, BMG, EMI, Warner Chappell, and Universal, five giant publishing companies, mostly owned by conglomerates that own major labels.

Thirty years ago, it was considered a potential breach of anti-trust laws for major labels to own music publishing companies. Generally, over the years the major record labels have been good about not giving special preference to songs or artists presented to them by their sister publishing companies. But as the home offices demand more from their Nashville divisions, who knows if that the separation will hold.

Yet the fact is, big and small publishing companies live side by side on Music Row. The dynamic is not one of big publishers pushing the little ones out of existence. The big guys are pleased to watch the little ones grow, taking chances with new writers, finding great songs, getting them recorded, and building great catalogs—catalogs that the major companies are then pleased to buy up for a pretty price.

"This town *is* a publishing town," Tomlinson says. "And I would say the time is perfect for a number of independent publishers to crank up, and if they will be modest in their approach and give good service to their writers, then they could actually pull writers from major publishers.

Because as the rosters have grown at the major publishing houses, some writers would simply rather be at a small house."

But Tomlinson believes in the future it will be the major publishers signing most of the new singer/songwriters, because they have the resources and facilities to develop them. "For example," he says, "here at Sony, we have a studio facility, an engineer is ready, and we have a line-item budget that we can use for production. That's hard for a small publisher to do. Some of the smaller publishers still use their demos to develop their writer-artists, which is great. We did that a lot at Acuff-Rose. What we typically did [at Acuff-Rose] was we'd sign a new writer-artist, and we'd use the process of demoing the songs they wrote to double as [production demos to get a record deal]. We'd spend a little more time on the demo. But the majors can actually say, 'Hey, here's ten grand. Just don't worry about whether you wrote 'em all or whether we publish 'em all. Go in and cut five great songs from the production budget.'"

Tomlinson loves to listen to the stories of the old characters that made the Row such a colorful place to be. Sadly, he says there are far fewer stories these days because there are far fewer real characters. "We've always had hillbillies, but now we have *refined* hillbillies. We have more subdued characters today for the most part, whereas in the '60s and the '70s, the word *subdued* would have never been used. They went balls-to-the-wall, whatever they wanted to do they did, and they had a big time doing it. Now, even Hank Williams [Jr.] has settled down!

Still, he is never at a loss to tell tales of Music Row and the cast of characters that made Nashville legend.

"The drinking stories of course are never-ending. Hillbillies never stop amazing me. There is no reality, there is no fiction, or comedy based on fiction, that can touch the reality of Music Row hillbillies. I had a writer—that I won't name—who spent some time at the V.A. clinic drying out. He'd been on marijuana, cocaine, alcohol, everything. I was in my early twenties then. They sent me over to the V.A. dry-out tank to pick him up. He had on one of those green uniforms that surgeons wear. He got in the car and he said, 'Troy, man, my life's changed. I've been here thirty days and my life has completely changed. No more cocaine, no more pills, no more alcohol. I've found the Lord—I'm a changed man.'

"I said, 'Man, that's fantastic. I really never thought there'd come a day when I would hear you say you weren't gonna, you know, smoke more pot.' He said, 'Hell, I didn't say nothin' 'bout no pot!'

"You can't make that up," he says.

"We had a white piano at Acuff-Rose," he recalls. "It was an old piano, and had that pleated-lookin' vinyl stuff on it with the gold tacks. Whitey Shafer wanted it for his music room, I guess, because it was white. And we decided to give it to him. He'd just bought a brand-new Toyota pickup, and he pulled it into the garage down there. Me and some ol' boys grabbed that white piano and got it down to the garage level, which was a bitch to do, but we got it down there. We went to set it up on his truck, on the tailgate, and the tailgate on this brand-new truck just folded in half. He says, '*D-d-d-don't* worry about it,' and we slid it on up in the truck and he said, 'That's *n-n-n-nothin'.*'

"I said, 'What do you mean?' He said, 'One time I bought a piano in Fort Worth and I was headed back home with it and I stopped and had a few *b-b-b-beers*. I pulled up to a major intersection and the light turned red and I stopped. I sat there for a couple of minutes at this major inter-section waitin' for the light to turn green and while I was sittin' there I *f-f-f-forgot* I had the piano in the back. So when the light turned green, I was so ready to go forward that I just nailed it, and the piano shot out the back of my tailgate and dropped into the middle of this intersection in Fort Worth.'

"I said, 'Golly, that had to be terrible.' He said, 'It was, but for just a moment, it sounded like a . . . *s-s-s-symphony.*'

"The real characters are the guys who are passionate about the music, passionate to the point that they'll tell you they're gonna whip your ass over it, and at the same time passionate enough to cry when they hear a melody that moves 'em, or a lyric that touches 'em. That's a character. The ones that we tell the stories on—those are the guys that are passionate.

"Corporations," Tomlinson intones darkly. "When we were a bunch of independent hillbillies owned by other independent hillbillies, we didn't see and live and breathe and spend as much time around New York and Los Angeles corporate people. As they bought us up, and we're around it more, we have to react in a more responsible way. Our society no longer tolerates behavior it used to wink at. Even in the early '80s, if you got pulled over, you were drinkin', if you could still say, 'Officer, I have been drinkin, but I'm two miles from home, he'd say, 'Get in that car, and you better not cross the line on the way home.' Twenty years later, we don't live in a culture like that. We live in a culture where if they pull you over and you've had a couple of drinks, you're going to jail. A lot of what made the characters in our business characters could be associated with a little alcohol. Since our culture has changed with regard to its acceptance of alcohol, that might have toned us down a little bit. You know what I mean?"

But Tomlinson also says that looks can be deceiving, and that Nashville might not be as uptown as it sometimes seems. "Aaron Tippin always said this: 'Troy, I know it seems like we're surrounded by a bunch of *them*, but always remember, there's more of *us* than there is of *them*.'"

Tomlinson has a keen sense of the history of his two decades on Music Row, but he especially relishes the early '90s, when country was pulling in sales numbers that dwarfed anything that came before.

"It looked like it was not gonna end," Tomlinson remembers. "The thing I remember about that period, for us [at Acuff-Rose] was, even as an independent, we couldn't help but get cuts. There were so many people recording, and if we went to an appointment, we were *gonna* get a cut. The cuts were doubling, year after year, and a lot of those people were selling platinum and above. All of a sudden we could make money off the sales of albums, even if we didn't get the singles. It was a wonderful time. There was a gold, or platinum, or multiplatinum party four days out of the week. I don't think we knew how good we had it. Not only were we too busy to think about how great it was, but when you're owned by a corporation, they always want more. And so I found us withholding good news and withholding the number of cuts month over month, because we knew that if I told them we had fifty in January, they'd want sixty in February. I was sandbagging it. We were busy trying to satisfy the corporate machine. I regret that I didn't take as much time as maybe we should have to celebrate how wonderful things were."

And then in the mid-'90s, the discomfiting signs crept into the daily life of the Music Row publisher, signaling that this sleigh ride, at least, was coming to an end.

"Record companies feel the hurt before publishers do," says Tomlinson. The reason is that record companies make all their money from sales, while publishers make much of their income from airplay and sync rights—income from use of songs in movies, jingles, etc.

"I remember beginning to have concerns when I sensed record company executives I trusted and admired, like Joe Galante, over lunch or in a casual conversation, pointing to problems with sales. That told me that I was gonna feel it a year or two later. I can remember specifically having a lunch where Joe came to our office, and he described some key indicators that he saw that were troublesome to him. When he left I said to the staff, 'If Galante is troubled, we better be as well.'

"So my first indicator of the slide was not somethin' I saw in a record store, or something I saw in SoundScan—it was record company executives beginning to be troubled. Tim DuBois, he was as hot as one could get, and when he began to be troubled, I began to be troubled." Tomlinson recalls that these troubled times began around '95 or '96.

The depression on Music Row continued for the remainder of the millennium, but Acuff-Rose did not feel the pain the way the labels did. "We were blessed because the standards we owned continued to get use in different ways." And nobody in Nashville had more authentic standards than Acuff-Rose, including the timeless songs of Hank Williams, Pee Wee King, Don Gibson, Roy Orbison, and others.

"Ringtones were beginning to come around. We put a lot of money and time and effort in film, and particularly in getting our songs used in television advertising. So as we saw the revenue from mechanicals drift downward, we saw performances continuing to go up. Goodness gracious, we had standard after standard used in toys!"

As the labels reduced their rosters and the number of sessions went down, songpluggers found it harder and harder to get songs cut. Publishers responded by reducing their writer rosters and songplugging staff.

"I think 2002 was the year I started thinking, maybe we bottomed.... Around 2002 or 2003, I started sensing in conversations with Joe that things were just a little more positive, things were just a little brighter than they had been. It was about that time that I began to think that it might be a good opportunity for some independent publishing companies to fire up, pick up some of these writers that had been let go in the tougher years, and begin to build up companies on them."

"9/11 had a lot to do with that," he says. "I think country music has typically served as a salve for hurtin' people, whether they're hurting in a relationship, or they've lost their job. The songs in country music—and the artists, even—seem to be common people singing songs about other common people.

"Pre-9/11 you know the world was flyin' down the superhighway, a lot of plastic, a lot of Tupperware. 9/11, in general, caused Americans to view what's important again. And when Americans look at what's important, they come back to some common denominators: their family, their faith, their friends, the simple things in life. Country music talks about family, friends, faith, the simple things in life. When the country needed it, the songs of country music—they were that salve, that ointment.

"And here's the other things. What we've seen is that more artists, even above and beyond that unbelievable innovative melody, they want a *real* lyric. *Don't give me plastic, I don't want plastic. Give me glass. Or give me steel. Give me something real I can hold on to.* I believe that tripped, almost like a light switch, right after 9/11. Starting with Alan Jackson, of course, with 'Where Were You When the World Stopped Turning.' Whether you were a red state or a blue state or a Republican or a Democrat, it didn't make any difference. Even in this chaos that our world was experiencing, that song was a comfort. I think Martina McBride has had the ability to do that consistently. Reba, for many years, has had that ability to relate on a very real level, with the circumstances of life, even tough ones—divorce, children caught up in divorce.

"Post-9/11—*real*. Gretchen Wilson comes out; she doesn't try to be someone she's not. I understand at a writing session John Rich said, 'Who are you?' She said, 'Well, I'm not a Barbie-type artist of course. I'm just a redneck woman.' And John Rich, being the great writer he is, picked up on that and they wrote a real song.

"Every Sony employee, whether it was publishing or record company, went to a meeting at the Country Music Hall of Fame, with some Sony New York executives, and Gretchen performed for us. I was sitting near the back, and I watched as every woman in that audience related to the song 'Redneck Woman'—whether they were young or old or skinny or larger or city or country, it didn't matter. There was something about the honesty and realness about that redneck woman singin' it that moved them."

Tomlinson feels very optimistic about Music Row's future, in spite of the fact that major changes are obviously on the way. "We still have the challenges of technology," he says. "But from a creative perspective it feels better right now than it's felt in a long time. That goes back to bein' *real*."

28

MURDER ON THE ROW

A few years ago a couple of veteran songwriters named Larry Cordle and Larry Shell wrote a song called "Murder on Music Row" that got a lot of airplay and put forth the idea that authentic country music was being murdered by those who would replace it with songs and records that are not country. It's an old argument that will be rehashed as long as there is a genre called country music.

"The people who complain about murder on Music Row might as well be makin' that argument about planes, trains, and automobiles," says Paul Worley, a Warner Bros. record executive who in his time has made his mark as a musician, studio executive, publishing executive, and record producer. "Man wasn't born with wings. Why is he flyin'?!"

In 2004, after a long career, Paul Worley was thinking that it was time to be out of sight and out of mind. "You know I was kind of thinking, 'Okay, well, it's probably about over for me. I'm fifty years old, you know....' And then I ran into John Rich and Big Kenny and the Muzikmafia.

"Here in the autumn of my career I've found what I believe to be the reason that I've been in the business all these years, and that is to hook in with this tribe of wonderful, talented people and help them reach their dream, which is to nurture and promote music of all genres from Nashville in a way that doesn't compromise the music. I didn't think it was gonna happen—I'd sorta given up on the dream.

"But it was a dream that I'd had in 1972. I was sure in 1972 and 1973 that I was going to be part of what was gonna export more than *just* country music from Nashville. Music City was gonna truly be *Music* City, not *country* music city. I thought I was gonna be one of the artists that did that. It didn't happen. And then I thought I was gonna be one of the session musicians that did that, and that didn't happen either. I was a session musician, but I ended up makin' country music because that's how you can make a living.

"Then I thought I was gonna be the producer who made it happen. And when I was at Tree I thought, I was gonna be the publisher that did it. Buddy Killen had Joe Tex, Bobby Marchand, Paul Kelly. They were always on the cutting edge.

"Country music is not a full meal for me. A full meal, you got your appetizers, your entrée, and your dessert. I grew up in Nashville. I knew John R. [an R&B disc jockey treasured throughout much of the South], and I listened to WLAC and WKDF, and Scott Shannon, who's now the biggest rock jock in New York. And I also listened to country music. It's always *all* been here.

"Big & Rich reminded me of the dream, by showin' me it was their dream too, but they were living it. They were doing it.

"The Muzikmafia is a tribe. It exists to nurture and foster creativity, with no limits. We do music of every kind—we blend and mix genres of music. Cowboy Troy is a six-foot-four black rappin' cowboy from Dallas. Where else but on Raybaw Records, which is the Muzikmafia record label [an imprint of Warner Bros.]? *Raybaw* stands for 'Red and yellow, black and white.' Their whole thing is 'Music without prejudice,' approaching the world from a spiritual and musical nonprejudicial way.

"We owe it to ourselves as creative people to let the creator in, to not block the creator with any preconceived notions about what we ought or ought not to be doing with music, we ought to just let the music do it to us.

"There are no two people less alike than John and Kenny. The guys are negative images of each other. John's got one of the sharpest and biggest brains I've ever been around. He's got that confidence that only can come from the Texas prairie. He's an amazing force. I look at how good he is, as prolific as he is. Hard, hard drivin'. Kenny, on the other hand, is about soul, he's about connection to the universe, and sort of channeling that universal energy through himself. His mind is amazing in its ability to rhyme and reason at the same time. Kenny's more mellow. So you've got those two completely different sets of energies and two completely different views of the universe, and yet they love each other and they fit together like *yin* and *yang*.

"The four godfathers of the Mafia are John Rich, Kenny Alphin, Jon Nicholson, and Corey Gierman. Corey's been a publisher, A&R guy, and he's also the chief organizer of all the Muzikmafia events. He's the center of it all. Those four are the principals of Raybaw."

Okay, so a couple of guys get together, declare that they are rebels, defiant, outlaws.... Been done before, right? Remember, in the mid-'70s, there was an in-group actually called the Outlaws, defying all the conventions, living hard, and telling the record labels to go to hell. But for all their honest-to-goodness attitude and down-to-earth, bad-ass songs and unbridled talent, that outlaw movement grew out of an album conceived in an office at RCA. The Muzikmafia was a self-created group of frustrated artists who set up business in a place called the Pub of Love, just this side of the new millennium, and they've gone on from there.

Worley: "Out of artistic frustration Corey and the other three principals of the Mafia said, 'You know what, we're gonna start playin' for ourselves, just so that we can feed our souls and play our music to each other. Where can we do it?' And they started in some people's living rooms and then it was like, 'Ah, you know, we need more space, so there's this little tiny place across from 12th and Porter called the Pub of Love, itty-bitty. We'll play on Tuesday nights at ten, guarantee we're not gonna get in anybody's way. Tuesday night's the deadest night of the week. No industry people'll ever come. It'll just be us and our friends and no outsiders.

"And guess what? It started to grow. They outgrew the Pub of Love. Then they moved to a bigger club, and a bigger club, and a bigger club."

What they've done is helped to shatter country music's nasty periodic habit of painting by the numbers. While it may not be everyone's idea of "country," you would think that the whole industry on Music Row would be rooting hard for the success of the Muzikmafia and Warner Bros. because it opens up so many possibilities for the industry.

"But they don't," says Worley. "And they won't. What's happening in Nashville now, this taking pleasure in other people's pain, is what killed Memphis. It killed it. I watched it happen. I watched 'em divide into camps, and if you worked for this camp, you couldn't work for that camp, and if you were with this group, you were blackballed from that group. Memphis is dead."

And you see a certain amount of that in this town now? "Absolutely!" he says. "Are you kidding me? I know everybody thinks I'm a total fool and idiot for signing Big & Rich, I know that! They think it's a one-off—it'll go away. They might be right! I don't know."

But fortunately, Warner Bros. was thinking in ways that complemented the mindset of these iconoclasts.

"The classic model is that every label has a Nashville division," Worley notes. "When I came in, I thought, okay, I'll be the head of the Nashville Division at Warner Bros. It took Tom Whalley [chairman of Warner Bros. Records] two years to beat that notion out of my head, for me to understand that what he was creating was a *nondivisional* record company. He said, 'I don't like the word *division*. It comes from the word *divide*. I don't want anybody to be divided. We're in the music business. Music is the nondivisional thing that human beings have in common. I don't want a divisional company.'

"He's developed a culture at Warner Bros. that allows us to know who our counterparts are in Burbank and in New York, and how to put together a marketing plan with them that we can go after. We listen to each other. We really do have that kind of company, and it's the only one of the majors that I know of, the rest of them all retain their divisional structure. That structure at Warner Bros. made us uniquely right for a label like Raybaw.

"In radio, we're promoting Cowboy Troy through the country funnel because even though it's rap or hip-hop, it doesn't fit on those channels. Musically it fits in country a lot more because it's real musicians, a real band, real grooves. It's all hooks. The songs are structured like classic country songs, with verses and choruses and breakdowns, but the verses are rapped, and the choruses are sung by Big & Rich, by the 'tribe'....

"We're signing a kid named Chance, a white hip-hop artist with sort of Southern white hooks. We represent the painting of Rachel Kice. She started showing up in the early days at the Pub of Love, and would start painting the event.

"The marketing on Big & Rich is very wide," says Worley. "We knew that it was gonna be a tough sell at radio. Didn't really know how tough or what. You know we still haven't had a Top 5 single." This is significant because in this day and age there are still country artists that get number-one singles, yet their albums don't make it past the half-million mark, while Big & Rich is multi-platinum on their first album.

"You know, we'd like to have a number-one single, but it's not the end-all," he adds. Country artists who can sell big numbers without huge radio hits, "have a career. They've got real fans that really care about them, care about what they stand for. The guys have always made really good decisions about who they work with and who they surround themselves with, so they've got great management, Dale Morris and Associates. They work with Mark Oswald within that organization. Mark's a very talented promoter, knows the concert promotion business, knows the video promotion business. Early on, we were able to get a strategic alliance with Chevy, so we were able to get an infusion of some capitol and some advertising opportunities even before they had a hit."

So goes the country music business today. There's a lot to breaking an act that is not directly connected to radio. And then there's the Tim McGraw connection.

"Tim fell in love with the music, and put the guys on his tour for no good reason, except that he loved the music, because they weren't gonna put any butts in seats. But Tim is that way. He feels secure in who he is and what he's doin' and he likes to be in the vanguard of what's goin' on. So early on, even before they had a hit, they were able to go out and get in front of a lot of people"

Worley does not see much sense in the laments of those who demand that country music defy the future and remain as it has always been—whatever that is. Country has kept faith with its past, he insists, because "the lyric is very important in country music. That's an element that it owns, more so than any other genre of music. It's not just music, but what it's saying about life is equally important. It's evolved just like everything else has evolved, I mean, they don't plant fields with mules and wooden plows anymore! For God's sakes, *they've got air-conditioning on the tractors. The world is coming to an end! We don't have to sweat anymore!* They should have to dig in the earth the way their ancestors used to.... In fact, *let's bring back slavery. For God's sake!'"*

For all of the hip-hop and hard-rock aggression that is infiltrating Nashville, thanks to the Muzikmafia, the leading edge of the cutting edge of country just may be a wild-ridin', redneck woman.

"Big & Rich were out terrorizing the town one night," Worley remembers. "And Gretchen Wilson was tending bar at B.B. King's [Blues Club & Grill] downtown. They found her down there, and then they heard her sing, and John just pursued her and started writin' songs with her."

Gretchen's producer is Mark Wright. Wright is from Fayetteville, Arkansas, and was one of the earlier attendees of Belmont University's music program. He came to Music Row in 1976, and began hanging out at Sound Stage studios, where one of the owners was a Belmont grad. Another owner of the company was Gary Paxton, a noted songwriter, producer, and publisher who helped keep the focus of Sound Stage on Christian music.

"Gary would see me in the hallways and basically tell me, 'You can sell about anything. Why don't you come and work for me? I've got a country catalog of all my old country songs'—stuff he wrote before he became a Christian, 'Woman, Sensuous Woman,' and 'Honeymoon Feelin'.' He asked me to start pitchin' them."

At that time, Paxton was producing Vern Gosdin for Elektra. "Gary said, 'You know what you need to do? All these publishers wanna pitch me songs for Vern, you oughta start takin' appointments with *those guys* and meetin' every one of 'em. So I was pitchin' Gary's songs back to them while they were pitchin' songs for Vern."

Eventually Wright found himself writing for Bill Hall, but Wright wanted to be a producer. "Hall did not feel like they should be spendin' money developing producers. He was still about writin' the song, gettin' it cut," recalls Wright. Wright wound up over at a Waylon Holyfield/United Artists Publishing co-venture with Jimmy Gilmer, best known to the public for his moment as a pop hero with his hit recording of "Sugar Shack" in 1963, but later a very successful publishing executive and talent manager. "I was able to sign on there as a writer," says Wright, "but they gave me a revolving producer budget so I could go and develop artists.

"The first guy I signed was T. Graham Brown, cut a bunch of sides on him and got him a deal at Capitol. They wouldn't let me produce the records—[Lynn] Shults and them guys didn't think I had enough experience—which was okay. Hell, I was just twenty-two years old at the time. Between about '82 and '84 was when I met Tony Brown and Norro. I had a hit that I wrote for Charly McClain and Mickey Gilley, 'Paradise Tonight,' my first number-one, in 1983. And Norro came in, said, 'You know what? I wanna let you get into the studio and piddle around with this, 'cause I want it to sound like your demo.'

"He and I became buddies, and he started lettin' me hang out at the studio. That kind of all segued into Joe Galante getting wind of my production. Norro started tellin' Joe, 'Listen to this kid.' Tony was workin' there at RCA and he was kinda high on helpin' me, sayin' we need some fresh blood. At the time there wasn't a lot of young people, everybody there had been doin' it for fifteen or twenty years, the same people. It was a little taboo for a twenty-two-year-old kid to be in there makin' records. I got hired in '84 as a staff producer by RCA."

During his early years at RCA, Wright produced a wide variety of acts for the label. "Basically I did what I was told to do," he says. And then one day a young kid named Clint Black walked into his office.

"Joe said, 'Look, here's this kid, are there any good songs here?' This kid had a twenty-song demo, and I put it on, and I went, 'Good Lord! This kid's like twenty years old or nineteen years old, and he's writin' these songs.... His first album was already written!

"So we flew to Houston and [producer James] Stroud was already workin' with him through Bill Ham [best known as Z.Z. Top's manager]. Stroud and I did that record together, first time we'd ever worked together," recalls Wright. The album was *Killin' Time*, which yielded five number-one hits. "It sold two or three million records right out of the chute. That was right before Garth got hot.

"Clint had the early lead. I always say the difference was the last single of Garth's first album, 'The Dance,' and the first single of his second album was 'Friends in Low Places.' When those two songs came out back to back, Garth went to about eight million units, just blew right past everybody. That was '89, that's even before Brooks & Dunn, and before Alan, but that was the beginning of *The Run*."

The Run was that golden age of country sales, the first half of the '90s when it seemed the labels couldn't miss and a million sales was the minimum measure of a successful new act.

In spite of Clint's amazing success, Wright only produced that one album on him. "Then I got fired," Wright says with a rueful smile. "I got relieved of my duties in about '89."

Why? Let's just say Wright hadn't quite climbed out of his adolescence, and his presence in the workplace was less than reliable. "Joe Galante always said, 'You know I woulda fired you sooner if I could have found you.' Ah, I was writin' a lot and producin' a lot and I didn't wanna be an executive at the time. I really didn't. I really thought I should just be creative. I didn't think I should have to go to any meetings.

"I went out on my own for about five years, but I was kind of an A&R guy for Tony Brown." And he came through for Brown. He found Mark

Chesnutt. The first album Wright produced on him went platinum, and all told, the collaboration sold seven or eight million records.

"I had a publishing company with EMI, turned around, and sold that company back to EMI. That got me healthy with my ex-wife. I got everybody paid off, I got everybody off my ass, you know. Basically, it's just one of those deals where you just gotta go clean up. Every once in a while you gotta stop and take a shower.

"In '94, I was workin' for Tony, and Tony and Bruce [Hinton, head of the Nashville division of MCA] had those big years. I mean, they had Vince, Reba, George, and that Wynonna album. They were sellin' two million records on everything they put out. They were approachin' two-hundred-million-dollar years.

"Tony calls me and says, 'Bruce and I are gonna start another label. Why don't you come talk to us about it. And I did, and they let Shelia and me have the new Decca label, and that went 'til about '98, maybe."

Shelia was Shelia Shipley Biddy, credited with being the first woman to ever run a major country record label. Early experience at Monument Records had eventually led to RCA, where under Joe Galante, she became one of the first successful female promotion executives in the history of country music. By the time she became part of the MCA team, she had achieved the reputation of someone who met whatever challenge a label could throw at her. So MCA gave her Decca to run, and although country was heading into a downturn, Shipley Biddy and Wright had it moving in the right direction.

"It actually got to where it turned the corner and was makin' money the last two years," says Wright. "The first hit act we had was probably Rhett Akins, and we moved Chesnutt over [from sister label MCA]. Then we signed Gary Allen, and then Lee Ann Womack. Actually we were havin' platinum records on Lee Ann and gold-plus on Gary."

The reason, Wright says, for the demise of Decca was the merger between MCA and Polygram, which made the MCA brain trust feel the need to cut down on the number of imprints they had to deal with. So in spite of the quick success of Decca, the new label with the old name was gone.

"I'll never forget, Bruce called me in his office and said, 'We're gonna close Decca.' I'm just like, well, shit, I'm out of a gig. I'm gonna have to go back to bein' an independent producer, songwritin' again, scrapin' around, tryin' to figure what I'm gonna do. And he says, 'We're gonna have to close down, but your wife and I decided that we shouldn't put you back on the street, so you're gonna come to MCA as senior vice president of A&R.'"

Wright's gig at MCA lasted from 1994 to 2003, a long run for an independent character like Mark. But then they decided to consolidate Mercury and MCA. The new executive lineup left Wright in a difficult position, with a long time to go on his contract.

"Just pay me," he told his new boss, Luke Lewis.

"The very next day after I'd had that conversation John Grady calls me and says, 'This is kinda confidential, but I'm gonna go to work for Sony. Don Ienner wants me to take over this Nashville division. Would you come and be my partner on the creative side?

By the time Wright arrived at Sony, the label was in a bit of an uproar, thanks to squabbles between the Nashville office and the label's most successful act, the Dixie Chicks.

"They were now reporting to New York," Wright recalls. "They were no longer recording for the Nashville office." This left Nashville Sony without a big moneymaker for their balance sheet. "They had focused a lot of their energies on the Chicks, and when that fell apart, they didn't have plan B. You gotta build your business with a broad base, especially when you're dealin' with artists and public tastes....

"We need to have four or five of those things, so if one of them goes away, your business isn't gone. That's what we're workin' on now. Fortunately, we have Gretchen Wilson, who's already sold over four million records. That's like breakin' four platinum acts.

"I'd heard about Gretchen, I'd heard her sing demos when I was at MCA. We'd talked about doin' somethin' there, and at that point, I didn't feel that I was gonna probably be around, so I just didn't pursue it. I just kind of quietly laid back and waited. And one day [after I'd got to Sony] I called Dale Morris and he said, 'We got some new stuff you need to hear. They came in and set up in Grady's office and played 'Holdin' You Holds Me Together,' 'I'm Here for the Party,' and 'Redneck Woman,' and we just went, 'Yeah, let's go make a record!' The rest is big-time history.

With as big a hit act as Gretchen leading the way, Wright is understandably optimistic about country music's future. "I see radio being a lot more receptive to new sounds," he says. "Radio got to be at a point where if you weren't makin' a record that sounded *like the radio*, you couldn't get on the radio. Now we're makin' records that don't sound like the radio, and radio's playin' them, and the people are comin' in droves.

"They just wait 'til the ratings get so bad that they have to start opening up to new ideas. What's going on now reminds me of the '80s. A bunch of people sayin', 'Hey, we're all in the damn tank here, numbers are in the tank, you're in the tank, the ratings are in the tank, the sales are in the tank, bookings are in the tank—we gotta just do somethin'. Why don't we maybe go back to the creative community and see what they've got?' What happens is the creative community always gets it goin', and then the business community takes it, just starts marketing and marketing and marketing it. And then they forget about the creative people....

"We have to go through it every time. It happens in every format, it doesn't just happen in country. It's called the *music business* because both sides wanna run it, the *music* people wanna run it, the *business* people wanna run it. What you gotta do is all be together and run it together. But that'll never happen.

"Nothin' against radio. Their job is not to lose listeners. And I understand that. But I gotta tell you, with satellite radio and all sorts of other stuff comin', people playin' more adventurous stuff, and givin' some outlets to more inventive thinking, they're gonna have to change their ratio of safe versus risky. And I think they will. I'm a believer in people's adaptability. I believe the human spirit wants to be part of something successful, as opposed to just being right all the time."

29

"IF IT IS NOT KNOWN FOR MUSIC, IT WILL NOT BE KNOWN FOR ANYTHING"

"At some point the money people and the music people have to make some kind of accommodation with one another. There has always been, even to this day, a sort of ill-defined but substantial element of upper-class Nashville that struggles against the image of country music as the face of Nashville. But this is what gives Nashville its imprimatur in the world. You could go from here to Boston talking about Nashville as the 'Athens of the South' or the 'Wall Street of the South,' and you'd just get puzzled looks. But you just say 'Nashville' in Bangkok and people will say, 'Ah, Dolly Parton! Ah, country music!'"

John Egerton is an award-winning author who has been chronicling the social history of Middle Tennessee and the South for many years.

"If wealthy white Nashville, through the Chamber of Commerce or whatever institutions, doesn't find ways to embrace the music industry, recognize it, and value it as our label—Music City—then not only will the label go by the boards, but the city will, too. Fifty years from now, if we're not known for our music worldwide, we won't be known for anything. We'll just be another flyover city, where nothing out of the ordinary goes on."

In 1925, when WSM started the *Grand Ole Opry*, Egerton points out, "The insurance company owned the radio station. All they were interested in was selling insurance. The radio station was simply another way to put salesmen on the street. You save a lot of shoe leather, expense accounts, when you're selling over the radio. They had an interest in using music as a way to open the door to a lot of people to whom they could sell insurance.

"That story is well known. The part that fascinates me is, if you allow for, fifteen or twenty years to pass, from, say, 1925 to 1945, Nashville had twenty years to get used to the idea that this music on the radio station was gonna be a big part of Nashville.

"But you had this sort of pseudo-elite of Nashville society, including the people who owned the insurance companies and the banks and so forth, who never thought that they were gonna have to be interlocked with these music makers. All they were interested in was the money the music could generate for them.

"So this conflict was there. And if you take that twenty-year period during which radio became a common phenomenon, we go through a depression and a world war, and then we finally get to a place where the prospect of prosperity was at hand. People are at home, new jobs are being created, and naturally, this music is gonna blossom because suddenly everybody's got radios—even in their cars! Television is just around the corner, that's gonna ramp it up some more. And so we have the growth of this industry, which is generating lots of money. It's making big-name stars out of lots of people, and the same old folks or their sons and daughters are still running this show in Belle Meade and Jackson Boulevard and Union Street downtown.

"My big gripe with the elite in Nashville is that they have never been able to embrace the reality of the music industry. It's a no-brainer. But Nashville has come to the twenty-first century without ever fully acknowledging how unique it is. Nashville *is* Music City. Nobody else can claim that. But Nashville itself doesn't know what to do with it! And I would dare say that country music doesn't know what to do with it, either. They get hung up on *How country is it?* And of course that's made harder by the fact that Americans in general have very stereotypical views of country music and of the South. The depth of that ignorance is still pretty abysmal.

"Much of that ignorance," Egerton asserts, "is willful. Many Americans don't want to be disabused of those stereotypes. Every time something weird happens down here, the people in the North will say, 'You see? That's what I'm talking about. Those people really are a little bit off.'

"Part of this is a rural-urban thing. Part of it is a North-South thing. Part of it is a black-white thing. Part of it is an East-West thing. And all of that gets mixed up together. And we down here, our problem is, we still can't decide how we define *ourselves*. Are we gonna be okay being Southerners? Well, I want to define it my way, but when I go North, I am as staunch a defender of the South as you're gonna run into. And then

I get back down here and I get into near fistfights with people whose attitudes and behavior I think are just feeding the negative stereotypes."

"But look how many people in the music business have moved here from California and New York because of the ambience, because here is this critical mass of highly skilled professional people and all this infrastructure. That, and 'I can do anything in Nashville I could in New York or Los Angeles, so why live in those places if you I can live here?' That phenomenon should never go away. We should be feeding that," says Egerton.

The Nashville Convention and Visitors Bureau has recently come to see it Egerton's way. In 2005, it made "Music City" an official part of their message to the outside world. Bart Herbison, executive director of the Nashville Songwriters Association International, says that in recent years his organization and the Convention and Visitors Bureau have been working together more closely.

Then there's this odd confluence of forces: Downtown, close to Lower Broadway, where Tootsie's and other honky-tonks still sell longnecks and country music, the new state-of-the-art Schermerhorn Symphony Center is nearing completion, just a short walk from both the Country Music Hall of Fame and the Musicians Hall of Fame and Museum. The highly regarded Nashville Symphony has in the past done programs with Nashville's country and gospel artists, and perhaps the shared business interests of these three institutions will help move the Nashville elite a bit closer to the music community.

"It's about a mile from Music Row to the central business district," Herbison has said, "but it might as well be three thousand."

Music Row has given America much of its favorite music over the past fifty years. The Nashville recordings of Elvis Presley, Jim Reeves, Brenda Lee, the Everly Brothers, Patsy Cline, Marty Robbins, Johnny Horton, Johnny Cash, Roy Orbison, Floyd Cramer, Boots Randolph, Roger Miller, Bob Dylan, Joan Baez, Tammy Wynette, Crystal Gayle, Kenny Rogers, Waylon Jennings, Willie Nelson, Dan Fogelberg, Jimmy Buffet, Neil Young, Garth Brooks, Big and Rich, and so many others have transcended genre and become a part of the mainstream American music catalog.

Six decades after the beginning of the Nashville recording industry, and five decades after Owen and Harold Bradley built their studio on 16th Avenue South, Music Row survives. In fact it, thrives. There is nothing like it in the world.

And the music it produces year in and year out is meant not just for the inhabitants of our fast-disappearing rural South. Rather, it is a Southern gift to American music, and American culture. The men and women who built Music Row built it to last, because they built it on music that endures. More than any other music, country is a mirror of the American dream.

Permissions for *How Nashville Became Music City, U.S.A.* CD

"Bread and Butter"
Larry Parks (BMI), Jay Turnbow (BMI)
Sony/ATV Acuff-Rose Music (BMI)
Copyright © 1964 (Renewed 1992) Sony/ATV Songs LLC. All rights administered by Sony/ATV Music Publishing, 8 Music Square West, Nashville, TN 37203. All rights reserved. Used by permission.

"Bye Bye Love"
Boudleaux and Felice Bryant
Copyright © 1957 (Renewed 1985) by House of Bryant Publications, LLC.

"Walkin' After Midnight"
Alan Block (BMI), Don Hecht (BMI)
Sony/ATV Acuff-Rose Music (BMI)
Copyright © 1956 (Renewed 1984) Sony/ATV Songs LLC. All rights administered by Sony/ATV Music Publishing. All rights reserved. Used by permission.

"Crazy"
Willie Nelson (BMI)
Sony/ATV Tree Publishing (BMI)
Copyright © 1961 (Renewed 1989) Sony/ATV Songs LLC. All rights administered by Sony/ATV Music Publishing. All rights reserved. Used by permission.

"King of the Road"
Roger Miller (BMI)
Sony/ATV Tree Publishing (BMI)
Copyright © 1964 (Renewed 1992) Sony/ATV Songs LLC. All rights administered by Sony/ATV Music Publishing. All rights reserved. Used by permission.

"Heaven's Just a Sin Away"
Jerry Gillespie (SESAC)
Copyright © 1977 (Renewed) Sony/ATV Tree Publishing/Big Yellow Dog Music. All rights administered by Sony/ATV Music Publishing. All rights reserved. Used by permission

"If We Make It Through December"
Merle Haggard (BMI)
Sony/ATV Tree Publishing (BMI)
Copyright © 1973 (Renewed 2001) Sony/ATV Songs LLC. All rights administered by Sony/ATV Music Publishing. All rights reserved. Used by permission.

"Ain't Gonna Bump No More (With No Big Fat Woman)"
Buddy Killen (BMI), Bennie McGinty (BMI)
Sony/ATV Tree Publishing (BMI)
Copyright © 1976 (Renewed 2004) Sony/ATV Songs LLC. All rights administered by Sony/ATV Music Publishing. All rights reserved. Used by permission.

"He Stopped Loving Her Today"
Bobby Braddock (BMI), Claude Putman Jr. (BMI)
Sony/ATV Tree Publishing (BMI)
Copyright © 1984 Sony/ATV Songs LLC. All rights administered by Sony/ATV Music Publishing. All rights reserved. Used by permission.

"I Wanna Talk About Me"
Bobby Braddock (BMI)
Sony/ATV Tree Publishing (BMI)
Copyright © 2000 Sony/ATV Songs LLC. All rights administered by Sony/ATV Music Publishing. All rights reserved. Used by permission.

INDEX

How Nashville Became Music City, U.S.A. Song List

1. "Bread and Butter"—Newbeats pop hit on Acuff-Rose's Hickory record label. Lead singer Larry Henley would later co-write several classics, most notably "Wind Beneath My Wings."

2. "Bye Bye Love"—Boudleaux and Felice Bryant demo. The husband-and-wife team would write many of the Everlys' most memorable songs, including "Wake Up Little Suzy" and "All I Have to Do Is Dream," as well as the bluegrass standard "Rocky Top."

3. "Walkin' After Midnight"—Patsy Cline. Patsy Cline's first hit, released in 1957 on 4 Star Records.

4. "Crazy"—Willie Nelson demo. This song became Patsy Cline's biggest pop single and one of the top earning copyrights in the history of country music.

5. "King of the Road"—Roger Miller recut. Roger Miller's signature song: number one, country, for five weeks, and number four on the pop charts.

6. "Heaven's Just a Sin Away"—The Kendalls recut. Number one, country, in 1977, and one of the best selling country hits ever released on an independent label.

7. "If We Make It Through December"—Merle Haggard recut. Number one, country, in the mid-'70s and the highest charting pop record in Merle's career at number twenty-eight.

8. "Ain't Gonna Bump No More (With No Big Fat Woman)"—Joe Tex (master for Dial Records). R&B and pop sensation in 1972 for this gifted artist, produced by Buddy Killen for his Music Row–based Dial Records.

9. "He Stopped Loving Her Today"—Bobby Braddock demo. Written by Braddock and Curly Putman. A number-one country smash for George Jones back in 1980 and often considered the greatest country song of all time.

10. "I Wanna Talk About Me"—Bobby Braddock demo. Number-one country hit for Toby Keith in 2002. This song did as much as any song to make him one of country's top earning stars of today.